History as a Visual Art
in the Twelfth-Century Renaissance

The force of imaginative play in selecting, omitting, and shaping historical fact is illustrated by this figure of a monk calmly writing as he sits on a dragon's back. The scribe holds two implements, a pen for writing and a scraper for coordinating eye and hand, making erasures, and sharpening the pen. See the lower figures in figure 8 for other representations of these implements being used to shape expression. The figure, in brass, was made in Germany during the third quarter of the twelfth century. *The Metropolitan Museum of Art, New York. The Jack and Belle Linsky Collection, 1982. (1982.60.396.)*

# History as a Visual Art
# in the Twelfth-Century Renaissance

*Karl F. Morrison*

PRINCETON UNIVERSITY PRESS

PRINCETON, NEW JERSEY

*Library of Congress Cataloging-in-Publication Data*

Morrison, Karl Frederick.
History as a visual art in the twelfth-century renaissance / Karl
F. Morrison.
1. Aesthetics, Medieval. 2. Historiography. 3. Cognition.
4. Kingdom of God. 5. Women. 6. Time. I. Title.
BH131.M67   1990   111'.85'09409021—dc20   90-8251

ISBN 0-691-05582-3 (alk. paper)

Publication of this book has been aided by the Whitney Darrow
Fund of Princeton University Press

This book has been composed in Linotron Galliard

Princeton University Press books are printed on acid-free paper
and meet the guidelines for permanence and durability of the
Committee on Production Guidelines for Book Longevity of the
Council on Library Resources

Printed in the United States of America by Princeton University Press,
Princeton, New Jersey

1   3   5   7   9   10   8   6   4   2

# To My Colleagues

*in the Kenneth Spencer*

*Research Library*

*at the*

*University of Kansas*

More than the godlike gleams of sculptured stone,
More than the golden rhythms the poet weaves,
Who knows if a good act unknown, some wound's
Balsam, shines not with brighter lasting beams?

—*Kostes Palamas, "Thought," trans. Phoutrides*

# CONTENTS

# LIST OF ILLUSTRATIONS

# PREFACE

---

In the days of old, those Greeks who were considered
wise spoke their sayings not straight out but in
riddles. . . .
—Pausanias, *Description of Greece*, 8.8.3, trans. Jones and
Ormerod

The Gauls are terrifying in aspect and their voices are
deep and altogether harsh. When they meet together,
they converse with few words and in riddles, hinting
darkly at things for the most part and using one word
when they mean another. . . .
—Diodorus Siculus, *Histories*, 5.31.1, trans. Oldfather

WHEN WE take a work of art into our hands, we can discover many things
about its physical properties, but little about why it exists. The artist
kneaded both motives and creative processes into the very substance of the
work. Such things were as fundamental to the act of making as the formal
design and the materials used. Yet concerning these motives and processes
the object is mute. The muteness exists even when we study contemporary
works from our own cultures, and much more completely when we occupy
ourselves with fragmentary survivals of vanished ages. If we are to understand, even indirectly, the heart and mind of a people, we must find some
way to explore their silences.

These essays are devoted to a particular kind of work: historical writings.
Through histories, members of a society reflect upon—in fact, re-create—
their own collective experience. Therefore, what the authors tell about motives, in words and silences, illuminates not only the reasons for which the
particular histories were written, but also the impulses for a broad range
of creative efforts in their societies.

I have written about works composed at a crucial, formative moment in
European culture: the so-called Renaissance of the twelfth century. The
imperfections that modern readers find in these writings are sure signs that
what they expect from a literary work, particularly from a historical inquiry, differs widely from what writers and their intended audiences expected in twelfth-century Europe. For example, many of the texts combine
poetry and prose. They regularly lack any architectonic order; never complete and self-explanatory in themselves, they appear episodic, miscellane-

ous compilations, and, given that some of the most distinguished works were revised by their authors, this appearance cannot have been the result of accident or haste. Even the most relentlessly honest writers suppressed important information. Whole classes of dominant actors in history were omitted, partially or entirely: Jews (who were outside Christian society), as well as women, heretics, artisans, and peasants (who were within it). Moreover, even writers who in many respects satisfy post-Enlightenment demands for rational judgment display a perplexing mixture of criticism and credulity. Finally, despite the astonishing wealth of historical writings composed in the twelfth-century Renaissance, it has been possible for one of the most acute modern scholars, R. W. Southern, to conclude that "the intellectual climate of the twelfth century was not generally favorable to historical thought." The impelling drive of the age toward systematization, which scholastic philosophy was invented to serve, he continued, was "profoundly unhistorical in [its] approach to knowledge."[1]

It would be wrong to ignore a hint—from the ninth century, to be sure—that highly developed ways of understanding produced this segmentation and idiosyncrasy. As he interpreted the parable of the Prodigal Son, John Scotus Eriugena found that it was possible to assign more than one symbolic meaning to characters in the parable. How, he asked, was this possible? The solution, he answered, was difficult. Composition was one factor. While some parables were written in a direct, uniform way, without any transition from one thing into another figure of speech, the structures of others did provide such transitions, which were invisible in the written texts. Multiplicity could also enter by way of interpretation. Commentaries on the parable of the Prodigal Son illustrated how some interpreters (but not others) explicated the "transition into diverse figures."[2] I contend that twelfth-century historical writers likewise assumed transitions, or encoded framing structures, analogous with what John called *transitus parabolarum*, and that those transitions provided for the intended audiences a unity and beauty hidden from modern eyes.

Without a sense of those invisible transitions, so far as this randomly assorted evidence is concerned, "what the Middle Ages engender is a cluster of questions."[3] Something impatient and restless, something hostile to the classical order of beginning, middle, and end is built into these texts. Their authors, and their intended audiences, worked according to models of intelligibility that rejected the idea of the self-explanatory masterpiece,

---

[1] R. W. Southern, "Aspects of the European Tradition of Historical Writing, 2: Hugh of St. Victor and the Idea of Historical Development," *Transactions of the Royal Historical Society*, 5th series, 21 (1971): 163.

[2] *Periphyseon*, 5; Migne *PL* 122:1008.

[3] Paul Zumthor, *Speaking of the Middle Ages*, trans. Sarah White (Lincoln: University of Nebraska Press, 1986), p. 10.

literary or otherwise. Although the works lacked the classical dramatic unity of beginning, middle, and end, they yet were intended to have dramatic effects. Over and over, their authors drew analogies between history and theater. Both were spectacles. And in their selection and appraisal of evidence—in their arbitrary suppressions and puzzling combination of criticism and credulity, writers plainly thought that they were working, in some way, as dramatists did. They were selecting, trimming, and arranging materials to portray, rather than to document, experience. One object of drama is to confound the reason, to present to the imagination, not single meanings, but multiple, perhaps indefinitely multiple, ones—some unanticipated by the authors themselves.

Thus, these artifacts of twelfth-century European culture present some general interpretive challenges in addition to their specific textual riddles. In their native habitats, they belonged to a general branch of activity called literature, and they were not entirely different from poetry, as the insertion of verse sections and, indeed, the composition of some histories in verse, indicate. It is perhaps extreme, but not untrue, to say that the culture delivered "an entirely poeticized history, and . . . a poetry unthinkable otherwise than as history."[4]

To be sure, in an era when the compartmentalization of the arts was unthinkable, the general interpretive challenges presented by these historical writings were considered by contemporaries to be common to all the arts of the imagination. They all were guided by principles of play and imitation and ruled by esthetic judgment.

Our first task, then, is to examine how people thought about thinking, that is, how, in the twelfth century, ideas about how the mind worked both explained and determined forms of artistic expression, including historical writing. The subject of cognition, of course, involves meaning, both in what is said in the words and in what is implied between the lines and words of speech. The subject of meaning, in turn, leads to imagination itself, that speculative faculty of the mind that always operates in the silences of works of art (including texts) by inseminating such material forms as words with meaning.

The principle that emerges, as I have already implied, is that art's coherence was not in the work, but rather in the actual processes of esthetic judgment by which it was composed, and in the responses of the intended audience, that is, in the spectator rather than in the spectacle. One consequence is that understanding was recognized as an act that took place in a wide context, indeed within the whole constellation of images provided by culture; and that it was performed by individuals in their particular contexts and could be repeatedly performed by any of them in, as we could

----

[4] Ibid., p. 25.

say, different frames of mind—a different drama at each performance. Such
surprise and variety were among the pleasures of history.

In the view of one scholar, "we have simply lost contact, albeit willingly
and rightly, with everything that could allow us to approach medieval histories naturally and directly."[5] Thus far, I have identified one reason for
that lost contact: for twelfth-century writers, understanding was not exclusively linguistic or, consequently, identical with explanation and interpretation. For them, there was more in a text than words.[6] There were also
spaces between the words and the lines, and they were by no means empty.
The spaces were inhabited by what was said but not uttered, assumptions,
implications, and suppressions prior to the text. These unuttered, and
therefore negative, values in the silences shaped, and still inform, the
words. The words give cues. Following them, the imagination plays, mimetically yet speculatively, in those silences. I shall later define a nuclear
perspective from which the imagination did its work in the twelfth century,
a point of view effaced by the Renaissance of the fourteenth and fifteenth
centuries.

So much for general propositions. In the first section of this essay, on
digesting history, as well as in another work,[7] I have suggested in general
the importance of exploring the unsaid in the uttered. It seems only right
to attempt to enter those silences where, to adapt a sentence of Bernard of
Clairvaux,[8] words were impregnated with meaning. Today, one commonly
expects a linear narrative in historical accounts. However, to recover the
perspective from which twelfth-century histories were written, one is
obliged to explore them from the nucleus, the hub of the wheel. In the
following essays, I have studied three subjects that were encompassed by

[5] Nancy F. Partner, *Serious Entertainments: The Writing of History in Twelfth-Century England* (Chicago: University of Chicago Press, 1977), p. 4.

[6] In working out the ideas indicated above, I have incurred a large obligation to scholars
who take the opposite point of view. I should mention especially Brian Stock's book, *The
Implications of Literacy: Written Language and Models of Interpretation in the Eleventh and
Twelfth Centuries* (Princeton, N.J.: Princeton University Press, 1983). I have been encouraged to follow a different trail, partly because of the exceptions to exclusively linguistic paradigms of understanding that those scholars have discovered. Jesse M. Gellrich develops a
cogent argument for considering "conditions of signifying" at one with the " 'textuality' of
traditions" in literary and other art forms. Setting forth the book as a general metaphor of
structure, he discounts the role of discourse to challenge and negate its own powers and
functions of signification. Yet, in discussions of Augustine and Dante, he refers to modes of
understanding that surpass or elude speech. Jesse M. Gellrich, *The Idea of the Book in the
Middle Ages: Language Theory, Mythology, and Fiction* (Ithaca, N.Y.: Cornell University Press,
1985), pp. 19, 113, 119, 142–43, 146, 162, 164.

[7] *"I Am You": The Hermeneutics of Empathy in Western Literature, Theology, and Art* (Princeton, N.J.: Princeton University Press, 1988), esp. chap. 2, "The Negative Content," pp. 33–
40, and pt. 3, "Understanding Understanding: The Silence of Words," pp. 169–266.

[8] Chap. 3, n. 69. See also chap. 3, n. 59.

the nuclear perspective and that are present in texts but by some necessity or other are absent from the words. In this pursuit of mentalities in the twelfth-century "Renaissance," I have continually been reminded that the authors of the historical writings that I was studying habitually and acutely distinguished between the sense and the words of texts.

This distinction between sense and words was born of experience in a society that was at least bilingual. It also resulted from daily meditation on symbolism in Scripture. As we shall find in considering the "digestion" of experience into history, both exercises—in translation and in exegesis—trained readers to expect the essence of a text to be latent, and perhaps concealed, in the words. Authors believed, for example, that the essence of Scripture was not expressed in the words of Holy Writ.

The conviction that sense was unexhausted, if not actually unrealized, in words established a point of convergence between historical writing and other enterprises in which much was said, but unexpressed, namely, in the visual and performing arts. In the minds of these authors, understanding history was an esthetic, cognitive venture in which imagination was recognized as the speculative faculty of the mind in all the arts, including historical writing. In that esthetic, there was a characteristic acceptance of violence as a medium of beauty. This is in general the argument of the first section.

There are many reasons why one may avoid taking note of what one sees. Not all silences are the same; for example, they may arise from different mental operations.

In the second section, to illustrate the variety of silences in which criticism served as a means to epiphany, I have chosen three of the most obvious subjects: the Kingdom of God, a subject that the authors apprehended intuitively, as a "holy secret"; women, a subject that they comprehended with dread and fascination; and time, a subject about which they reduced themselves to silence by indefinitely multiplying categories of "the times." In each case, some mode of understanding was achieved by imaginative play, and some esthetic judgment was formed by critical methods. But silence ensued because those quite different judgments hindered the functions of interpreting, explaining, or even describing. The subjects were excluded from epiphanies reported in the texts and in visual representations, though not from epiphanies enacted between the lines.

The discussion of time underscores, even more sharply than that of the Kingdom of God and women, some of the traces of composition of beauty through violence, including death as a transformation into beauty. For the pattern of words and silences forms a mold for readers' attention into which they pour their times; and that mold itself is shaped, as though by a lost wax process, by the author's experience, or expectation, of readers' *tempi*. Traces of these hermeneutic molds can be recovered. To be sure, the words of the texts in question provide an added reason for exploring time as an inhabitant of the spaces between them. For the authors wrote about events as if they were not defined by coordinates of time and space, as though they were in some way governed by "untimeliness" (*inactualité*), and even as though they were not at all phenomena.

Whatever else they suggest, these studies demonstrate that the words are always one fragment of a text. The other, completing fragment is the understanding that voices the unspoken and visualizes the undepicted, perhaps to reject it.[9]

There is yet something to say before our exploration begins. The estrangement of Eastern and Western peoples has become proverbial. In Western stereotypes, the Orient is a land of unfathomable calmness, danger, and mystery, whereas the West is one of urgency, hope, and pragmatism. Oriental ostentation, cruelty, and despotism is opposed to Occidental nobility, sacrifice, and freedom. Although actual experience repeatedly demonstrates the inadequacy of these stereotypes, yet, in its signifying triteness, the refrain persists,

> East is East and West is West, and never
>     the twain shall meet
> Till Earth and Sky stand presently at
>     God's great Judgment Seat. . . .
>                 Rudyard Kipling, *The Ballad of East and West*

Investigations in various areas—including art, mysticism, philosophy, and science—have underscored the importance of cultural borrowing between East and West through the centuries. Yet there are also areas in which universal dilemmas were separately encountered in both hemispheres and answered with similar responses. Frequently, such responses did not become dominant. But even when assigned subordinate roles to play, they remained idioms in the give-and-take of their own cultures, alternatives to vernaculars that held sway. As irritants, if for no other reason, they held a latent promise of discourse with ways of knowing that were geographically distant, but not alien.

---

[9] See Walter Benjamin, "Charles Baudelaire, Tableaux parisiens. Deutsche Übertragung mit einem Vorwort über die Aufgabe des Übersetzers," in *Walter Benjamin: Gesammelte Schriften*, ed. Tillman Rexroth (Frankfurt am Main: Suhrkamp, 1972), vol. 4, pt. 1, p. 18: "Wie nämlich Scherben eines Gefässes, um sich zusammenfügen zu lassen, in den kleinsten Einzelheiten einander zu folgen, doch nicht so zu gleichen haben, so muss, anstatt dem Sinn des Originals sich ähnlich zu machen, die Übersetzung liebend vielmehr und bis ins Einzelne hinein dessen Art des Meinens in der eigenen Sprache sich anbilden, um so beide wie Scherben als Bruchstück eines Gefässes, als Bruchstück einer grösseren Sprache erkennbar zu machen." Cf. also my article, "Interpreting the Fragment," in *Hermeneutics and Medieval Culture* ed. Patrick J. Gallacher and Helen Damico (Albany: State University of New York Press, 1989), pp. 27–37.

In another study, *"I Am You,"* I explored an idea of the sort that provides an alternative to the concept of isolated individualism in the West. As a simple declarative sentence, "I am you" summed up an idea of human bonding that in Antiquity may have been reinforced by contact with Vedic thought. Generally a subordinate motif for centuries in many areas of inquiry, that way of thinking persisted wherever compassion, or empathy, was considered basic to understanding. It gained strength in modern times among artists and writers (for example, German Idealist philosophers and, through them, Hermann Hesse and Thomas Mann) who sought enlightenment from the East. However subordinate it may sometimes have been, or however opposed to the institutional values of the West, the tradition summed up in "I am you" was always there, witnessing to a common humanity, an embracing of wisdom and compassion.

The present study likewise explores an area of common human venture, one in which similarities between Eastern and Western ways of thinking have not generally been taken into account. The anomalies of historical writing brought us, not to reason and logic, but to imagination and feeling—to imagination, that speculative faculty of the mind that always operates in the silences of works of art (including texts), infusing material forms such as words with meaning that cannot always be predicted. What seems evident from our texts and the circumstances in which they were written is that coherence was not sought in the work but rather in the actual processes of esthetic judgment by which it was composed, and in the responses of the intended audience, that is, in the spectator, rather than in the spectacle. The figures in the texts are devices to be used for moving into the silences between the lines. The spectator moves from observation to meaning by imagination, the power to visualize. We have come to a point where the premise that all understanding is linguistic fails, together with the equation of understanding with interpretation. At this point, the ways of thinking that prompted these historical writings duplicate some Oriental ways of thinking.

For us, the silences, not the texts, are problematic. Why did twelfth-century writers regard silences so differently from us, as containers of things, rather than as absences? The practice of allegorical interpretation—reading sense into the words—was not a justification but a practice that rested on fundamental propositions. I wish to suggest here, and to demonstrate in the following chapters, that the silences and other devices of narrative discoordination express a critical method designed to achieve a distinct object: spiritual enlightenment. No less than other artifacts of twelfth-century cult, historical writings were intended to enhance the discipline of the soul, its purification, its re-creation, its final union with God. The methods employed to serve that end were complex. A religion of mystery, Christianity employed cognitive methods in order to transcend them;

the objects of its desire passed all intellective understanding. Thus, the syntax of Christian doctrine was a deliberate, calculated use of paradox and enigma to baffle attempts to establish an order that was compelling because of its logical coherence. Opposites coincided; and, at the point of coincidence, necessity and freedom, being and nonbeing, were identical. Contradictions resolved in harmony.

Bafflement derived from the origins, as well as from the ends, of belief. As Thomas Aquinas wrote, the articles of faith, the principles of sacred doctrine (unlike the principles of other sciences), could not be demonstrated by argument, since they were divinely revealed. One could argue with an unbeliever or a heretic only if the opponent accepted "some at least of the truths obtained through divine revelation."[10]

Most telling of all, the methods of reasoning were carefully constructed to lead to "learned ignorance," or, supremely, to what mystics called the darkness of divine illumination, a state of unknowing. The positive way of affirmation was completed by the negative way, denying the adequacy of what had been or could be affirmed. Evidently, ways of knowing that were accessible to the faculties of human nature had to be used, including sensory perception, inference, acceptance of authority, and comparison. And yet these faculties were employed to strip away perceptions, inferences, knowledge of authorities, memories, and conscious thought and, finally, to enter a state of nonperception or noncognition.

The result of that transition was apprehension of nonexistence, in two senses. In the suspension of mental faculties, sometimes described as the sleep of contemplation, the mind apprehended the nonexistence of God; for, in its perfection, God's being corresponded with no mode of existence conceivable by human powers. The mind also apprehended the nonexistence of all things other than God. Only God truly was. The world and its creatures were real only in their dependence upon God for existence, and in the degree to which they participated in His Being, which was also His Goodness. Thus, it was argued, evil did not exist; persons who wished to do evil wished their own nonexistence and did not exist in so far as they were evil.

Of course, other kinds of nonexistence came into play. The time before an individual came into being was the moment of that individual's nonexistence, extending eternally backward. A period of nonexistence also followed an individual's death or destruction. But each case presented modifying questions—whether, for example, individuals existed in the mind of God before they took physical shape in the world, and whether individuals (apart from those endowed with immortal souls) ceased to exist with their physical bodies. Nonexistence through destruction achieved special impor-

---

[10] Thomas Aquinas, *Summa Theologiae*, P. 1, Q. l, art. 8.

tance because of the centrality of death in Christian doctrine, notably through the doctrine that spiritual unity was achieved through sacrifice, which destroyed the old being and rendered it new.

Thus, a developed repertory of nonexistences was recognized, and a rich vocabulary for speaking of it was put to use. The methods of criticism were deployed to achieve noncognitive epiphanies; and epiphanies revealed the mysteries of nonexistence.

It is important to emphasize another characteristic quite foreign to post-Enlightenment insistence that words should be used in a plain, clear style. The methods that authors used affirmed linguistic understanding in order to negate it. The dominant method of progress was not rational and linguistic, but emotional and visual. Ancient questions and ancient skepticisms remained vivid: Could things be known as they were? (What correspondence, if any, was there between experience and thought?) Was memory knowledge? (Since memory was only the imperfect image of a past event, was knowledge real only in the present, at the actual moment of experience?) If things could be known as they were, could a person express them in words? (What was the degree of correspondence between what could be known and what could be said?) And, finally, could one person ever really understand what another said, as the speaker intended?

These ancient, basic doubts about the possibility and limits of communication played important roles in the methods of noncognition, or learned ignorance. But by impugning the authenticity of speech, authors assigned great creative power to visualization, which is also to say, imagination. When writers considered the works of any art, they grasped an essential truth: that the creative act occurs first in a person's desire, or feelings, then in the mind, and, last of all, in a physical event. The architect first wishes to design a house; then imagines how it will look; and, finally, draws the plans. In this way, existence is called forth from nonbeing.

What is unseen and unseeable becomes manifest. Relationships are forged and thereby meanings—and values—are altered. However, the authors of the texts with which we are concerned believed that the order of things was not exhausted by these affirmations of the power of the artist. A great arc led up, in self-assertion, from creative desire through thought to deed; but it also led further—to fulfillment in self-renunciation. Beyond the painting was the beauty of the painting; beyond the poem was the poetry in the words. The arc led from individual works to the transcendence of individual forms and finite relationships. It led from individuals to the universal One, the wisdom, energy, and empowering love in which all things that lived and moved had their being. The walls encasing the mode of nonexistence conceded to individuals were broken down, and passage was opened to the quite different mode of the nonexistence that was the One.

We should note that the authors of the texts under review were taught this method of alternating assertion and renunciation by the ascetic disciplines under which they lived. The objects of rituals of penance and the practices of spiritual contrition and physical mortification, prayer and meditation (including the daily canonical hours), chants, and obedience were to annihilate the will, to deliver it up the instrument of others. The conspicuous waste of ecclesiastical opulence served a morality of abject self-denial. The goal of sacrificial annihilation was to become one with the Creator of all that is, the Life of all lives.

Although the terms are unfamiliar in discussions of Western spirituality, the goal of apprehending nonexistence through noncognition, as I have described it, is entirely familiar. The broad similarities to structures of Eastern thought, including Buddhism and Vedic philosophies are not commonly taken into account. Beyond question, immense differences exist among these systems of thought, not least the distance dividing the elaborate Trinitarian theology (combined with a juristic doctrine of sin) in Christianity, the pantheism of Vedic philosophy designed to affirm the being of Brahman, and the atheism of Buddhist doctrine.

And yet, by different paths, such systems lead alike to the destruction of metaphysical ideas, to the negation of logic as a structure of words (except as a means of public discourse), and to the ascetic quest for nothingness. Together with the reduction of discourse to silence, they also have in common an elaborate discipline of visualization. Inventions of the visual arts and the practice of imagining forms in the mind are embraced as preliminary tools, useful above all for those in the elementary stages of spiritual training. They illustrate how all forms return to the nonexistence from which they came. The elaborate development of methods of discourse employing perception, inference, authority, and comparison to achieve states of noncognitive knowledge—in which the science of noncognition apprehends nonexistence—figures in Eastern as well as Western spirituality. Both Eastern and Western systems use deliberate bafflement of the intellect with doctrines of opposites that coincide and become identical. One is struck also by their common striving for a redemption entered through the gates of death. In Christianity, the destruction is a sacrifice in which individuals join their sufferings to those of Christ (as one poet wrote, the person is "clad in Christis skin"[11]); in Vedic thought, it is release from rebirth to individual and physical (or sensuous) life; and in Buddhism, it is the emancipation from craving and pain, which also extinguishes individual existence.

In all three, contemplation and detachment, clinging to nothing, was

[11] "Gold and all this werdis win," in *Medieval English Lyrics: A Critical Anthology* ed. R. T. Davies (Evanston, Ill.: Northwestern University Press, 1964), no. 49, p. 130.

fundamental to the way of perfection. Existence was illusory, a thing of passing shadows; being was eternal, the antithesis of existence. Visualization, assisted by the full repertory of representational arts, was a means to pass from the phantom existence of this world into the real, but encompassing, darkness of divine being, known metaphorically as light, beyond sensation, conceptions, and consciousness. In all, individual life was seen under two aspects: it had an enduring nonexistence by virtue of its participation in the ground of all being; and it had existence that perished by virtue of its finitude. Christian theologians taught that the world, created from nothing, tended always to return to its elemental nothing; only God's continual providence kept it from instant dissolution. In the ceaseless destruction of the old and evocation of the new, art provided the viewer with a parable of the tendency of created forms to turn away from being (nonexistent because human minds could not grasp it) and return to the blank and shapeless existence (nonexistent because it lacked true being) from which they had momentarily been called.

In the following essays, I do not attempt to establish correspondences between the spirituality of Western historical writing in the twelfth century and Oriental religions. However, much discussion turns on the silences in the texts. I have emphasized the parallels between Eastern and Western religions at the outset in order to suggest that those silences, and some of the anomalies that I mentioned, were not entirely fortuitous or the results of authorial ineptitude, but that they derived from methods of understanding that are well established and constitute part of the common legacy of human aspiration.

Even by way of introduction, I cannot ignore the fact that in the West there emerged from those silences an esthetic in which violence was cognate with beauty. It has been argued that, during the eleventh and twelfth centuries, a "persecuting mentality" formed in Europe. Educational and institutional changes, the emergence of a class of legally trained administrators and the formation of bureaucracies in the service of "national" monarchs, so the argument runs, permanently consolidated the West into "a persecuting society" that was not slow in consuming victims.[12] The interlace of beauty and violence, including death, may mark a point of similarity from which East and West departed in separate paths.

To many philologists of the nineteenth and twentieth centuries, the text was a sacred object, integral and inviolate. From them comes, indirectly and with many elaborations, the proposition that all understanding is linguistic. Yet, the sanctification of the text was very far from the way of understanding apparent in the writings with which we are concerned. Ac-

---

[12] R. I. Moore, *The Formation of a Persecuting Society: Power and Deviance in Western Europe, 950–1250* (Oxford: Blackwell, 1987), pp. 3, 5, 138–40, 145.

cording to this point of view, the text was to be taken as an element in a wide and shifting constellation, and the reader was not to stand apart and revere it, but rather to enter into it and rearrange it in the play of imitation and esthetic judgment.

One telling sign of this point of view is the prominence of the circle as a metaphor in twelfth-century writings. Their authors conceived of cycles in which patterns of meaning—but not specific phenomena—were repeated. These included the play of Fortune's Wheel; the cycles of sacred revelation, repeated yet advancing through prophecy and fulfillment; and the "crown" of the Lord's Year, rounding all existence from Creation to the Last Judgment. Not surprisingly, processes of understanding were portrayed as cycles, and historical writings, reflections on events in the world and mind, were also described as crowns, braided wreaths, or woven objects composed of repeating patterns. Beyond question, the dominance of cycles as a pattern of thought in these texts lay behind the timelessness and spacelessness—the lack of a third dimension—in twelfth-century art. The slow introduction of three-dimensionality in Western painting during the fourteenth and fifteenth centuries marks a departure from these cyclical preconceptions and from another parallel with Eastern asceticism and its art.

Cyclical conceptions of events have long since dropped out of the historical vocabulary. That they characterized twelfth-century thinking is a clue to a yet wider difference, namely, the equation between understanding and interpretation in contemporary thought (whenever both are assumed to be linguistic) and the ideas in the twelfth century that understanding was not linguistic and that some ways of high understanding defied—indeed, were invented to thwart—explanation, interpretation, or commentary in the equation of wisdom with piety. That these native analogues to Oriental explorations of mind and heart have dropped out of the West's historical vocabulary at a time when distances between cultures narrow day by day is reason enough to re-examine them. For it is, after a fashion, true that "we understand one another, if at all, only through analogy."[13]

[13] David Tracy, *The Analogical Imagination: Christian Theology and the Culture of Pluralism* (New York: Crossroad, 1981), p. 454.

# ACKNOWLEDGMENTS

THE GREATEST part of this book was written at the University of Kansas, where I had the good fortune to inhabit the Kenneth Spencer Research Library. With the dedication, I hope to recognize, as well as a scholar can, a heavy obligation to Professor Alexandra Mason, the director of the library, and my other colleagues there. I am also profoundly grateful to the University of Kansas for enabling me, through funds attached to the Ahmanson-Murphy professorship of Medieval and Renaissance History, to accomplish tasks that would otherwise have been daunting to contemplate. Running conversations on the Hill with Professor Alan Sica and Professor and Mrs. John Brushwood helped me clarify a number of ideas set forth here.

The prehistory of this book includes a study of mimesis as a traditional strategy of reform in Western culture, another closely related work on empathetic hermeneutics, and a series of articles on twelfth-century historical writings. The present enterprise therefore benefited from encouragement given to earlier and simultaneous ones, but it also answered new calls. Some of the chapters began life as lectures; the section on "Digesting History" started as a review article that expanded beyond the limits of that genre. I am grateful to the sponsors of the lectures and to Professor Edward Cook, who invited me to attempt the review article and whose confidence, I hope, will be repaid in these pages.

Other guests of the Monumenta Germaniae Historica will understand the paradox of delightful obligation that ensued from the time that I spent in the reading room on the Ludwigstrasse. The resources of the Institute's library and the unfailing courtesy of its members immeasurably accelerated my work.

Professors Rudolf Bell and Martha Carlin, my new colleagues at Rutgers University, exhibited many virtues, not least compassion, leading me through the ominous thickets of word processing. That they had any prior knowledge to build upon was due to the generosity of the Office of Academic Affairs at the University of Kansas, and to the expert, enheartening, and always kind instruction of Ms. Janet Crow, in the Department of History and later at the Hall Center for the Humanities there. Professors Marcia Colish and Winthrop Wetherbee gave most needed and welcome advice on the whole manuscript, and Drs. Adelaide Bennett and Lois Drewer, at the Index of Christian Art in Princeton, greatly helped me on matters of iconography. I do not wish any of them to be inculpated by their kindness.

I gratefully acknowledge further obligations to the Guggenheim Foundation for a fellowship given to assist this work (1986–87); to Rutgers for subventions attached to my research as the Lessing Professor of History and Poetics (State of New Jersey professorship); to the Institute of Advanced Study, where I had the honor to be a visitor during the summer of 1988; and to Professor Giles Constable, of the Institute, for his encouragement. The vagabondage allowed by these benefactions and the ones already mentioned allowed me to consult the following libraries, the patience and resourcefulness of whose representatives I have every reason to remember: the University of Kansas, Rutgers, the New Brunswick Seminary, Princeton University, the Princeton Theological Seminary, the Institute for Advanced Study, the Monumenta Germaniae Historica, the Bayerische Staatsbibliothek, the British Library, and the Victoria and Albert Museum.

The epigraph to the book is from Kostes Palamas, "Thought," in *Life Immovable, First Part*, trans. Aristides E. Phoutrides (Cambridge, Mass.: Harvard University Press, 1919), p. 211. The epigraphs at the beginning of the Preface are from, respectively, Pausanias, *Description of Greece*, 8.8.3, trans. W.H.S. Jones and H. A. Ormerod (Cambridge, Mass.: Harvard University Press), p. 381; and Diodorus Siculus, *Histories*, 5.31.1, trans. C. H. Oldfather (Cambridge, Mass.: Harvard University Press), p. 177.

It remains to acknowledge the kindness of those who have permitted me to use illustrations: the British Library; the British Museum; Diözesanmuseum Bamberg; Essen Domschatz; Herzog Anton Ulrich-Museum, Braunschweig; John Calmann and King Ltd.; The Metropolitan Museum of Art, New York; Dr. Barnett Miller; The Pierpont Morgan Library, New York; and Princeton University Library.

# ABBREVIATIONS

| | |
|---|---|
| *Corp. Christ., ser. lat.* | *Corpus Christianorum, series latina* |
| *CSEL* | *Corpus Scriptorum Ecclesiasticorum Latinorum* |
| Mansi | Giovanni Dominico Mansi, *Sanctorum Conciliorum Nova et Amplissima Collectio* |
| Migne | J. P. Migne, *Patrologiae Cursus Completus* |
| *PL* | *series latina* |
| *MGH* | *Monumenta Germaniae Historica* |
| *Ldl* | *Libelli de lite* |
| *SS* | *Scriptores* |
| *SSrrG* | *Scriptores rerum Germanicarum in usum Scholarum* |

## PART I

# Digesting History

## Chapter 1

# INTERPRETERS AT THE FEAST, OR A DIALOGUE
# BETWEEN ANCIENTS AND MODERNS

SOME FRIENDS have suggested that I begin these inquiries with a word about method. By what method can we apprehend a way of understanding that is not linguistic, and that is not equivalent with interpretation? The idea of an introduction on this subject is appealing. However, in some important ways, every text discussed or referred to in the following pages requires the development of a special method. When I work with texts, I read them to grasp the message of the letter and also to explore what is unsaid between the lines of written words. Sometimes this work requires attention to the formal organization of a treatise. This is true, for example, if the number of chapter (or book) divisions corresponds with some part of a symbolic code worked out by numerologists, or if an author followed a repetitive pattern of organization. Sometimes it requires attention to elements of composition other than deliberately calculated ones. Authors can unconsciously indicate their casts of mind by the frequency with which they quote certain "test passages" from Scripture, or by the kinds of metaphors they use, for example, metaphors of predatory animals, plants, or games.

But, always, thoughtful readers have to interrogate the texts before them, searching out negative values as well as positive ones. What do these authors tell us when their narratives plainly suppress information that was at hand, or when, in their effort to preserve the memory of events, they committed significant actors (such as women) to the river of forgetfulness? Let us say that I have tried to learn how to interrogate texts so that they can answer from their silences as well as from their words and, above all, I have tried to bring to the surface the ways of thinking and feeling that dictated the shapes that their formal structures eventually took. My object is to recover both abstract ways of thinking about the creative process and traces left by the creative process itself in works of art.

I am not sure that this endeavor can be redacted into method. "Method," after all, is a rational and scientific word. We have to deal with ways of feeling perhaps even more than with ways of reasoning, with esthetics more than logic. And, although the works with which I have been con-

cerned were tailored to esthetics quite different from his, I am persuaded
that Hans-Georg Gadamer's general rule applies to them:

> From its historical origin, the problem of hermeneutics goes beyond the limits
> that the concept of method sets to modern science. . . . The hermeneutic phe-
> nomenon is basically not a problem of method at all. . . . It is concerned to
> seek that experience of truth that transcends the sphere of the control of sci-
> entific method wherever it is to be found, and to inquire into its legitimacy.
> Hence, the human sciences are joined with modes of experience which lie out-
> side science: with the experience of philosophy, of art, and of history itself.[1]

Or, as other writers conclude, general method does not have "more than
heuristic value"; for subject matter "takes hermeneutic precedence over the
method to allow for a whole spectrum of possible particular correlatives
. . . depending on the subject matter itself."[2] Method has little hold on
what once was called the god-intoxicated poet.

But I cannot follow these reservations so far as to deny the possibility of
hermeneutical study. Some silences have much to say, if we can listen to
them. We take our stand at a point from which we can see the creative work
of critics diverge from that of artists (whether authors, painters, or per-
formers). Apart from the maker and the critic, the audience intended by
the maker has to be considered, and then distinguished from the procession of unintended audiences through the centuries. Therefore, we shall
also have to gain some perspective on ways in which one puts, or finds,
feeling (esthetic judgment) inside a work, that is, on how a reader's or
spectator's imagination plays inside the artwork. But what entices the
imagination to go inside the work, to play in and with it, in the first place?
What drew Hamlet's uncle into the words and gestures of the play so as to
make it a trap wherein to catch the conscience of the King? And, con-
versely, what at any given moment are the barriers to empathetic participation? There is no way to avoid asking for whom, and under what conditions, the outer shell defining a work's capacities became a net in which
the imagination was snared.

If, indeed, every text requires its own method, any discussion would be
very diffuse. However, readers accustomed to the normal, and reasonable,
expectation of critical method may find useful some further explanation of
why that expectation could be misplaced if it were directed toward the
materials here being reviewed. Consequently, under the guise of the following fable, I should like to explain the omission of a statement of critical

---

[1] Hans Georg Gadamer, *Truth and Method,* trans. Garrett Barden and John Cumming
(New York: Crossroad, 1985), pp. xi–xiii. I am obliged to Professors James Ross Sweeney
and Vickie Ziegler for the occasion of this inquiry.

[2] David Tracy, *The Analogical Imagination: Christian Theology and the Culture of Pluralism*
(New York: Crossroad, 1981), p. 406, commenting on the work of Langdon Gilkey.

method and, at the same time, indicate the contours of a hermeneutics of nonlinguistic understanding.

. . .

The tradition of the symposium was a long one in the West. Both Hebraism and Hellenism conveyed this institution—a feast that counted philosophical discourse among its pleasures—to the post-Roman world. There, surrounded with religious persons and literati as they reclined at table, great prelates rejoiced in exchanges of light banter, in debate and conversation about histories of kings and judgments of philosophers, about natural sciences (including arithmetic and astronomy), about Scripture and the teachings of the holy Fathers—in short, about God and the world. Some passed the whole night in such diversions, until cockcrow, and slept through the daylight hours.[3]

Other interpretive diversions at these feasts were linguistic only in part, or not at all. The entourage might include (among many others) physicians and actors, interpreters of dreams, casters of horoscopes, bibliomancers, craftsmen who supplied the ornaments and vessels of the table, musicians, and even "pantomimes, who are wont to entertain common folk with obscene gestures of [their] bodies."[4] The bishop himself might be adept in several of these kinds of interpretive ventures, and in one other to which I wish particularly to draw your attention: the casting of dice.[5]

Let us imagine a symposium at the table of Archbishop Adalbert of Hamburg-Bremen (1043–72). Anticipating a journey, the archbishop has just taken the auspices, and he has settled in for an evening of discourse and dice. A handsome man, yet resolutely chaste, he exults in the nobility of his descent and in the splendor and power of his see, which he takes pains to display in many enterprises. He glories in sumptuous liturgies, with thundering choirs and clouds of incense. He boasts that he will rebuild in gold, and in the exotic model of Benevento, the church that his

[3] Cf. Balderic, *Gesta Alberonis*, chap. 26; *MGH, SS* 8, pp. 256–57. Adam of Bremen, *Gesta Hammaburgensis Ecclesiae Pontificum*, 3.39(38); *MGH, SSrrG*, pp. 182–83. Ordericus Vitalis, *Ecclesiastical History* 5.3; Marjorie Chibnall, ed. and trans., *The Ecclesiastical History of Ordericus Vitalis*, 6 vols. (Oxford: Clarendon, 1968–80), 3:20, 23. See also chap. 6, n. 103.

[4] Cf. Adam of Bremen, *Gesta Hammaburgensis Ecclesiae Pontificum*, 3.36(35), 39(38); *MGH, SSrrG*, pp. 179, 182, 183. Carthaginians in the time of St. Augustine needed a narrator to tell them what the gestures of mimers represented. *De Doctrina Christiana*, 2.25.38; *Corp. Christ., ser. lat.*, 32, p. 60.

[5] E.g., Gilbert Maminot, bishop of Lisieux, about whom Ordericus Vitalis did not tell all, *The Ecclesiastical History of Ordericus Vitalis*, 5.3, 9.2; Marjorie Chibnall, ed., 3:18–20, 5:8–10 (*horoscopus, medicus, phisicus, multarum artium peritissimus*). Adalbert of Hamburg-Bremen, Adam of Bremen, *Gesta Hammaburgensis Ecclesiae Pontificum*, 2(2); *MGH, SSrrG*, p. 144: "vir . . . multarum artium suppellictile."

predecessors had built in silver.[6] The dark days are still ahead when his rapacious and corrupt agents will bestow on harlots the jewels pried out of crosses, and, suspecting that he resorted to magical arts, his people will hiss at him as they hissed at heretics.[7] Then, beset by enemies, stripped of the vice-regal powers that he adored, and barred from the papacy that he coveted, Adalbert to some seemed to have gone insane. But in these earlier times, he left no demand of opulent hospitality unattended so that he could gain, not only the reward of virtue from God, but also unstinting praise from men.

He played at dice. Given the splendor with which he surrounded himself, we must imagine that his gaming set was not of ordinary wood, bone, or even ivory, but that it was of some costly material, like the dice set of rock crystal recorded as a gift to the monastery of St. Hubert in Angers.[8] There is no need to imagine that he cast his dice with a great apparatus such as copyists of the Utrecht Psalter placed at the foot of the Cross. It is enough to think that they were presented to him on a *tazza*, in precious metal, rather like that represented in Abbess Herrad's *Hortus Deliciarum*.[9] We are not concerned, for the moment, with this reminiscence of Petronian luxury.[10] We are not even concerned with the fact that dice-playing, in which Adalbert passed whole nights, had been steadily forbidden to all clergy from late Antiquity onward, and that universal and local acts of legislation continued to repeat this prohibition long after Adalbert's day.[11] We are concerned with the playing. Above all, it is stochastic; it is kinesthetic. According to Isidore of Seville, some considered it allegorical, since they played on a board marked to represent past, present, and future.[12]

[6] Adam of Bremen, *Gesta Hammaburgensis Ecclesiae Pontificum*, 3.1(1), 39(38), 46(45); *MGH, SSrrG*, pp. 143, 182, 189.

[7] Adam of Bremen, *Gesta Hammaburgensis Ecclesiae Pontificum*, 3.46(45), 47(46), 49(48), 63(62); *MGH, SSrrG*, pp. 190, 192, 208–9.

[8] *Chronicon S. Huberti Andaginensis*, chap. 83(103); *MGH, SS* 8, p. 615. The set was given by Duke Godfrey of Lorraine as he set out as a crusader, bound for Jerusalem (1096).

[9] The casting machine, copied from the Utrecht Psalter, appears in Trinity College Cambridge MS. R. 17.1, folio 36v (KJV Psalm 22). I am obliged to Dr. Adelaide Bennett for this reference. Rosalie Green et al., eds., *Herrad of Hohenbourg: Hortus Deliciarum*, 2 vols., Studies of the Warburg Institute, vol. 36 (London: Warburg Institute, 1979), vol. 1, illustration nos. 213, 239, pp. 175, 184; vol. 2, pp. 268, 308.

[10] Petronius records crystal dice (*tesserae*) with counters (*calculi*) of gold and silver coins. *Satyricon* 33; Konrad Müller, ed., *Petronii Arbitri Satyricon* (Munich: Heimeran, 1961), p. 31.

[11] Council of Elvira, chap. 79; Mansi, 2:388. The Council did not limit its prohibition to clergy and religious. *Nov. Just.*, 123.10. Fourth Lateran Council, chap. 16; Mansi, 22:1003, 1006. Matthew Paris, *Chronica Majora, Additamenta*, 120, s. 19; in Henry Richards Luard, ed., *Matthaei Parisiensis . . . Chronica Majora*, Rolls Series, no. 57 (London: Longman, 1882), 6:243.

[12] *Etymol.* 18.60.1, 18.65.1; W. M. Lindsay, ed., *Isidori Hispalensis Episcopi Etymologiarum sive Originum Libri XX* (Oxford: Clarendon, 1911), 2:n.p.

That was certainly the view of casters who resorted to dice, as well as to auguries and dreams, for prognostication.

But figural interpretation is more distant from the stochastic action—the surprise in the play—than the archbishop's fist, smashing the face of his opponent bloody.[13] The casting of those glittering crystal cubes, the allegory and the fist, not to mention the response of the bloodied victim, are expressions of the awe and passion at the point where gambling intersects with prognostication, ritual acts prescribed by the divinatory cults of hazard and prophecy. But it is also true that they address the climactic surprise in different ways, some with the logical game of language, others in modes of play closed to reason but open to instinct and intuition.

I cannot tell you the hour, since the waterclock has frozen. The barriers of physical time have been cracked through, and we have passed into the unity of psychic time.[14]

Other participants in this imaginary symposium stand at a little distance from the gaming board. Villard d'Honnecourt is there, drawing on a little sheet of vellum, and a Goliardic poetaster smirking over his latest blasphemy, "The Gamblers' Mass," together with a visitor from overseas, John of Salisbury, who is taking notes for his inventory of courtly follies. Villard ends with a sketch; the Goliard, with a composite of melody, rhythm, and language; and John of Salisbury, with a rhetorical disquisition.[15] Each has played a different game, kinesthetic to be sure, like the cast of the dice and the blow to the face, but far removed from the stochastic (or, more precisely, aleatory) action at the board. Their works stand generalized, abstract; they lack the passion for the unforeseen, the awe of divination, the surprise of the throw and the smashing fist. Every work is interpretive, of course, but in a different medium, shaped by the peculiar conditions, limits, and possibilities of that medium. Every work is a memorial of how one game was played and an excuse for others but a souvenir, and not itself the play of imagination, a footprint, but not the pacing.

A crowd of critics have been observing Adalbert's game and the *jeux d'esprit* contributed by Villard, the scholiast, and John to the feast. They are envoys from a distant land, ruled by Queen Entelechy, and, as ambassadors, they wear golden chains of signification. Their queen considers surprise an unpleasant lapse of reason against which one should be both fore-

---

[13] Adam of Bremen, *Gesta Hammaburgensis Ecclesiae Pontificum*, 3.38(37), 3.62(61); *MGH, SSrrG*, pp. 180, 208.

[14] I am obliged to Professor Gwenyth Hood for this expression from science fiction.

[15] J.B.A. Lassus, *Album de Villard de Honnecourt* (reprint, Paris: Léonce Laget, 1968), pl. 16. *Officium Ludorum*, in *Carmina Burana*, no. 215. Carl Fischer, *Carmina Burana: Die Gedichte des Codex Buranus Lateinisch und Deutsch* (Zurich: Artemis, 1974), pp. 628–32. John of Salisbury, *Policraticus*, 1.5; Clement C. J. Webb, ed., *Ioannis Saresberiensis Episcopi Carnotensis Policratici . . . Libri VIII* (Oxford: Clarendon, 1909), 1:35–38.

warned and forearmed. As she said in one of her notable allocutions: "What occasions the aberrations of human cogitations through the perplexing labyrinths and abysses of admiration is not the source of the effects, which sagacious mortals visibly experience to be the consequential result of natural causes. 'Tis the novelty of the experiment which makes impressions on their conceptive, cogitative faculties; that do not previse the facility of the operation adequately, with a subact and sedate intellection, associated with diligent study." Dismissive of surprise, the queen also does not countenance divination, for all understanding depends upon the "ratiocinating faculty."[16] She is not, like Adalbert, a person for whom the greater the stakes, the more irresistible the game, and for whom the most compelling stake is honor. Although they sacrifice on different altars—to Structuralism and Deconstruction, for example—Entelechites practice homotextuality in common. Theirs is "one of those cultures where it is believed that intelligence is located in the mouth, not in the brain."[17]

As far as homotextualists are concerned, Villard's sketch, the scholiast's song, and John's discourse are equal and equivalent. A scholar named Gombrich, who sometimes travels with the Entelechites, takes up Villard's sketch. Naturally, he regards it as a text, an ideograph or a pictograph. The point of departure for interpreting the work, as he said when he saw a sketch Villard made of the Wheel of Fortune, is the character of the drawing as a means of transcribing "the philosophical distinction between 'universals' and 'particulars.' " Its abstract schematization, he said, was a device by which viewers could apply to themselves concepts generalized in the drawing.[18] The whole enterprise of interpretation depended upon "the language of art."

Gadamer, on this occasion, agrees: "The experience of art must not be side-tracked into the uncommittedness of the aesthetic awareness." "Language is the universal medium in which understanding itself is realized. The mode of realization of understanding is interpretation. . . . All understanding is interpretation, and all interpretation takes place in the medium of language, which would allow the object to come into words and yet is at the same time the interpreter's own language." Consequently, what ob-

[16] François Rabelais, *Gargantua and Pantagruel*, ed. Donald Douglas (New York: Modern Library, 1928), 4.15, 17, pp. 478, 486.

[17] I borrow the term "homotextuality" from John O'Neill, "Homotextuality: Barthes on Barthes, Fragments (RB), with a Footnote," in *Hermeneutics: Questions and Prospects*, ed. Gary Shapiro and Alan Sica (Amherst: University of Massachusetts Press, 1984), pp. 165–82. Professor Sica kindly drew my attention to this essay. The quotation is from Richard A. Shweder, "The How of the Word," review of *Works and Lives* by Clifford Geertz, *New York Times*, 28 Feb. 1988, Book Review Section, p. 13.

[18] E. H. Gombrich, *Art and Illusion: A Study in the Psychology of Pictorial Representation*, 2d ed., Bollingen Series 35 (Princeton, N.J: Princeton University Press, 1969), pp. 78–79, 152, 291.

jects as texts mean is what they mean when we understand them, whether or not "we can gain from the tradition a picture of the author and whether or not the historical interpretation of the literary source is our concern." Whether the "text" is picture or writing, "the horizon of understanding cannot be limited either by what the writer had originally in mind, or by the horizon of the person to whom the text was originally addressed." Interpreting is a game of language, a form of translation, in fact, in which the interpreter brings "himself and his own concepts into the interpretation . . . so that the meaning of the text can really be made to speak for us." Thus, "the text that is understood historically is forced to abandon its claim that it is uttering something true," even though, inasmuch as language bears its own truth within it, interpreters are drawn into "the truth of play," played in fact by the game of language, a continuing and changing "event of truth."[19]

This speech, Rabelais said scornfully, gave a general idea of why Entelechy was also known as "Whims," and why the only way to arrive safely in her land was "to trust to the whirlpool and be led by the current." If Entelechy never ate anything at dinner but such discourse as this—the sounds of language, categories, abstractions, antitheses, transcendent prolepses "and such other light food"—it was no wonder "that she never visited a close-stool but by proxy."[20]

A murmuring also rose from the others, whose life-styles did not include homotextuality. How, they wondered, could Gombrich "read" Villard's sketches as "ideograms" or "hieroglyphs" since they did not correspond with spoken words, had no syntax, and lacked the long duration and malleability of a common language? Villard himself points out, with some irritation, that Gombrich has rested his theories on drawings that are no more than sketches. The drawing of dice-players is one of many trial runs in which he practiced representations of draperies, anatomic proportions, and perspectives. Indeed, the sketchiness of the Wheel of Fortune that Gombrich judged a transcription of logical propositions was nothing more than a test run abandoned in midflight, if anything, hardly more than a stage toward a completed picture, with modeling and color, such as the representation of Fortune's Wheel in the manuscript of the *Carmina Burana*.

Learnedly quoting Ovid, Giraldus Cambrensis says that what we have here is art practicing its major function: to conceal itself.[21] Villard was just practicing his eye-to-hand coordination when he drew the dice-players with two unrelated animals on the recto of a sheet of vellum and added

[19] Gadamer, *Truth and Method*, pp. 87, 270, 350, 351, 356, 358, 364, 446.

[20] Rabelais, *Gargantua and Pantagruel*, 4.13, 14, 15, 18, pp. 470, 476, 479, 489.

[21] *Topographia Hibernica*, dist. 3, chap. 11; James F. Dimock, ed., *Giraldi Cambrensis Opera*, Rolls Series, no. 21 (London: Longmans, 1867), 5:153–55. Ovid, *Ars Amatoria*, 2.313.

other doodlings later. Later, Villard turned the page upside down and filled it with two other subjects: a mechanical fountain and a labyrinth. Then, he drew, on the verso, a ground plan of a tower at Laon, a sketch of some evidently unrelated structure, and to be sure, there was also upside down—probably the first drawing done on the page—a man's head.

The long, continuing debate over iconoclasm kept alive the distinctions between writing, which was self-explanatory, and visual images, which were not. One such distinction was that the representative function of literary works respected the integrity of the letter, while the representative function of visual images demanded suspension of disbelief—the acceptance of an image *as if* it were the absent subject. This difference lay at the heart of the topos of lying painters. Thus, while literary texts required a hermeneutic of understanding, visual images required one of deliberate, stylized misunderstanding.

In Villard's case, the verbal elements on the page made the textuality of the pictures all the more dubious: the elaborate comments on the mechanical bird on the page with the dice-players (about whom there are no words) and, on the page with Fortune's Wheel, apart from a simple caption, a reference to two heads on the recto of the next sheet and two recipes, the one for a ceramic paste and the other for a depilatory ointment.

The defence of homotextuality brought fire to the eyes of others. They were hostile to Gadamer's doctrine that all interpretation, being linguistic, was also translation. To the contrary, they argued that even verbal translation—much less any possible transaction between sights and sounds—was, so to speak, dicey. Experienced translators such as Jerome and Bede observed that beauty and elegance of expression could not be conveyed from the original to the translation.[22] Adam of Perseigne added that there were gains as well as losses. Any statement, he said, translated from one language to another, hardly ever retained its original savor and coherence (*sapiditas et compositio*), just as a liquor poured from one vessel into another sometimes changed in color, taste, or fragrance.[23] The proposition that all understanding was linguistic also provoked doubts among the French and Germans from Lorraine, who were frustrated in their efforts to barb each other with "bitter and envious jokes,"[24] and to Archbishop Albero of Trier, who never mastered German, French being his native language, and who consequently spoke haltingly when he preached to the people, and was

---

[22] Jerome, *De Optimo Genere Interpretandi*, chap. 5; Migne *PL* 22:571–72. Bede, *Bede's Ecclesiastical History of the English People*, 4.24; Bertram Colgrave and R.A.B. Mynors, eds. and trans. (Oxford: Clarendon, 1969), p. 416.

[23] *Ep. 30*, to Blanche of Champagne; Migne *PL* 211:691–92. I am obliged to Professor Giles Constable for this reference.

[24] Otto of Freising, *Chronicon*, 7.5; *MGH*, *SSrrG*, p. 315.

hardly ever able to expound the deep subjects that he broached, entrusting everything to proverbs and similitudes.[25]

One reveler chimed in that Augustine considered understanding to be the tossing back and forth in the mind by which an unspoken and unspeakable word or concept took shape in the mind, and interpretation the quite different recollection and explanation that followed.[26] Indeed, Wibert of Gembloux added, he had lately received a letter from Hildegard of Bingen who wrote that when she received a vision, she saw, heard, and knew all at the same time—in her peculiar wisdom, she said "know" instead of "understand"—and that the verbal interpretation followed as a work of memory.[27] Whether it was the miraculous enlightenment of a saint or the "candle of the Lord" (reason) set alight by the Creator in the mind of every person who came into the world, understanding was a charism. Interpretation was a venture.

At this, the Adalbertines took up, rather heatedly, the Entelechites' propositions that to understand was to interpret and that objects yielded truth to critics when and as they interpreted them. "Words feed not the soul," Thomas à Kempis asserted, with a sweet, sad smile.[28] Understanding truth, Bernard of Clairvaux added, is not a matter of knowing so much as it is one of feeling, since this understanding, as a song "is not noise of the mouth, but jubilation of the heart, not a sound of the lips, but a churning of joys, a harmony, not of voices, but of wills. It is not heard outside, for the sound does not break forth for all to hear. Only she [the soul] who sings can hear it, and He to whom it is sung, namely the Bridegroom and the Bride."[29] And surely our host, Adalbert, distinguished between words (interpretation) and the power in words (understanding) when he appointed special psalms to be sung to bring vengeance down on the enemies of the church.[30]

With a strong Tuscan accent, a figure murmured from the shadows that he had grappled in vain with a whole library of interpretations:

> Like a geometer, who will attempt
> With all his power and mind to square the circle,

[25] Balderic, *Gesta Alberonis*, chap. 26; *MGH, SS* 8, p. 257.

[26] *De Trinitate*, 15.15.25; *Corp. Christ., ser. lat.*, 50A, p. 499.

[27] Jean Baptiste Pitra, ed., *Analecta Sacra*, Analecta Sanctae Hildegardis Opera (Cassino: Monte Cassino, 1882), vol. 8, *ep. nov.* 2, p. 333: "simul video, audio, scio, et quasi in momento hoc quod scio, disco. . . ."

[28] *Imitation of Christ*, 1.2; Richard Whitford, trans. and Edward J. Klein, ed. (New York: Harper, 1941), p. 5.

[29] *Sermones super Cantica Canticorum, Sermo 1*, 6.11; Jean Leclercq et al., eds., *S. Bernardi Opera* (Rome: Editiones Cistercienses, 1957), 1:7–8.

[30] Adam of Bremen, *Gesta Hammaburgensis Ecclesiae Pontificum*, 3.55(54); *MGH, SSrrG*, p. 200.

Yet cannot find the principle he needs:
Just so was I, at that phenomenon.

. . . . . . . . . .

Too feeble for such flights were my own wings:
But by a lightening flash my mind was struck—
And thus came the fulfilment of my wish.
     My power now failed that fantasy sublime:
My will and my desire were both revolved
As is a wheel in even motion driven,
By Love, which moves the sun and other stars.[31]

Many were perplexed by their own experience of the indeterminacy, deceptiveness, or impossibility of translation.[32] Surely, they suggested, if interpretation were linguistic, understanding could not be; and if translation
were the way to move back and forth between verbal and visual images, it
must somehow find a common locus, if not in the reason, then in the feelings. In the same way, literary texts served the needs of monastic *lectio*;
pictures, those of prayer; and both together, the exercise of contemplation.[33] The effects of the arts entered the "stomach" (or "cistern") of memory. They entered by different conduits—the five senses. But in that "stomach" they were rendered homogenous; from it, rumination brought them
up, mingled and in the process the feelings made sense of what the senses
had delivered. The issue was not the priority of one sensory conduit over
another, but rather how cognition oscillated between a person's outer and
inner faculties, how the contents of the stomach were digested, retrieved
and redigested, and how it was possible for a cult, and a person, devoted
to mortification of the senses to live in settings of extreme splendor and,
indeed, to find the physical necessary to the dynamics of spiritual enlightenment.[34]

At this point, the conversation takes a metalinguistic turn. "The Entelechites are counterstriking our coins in their own workshops," the Adalber-

[31] Dante, *Paradiso*, trans. Lawrence Grant White (New York: Pantheon, 1958), canto 33,
lines 136–45, n.p.

[32] E. g., Pierre Antoine Motteux, trans., *Pantagruel's Voyage to the Oracle of the Bottle* (London: James Woodward, 1708), p. iii: "Yet there was no small difficulty in doing Rabelais
justice. . . . The obsolete words and turns of phrase, and dark subjects, often as darkly treated,
make the sense hard to be understood even by a Frenchman, and it cannot be easy to give it
the free and easy air of an original; for even what seems most common talk in one language
is what's often the most difficult to be made so in another."

[33] Bertrand of Pontigny, *Vita S. Edmundi Archiepiscopi Cantuariensis*; in Edmond Martène,
ed., *Thesaurus Novus Anecdotorum* (Paris: Delaulne, 1717), 3:201.

[34] Cf. David Michael Levin, "Mudra as Thinking: Developing Our Wisdom-of-Being in
Gesture and Movement," in *Heidegger and Asian Thought*, ed. Graham Parkes (Honolulu:
University of Hawaii Press, 1987), p. 245.

tines complained.[35] They are like foreigners, Giraldus added, who listen to Irish music without knowing anything of its subtlety or the skill with which the art conceals itself, and who hear only confused and ill-ordered racket, instead of the intricate, sweet, and joyful harmony that is there.[36] The interpreter, for the Entelechites, is a good Cartesian, in whose universe the "rationating faculty" reigns. But for the Adalbertines truth can be met only where they confront impossibility. "I thank you, my God, because you have made clear to me that there is no way of drawing near to you other than the one that seems wholly inaccessible and impossible to all human beings, even to the most learned philosophers. . . . And you have given me the spirit, Lord, who are the food of the strong, to do violence to myself, because impossibility coincides with necessity, and I have discovered that the place in which you are found unveiled is encircled with the coincidence of contradictories, and this is the wall of the Paradise in which you dwell. The most exalted spirit of Reason guards its gate; unless he is vanquished, the way in will not lie open."[37]

The Adalbertines protested that they did "digest truth" in their works,[38] and that much of what they said was not in the logic of the language, but in the alogical spaces between the lines. The intuitive, aleatory, and surprising play of art took place in those silences, where esthetic choices could also be moral choices. The word was mum.

They turned to the Entelechites with a question: Given the pervasiveness of dice-casting in every level of society, why do you think that women are so conspicuously absent from the dice tables in our works of art? The representations of women playing chess or backgammon are not uncommon, but this is not so of women casting dice—it does not matter whether the women are with women or with men.[39] Alarmed that she would carry her zeal for chastity to extremes, Christina of Markyate's parents delegated her as cupbearer at a feast where they were guests of honor. They hoped that the abundance of food and drink, alluring music, and the flattery of the

<hr />

[35] Cf. *Martyrium Arnoldi Archiepiscopi Mogontini*; in Johann Friedrich Böhmer, ed., *Fontes Rerum Germanicarum* (Stuttgart: Cotta, 1855), 3:288: ". . . erantque principes coniurationis Burcardus prepositus et nepotes sui, filii Mengoti, et Hartmannus maior prepositus, in cuius fabrica omnem hanc iniquitatis cudebant monetam. . . ."

[36] Giraldus Cambrensis, *Topographia Hibernica*, dist. 3, chap. 11; Dimock, ed., p. 154.

[37] Nicholas of Cusa, *De Visione Dei*, chap. 9; *Nicolai Cusae Cardinalis Opera* (Paris, 1515; reprint, Frankfurt am Main: Minerva, 1962), vol. 1, fol. CIIIr. See also Jasper Hopkins, *Nicholas of Cusa's Dialectical Mysticism* (Minneapolis, Minn.: Banning Press, ca. 1985), p. 160.

[38] E. g., continuator of Sigebert of Gembloux, *Chronicon* (a. 1137); *MGH, SS* 6, p. 386. See also chap. 2, n. 1; chap. 7, n. 12.

[39] For the story that Cleopatra played dice and other games with Antony to divert him and to keep him with her, see L. Becq de Fouguières, *Les Jeux des Anciens* (Paris: Reinwald, 1869), p. 321. See also chap. 2, nn. 28–29, 37–43, 48, 49; chap. 6, nn. 3, 35, 48.

guests would ripen her for seduction. Who could doubt that dice were in their picture?[40]

In addition, the celebrated vitrologist, Wolfgang of Marburg, recalled seeing great windows at Chartres and Bourges. They depicted the Prodigal Son among prostitutes, but not playing dice with them. They also depicted him at different games and at different boards, in each case losing his shirt to another man.[41] Do you think that the concubines of priests—who, to Gerhoch of Reichersberg's disgust, flocked to watch when those ministers of the altar turned houses of prayer into theaters—abstained from casting,[42] or that the Margravine Itha of Austria, journeying with crusaders to Jerusalem and treacherously captured by the Saracens,[43] also abstained, or that the wife of Hugh the Barber did not play with him, a man who, abruptly stricken blind, was restored to sight when he prayed to be able again to see those playing at dice and play with them?[44] It is not necessary to think that Bishop William Longchamps carried a dice-set with him to complete the masquerade when he escaped from Dover disguised as a merchant woman—or was it a prostitute?[45] But if women were absent from the dice table as our works indicate, how can one understand the charge that dice-playing was itself effeminate, and that with other like practices it gave fathers degenerate heirs who dishonored the male sex with womanly softness?[46] Dice-play with Jews was left out of narratives almost as completely as dice-play with women. Were not the reasons for this also moral?[47]

With parallel customs of his native Cyprus in mind, Theophanis of

[40] C. H. Talbot, ed. and trans., *The Life of Christina of Markyate A Twelfth Century Recluse* (Oxford: Clarendon, 1959), chaps. 8, 9, p. 48. Herrad of Hohenbourg's *Hortus Deliciarum* represents women present in illuminations of the Marriage at Cana, Esther's feast, and the story of Dives and Lazarus.

[41] Wolfgang Kemp, "Narrative Structures in Medieval Stained Glass" (Paper delivered at symposium, "Meaning and Understanding in Medieval Narratives: An Interdisciplinary Conference," The Pennsylvania State University, 15 April 1988).

[42] *De Investigatione Antichristi*, 1.5; *MGH, Ldl* 3, pp. 315–16.

[43] Otto of Freising, *Chronicon*, 7.7; *MGH, SSrrG*, pp. 316–17.

[44] *De Miraculis S. Thomae de Cantilupe*, ss. 18–22; *Acta Sanctorum*, 2 Oct., 1:698–99. Hugh also prayed that his sight be restored so that he could see the elevation of the Eucharistic host and walk unaided. For a general summary of the testimony that Hugh gave in Thomas's canonization process, see Meryl Jancey, "A Servant Speaks of His Master: Hugh le Barber's Evidence in 1307," in *St. Thomas Cantilupe, Bishop of Hereford: Essays in His Honour*, ed. Meryl Jancey (Hereford: Friends of Hereford Cathedral, 1982), esp. pp. 200–201.

[45] Giraldus Cambrensis, *De Vita Galfridi Archiepiscopi Eboracensis*, 2.12; J. S. Brewer, ed., *Giraldi Cambrensis Opera*, Rolls Series, no. 21 (London: Longman, 1873), 4:410–11.

[46] John of Salisbury, *Policraticus*, 1.5; Webb, ed., 1:38. Ordericus Vitalis, *The Ecclesiastical History of Ordericus Vitalis*, 8.10; Marjorie Chibnall, ed., 4:188.

[47] Cf. Jacques de Vitry, in Thomas Frederick Crane, ed., *The Exempla or Illustrative Stories from the Sermones Vulgares of Jacques de Vitry*, Folklore Society Publications, no. 26 (London: Nutt, 1890), p. 91.

Dhiorios observed that the play of honor and revenge, which defined manhood, naturally excluded those who had no part in the vying of men against men that proved valor. Women—and Jews, for that matter—had no more share in simulated battles, like those of dice play, than in real ones. Not for them were the lust for military glory or exhilaration in the spoils of victory.[48] Such as they could never be esteemed worthy foes; never, through bravery, strength, and wit, step forth as possible allies in the cycles of violence that honor demanded. The "woman's heart" was no commendation for a warrior. As to women's commensality—when families gather or guests receive hospitality, women may dine with men. Generally, they enhance the manly display of their lords by preparing and serving food and by otherwise adorning banquets with ceremonial acts of courtesy assigned to them. According to the norm, women and children eat what the men leave behind; for it is ignoble for those who cannot be companions at arms to eat in the presence of men.

The crystal dice gave another excuse to probe the silences between the lines. Raising their magic mirror with a portrait of Sausurre on the back, the Entelechites went straight to the heart of the matter: the bundle of relations knitting *parole*, *langue*, and *language*, and, especially, the symmetries between units of speech smaller than a sentence (the purview of linguistics) and those at least as large as a sentence (the domain of language, narrative, and myth). Resorting to the materials at hand, they agreed that the intersection of esthetic and moral judgment did leave traces in the words of texts.

They pointed to written evidence that crystal was made of water that, long frozen, congealed into permanent hardness. Its transmutation from water into a precious stone made it a symbol of the transformation achieved by grace in baptism; of the fluidity of the angels' free will before the fall of Lucifer when, by way of reward, the will of the holy angels was hardened so that they could never fall; and of the body of Christ, which after the resurrection was changed from the mutable weakness of corruption into the permanence of incorruption. Through the crystal of the dice, Entelechites argued, the Archbishop could behold the glassy sea revealed in the Apocalypse, stretching before the throne guarded by four beasts (Rev. 4:6), and those same beasts, envisioned by the Prophet Ezekiel, bearing upon their heads a likeness of the firmament "as the color of terrible crystal" (Ezek. 1:22). It was right that this stone of purity and Apocalyptic transparence should be used to make new fire on the feasts of the Purification of the Blessed Virgin and for the Easter Vigil. It was also right that, to plotters of the zodiac, crystal was the stone of Venus. Surely the Arch-

---

[48] Cf. William Fitzstephen, *Vita S. Thomae Cantuariensis Archiepiscopi*, prol.; Migne *PL* 190:110.

bishop knew the highest throw of the dice was called "the throw of Venus"—all the more lucky when (like the secret bed of Tristan and Iseult) they were made of Venus's stone.[49]

This implied slur on Adalbert, that "lover of chastity," [50] provoked cries of outrage. Why refer to the bed of adulterers, and not to the wonderful discoveries of St. Brendan, the chapel in the monastery of St. Ailbe, furnished with thrones, altars, and Eucharistic vessels of pure crystal, and with crystal lamps, besides, in which material substance burned with spiritual light. Why not refer, the defenders of chastity continued, to the immense column of crystal, bearing a womb-like canopy, that Brendan and his companions found penetrating through the midst of the ocean?[51] The Adalbertines protested that the Entelechites again had kept their eyes glued to functions and logic and words, without paying attention to the great virtue of uselessness, to material evidence without regard for the feeling in the text. The words themselves, no less than the crystal dice, and the feast served a culture of conspicuous waste, in which honor—including the honor of God—was a keystone of social order, entailing all that was grand, resplendent, and glorious. Correspondingly, the esthetic of nobility and the morality of rank fused under the sanction of vengeance.

Whatever could be said about their allegorical significance, Adalbert's dice were small monuments of the conspicuous waste that resulted. Such waste served as fuel for honor's sake and vengeance, fortified by anger,

[49] Rhabanus Maurus, *De Universo*, chap. 9; Migne *PL* 111:472–73. See Peter Kitson's judgment that Rhabanus's materials were largely taken from Bede. Peter Kitson, "Lapidary Traditions in Anglo-Saxon England," *Anglo-Saxon England* 7 (1978): 22. I am obliged to Dr. Richard Clement for directing me to Kitson's article. Peter Damian repeated the fire and ice association in *ep. 10*; *MGH*, Die Briefe der deutschen Kaiserzeit, Bd. 1, Teil 1, p. 131: "Nam si christallum, quod absque ulla quaestione obdurescit a glacie, radio solis apponitur, nulli dubium quin ex eo ignis protinus oriatur." See also Rupert of Deutz, *Commentum in Apocalypsim* 12.21; Migne *PL* 169:1196: "Per jaspidem ergo virtutum pulchritudinem; per crystallum fidei quam in baptismo percepit conservatam intelligimus puritatem." Rupert repeated the Christological symbolism in *Commentum in Apocalypsim*, 3.4; Migne *PL* 169:910–11. Herrad of Hohenburg quoted another passage from Rupert's *De Divinis Officiis*, comparing the body of Christ with crystal (containing a quotation from Gregory the Great on Ezekiel's vision), *Hortus Deliciarum*, text no. 591, 2:292. See also ibid., text no. 739, 2:350. Charles DuCange (revised), *Glossarium Mediae et Infirmae Latinitatis* (Paris, Didot, 1842), 2:664: *s.v.* "cristallum." Real Academia de la Historia, *Lapidario del rey d. Alfonso X* (Madrid: La Iberia, 1881), pp. 66, 104–6. See also the second stone of Jupiter (p. 102) and an emblem of the first phase of the sign of Libra and of the fifth degree in the sign of Cancer (pp. 32, 28, 60–61, 69, 96–97). Gottfried von Strassburg, *Tristan*, chap. 26, trans. A. T. Hatto (Baltimore, Md.: Penguin Books, 1960), p. 264.

[50] Adam of Bremen, *Gesta Hammaburgensis Ecclesiae Pontificum*, 3.2(2), 3.30(29); *MGH*, *SSrrG*, pp. 144, 173.

[51] "The Voyage of St Brendan," chaps. 12, 21–22, in *Lives of the Saints* trans. J. F. Webb (Harmondsworth, Eng.: Penguin, 1965), pp. 47–49, 58–60. I am obliged to Mr. Larry Watkins for these references.

hatred, resentment, envy, and fear. It was not an accident, the Adalbertines observed, that understanding higher truths was so often called a kind of intoxication, or that the audience response, so often sought and gained, was tears.

What the Entelechites found in the words of the text was structure, the fluidity of water or the hardness of crystal, and not the apocalyptic transformation in between. They saw in words the rules of the game and not the surprise in play, the order of composition and not the divinatory breath of the poet, thrilling through his harp.[52] "But all these things can be seen with the eyes, rather than written with the pen," that is, "seen" at the point where all the arts intersect, "seen" with the eye of intuition moving uncannily between the lines, experiencing, understanding, but not knowing.[53]

The Entelechites were after architecture—*what* in the syntax of things makes the potential actual. The Adalbertines were after alchemy—*how* the actual was transmuted, took shape, was performed in the potential. Observing the parting of ways between "what" and "how," the Entelechites thought that meaning was a noun. To the contrary, the Adalbertines insisted, it was really a gerund and should be written with a hyphen—"meaning"—to denote a work, whether text or painting, doing its job as a mean, or means.

Another faction of Adalbertines rose to the occasion with the words "structural amnesia" on their lips. The "stomach" of memory was also the "stomach" of forgetfulness.[54] Surely, they said, taking in the meaning in a text—or a picture or song—involved both a *via positiva* and a *via negativa*. It required analysis of the logical structures relating units of speech. But absorption also required forgetting. In fact, they said interpretation itself becomes possible only by ignoring basic facts, perhaps "leaving out as much as it takes in."[55]

With grave solemnity, they raised their magic mirror with a triple portrait of Longinus, Suger, and John Ruskin on the back. Beyond the constitutive units of *parole, langue,* and *language,* the asymmetries of their creed professed a structural amnesia that must be counterbalanced by affective and pathetic fallacies. Affective fallacy, above all, operating in the silences of words, was essential if those who understood were to take their

---

[52] Cf. "Sweet in goodly fellowship," in John Addington Symonds, *Wine, Women, and Song* (New York: G. P. Putnam's Sons, n.d.), p. 151.

[53] Cf. Adam of Bremen, *Gesta Hammaburgensis Ecclesiae Pontificum*, 3.34(33); *MGH, SSrrG*, p. 176. Bernard of Clairvaux, *Sermones super Cantica Canticorum, Sermo 1*, 6.11; Leclercq et al., eds., *S. Bernardi Opera*, 1:7.

[54] For the much rarer phrase, "stomach of forgetfulness," see *Martyrium Arnoldi Archiepiscopi Magontini*; Böhmer, ed., p. 275: "de ventre oblivionis."

[55] Susan R. Horton, *Interpreting Interpreting: Interpreting Dickens's Dombey* (Baltimore, Md.: The Johns Hopkins University Press, 1979), pp. 4–6.

proper place inside the work, and if their lives were to be in-formed by it.[56] To understand is not to interpret, but to absorb and be absorbed. Did the Entelechites actually think that suspending the rules of the game of language so that these fallacies could work their double-play was equivalent to cheating at dice?

Rabelais shouted his agreement. The joint voyage of discovery taken by Pantagruel and Panurge, from their prognostic dice casting on, he bellowed growing quite red in the face, led finally to the shrine of the sacred bottle, which uttered a Panomphean (or metalinguistic) word—"Trinc." To interpret the oracle, the High Priestess, Bacbuc, did not fill Panurge up through his ears with fine words and cant. "Here," she said, "we really incorporate our precepts at the mouth," and gave him a flask of best Falernian (disguised as a silver book) to swallow, every drop. In this way, he reached his goal of truth intoxicated with poetic fury. Cult and cognition were twins. Some whispered that this was so too in heaven, where the blessed perceive the thoughts of one another directly, without the meaning of words.

A real *contretemps* was brewing, for the Entelechites were certainly not wordless. With all the power of developed homotextuality, Gadamer stood and intoned: "The hermeneutical experience is the corrective by means of which the thinking reason escapes the prison of language, and it is itself constituted linguistically." The "hermeneutical experience" of politics, Giraldus said with an unpleasant laugh, is nothing but a crapshoot.[57]

Seizing the metalinguistic possibilities of self-reconstitution with both hands, some Entelechites began to mock Rabelais, chanting in a mixed Aeolian and Doric mode: "O how glorious is the Lord's lamp—the cup of drunkenness—in the strong man's hand!" They set up a versicle, intoning the words of Christ: "Can ye drink of this cup, in its kind, whereof I am to drink," improvising the response: "You bet we can! Ha ha, hee hee! Get on with it!"[58]

The other happy Entelechites reclining at dinner shouted their approval, which displeased the Archbishop.[59] And so, nodding to his brethren, who were also present, he ordered the cantor to set the antiphon, "Sing ye to us a hymn." But the Entelechites again broke out into boisterous shouts, mer-

---

[56] Cf. Bernard of Clairvaux, *Sermones super Cantica Canticorum, Sermo I*, 1.2; Leclercq et al., eds., *S. Bernardi Opera*, 1:3.

[57] Gadamer, *Truth and Method*, p. 363. Giraldus Cambrensis, *Itinerarium Kambriae*, pref. prima; James F. Dimock, ed., *Giraldi Cambrensis Opera*, Rolls Series, no. 21 (London: Longman, 1868), 6:6.

[58] *Apocalypsis Goliae Episcopi*, lines 365–72, in Walter Map, *The Latin Poems commonly attributed to Walter Mapes*, ed. Thomas Wright, Camden Society Publications, no. 16 (London: Nichols, 1841), p. 17.

[59] Much in this paragraph is drawn from Adam of Bremen, *Gesta Hammaburgensis Ecclesiae Pontificum*, 3.70(68); *MGH, SSrrG*, pp. 217–18.

rily knocking against each other as the game of language threw them into play. Adalbert then had the clergy begin: "We waited for peace and it did not come." A third time, they again set up a bellowing in their cups. Greatly angered, Adalbert ordered the table to be cleared. Defending Rabelais in a loud voice, he said:

> When tasteless France provoked our Author's gall,
>
> . . . . . . . . . . . . . . . . .
>
> The great physician wrote with artful rage
> To cure the vicious palate of the age.
> Bitter the med'cine was, but kindly he,
> To make it relish, gave it an allay:
> Sweet'ned with seeming nonsense, down it went,
>
> . . . . . . . . . . . . . . . . .
>
> . . . pleasantry and rage
> Were wisely mingled in the double-meaning page.
> Mirth seem'd predominant and most it work'd;
> The fable tickled, but the moral lurk'd.[60]

The guests fell about reconstituting themselves linguistically. Overwhelmed by the pathos of historical distance, Adalbert shut himself in the oratory and wept bitterly.

Rabelais trimmed his lantern, and winked.

"But don't you see what has happened?" said Giraldus Cambrensis, always eager to have the last word. "It is the same in literature as in the history of chess. In the old days, those who played well played alone, and with all the pieces. But now modern players find all those moves too boring. They have changed the rules and made the game shorter and less tedious. They have dropped the ponderous niceties of the old etiquette and, using fewer pieces, have divided them among more than one player."[61] No one player, anymore, has all the pieces.

---

[60] Robert Gale, "On Mr. Motteux's Translation of the Two Last Books of Rabelais, and His Key to the Whole," in Motteux, *Pantagruel's Voyage*, pp. ix–x.

[61] Giraldus Cambrensis, *Gemma Ecclesiastica*, 2.37; J. S. Brewer, ed., *Giraldi Cambrensis Opera*, Rolls Series, no. 21 (London: Longman, 1862), 2:356.

## Chapter 2

# HISTORY AS AN ART OF THE IMAGINATION

EVERY STUDY has its fascination. The fascination of history is power. In one aspect, power is wielded over the outer world of human destinies, over the conditions and possibilities of life itself. Histories of politics and war are among the branches of inquiry devoted to this aspect. In another, power is represented in the inner world, where mind and heart imagine what they have sought in the physical world and what it has disclosed to them. Investigation into the inner world has unfolded into histories of religions, of ideas, and (not least) moralities, apart from many other forms.

Writing in general and the writing of history in particular are by no means universal among the cultures of the world. Yet where they occur, they have formed bridges between these two quite different spheres: that of power as wielded and that of power as represented. The texts that resulted give evidence of how, in specific circumstances, some persons were able to use tools of criticism in order to translate acts of physical power into epiphanies of understanding. Thus, historical texts are anthropological evidence of the first magnitude. They stand at the juncture where physical experience is changed into cultural.

A historical text is, so to speak, the evidence left at the scene of an important event, an act by which, in the past, a mind informed experience with meaning, or, to put it another way, that mind translated experience into information which in its turn was a stepping-stone to epiphany. Ways of appraising such evidence—vestigial remains of the circumstances that made the event possible—must vary from one culture to another, and, in some respects, from case to case.

The subject of these essays is historical writing in western Europe—put broadly, between Antiquity and the Renaissance of the fourteenth century, and, more precisely, in the eleventh and twelfth centuries. That moment has been considered a Renaissance of sorts and an indispensable preliminary to the cultural transformations of the fourteenth and fifteenth centuries. Then, as enduring institutions crucial to the organization of political and institutional power took shape, reflections on the history of those institutions had one, quite distinctive, anthropological trait: they were artifacts of religious cult. The critical methods by which experience was digested into epiphany were not only cultural but also cultic.

I should emphasize that, while authors with whom we are concerned used the word "digest" in a common rhetorical sense, the arrangement of materials, to describe what they were about[1] they also employed it and the word "rumination," sometimes with very literal elaborations of both words, to describe their absorptive meditations on Scripture and its pre-dicaments.[2] For them, the word "digestion" provided an analogue, not only to the biological functions of absorption and expulsion, but also to the experience of delight. They knew that, by digestion, the part of body of the eaten that was not rejected changed into that of the eater.[3] They also knew the delight of rumination, chewing over the variety that a subject could offer when considered from different aspects or levels of interpreta-tion; it was the pleasure that came from detecting and unfolding intracta-ble riddles.

The chronological center of our attention is the eleventh and twelfth centuries, that moment of "Renaissance," or "proto-Renaissance," during which many enduring characteristics of European intellectual and political life took shape. Indeed, we hope to recover some aspects of thought which—on the one hand, encased in institutions and, on the other, rami-fied in countless unpredictable ways through individual minds—quickened that vast creative enterprise. However, it is essential to recognize that, whatever elaborations the ways of thinking with which we are to deal re-

---

[1] Cf. continuator of Sigebert of Gembloux, *Chronicon (a.* 1137); *MGH, SS* 6, p. 386: "bre-viter digesta veritas." Giraldus Cambrensis, *Expugnatio Hibernica*, pref. ep.; James F. Dimock, ed., *Giraldi Cambrensis Opera*, Rolls Series, no. 21 (London: Longman, 1867), 5:222–23: "Legendi namque studio, quasi quotidiano cibo, aliter et pinguescit oratio," followed after a long space by the phrase "digestam historiam" (p. 224). Giraldus employed a similar meta-phor in *De Jure et Statu Menevensis Ecclesiae*, pref.; J. S. Brewer, ed., *Giraldi Cambrensis Opera*, Rolls Series, no. 21 (London: Longman, 1863), 3:117–18.

[2] E.g., Hermannus quondam Judaeus, *Opusculum de Conversione Sua*, chap. 2; *MGH*, Quel-len zur Geistesgeschichte des Mittelalters, 4:74: "Ego autem episcopum hec et huiusmodi in populo declamantem tanto avidius ac delectabilius audiebam, quanto et ea, que de veteris instrumenti memorabat historiis, sepe in hebraicis lecta codicibus memoriter retinebam. Sciens etiam animalia non ruminantia a lege inter immunda deputari, quecumque mihi ex illius predicatione audita placuerant, in ventrem memorie sepius mecum ruminanda transmisi. . . ." See also ibid., chap. 21, p. 125.

[3] Some verses of Scripture led commentators to apply the metaphor of digestion to the exercise of reading or hearing. Cf. Rupert of Deutz, *Commentum in Apocalypsim*, 2. prol., 6.10; Migne *PL* 169:866, 1015. (Rupert used the word "digest" elsewhere to mean "dis-played" or "arranged." St. John the Divine "digestas operum Dei rationes mysticas coram se conspiciat." *Commentum in Apocalypsim*, 5.8; Migne *PL* 169:969–70. The ancient metaphor for anthologists—a bee gathering nectar and producing honey—was also current. E.g., Her-rad of Hohenburg, *Hortus Deliciarum*, Green et al., eds., Studies of the Warburg Institute, vol. 36 (London: Warburg Institute, 1979), text no. 2, 2:4, referring both to Herrad as collector and to readers as consumers. Othloh of St. Emmeram's inventory of his writings is replete with metaphors of cooking and banqueting. *Liber de Tentationibus et Scriptis*, pt. 2; Migne *PL* 146:51–58. The analogy of digestion was given an unusual, if fitting, application by Gerhoch of Reichersberg, *Tractatus in Ps. 22:* 5 (Migne *PL* 193:1051): At the Eucharist, Christians consume and are consumed by Christ, becoming his body as a dove becomes part of the body of the falcon that devours it.

ceived in the eleventh and twelfth centuries, they belonged to a common heritage. To emphasize the fact that we are considering one moment in the unfolding of a tradition, and thus the fact that historical writers at that moment were using and improvising upon a common repertoire of ideas delivered to them by the past, I shall devote considerable attention to the Venerable Bede (ca. 673–735).

Indeed, the earliest texts considered in this essay are Bede's. Although the latest given detailed attention is by Matthew Paris (ca. 1200–59), the esthetic process of digestion that arose in cult texts also served Chaucer (ca. 1340–1400) as he performed the double historical task of evoking a remote, pre-Christian past and thereby consciously defining his place in a chain of masters that included Boethius, Dante, and Boccaccio. Consequently, I shall briefly extend my remarks on historical texts beyond Matthew Paris to include Chaucer, who witnessed to the earlier process just as Renaissance norms of historiography were taking shape.

Certain limits need to be drawn at the outset. The phrase "monkish historians," a souvenir of the Enlightenment, expresses a stereotype: the idea that historical writing was a normal and regular, if not an inevitable, aspect of Christian tradition, notably as it was transmitted in monastic institutions. Yet this was not so. To be sure, surviving texts set forth numerous motives for writing histories, including the moral improvement of readers and the preservation of notable deeds from oblivion.[4] But they also record such inhibitions against historical writing as the savagery of critics and the dangers incurred by recording what others wished to be buried in silence.[5] In some cases, writers were specifically forbidden to complete their tasks, as when Anselm of Canterbury commanded Eadmer to cease and desist from writing the Archbishop's biography, a task, however, in which Eadmer clandestinely persisted.[6] Some areas are inexplicably historyless. This is the case, for example, with Toulouse for two centuries (840–1050), de-

[4] Southern took account of different objectives with his categories of "classical imitators," "scientific students," and "prophetic historians." The first wished to extract moral lessons and "the destinies of peoples" from past experience. The second took it upon themselves to disclose a "divine plan" working itself out in history and to demonstrate that Scriptural authority and secular accounts mutually corroborated one another. The last examined the past to determine which Scriptural prophecies had been fulfilled and which were yet to be accomplished. See the summary in R. W. Southern, "Aspects of the European Tradition of Historical Writing, 4: The Sense of the Past," *Transactions of the Royal Historical Society*, 5th series, 23 (1973): 243. Of course, one and the same author could work in all three modes.

[5] E.g., Ordericus Vitalis, *Ecclesiastical History*, 6.1; Marjorie Chibnall, ed. and trans., *The Ecclesiastical History of Ordericus Vitalis*, 6 vols. (Oxford: Oxford University Press, 1968–80), 3:212. William of Malmesbury, *De Gestis Regum Anglorum*, 4. prol.; William Stubbs, ed. Rolls Series, no. 90 (London: Stationary Office, 1889), 2:357. See chap. 1, n. 5; chap. 5, n. 32; chap. 6, n. 2; chap. 7, nn. 11–22.

[6] R. W. Southern, *St. Anselm and His Biographer: A Study of Monastic Life and Thought, 1059–c. 1130* (Cambridge: Cambridge University Press, 1963), pp. 300–301, 315.

spite the presence of a literate, well-organized society fully aware of the importance of documentation, as the abundance of its charters plainly demonstrates.[7]

Moreover, the disciplines of some orders or religious houses forbade literary exercises such as historical writing because they were considered opposed to simplicity and conducive to the dangerous vanity "of deep and pompous rhetoric." Instances are known in which this prohibition extended, not merely to literary composition, but even to copying books of prayers and meditations without permission of monastic superiors.

Under such circumstances, it was possible for members of a monastic community to read histories and, in fact, to encourage others not of their number to write them. But within their walls, writing history fell under an ascetic prohibition like that against "sculptures and superfluous paintings," which were banished, except perhaps for "painted wooden crosses," which were thought useful for "good meditation and the discipline of religious gravity." The Benedictine Order stands virtually alone in the number of individual historical works composed by its members, and in the collective enterprise of a tradition of historical writing.[8]

Above all, even among Benedictines, ascetic contempt of the world militated against placing too great a value on secular events. One delight that contemplating the misery of a sinful world produced was *delectatio morosa*. The conventional antipathy between true believers and the world was normative for connoisseurs of history and its writers in the period under review. Indeed, it was elevated for them by the ritual obligation of monks and clerics to keep themselves pure from the defilements of this life.[9] It was perfectly consistent for historical writers to hope that their works would enhance the salvation of many by recalling them to penance, secure the intercessory prayers of others for themselves, and redound to the glory and

[7] Professor Archibald Lewis kindly reminded me of this Toulousan paradox.

[8] On the Cistercian restriction of historical writings, which prompted Abbot Ernald of Rievaulx to incite William of Newburgh to write his *Historia Regum Anglorum*, see Antonia Gransden, *Historical Writing in England, c. 550 to c. 1307* (Ithaca, N.Y.: Cornell University Press, 1974), p. 263. F. M. Powicke, in *The Life of Ailred of Rievaulx by Walter Daniel* (London: Nelson, 1950), pp. lxxxiii–lxxxiv. William of Newburgh, *Historia Regum Anglorum, ep. ad Ernaldum*, in Richard Howlett, ed., *Chronicles of the Reigns of Stephen, Henry II, and Richard I.*, Rolls Series, no. 82 (London: Longman, 1884), 1:3–4. There is, however, no surviving indication that Otto of Freising, devout Cistercian abbot that he was, sought approval of his Order's general chapter for his historical writings. The prohibitions of copying books and visual representations cited above derive from the Gilbertine Order. See *Capitula de Canonicis et Noviciis et Eorum Aetate, et Laicis Canonicis*, chaps. 15, 19, in William Dugdale, ed., *Monasticon Anglicanum* (London: Longman, 1830), vol. 6, pt. 2, pp. 1*, *1–*1:.

[9] Cf. Bede, *Commentary on James 1*: 27; David Hurst, trans., *Bede the Venerable: Commentary on the Seven Catholic Epistles*, Cistercian Studies Series, no. 82 (Kalamazoo, Mich.: Cistercian Publications, 1985), p. 21.

praise of God.[10] But a paradox arose when they contemplated events knowing that even the mightiest of this world would quickly pass away as if they had never been. "If we desire to hear the voice of God the Father," Bede wrote, "if we desire to behold the majesty of His consubstantial Son, let us earnestly shun the perverse and useless things of mortals, let us earnestly avert our eyes from the gross emptiness of spectacles in this failing world. . . ."[11]

Giraldus Cambrensis' career illustrated how truthfully he wrote when he said that he had spent his youth in historical inquiries so that he could give his ripest maturity to explicating sacred knowledge. And Matthew Paris reduced worldly events to scale by dismissing them, even as he wrote about them, as outcroppings of a killer instinct, a dog-eat-dog fight over a bone, in which lunging attackers, also the attacked, soon forgot about the bone and gnashed one another.[12] More than one historical writer, meditating on the uncertainties and injustices of this world confronted the great predicament: whether blind Fortune, with her aimlessly fluttering wings, ruled human affairs, or a divine providence, giving to each according to his just merits. For surely anyone could see the wicked and ill-deserving raised up on high, and exalted with position and honor, while others, exemplary in their virtue, were pinioned by adversity and tormented by tribulation and grief.[13] While *Schadenfreude* might reward the virtuous when they studied history as a morality play, doubt (Giraldus used the word "*ambiguitas*") might also arise to cloud their delight.

If we recognize that historical writing as distinct from historical thinking

[10] Bede, *Bede's Ecclesiastical History of the English People*, pref.; 4.30; 5.13, 14, 24; Bertram Colgrave and R.A.B. Mynors, eds. and trans. (Oxford: Clarendon, 1969), pp. 6, 444, 502, 504, 570.

[11] *Hom. I.* 24 (*In Quadragesima*) and *II.* 2 (*In Quadragesima*); *Corp. Christ., ser. lat.*, 122, pp. 177, 195. See also chap. 3, n. 96; chap. 5, n. 38; chap. 6, n. 58; chap. 7, n. 62.

[12] *Descriptio Kambriae*, praef. prima; James F. Dimock, ed., *Giraldi Cambrensis Opera*, Rolls Series, no. 21 (London: Longman, 1868), 6:158. *Chronica majora* (a. 1252), in *Matthaei Parisiensis Monachi Sancti Albani Chronica Majora*; Henry Richards Luard, ed., 7 vols., Rolls Series, no. 57 (London: Longman, 1872–83). The present reference occurs in 5:357.

[13] Giraldus Cambrensis, *De Vita Galfridi Archiepiscopi Eboracensis, introitus primus*; J. S. Brewer, ed., *Giraldi Cambrensis Opera*, Rolls Series, no. 21 (London: Longman, 1873), 4:357. See also *Chronicon S. Huberti Andaginensis* (a. 1095), chap. 76(96); *MGH, SS* 8, p. 611: "Rerum quidem exitus prudentia metitur, sed alieno decepti errore rotam fortunae nos quoque aliquandiu revolvimus, et maximos labores frustra fatigati expendimus. Erit certe hoc aeterni Iudicis vindicare, pro cuius fide maxime proposuimus inimicis eius displicere." The argument had yet to be developed "that all *fortuna* ('fortune') is reducible to God," or at least it had yet to be discovered in "the Stoics, together with Aristotle and his Arabian interpreters" as upheld by "the best of the pagan authorities on that subject." A. J. Minnis, *Chaucer and Pagan Antiquity*, Chaucer Studies, vol. 8 (Cambridge: D. S. Brewer, 1982), p. 44, referring to Bradwardine.

was not an indispensable part of medieval culture, we must also conclude that the ways of thinking that made historical writing possible were not invariable and universal norms. Plainly, those ways of thinking could be discarded and indeed forbidden in some areas by the same cult that made them possible in others. Therefore, to assess historical writing as a cultural artifact requires examining with particular care the principles of criticism by which some writers digested experience into epiphany.

## REPRESENTATION, NOT DOCUMENTATION

How can we explore this complex matter? Two general characteristics of historical texts in our period will serve as clues for beginning the investigation. They are traces left by the digestive methods behind the texts. The first is a formal characteristic of what recent critics call "the structure of discourse." In general, texts have no unified narrative structure. Certainly, authors were capable of portraying individual scenes with great narrative detail and power. For example, Giraldus Cambrensis described Geoffrey of York, the second son of Henry II of England, at his father's deathbed, sitting beside the anguished King and supporting his head and shoulders. A knight supported Henry's feet in his lap while with a whisk Geoffrey brushed the flies from his father's face.[14] Yet Giraldus did not conceive his account of Geoffrey's troubles and vindication as an organic whole with a beginning, middle, and end. Rather, he constructed it as a series of segmented episodes, each organized (as he said explicitly in another instance) by glancing over the materials cursorily, garnering them by the power of the pen, and binding them up in a bundle (*fasciculus*).[15] Other writers employed categories of organization distinct from events or deeds. For example, William of Malmesbury organized his accounts of kings and bishops according to geographical divisions. But this too was a method of composition by fascicles, a segmented order, and, as William acknowledged, it required duplicating information when the same event figured in

[14] *De Vita Galfridi Archiepiscopi Eboracensis*, 1.5; J. S. Brewer, ed., p. 370. In a vision, Christina of Markyate similarly held the head of the Blessed Virgin, who had appeared to her as queen. C. H. Talbot, ed. and trans., *The Life of Christina of Markyate A Twelfth Century Recluse* (Oxford: Clarendon, 1959), chap. 25, p. 76. For a much earlier example of this kind of intimacy, see Benedicta Ward, ed. and trans., *The Sayings of the Desert Fathers* (London: Mowbray, 1975), Poemen no. 92, p. 151.

[15] *De Vita Galfridi Archiepiscopi Eboracensis*, 2.19; Brewer, ed., p. 420. Concerning the Venerable Bede, cf. Joel T. Rosenthal, "Bede's *Life of Cuthbert*: Preparatory to *The Ecclesiastical History*," *Catholic Historical Review* 68 (1982): 602: "The text of *The Ecclesiastical History* is actually a consummate blend of narrative passages and biographical or hagiographical excursions. . . . a prose version of antiphonal presentation." On the anecdotal organization of the *Life of Cuthbert*, see Rosenthal, p. 605.

the histories of more than one region.[16] Like artists, authors consciously intruded "discoordinating narrative devices" into their works.[17]

Even in the rare instances when authors imposed themes of architectonic unity on their materials, the project of a progressively unfolding narrative is thwarted by the disconnected, wayward character of their basic organization: that of anthology. Such is notably the case, for example, in Otto of Freising's *Chronicle*. There, the overarching theme—that history was the story of conflict between Jerusalem, the city of Christ, and Babylon, the evil city, a conflict moving toward the Last Judgment—was on the whole relegated not to the substance of the evidence but to introductory and concluding remarks. Even so, Otto found himself inextricably tangled in difficulties between the atomistic materials that he anthologized into chapters and books and the broad theories that he wished them to demonstrate and that he appears to have imposed upon them, almost as decorative afterthoughts, in revision.

In a different sense, historical writers were like "the courtly poet [who] did not create a poem, [but] found its parts and put them together—he was a *trouvère*." Exactly how far our texts were from the norm of a masterpiece—a work that is complete and whole in itself—is indicated by a number of characteristics of historical works: for example, by the continuation of chronicles by a series of authors (in a manner reminiscent of the chain letter), each author writing in his own style; by the submission of a work to a reader, or a community of readers, for emendation; and by the requests

[16] William of Malmesbury, *De Gestis Pontificum Anglorum*, 2. prol.; N.E.S.A. Hamilton, ed., Rolls Series, no. 52 (London: Longman, 1870), p. 139. On early twelfth-century English monastic writers in general, see R. W. Southern, "Aspects of the European Tradition of Historical Writing, 4: The Sense of the Past," *Transactions of the Royal Historical Society*, 5th series, 23 (1973): 256: "They rejected both the form and the rhetoric of classical models. They accepted unpredictable confusion as the ordinary state of men in history, and they found a uniting thread, not in the working out of a grand design, but in the memories of small communities accumulating over several centuries. Their only contribution to universal history was to fit these microscopically small events into the system of earlier scholars. They took no account of the end of the world. . . ."

[17] Stephen G. Nichols, Jr., *Romanesque Signs: Early Medieval Narrative and Iconography* (New Haven, Conn.: Yale University Press, 1983), p. 47. Meyer Schapiro, "The Sculptures of Souillac," in *Romanesque Art* (New York: Braziller, 1977), p. 104. The idea that "medieval narrative seems terribly slack and fallen-off from any aesthetic or intellectual standard" is cogently argued by Nancy F. Partner, "The New Cornificius: Medieval History and the Artifice of Words," in *Classical Rhetoric and Medieval Historiography*, ed. Ernst Breisach, Studies in Medieval Culture, no. 19 (Kalamazoo, Mich.: Medieval Institute, 1985), pp. 15–16. Because I consider visualization an important part of the ways of understanding embodied in these writings, I cannot accept to the letter Partner's view that "analogies with the visual arts have an immediate suggestiveness, but do not stand close inspection" (ibid., p. 18). Partner, at this stage in her argument, was drawing analogies between twelfth-century historiography and the modern art of cinematography, not between twelfth-century historical writings and contemporary works of art in other media.

of authors that readers send them additional information, which in one case William of Malmesbury promised to insert in the margins of his manuscript.[18]

In the preface to his biography of St. Cuthbert, Bede set down an unusually complete description of redactive criticism at work. He described the procedure by which he wrote the *Life*, first taking notes from those who had known Cuthbert, then arranging the notes in order (by fascicles) and submitting them to the saint's companions for reading and revision, and setting down a draft biography that incorporated their judgments. This latter document he sent to the Bishop and community of Lindisfarne for their collective scrutiny.

Bede wrote that he committed nothing to the final draft that was not approved by common consent of the brethren. He regarded his work as "considered and complete." And still, as Bede himself wrote, the brethren in their scrutiny had recalled many new facts that were by no means inferior to what he had recorded, and that would have deserved inclusion if they could have been added without jeopardy to the congruity and beauty of the book as it already stood. Although he excluded the new data for esthetic reasons, preserving the wholeness of his text, he plainly knew that his omissions ensured that redactive criticism, expanding and altering his text, would continue among the brethren of Lindisfarne. He provided another spur to redactive criticism by readers when he composed a metrical version of the *Life* which differed from the prose version in some regards.[19] From the first stage of composition to the last, Bede composed in fascicles, and centuries later Matthew Paris still employed this method of segmented

---

[18] Douglas Kelly, *Medieval Imagination: Rhetoric and the Poetry of Courtly Love* (Madison: University of Wisconsin Press, 1978), p. xii. *De Gestis Regum Anglorum*, 2. prol.; Stubbs ed., 1:104. One author's willingness to alter his work if readers found aberrant doctrines occurs in the *Vitis Mystica*; Migne *PL* 184:740: "sed nos magis legentem volentes sitientem relinquere, quam fastidientem, hic huic sermoni terminum imponimus, parati emendare, demere, et mutari, sicubi contra fidem et contra sacras Scripturas aliquid diximus. . . ." See also Caesarius of Heisterbach's testimony to the moral benefits of redactive criticism. *Dialogus Miraculorum*, 12.59; Joseph Strange, ed., *Caesarii Heisterbacensis Monachi Ordinis Cisterciensis Dialogus Miraculorum* (Cologne: Heberle, 1851), 2:346: "Codicis exigui stilus auctorem reticescens / Ingeror in medium, veluti nova verbula spargens / Sic ut mitis amor terat aspera, mitius illa / Corrigat, ac mores addat nota vera salubres." Someone, evidently Ordericus Vitalis, composed his interpolations into William of Jumièges's *Chronicle* in rhymed prose, and a anonymous editor expanded the conclusion of Bede's *Ecclesiastical History* to produce in Old English "a text of composite authorship and mixed form, prose followed by alliterative verse." Élizabeth M. C. Van Houts, "Quelques remarques sur les interpolations attribuées à Orderic Vital dans les *Gesta Normannorum Ducum* de Guillaume de Jumièges," *Revue d'histoire des Textes* 8 (1978): 214. Fred C. Robinson, " 'Bede's' Envoi to the Old English *History*: An Experiment in Editing," *Studies in Philology*, Texts and Studies 78, n.s. 5 (1981): 5.

[19] *Vita Sancti Cuthberti*, prol.; Bertram Colgrave, ed., *Two Lives of Saint Cuthbert* (Cambridge: Cambridge University Press, 1985), pp. 142–47.

composition, as we can see in the revisions that he wrote on, or affixed to, surviving manuscripts. The "fascicle" method of composition invited the redactive imagination to play in narrative gaps and in such incompleteness as marked individual works. The completed work was not an integrated whole, but rather an album, one made up (at least in part like contemporary photograph albums) of visual images.

There is, of course, an analogy to the fascicle method in the visual arts and in architecture. I refer to the composition of objects by the use of separate elements—for example, ancient cameos, pagan ivories, and enamelled plaques—that could later be broken apart and recombined in another composition. Abbot Suger of St. Denis was a master of recombinant art, both in the architecture of his monastery and in the works of art described by him, some of which survive. A twelfth-century cross composed largely of enamelled plaques indicates how the pictorial narrative of a program could be changed not by radical destruction, but by the substitution of a new segment for one originally included.[20]

In addition to the formal method of digesting information into fascicles, the way in which the subject of power was treated provides a clue for investigating the passage from experience to epiphany by way of criticism. Historical writings were essays on power, but as representations they by no means replicated the actual state of affairs. The process of digesting was, among other things, an exercise in theodicy and selective omission.

Theodicy appears as an organizing principle most regularly in the dyad of honor and revenge. The entire history of the world followed upon the assault made by Adam, in his disobedience, upon the honor of God, and the whole work of saints was to serve the honor of God and the utility of his Church, yearning always to see the King of Glory in his beauty, and not through types and shadows. The Creator had enfleshed nothing stable, nothing lasting, in this world, precisely so that he could the more readily provoke human minds to turn to the true and lasting good, which was himself, by contemplating the terror and anguish of universal mutability of things that were made. The discerning eye saw God's hidden judgment behind the changefulness of this world, a power ever ready to break the proud and cast them headlong from their heights into ruin. Experience recorded in histories documented how divine vengeance fell upon those who denied God and his servants their due honor—upon scoffers, despisers of relics, enemies of saints, and prelates who despoiled churches. Such were the powerful upon whom God visited the suffering of powerful torments, idols set up by themselves and demolished by the finger of God as

[20] The cross is now in the Victoria and Albert Museum (inv. 7234–1860). It is catalogued as "Mosan and North German, with fifteenth-century additions." See chap. 4, n. 44 and figure 5.

the Golden Calf had fallen at Moses' nod. Set over men, they had ruled with tyranny and terror, but they were laid low by the swift vengeance of God's right hand, made laughingstocks before all, objects of opprobrium and revulsion. The silence in heaven for the space of half an hour, revealed in the Apocalypse, would be the moment when those who had killed the saints would themselves be eliminated, so that they could kill no more.[21]

To be sure, for a time, seeking their conversion rather than their destruction, God might delay punishment, or administer only the loving, chastening blows with which he terrified and chastised his children. They might, in their obdurate injustice, appear to triumph over his true servants, as did Henry II in Becket's murder. But if they failed to repent, there was laid up for them a vengeance that would smite and edify the whole world with astonishment.[22] The hiddenness of justice, equated with vengeance, was a dominant theme.

Selective omission, guided by other principles of hiddenness, also shaped the representation of power. Authors frequently asserted that they had relied on trustworthy witnesses or recounted what they themselves had seen. Yet, even the most balanced accounts were limited precisely by their authors' perspectives. For example, as he digested his survey of the contemporary Church, Giraldus Cambrensis omitted almost everything except monastic institutions: "But even of monasticism he is not either a faithful or comprehensive chronicler, nor yet an earnest satirist. His picture of it is

---

[21] On the Apocalyptic moment, Rupert of Deutz, *Commentum in Apocalypsim*, 4.8; Migne *PL* 169:970. An example of divine vengeance in hagiography occurs in the punishments of bodily and spiritual anguish, and the loss of good repute, visited upon the detractors of Christina of Markyate. Talbot, ed. and trans., *The Life of Christian of Markyate*, chap. 75, p. 172: "Tantum autem Christus suam zelabat ancillam ut si qui eam infestarent aut cita corrigerentur penitencia, aut incommodo corporis aliquo multarentur, ita ut audiremus de illis aliquem cecitate percussum, alium absque viatico viam universe carnis ingressum, alios invidia tabescentes omnem fere qua prius claruerant religionis opinionem amisisse." The character of honor and vengeance in twelfth-century narrative needs to be added to Nichols's emphasis on the importance of a "hostile world and its would-be negating rhetoric" to historical and epic literature. Nichols, *Romanesque Signs*, in the chapters on Charlemagne and Roland as epic figures and, esp., p. 125. The substitution of divine vengeance as an organizational principle for chronology is noted by Donald J. Wilcox, "The Sense of Time in Western Historical Narratives from Eusebius to Machiavelli," in *Classical Rhetoric and Medieval Historiography*, ed. Ernst Breisach, Studies in Medieval Culture, no. 19 (Kalamazoo, Mich.: Medieval Institute, 1985), pp. 174, 176.

[22] E.g., Ebo, *Vita S. Ottonis Episcopi Babenbergensis*, 3.13; Jan Wikarjak, ed., Monumenta Poloniae Historica, n.s., vol. 7, fasc. 2 (Warsaw: Państwowe Wydawnictwo Naukowe, 1969), p. 117. Herbord, *Dialogus de Vita S. Ottonis Episcopi Babenbergensis*, 2.23, 34, 3.15; Jan Wikarjak, ed., Monumenta Poloniae Historica, n.s., vol. 7, fasc. 3 (Warsaw: Państwowe Wydawnictwo Naukowe, 1974), pp. 103–4, 127, 176. Giraldus Cambrensis, *De Vita Galfridi Archiepiscopi Eboracensis*, 2. prol., 19; J. S. Brewer, ed., pp. 386, 420, 430. *De Principis Instructione*, dist. 2, pref.; George F. Warner, ed., *Giraldi Cambrensis Opera*, Rolls Series, no. 21 (London: Eyre and Spottiswoode, 1891), 8:153.

derived from the most contracted view, and the most meagre materials."[23]
Giraldus's prejudices against the Cistercians and the Angevins produced
both omissions and inclusions that betray neither an exercise of impartial
judgment nor a wish to enable readers to form their own opinions.

William of Malmesbury was evidently a more detached observer than
Giraldus. And yet much of importance is merely implied in his statement
that he would relate what would incite the sluggish and move the diligent
to imitation, what would be useful to contemporaries and delightful to
later generations. But, he continued, he would not waste much time on
things that would bring no one any benefit, or that would offend readers
and give rise to hatred for the writer. Further, he would say as little as he
could about the bad without impairing the truth and praise the good as
much as possible without venturing into windy flights of rhetoric. He saw
no conflict between his wish to avoid saying too much and his wish to say
nothing except the truth. This moderation, he added, would enable authentic judges to declare him neither timid nor inelegant.[24] Evidently, he
did not consider that events seldom conform to the golden mean.

As we shall see, William's wish to display elegance expressed a common
attitude, one that employed principles of hiddenness to make historical
writing a branch of esthetics. What concerns us now, however, is the scale
of omission that distinguished the actual structure of power in society from
the concealing representation of power, not only in William's historical
works, but, indeed, in others generally. The anonymous author of the *Life*
of Christina of Markyate identified a number of reasons for suppression: it
was "necessary" for him to keep the name of a cleric who befriended Christina secret; he had been ordered to suppress the name of a particular monk;
by their malice and the envy of the demons who were urging them on,
Christina's enemies brought the infamy of forgetfulness on themselves; he
would not pollute the air by naming a cleric who tried to seduce Christina.[25] A biographer of William the Conqueror was more diplomatic when
he wrote that he had passed over very many of William's deeds so as to
avoid weighing down the reader with a huge codex, or because he just did
not know enough about a particular matter. He would reserve some things
for conversation. Given the way in which he sculptured his materials,
therefore, a certain irony pervades the contrast that the biographer drew
between the historical writer like himself and the poet, who could bring
forth beautiful things from his heart and expand what he knew with fig-

[23] J. S. Brewer, ed., *Giraldi Cambrensis Opera*, Rolls Series, no. 21 (London: Longman,
1863), 4:xiv, regarding the *Speculum Ecclesiae*. See also chap. 1, nn. 39–43; chap. 6, nn. 3,
48.

[24] *De Gestis Regum Anglorum*, 3. prol.; Stubbs, ed., 2:283–284.

[25] Talbot, ed. and trans., *The Life of Christina of Markyate A Recluse of the Twelfth Century*,
chaps. 26, 43, 76; pp. 78, 114, 172.

ments of the imagination. Unlike a poet, he said, he could not deviate one step from the path of truth; in purity, he praised the Duke and King to whom nothing impure was ever beautiful.[26]

The digestive process that characterized these texts was a mnemonic exercise that kept whole categories of people outside the borders of history, tendentiously including some as exemplars of what was alien and threatening and marginally including others only by virtue of some abstraction.[27] This categorization can most readily be illustrated by pointing to how generally women and Jews were digested out of accounts rather than absorbed into them. In his *Ecclesiastical History*, for example, Bede scarcely referred to Jews at all. Adherents to the old British and Celtic forms of Christianity were reckoned enemies of truth, whose conversion was to be rejoiced over and whose recalcitrance, despised. Guided perhaps by his proposition that Eve (or woman) represented flesh and Adam (or man) spirit—respectively, the lower and higher parts of human nature[28]—Bede included relatively few women in his history. On the whole, they were qualified for inclusion by virtue of their kinship to a ruler; their distinction as nuns or abbesses; their exemplary holiness (Aethlthryth and Hild are examples); or some combination of these features, as in the virtue of the daughter of a king who became an abbess.[29]

On balance, the writers with whom we are concerned considered Jews alien and hostile to Christian society; consequently, they were thought to have chiefly an adversarial role in Christian history after the advent of Christ had ended their prophetic functions. By contrast, Christian women held and exercised immense powers in medieval society.[30] Yet the task of

[26] William of Poitiers, *Gesta Guillelmi Ducis Normannorum et Regis Angliae*, pt. 1, chap. 20; Raymonde Foreville, ed., Les classiques de l'histoire de France au Moyen Âge, vol. 23 (Paris: "Les belles lettres," 1952), p. 44.

[27] For two studies of historical bias, see Ilona Opelt, "Slavenbeschimpfungen in Helmolds *Chronik*," *Mittellateinisches Jahrbuch* 19 (1984): 162–69 (especially concerning Helmold's emphasis on the greed of the Slavs and horrific martyrdoms and betrayals allegedly perpetrated by them, pp. 163–64) and Williel R. Thomson, "The Image of the Mendicants in the Chronicles of Matthew Paris," *Archivum Franciscanum Historicum* 70 (1977): 3–34. Thomson defends Matthew's veracity, but concludes that his hostility toward the mendicants expressed a common attitude among Benedictines, Augustinians, and Cistercians.

[28] Cf. Bede, *Ecclesiastical History*, 1.27; Colgrave and Mynors, eds., p. 100.

[29] On Bede's tailoring materials to serve the objective of political unity, see H.E.J. Cowdrey, "Bede and the 'English People,' " *Journal of Religious History* 11 (1980–81): esp. 507–8, 522: Bede purchased the clarity of his presentation at the cost of "over-simplification." "The artificiality of Bede's scheme of peoples," Cowdrey holds, must (together with his "Northumbrian bias") have been evident to contemporary readers and weakened its persuasiveness. The burden of details, however, may have given weight to his "artificial" portrayal of unity.

[30] See also chap. 1, nn. 38–44; chap. 6, nn. 3, 35. Although women did not figure among historical writers in the twelfth century, their eminence and power indicates that some quali-

historical writers was not to document the distribution of power, but to represent it. Thus, in his 325 surviving letters, John of Salisbury from time to time alluded to the decisive parts that women played in political and social affairs, but such references in his letters and his historical writings are sparse, and none of his correspondents was a woman. Giraldus Cambrensis may have touched one cause of this concealment in explaining why in Ireland female hawks excelled male in power and violence. The female sex, he commented, was stronger than the male in all malice. Scripture and Cicero alike witnessed to the implacable and unshrinking malice of women who, Giraldus added, always toiled in any conceivable way to overcome men, deprive them of their proper virility, and render them effeminate. His consolation was that God had chosen the weak of the world to confound the strong (1 Cor. 1:27). Ironically, a woman gave visual expression to this idea. In her extraordinary *Hortus Deliciarum*, the Abbess Herrad of Hohenburg set forth an apparently unprecedented series of three illuminations depicting the myth of Ulysses and the Sirens. She had the Sirens represented as hybrid beasts—women from the waist up and predators with deadly talons from the waist down. Men were their prey; beauty was the enticement to destruction. Quoting Honorius Augustodunensis, Herrad used the myth of the Sirens to illustrate the conviction that nothing estranged men's minds from God more than love of women.[31]

---

fication is needed regarding this period for Natalie Zemon Davis's prerequisites for writing history, namely, availability of materials (including the ability to go to and seek out sources), experience in the discourse of historical writing, and personal identification by the writers with areas of historical inquiry, notably, in the premodern period, with politics and religion. Natalie Zemon Davis, "Gender and Genre: Women as Historical Writers, 1400–1820," in *Beyond Their Sex: Learned Women of the European Past*, ed. Patricia H. Labalme (New York: New York University Press, 1980), pp. 154–57.

[31] Giraldus Cambrensis, *Topographia Hiberniae*, dist. 1, chap. 12; Dimock, ed., p. 36. Evidence of Giraldus Cambrensis's misogyny also appears in his studied revisions of two saints' lives. Robert Bartlett, "Rewriting Saints' *Lives*: The Case of Gerald of Wales," *Speculum*, 58 (1983): 602–3. For Herrad of Hohenburg's illuminations, see illustrations 297–99 in Rosalie Green et al., eds., *Herrad of Hohenbourg: Hortus Deliciarum*, Studies of the Warburg Institute, vol. 36 (London: Warburg Institute, 1979), 2:365–66. See also Marie-Thérèse d'Alverny's review of classical citations, employed in the twelfth century, to assert that all women, even the virtuous, were to be feared. "Comment les théologiens et les philosophes voient la femme," *Cahiers de civilisation médiévale, Xe–XIIe siècles* 20 (1977): 126–28. D'Alverny's article contains useful *précis* of positions taken by individual writers and some schools (especially the naturalist philosophers) in the twelfth century toward the nature and status of women. Her comments on Abelard should be read together with Mary M. McLaughlin, "Peter Abelard and the Dignity of Women: Twelfth-Century 'Feminism' in Theory and Practice," in *Pierre Abélard—Pierre le Vénérable: Les courants philosophiques, littéraires et artistiques en Occident au milieu du XIIe siècle*, ed. René Louis, Jean Jolivet, and Jean Chatillon Colloques Internationaux du Centre National de la Recherche Scientifique, no. 546 (Paris: Centre National de la Recherche Scientifique, 1975), portraying "inconsistencies" in Abelard's assertions of the dignity of women caused by his adherence to conventional ideas "of feminine

Men were characterized by strength, rationality, and self-control; women, by weakness, sensuality, and lust. But, in the literature of misogyny, the frailty of the strong and the triumph of the weak were recurrent themes. Men and women constituted different cohorts in society and in the struggle for existence.

There were ethnic as well as theological reasons for this distinction in a society moved by the cycles of vengeance that served the ruling ideal of honor. As I hope will become clear in later sections of this essay, the ethnic and theological reasons coincided in sacrifice, the keystone in the great structure of Christian cult. The sacrificial death of Christ was an act of violence by men against a man. But, in the perspective of the twelfth century, the victim was by no means alone. For the aggressors were acting, against their knowledge and will, for the honor of God, affronted by Adam's disobedience, avenged by the curse brought by Adam on the human race, and vindicated by Christ on the Cross and in the Last Judgment. Moreover, Christ, the victim, was not alone. Contrary to appearances, his death was an engagement between opposing cohorts, the perverse and the sanctified. Thus, in addition to the disqualifications for magistracy placed by Church law on women, the entire apparatus of male bonding, essential in feudal society (and in others well known to enthnographers), came to a focus in the central act of Christian cult. "Manly" women could be enrolled in Christ's cohort. Others could be virtuous spectators of the *militia*, or *comitatus*, of Christ in action; but even this role was denied unbelievers.

The conventions according to which Bede had digested characters into and out of history also guided two writers to whom we shall devote particular attention, Ordericus Vitalis (1075–ca. 1142) and Matthew Paris. Ordericus neglected to include vivid contemporary incidents in Jewish history that occurred in Normandy, the geographical heartland of his history.[32] The reason may be that, laying upon the Jews the guilt for the deaths of Christ and his martyrs, Ordericus sympathized with crusaders who considered Jews, heretics, and Muslims to be the enemies of God, all fervently to be hated.[33] Certainly, the crusaders forced upon his mind the condemnation of Christ and the stoning of St. Stephen by the Jews,[34] and emphasized the retributive justice with which, he believed, the Romans had de-

---

'weakness' " (pp. 305–6, 333). On the general theme of misogyny, cf. Geoffrey of Monmouth's revision of the legend of St. Ursula, portraying the Saint and her companions as marrying for money. Valerie I. J. Flint, "The *Historia Regum Britanniae* of Geoffrey of Monmouth: Parody and Its Purpose. A Suggestion," *Speculum* 54 (1979): 464–65. See chap. 1, nn. 38–44; below, n. 37.

[32] Marjorie Chibnall, *The World of Orderic Vitalis* (Oxford: Clarendon, 1984), pp. 155–56.

[33] *Ecclesiastical History*, 3; 4.6; Chibnall, ed., 2:188, 5:44.

[34] *Ecclesiastical History*, 9.15; Chibnall, ed., 5:156, 168. Cf. Book 7.7; Chibnall, ed., 4:24, where Ordericus represents Pope Gregory VII complaining that the Romans, in abusing him, completed the persecution of Christ begun by the Jews.

stroyed their kingdom and dispersed them.[35] The crusaders also revealed
to him the deceptiveness of the Muslims, represented by the baker whom,
he had heard, the Devil had inspired to poison the abbot of St. Euphemia
in Calabria.[36]

The world, represented by Ordericus, is almost free of women, even of
women saints or religious, even of exceptional abbesses and nuns such as
Bede portrayed.[37] Reversing the order of filial bonding set forth by Augustine and many of his followers, Ordericus was primarily attached to his
father, who sent him as a child from England to the monastery of St-Évroul, in Normandy. They were never reunited. About his mother, Ordericus recorded only that she was English, without adding her name or any
further details.[38] Inevitably, women appear in his chronicle in their dynastic relationships with eminent men, and once as the indirect source of a
magnificent Anglo-Saxon psalter in the treasury of St-Évroul.[39]

But these women, like the wife of St. Évroul himself, whose devotion
the Saint increased by his own conversion to the ascetic life, are represented as acting in the shadows of men.[40] Such is even the case concerning
the Empress Mathilda, whom Ordericus portrayed first as the pawn in
marriages arranged by her father, Henry I of England, and later as a servant
to the interests of her second husband, Geoffrey of Anjou, in his resistance
to Henry and subsequently in his war against King Stephen. Plainly, Ordericus considered Mathilda's victory over and imprisonment of Stephen a
triumph over a humble and merciful man, whom Ordericus continued to
regard as king, though imprisoned. King Stephen's defeat signaled the ruin
of a once opulent land and induced Ordericus in sadness to conclude his
history.[41] Ordericus recorded the atrocity with which King David of Scotland and his soldiers invaded the English border regions, killing young and
old alike, and disemboweling pregnant women with their swords.[42] The

[35] *Ecclesiastical History*, 3; Chibnall, ed., 2:188.

[36] *Ecclesiastical History*, 7.6; Chibnall, ed., 4:22.

[37] See Paul Rousset, "La femme et la famille dans l'*Histoire Ecclésiastique* d'Orderic Vital,"
*Zeitschrift für Schweizerische Kirchengeschichte*, 63 (1969): pp. 58–66, esp. on the types of
women (p. 62) and the importance of marriage and family in defining the individual woman.
A stereotypal fear of women's sexuality may be expressed in Ordericus's account of a vision
of the anguished dead, among whom was seen a large company of women mounted on horseback and tormented by fiery saddles because of their immoderate enjoyment of obscene delights. E. Mégier, "Deux exemples de 'prépurgatoire' chez les historiens: À propos de *La
naissance du Purgatoire* de Jacques Le Goff," *Cahiers de civilisation médiévale (Xe–XIIe siècles)*
28 (1985): 52. See chap. 1, nn. 38–44; chap. 6, nn. 3, 35; above, n. 31.

[38] *Ecclesiastical History*, 13.45; Chibnall, ed., 6:552. Chibnall, *The World of Orderic Vitalis*,
p. 9.

[39] *Ecclesiastical History*, 3.4; Chibnall, ed., 2:42, 216 (Godiva).

[40] *Ecclesiastical History*, 6.9; Chibnall, ed., 3:266.

[41] *Ecclesiastical History*, 13.18, 42, 45; Chibnall, ed., 6:444, 544, 550.

[42] *Ecclesiastical History*, 13.37; Chibnall, ed., 6:518.

possibility that something other than compassion moved him is implied by his fascination with thunderstorms near St-Évroul in August 1134. No males, he heard, were killed, but only females, whether human or animal; and he at once hastened out to verify with his own eyes how the blow of divine chastisement had fallen.[43]

Matthew Paris's digestion of events produced an account that likewise concealed by what it told. A Jew, he wrote, once a "devil," was converted, baptized and transformed into a Christian, thereby shrewdly escaping the punishment that he would have suffered if he had been convicted as a poisoner.[44] Matthew recorded accounts of how Jews of England had been accused of abducting, circumcising, and crucifying Christian boys out of their contempt for Christ.[45] He recorded the terrible vengeance exacted by communities that believed these accounts and the vast payments exacted from the Jews, even in less agitated circumstances, including one made by King Henry III, who as "a second Titus or Vespasian, sold the Jews [i.e., the right to demand exceptional payments from them] for some years to his brother, Earl Richard, so that the Earl might disembowel those whom the King had skinned."[46] Saracens and Tartars are also portrayed as enemies with whom no common ground could be supposed, the Tartars especially, whom God's vengeance had plunged into a mindless bestiality.[47]

Women appear in Matthew's accounts far more frequently than in Bede's or Ordericus's, perhaps because Matthew counted some aristocratic women in his circle and wrote and illuminated hagiographical works for them. He took exception to Bishop Robert Grosseteste of Lincoln's indiscreet habit of thundering dreadful threats against all religious, especially women, yet he commended the Bishop's zeal.[48] He portrayed some great women rulers, including Queen Blanche of Castille, but generally he drew them as agents of dynastic expansion and aggrandizement. He recorded their aristocratic births, inheritances, ceremonial functions, and deaths, fre-

---

[43] *Ecclesiastical History*, 13.16; Chibnall, ed., 6:436–38.

[44] *Chronica majora* (a. 1259); Luard, ed., 5:730. Cf. Matthew's reference to his fellow monk, William Pigun, as a living demon. "Concerning Abbot John I, the twenty-first Abbot," in Matthew Paris, *Chronicles of Matthew Paris: Monastic Life in the Thirteenth Century*, ed. and trans. Richard Vaughan (New York: St. Martin's, 1984), p. 17.

[45] For a parallel charge made against the Jews of Winchester in 1193, occurring in the *Cronicon* of Richard of Devizes, see Nancy F. Partner, *Serious Entertainments: The Writing of History in Twelfth-Century England* (Chicago: University of Chicago Press, 1977), pp. 175–78.

[46] *Chronica majora* (aa. 1234 [for an event of 1235], 1239, 1240, 1255, 1256); Luard ed., 3:305–6, 543; 4:30; 5:488, 516–19, 537, 546, 552.

[47] *Chronica majora* (a. 1240); Luard, ed., 4:78.

[48] *Chronica majora* (a. 1253); Luard, ed., 5:419. Matthew's attitude toward women is particularly interesting in view of the fact that St. Albans was a double monastery until 1140, when the nuns moved to a separate house at Sopwell. See above, n. 29.

quently in childbirth. But apart from the fleeting glory of this world, other somber themes were woven into these accounts. Matthew's xenophobia convinced him that dynastic marriages with French noblewomen were devices of Henry III to corrupt the moral fibre of English aristocrats. Besides, "women," French or other, were so called because they softened man and his stern disposition, and, in inducing effeminacy, as in many other cases, woman's baneful ways could be taken for granted.[49]

In the minds of our authors as they wrote their historical works, there gleamed the ambiguous ideal of the ascetic. On the one hand, his body was worn away by mortification, his will stripped by the nakedness of his vows of self-renunciation. On the other hand, he was imagined as a male athlete in full vigor, grappling with vices in the spiritual gymnasium, dripping with sweat in battle, as the Maccabees had done, for victory.[50]

## VISUALIZING *ISTORIE*

It should be clear by now that our subject, digestion, is a synonym for a kind of cognition that fuses beauty with violence. Given the authorial strategy of concealment, it should be apparent that the unity not present in the formal structure of the texts is to be found in ways of thinking that expected readers to construct unity by using their own imaginations in the gaps between fascicles and episodes. In a similar way, the perception of gaps in historical literature—of persons, generations, or areas unrepresented in written accounts—stimulated the compositions of histories themselves. Thus, such factual writers as Bede and William of Malmesbury saw a need for accounts of what was known but unwritten, and Geoffrey of Monmouth took the absence of histories as the point of departure for the illusory "depiction" that he perpetrated on "an age grown conscious of the past."[51] Gaps within works invited the play of historical imagination no less than gaps between them. Behind the omissions and inclusions by which historical writers composed their works, which were representations and not documentations of power, there stood critical methods and objectives that changed experience into information. And behind the apparatus of criticism, by which information was transformed into epiphany, there lay an elaborate understanding of how the mind worked, that is, of cogni-

---

[49] *Chronica majora* (a. 1244); Luard, ed., 4:349: "Ipsam igitur verbis elegantissimis petit et exhortatur, sciens quia *mulier*, quasi *molliens herum* dicitur, ut ipsa regis viri sui [animum] in hoc rigore et rancore, quem concepit erga episcopum Wintoniensem, studeat emollire." But one particularly degenerate noble woman, a "tireless persecutrix" of religious, was distinctly not mollifying. *Chronica majora* (a. 1256); Luard, ed., 5:554.

[50] William of Poitiers, *Gesta Guillelmi Ducis Normannorum et Regis Anglorum*, pt. 1, chap. 55; Foreville, ed., p. 134.

[51] R. William Leckie, Jr., *The Passage of Dominion: Geoffrey of Monmouth and the Periodization of Insular History in the Twelfth Century* (Toronto: University of Toronto Press, 1981), pp. 20, 25–27.

tion. John of Salisbury captured the essence of the pattern that cognition was thought to take in his phrase *"cognitio Dei et cultus"* (the process of apprehending God and the service due him).[52] In exploring ways of thought that made historical writing possible, it is important to establish that the same pattern extended through all the arts of the imagination, historical writing among them.

All art of which our writers took notice was scholarly; its creators and intended audiences were schooled in mimesis. Thus, they inclined to seek likeness in dissimilars, including dissimilar artistic genres and media. Common to the arts of imagination, the pattern of cognition depended on elaborate cross-references between verbal and visual signs and esthetic responses. It presupposed that human beings became aware of their own mental faculties when they applied those faculties in the image-making phase of cognition, that is, in an effort designed to reach and change the heart through the imagination. The writing of history was related to the goal and experience of conversion.

To say this much is to anticipate the conclusion that the ideas of thinking with which we are concerned lead to a paradox: that human cognition is both negated and completed by divine grace. Indeed, traces of this paradox appear in the reliance, expressed by many historical writers, on the inspiration of God to complete their works.[53]

One is struck by the constant value placed on realism in the arts. Even the advent of "Gothic naturalism" in sculpture and painting does not remove the effect, for modern viewers, of abstract stylization. And yet, when twelfth-century writers commented on works of their day, pagan as well as Christian, they admired paintings that seemed to stand off from the wall and walk, and the "incredible beauty" of figures, painted or carved, that seemed to live and breathe. Their comments duplicate those of ancient viewers who, looking at works in vastly different styles, also saw patterns that "seem to stand up and move about, as if they were real."[54] A similar

---

[52] *Vita Sancti Anselmi*, prol.; Migne *PL* 199:1009. Cf. *Metalogicon*, prol.; Clement C. J. Webb, ed., *Ioannis Saresberiensis Episcopi Carnotensis Metalogicon libri IIII* (Oxford: Clarendon, 1929), pp. 4–5: "notitia veri, amor boni, cultus Dei." Other examples of the phrase *cognitio Dei* occur in Rupert of Deutz, *Commentum in Apocalypsim*, 5.8; Migne *PL* 169:981: "Nobis enim lucet ira Dei et ad cognitionem proficit ejusdem Dei, quae illos tanquam facula consumpsit. . . ."; and Anselm of Havelberg, *Antikeimenon*, 1.13; Migne *PL* 188:1159–60. Commenting on the silence in heaven for the space of half an hour prophesied in the Apocalypse, Anselm wrote that the saved would contemplate God in his glory, without ever comprehending him: "Recte ergo media et non integra hora dicitur, quia licet ad sufficientem beatitudinem, tamen ad integram ipsius Dei cognitionem, qua immensa divinitas comprehendatur, nulli pertingere conceditur."

[53] E.g., Otto of Freising, *Chronicon*, prol.; *MGH, SSrrG*, pp. 8, 10. William of Malmesbury, *De Gestis Pontificum Anglorum*, 5. prol.; Hamilton, ed., p. 331, and *De Gestis Regum Anglorum*, 1. prol.; Stubbs, ed., 1:3.

[54] Rupert of Deutz, *Anulus*, bk. 4; Migne *PL* 170:607–8. Herbord, *Dialogus de Vita S. Ottonis Babenbergensis Episcopi*, 2.32; Wikarjak, ed., pp. 122–23. See also Ebo, *Vita S. Ottonis*

value on realism is present in drama and, to be sure, in historical writing. And this refrain across the sweep of so many different arts indicates an emphasis on the empathetic participation by the reader or spectator in the work of art, the cultivation, in them as well as in the artist or writer, of "the performing self."[55]

To speak of the imagination's power to reach and change the heart in this way is to adduce the emotions. The author's concern was echoed in many arts. One example comes from the visual arts. A prelate caused a great cross to be made of purest gold and adorned with flashing jewels, so that as it dazzled in the light it would bring penitence and salvation to the hearts of believers. Music, one of the most beloved arts in the twelfth century, offers other analogues. Christina of Markyate's parents, seeking to subvert her vow of chastity and thrust her into marriage, craftily exposed her at feasts to the sensuous melodies of the lyre and the suggestive, alluring songs of singers. To be sure, the same imaginative powers, differently directed, could be aroused by the voice of psalmody when it prepared the Lord's way to the heart, disclosing mysteries of prophecy to the ardent mind and infusing into the soul the grace of compunction. Thus, our grasp of the imaginative interplay between cognition and epiphany, with its interlacing of beauty and violence, can be enhanced by turning from historical texts to other kinds of evidence. In fact, the etymological affinity between "history," a verbal art, and the visual arts, and between "*istorie*" and historiation, (that is, pictorial decoration), encourages me to seek analogies in two other mnemonic artifacts, the Bury St. Edmunds Cross (ca. 1181–90) and a scene in the drama of Dante's (1265–1321) *Divine Comedy*.[56]

---

*Babenbergensis Episcopi*, 3.10; Wikarjak, ed., p. 111, on the beauty of these paintings and carvings on the pagan temple at Stettin. The citation of Theocritus's *Idylls, 15* is a translation by Matthew Arnold, "Pagan and Mediaeval Religious Sentiment," in *Essays in Criticism, First Series*, vol. 3 of *The Works of Matthew Arnold* (London: Macmillan, 1903), p. 224. See also chap. 6, n. 79; chap. 7, n. 27.

[55] Antonia Gransden, "Realistic Observation in Twelfth-Century England," *Speculum* 47 (1972): 29–51. Otto Pächt, *The Rise of Pictorial Narrative in Twelfth-Century England* (Oxford: Clarendon, 1962). Martin Stevens, "The Performing Self in Twelfth-Century Culture," *Viator* 9 (1978): 193–212.

[56] *Gesta Episcoporum Tullensium*, chap. 47 (on Bishop Pipo of Toul); *MGH, SS* 8, p. 647. Talbot, ed. and trans., *The Life of Christina of Markyate A Recluse of the Twelfth Century*, chap. 8, p. 48. *S. Ottonis Episcopi Babenbergensis Vita Prieflingensis*, chap. 3; Jan Wikarjak, ed., Monumenta Poloniae Historica, n.s., vol. 7, fasc. 1 (Warsaw: Państwowe Wydawnictwo Naukowe, 1966), p. 58. Cf. the association of the reform of psalmody (*dulcissime*) and the sponsorship of hagiography by Abbot Olpert of Gembloux. *Gesta Abbatum Gemblacensium*, "De Olperto Abbate," chap. 43; *MGH, SS* 8, pp. 540–41.

The issue is a "symbolic synesthesia that runs throughout the Christian tradition," especially "the general tendency within the tradition to symbolize significant sacred events in terms of a convergence of auditory and visual categories." David Chidester, "The Symbolism

On the basis of convincing, but circumstantial, evidence, the Cross is thought to have been made for the monastery of Bury St. Edmunds at the order of Abbot Samson (figures 1, 2). Samson is known to have added to the splendor of his community by careful rehabilitation of its buildings, by acquisition and illumination of manuscripts, by purchase of vestments and other liturgical furniture, and by execution of an elaborate program of paintings in the choir of the abbey church. Each of those paintings was accompanied by verses which Samson himself composed. The Bury St. Edmunds Cross is thought to have been among the treasures that he gathered. It is made of seven interlocking pieces of walrus tusk; the upright measures 22⅝ inches, and the crossbeam, 14¾ inches. Small as it is, its surfaces are covered with figures and legends.

The front carries one scene at each of the four extremities encircling the corpus of the Crucified: at the foot, Pilate judging Christ; at the left hand of the corpus, the deposition from the Cross and the entombment; at the right hand, the resurrection; and, at the head, Christ's ascension into heaven. Other figures on the upright enlarge upon the historical centrality of the Crucifixion. Above the scene of Pilate sitting in judgment, the foot of the Cross begins in Adam, beside whom sits, off center, a lamentably misshapen Eve, almost a caricature of a woman. Just above the head of the corpus, at the juncture of the two arms, the sculptor placed an elaborate medallion representing prophetic and apostolic testimonies to Christ (including the figures of Isaiah, Moses, the Apostles John and Peter, and, above the medallion, Jeremiah) and drawing the allegorical parallel between the brazen serpent, which Moses raised in the desert to cure the Israelites bitten by serpents, and Christ, raised upon a tree to cure those fatally wounded by sin. Between this medallion, with its centrifugal movement, and the Ascension scene, the sculptor represented the inscription

---

of Learning in St. Augustine," *Harvard Theological Review* 76 (1983): 77–78. To underscore the theme of synesthesia, Chidester quotes a statement by Augustine that for Christians "hearing is sight and sight hearing" (*Tractatus in Evangelium Iohannis*, 18.9, 10). Of course, a robust synesthesia was present in the pre-Christian identif.cation between text and sight. For example, Apuleius, *Golden Ass*, 8.32: ". . . I purpose to tell you the circumstance of every point, whereby such as are more learned than I (to whom fortune hath ministered more copious style) may paint it out in paper in form of an history." William Adlington. trans., *The Golden Ass of Apuleius* (London: Lehmann, 1946), p. 155. This analogy was common in medieval texts, e.g., *Vita Adalberonis Episcopi Wirziburgensis*, prol.; *MGH, SS* 12, p. 129. See the interesting discussion of reciprocal transformation between verbal and visual images in Françoise Bardon, "De la *Passio* à la Peinture: Analyse historique du récit verbal de la légende d'Ursule," *Revue belge d'archéologie et d'histoire de l'art* 52 (1983): esp. 44, 78. Bardon emphasizes the role of every painting as a new statement, interpreting the action in the picture (however ancient and stereotyped in literature) in relation to its own present and to contemporary culture and frames of mind. Cf. Nichols's useful term, "metaleptic chain of transpositions," to indicate the exchange between visual and verbal associations. Nichols, *Romanesque Signs*, p. 97.

*Figure 1.* The interplay of violence and beauty in historical imagination and the importance of the scroll as a compositional element are illustrated by the Bury St. Edmunds Cross. *The Metropolitan Museum of Art, New York. The Cloisters Collection, 1963. (63.12 recto.)*

*Figure 2.* The central medallion on the front of the Bury St. Edmunds Cross depicts Moses with the brazen serpent, an anagogical (or prophetic) reference to the corpus that once hung on the cross immediately below it. *The Metropolitan Museum of Art, New York. The Cloisters Collection, 1963. (63.12.)*

that Pilate ordered hung on the Cross, proclaiming Christ as King of the Jews (here punctuated by the hand of God in an attitude of blessing). Above the inscription, two figures represent Jews arguing that Pilate ought to have written, "He said that he was King of the Jews," and Pilate replying, "What I have written, I have written."

The reverse side of the Cross is also elaborately carved. It follows the same general pattern of one major representation at each of the four ends of the Cross, an elaborate central medallion with centrifugal lines, and figures decorating the arms. The four ends originally carried the symbols of the four Evangelists. (The plaque representing Matthew has been lost.) The central medallion represents the wounding of the Lamb of God by the Synagogue. The arms carry figures of twenty-one prophets, each with an inscription witnessing (so Christian exegetes taught) to Christ.

The decorative program is completed by Greek inscriptions on the three exposed sides of the plaques at the head of the cross, declaring Christ as Man (*Anthropos*), Messiah (*Christos*), and Ruler of all (*Pantocrator*), and by two other inscriptions in Latin, the one on the front and the other on the sides of the upright, declaring that the Jews had mocked Christ when, as God, he paid the penalty of death, and that in their foolish striving against his conquest of death the Synagogue had fallen into ruin.

Despite its smallness, therefore, the Cross displays 60 inscriptions and 109 figures (including the corpus). Given the anti-Jewish character of the decorative program, connections have quite naturally been drawn between the Cross' carvings and the stormy relations between Samson's monastery and its Jewish creditors. Those dealings culminated in an attack upon the Jewish community in 1189, when many were slaughtered and the survivors expelled from the town. The vehemence of the iconic program has also been understood in the light of Samson's own profound sorrow at the loss of Jerusalem in 1187, and his ardent desire to join the Third Crusade. Such a mood drew on a general cultural attitude rooted in the desire for vengeance on those whom tradition portrayed as the killers of Christ and his martyrs.

The theme of honor is set forth in the luxurious ivory, the opulent workmanship, the representation of Christ's triumph over his enemies, including death, and of course in the ritual function of the Cross as an object of adoration. Like the theme of honor, that of vengeance (seen both in Christ's propitiating self-sacrifice and in hostility against the Jews) is a tentative point of contact with the esthetic that I have detected in historical writings of the epoch. Closely related to these motifs, of course, is that of martyrdom in its literal and religious senses as witness. In the latter sense, suffering extends even unto death. The monastery of Bury St. Edmunds and all its splendors were dedicated to a martyr killed by the Danes, and its monks were easily able to recall how many of the prophets and apostles represented on the Cross had sealed their testimonies with pain and blood, and how their triumphs, which once appeared to be disgrace and death, redounded to the infamy and abasement of their enemies and blazed forth with dazzling majesty in the holiest shrines of Christendom. I shall return to the theme of retribution.

Another point of contact with the esthetic signs detected in twelfth-century historical writings is in the categories of people excluded from the representations. Few pagans, Jews, and women figure in the program. Of these categories, only a female personification of the Synagogue appears on the back side of the Cross. Pagans figure exclusively in the scenes depicting Christ before Pilate, Pilate's refusal to alter his inscription for the Cross, and the Roman soldiers smitten at the resurrection. Jews (i.e., those who could not be considered forerunners or founders of the Church) appear only as single figures, one pushing Christ forward in the judgment scene and another remonstrating with Pilate over the inscription. Women appear in the misshapen form of Eve and in the scenes portraying the Deposition, Resurrection, and Ascension. Seven out of 109 figures portray women, an index of how rare were the "manly" women recruited to Christ's cohorts.

Of greater weight, however, is the variety of ways in which the Cross expresses translation, not merely in the literal, spatial sense (as in Christ's ascent into heaven), or in the linguistic product (as in verses from Jerome's translation of the Scriptures), but as an esthetic strategy. I emphasize that I am using the word "translate" in the broad sense of "transform" or "render," and not in an exclusively linguistic meaning. The entire iconic program elaborated the theme of *sensus, non verba* ("meaning, not words"), the guiding axiom of advocates of liberal rather than literal translation. It plainly divided the world between those who could detect the *sensus* within the words and those who heard the words, but were unable to penetrate the preverbal (and previsual) perception that informed them. Pilate did not grasp the *sensus* of words spoken before his judgment seat any more than he grasped that of the inscription that he wrote with his own hand proclaiming Jesus as King of the Jews, or apprehended the Word of God that stood before him in the flesh.

The full weight of the inscriptions and figures is directed toward the blindness of the Jews to the truth revealed by their revered prophets, preserved in their own sacred texts, and fulfilled by words and actions before their very eyes. The deficiencies of verbal and visual images, even those gathered by eyewitness experience, is therefore essential to the decorative program; for its message is that neither pagans nor Jews had the critical judgment to translate the images of sensory experience into correct knowledge, much less to pass from authentic knowledge to epiphany.

Yet that double translation—from sensory images into knowledge and from knowledge into epiphany—had to be performed by those who believed in Christ. The Cross does not display the acts by which the heart was transformed by the imagination. It does provide evidence of the tools that a spectator required to perform them, namely, association by categories of likeness, contiguity, and contrast.

The program plays with foreign likeness, the dissimilar similarity that could disclose something latent, but not expressed on at least three levels: in the work; in the anagogical relations of Old Testament prophecy and

New Testament fulfillment; and in the moral analogues between the portrayals on the Cross and the immediate historical circumstances and emotional needs of the viewer. It also plays in space with contiguity that was not spatial but affective, using the centrifugal, or axial, movement of the focal medallions to indicate that, while the events of history followed a temporal sequence—from Adam to the Ascension—from another perspective all authentic witnesses were simultaneous and equidistant from the truth to which they testified.[57]

The contiguity of figures and inscriptions led, finally, to association by contrast. They preach the inversions of weakness into power, folly into wisdom, and death into life that were central to Christian and especially to ascetic doctrines of God's honor and hidden, retributive justice. To these, the program adds specifically the ironic inversion of Ham's playful mockery of his father, Noah, into a curse upon Ham, and its allegorical counterpart, the Jews' mockery of Jesus, into the vengeance exacted from them.

In a deeper hermeneutic sense, association by contrast prompted the juxtaposition of verbal and visual images, not as labels attached to identify pictures, but as parts of mixed dramatic style, components of a single visual rhythm. The program consists of a montage of isolated portrayals. The figures are iconic; the scenes, pericopic. The separate figures and scenes utter their individual speeches; the inscriptions appear on scrolls that unfold as words in the air. Each is a dramatic moment frozen on stage. The iconic program is in effect a compilation of witnesses in the act of witnessing. But the play leaves the plot to the imagination of the viewer.

The figures might be empty and the words, blank. The Jews witnessed to Christ without believing him. Pilate witnessed believing, but not believing in him. Prophets and apostles witnessed believing in him, and for them as for others who in love believed in him, the darkness of the images and the words mutually illuminated one another in esthetic recreation, in the affective passage from image to presence, from sensory experience to spiritual epiphany.

Thus, the Bury St. Edmunds Cross, like historical writings composed by the fascicle method, was a work of collection, a kind of album. Like them, it was neither self-explanatory nor self-contained. Applying to it the canons of integrity, proportion, and clarity requires the pursuit of references outside the work itself, notably to the cult it was designed to serve. Consequently, it establishes the possibility of translating verbal and visual images, or memories, into affective stimuli. But the mimetic acts of translation, from sensory images into right knowledge, from knowledge

---

[57] Cf. Gerhoch of Reichersberg, *Tractatus in Ps. 18*: 11; Migne *PL* 193:930. *Tractatus in Ps. 45*: 6; Migne *PL* 193:1575–76, and the related passage in *De Edificio Dei*, chap. 3; Migne *PL* 194:1203.

into epiphany, and from violence into beauty, depended upon the capacity of the spectator for the affective transport that it implied but did not express.

*Canto X* in Dante's *Purgatorio* also illustrates the double translation from sensory images through criticism to epiphany. In *Canto X*, Virgil and Dante reach the first terrace on the mountain of Purgatory. There they find three relief sculptures carved by God in the living marble. The first depicts the Annunciation; the second, David dancing before the Ark of the Covenant; and the last, a poor widow gaining retribution from the Emperor Trajan. The ostensible theme to which all the panels testify is humility, exemplified in the submission of the Blessed Virgin to God's will, the self-abasement of David the King before the Ark, and the obedience of Trajan, in all his power and magnificence, to the demand of the poorest of his subjects for justice.[58]

Vengeance, with honor, its counterweight, is a subsidiary theme. The Incarnation announced to the Virgin by an angel was the means of atoning for Adam's sin. The relief of David dancing before the Ark portrays the punishment of death visited upon Uzzah, when unauthorized he stretched forth his hand to keep the Ark from falling. It also implies another retaliatory judgment in its depiction of David's wife Michal, the daughter of Saul, gazing with contempt on her husband's self-abasement. When she mocked David for playing before the Lord, she was cursed with childlessness (2 Kings 7:23). The widow's petition was that the men who had murdered her son be punished. Trajan saw that justice was executed upon them. As the balance of the *Canto* indicates, Dante's overarching subject was the payment of debt through retributive justice that vindicated God's honor and proclaimed his glory. The three imaginary relief panels conjured up visual representations of that subject in sacred and profane history.

As in the historical texts and on the Bury St. Edmunds Cross, the reliefs constituted a collection, or montage, of detached scenes that were neither self-contained nor self-explanatory. Their cognitive and affective contents depended upon Scripture, patristic hagiography, and sacramental cult. The three panels did not constitute a single composition. No one of the reliefs could stand by itself. Virgil admonished Dante not to let his attention rest on one place (verse 46), and as Dante gazed at the plaques of the Annunciation and the widow before Trajan, he apprehended the verbal dialogues represented in the stone without captions. His imagination multiplied the visual images by the verbal ones. To his mind, the angel appeared, not as a silent visual image, but in a dramatic tableau uttering the word "Hail." Mary's reply, "Behold the handmaid of the Lord," Dante wrote, was

---

[58] On medieval recountings of the story of Trajan and the poor widow, see Minnis, *Chaucer and Pagan Antiquity*, pp. 53–54.

stamped into her visual image as clearly as a figure is stamped in wax. Likewise, Dante imagined the plaque showing Trajan as a dramatic spectacle; he appeared to hear the conversation between the widow and the Emperor. For God, the sculptor, had produced "this visible speech, new to us because it is not found here."

Dante supplied, in imagination, the verbal captions that the rhythm of the pictures required to translate the sensory images of the plaques into authentic knowledge, and that knowledge into awe before the hidden operations of divine honor and vengeance. In his account, the words constituted an inherent part of the visual image, a fusion that the pairing of words and inscriptions (as on the Bury St. Edmunds Cross) could only approximate. Augustine had called gestures, insignia, emblems and the like "visible words."[59] But Dante's acknowledgment that "visible speech" was not accessible on earth confirms the experience of translation between verbal and visual images and memories in human works of art that characterized both the chronicles and the visual representations found on the Bury St. Edmunds Cross. This experience of translation yielded a multiplication of images, an application of critical methods, and an epiphany that completed the passage from image to presence.

As the narrative of the *Divine Comedy* advances, the importance of this esthetic, and critical recreation, going mimetically beyond all mnemonic images to presence, becomes evident. Visual images, Dante observed, even the achievements of the greatest painters, suffered rapid obsolescence, exemplifying that for artists as for rulers earthly renown was no more than a puff of wind.[60] As to words, Dante confessed the inadequacy of speech to portray his own vision, and, indeed, despite all multiplication of verbal and visual images, the immediate experience of the divine light overwhelmed both memory and speech and quickly faded from him, leaving only the impression of its sweetness.[61] Words did not transcend the human condition; transcendence was opened only to those whom grace permitted to feel it, not to all and sundry by the mere telling.[62] Likewise, the visual images of the marble reliefs "spoke" to Dante in his penitence, which had begun to cure in him the sickness of mental vision that afflicted the proud. When he saw and heard them, his conversion had advanced to the point at which by feeling he knew, as the proud did not, that human beings were worms born to be transformed into an angelic butterfly but still imperfect in form. They were still to fly defenseless in the sight of justice, the retribution demanded by divine honor.[63]

---

[59] *De doctrina Christiana*, 2.3.4; *Corp. Christ.*, *ser. lat.*, 32, p. 34.
[60] Dante, *Purgatorio*, canto 11, lines 100–101.
[61] Dante, *Paradiso*, canto 23, lines 55–63, 94–96.
[62] Dante, *Paradiso*, canto 1, lines 70–72.
[63] Dante, *Paradiso*, canto 10, lines 124–29.

In the ninth century, Archbishop Agobard of Lyons had spoken of *"sculpturae historiatae"* recalled in Scripture.[64] Both the reliefs that Dante imagined and the carvings on the Bury St. Edmunds Cross were works of this sort. Living outside the monastic discipline and its cultic environment, Dante nonetheless portrayed the esthetic of violence and beauty that characterized the historical writings with which we are concerned. His account is characterized by the dramatic visualization of narrative in separate episodes, or icons; the compilation of those discrete images as mnemonic witnesses to a moral truth outside themselves; techniques of critical association by foreign likeness, affective contiguity, and assimilative contrast; and, finally, the multiplication of visual and verbal images and their translation by affective mimesis into epiphanies not open to all. The mind did not come to rest on one image, but played an intricate game of understanding in a field of many.

[64] Agobard of Lyons, *De Imaginibus Sanctorum,* chap. 21; Migne *PL* 104:216. See also chap. 7, n. 81.

## Chapter 3

# COGNITION AND CULT

THUS FAR, we have asserted that digesting history employed ways of thinking common to the arts of imagination. We have identified some characteristics of those patterns of thought in the mutual reflection of verbal and visual images, an interplay that enabled readers to construct unity in the gaps between the fragments that made up the text. In this way, we have begun to recover some invisible "transitions" like those which John Scotus Eriugena considered as providing a hidden framing structure in some parables (see Preface, n. 2). We are now in a position to examine, more precisely, the acts of translation by which writers thought it was possible to move from experience to information by way of criticism, from violence to beauty, and thence to epiphany.[1] Our point of departure for this stage of our inquiry will be the terms that defined their movement, namely, *cognitio Dei et cultus* (coming to know and venerate God). This was a great and arduous striving, since "God is said to inhabit darkness, not because he does inhabit darkness, but because his light, by the weight of its immensity, benumbs the earth-bound senses of our body."[2] Throughout, we shall need to remember that, in its quest for authenticity, the culture represented by those writers accepted a very wide array of proofs, some of which were supernatural. Thus, even though Bede did not refer to miracles as producing conversion, he did adduce them as a confirmation, benefit, and enrichment of it. And, in the twelfth century, the reverence given to such prophetic utterances as the Sibylline fragments and "Merlin's" prophecies by rulers and scholars of the highest intelligence and standing demonstrates that "we are not dealing with any popular mumbo jumbo, but with a matter of grave intellectual concern to serious and practical men. . . . It was not naivety which made men search the cloudy imagery of Merlin for some hint with a contemporary relevance. It was,

---

[1] Cf. the description by Leclercq of St. Bernard's doctrine of imagination as a passage "from experience to image and from image to style." However, in his consideration of how Bernard's ideas led to transcending both corporal necessity and this life, Leclercq certainly went beyond literary style. Jean Leclercq, "The Love of Beauty as a Means and an Expression of the Love of Truth," *Mittellateinisches Jahrbuch* 16 (1981): 69–72.

[2] C. H. Talbot, ed., *The Life of Christina of Markyate A Twelfth Century Recluse* (Oxford: Clarendon, 1959), chap. 81, p. 188.

rather, a too ambitious view of knowledge which is accessible to man."[3] Such was the cast of mind from which our histories arose and which they addressed.

## COGNITION

Ideas about history as an "instrument of cognition," and particularly as an instrument of cognition about God, evidently presupposed ideas about cognition in general. Everything that we have to say can be summed up in this way: the shape that histories received, as instruments, was set by the idea that thought itself—including the thought that they were meant to provoke—moved "only by degrees and as it were in fragments."[4] Like the writings that expressed it, thought itself was deemed to follow a segmentary order.

Among all the aspects of cognition, none was more difficult or fundamental than the relation of sensory data to thought. Did sensory experience accurately translate the jumbled outer world of things into the ordered inner world of ideas? Perhaps, as Bernard Silvestris wrote, the senses served the greater mental faculties as messengers from different quarters, delivering "the shapes of things" to the imagination, to be judged by reason and deposited in memory. Bernard considered the imagination the speculative power of the soul, and others were able to exemplify the speculative function with the paradigm of an architect, drawing upon the varied experience of material things to form in his mind the coherent plan (*forma*) that, in turn, would be translated into an actual house.[5] But how could similar

[3] Joel T. Rosenthal, "Bede's Use of Miracles in 'The Ecclesiastical History,' " *Traditio* 31 (1975): esp. 330–33. R. W. Southern, "Aspects of the European Tradition of Historical Writing, 3: History as Prophecy," *Transactions of the Royal Historical Society*, 5th series, 22 (1972): 167–68.

[4] William of Malmesbury, *De Gestis Pontificum Anglorum*, 5.187; N.E.S.A. Hamilton, ed., *Willelmi Malmesbiriensis Monachi de Gestis Pontificum Anglorum*, Rolls Series, no. 52 (London: Stationary Office, 1870), p. 331: "cognitionis instrumentum." Guigo II, "Meditation 10," in *The Ladder of Monks (A Letter on the Contemplative Life) and Twelve Meditations*, trans. Edmund Colledge and James Walsh (Kalamazoo, Mich.: Cistercian Publications, 1981), p. 121.

[5] *The Cosmographia of Bernardus Silvestris*, chaps. 13, 14; Winthrop Wetherbee, trans. (New York: Columbia University Press, 1975), pp. 122–23. Letter of Robert Grosseteste to Master Adam Rufus, *ep.* 1, in Henry Richards Luard, ed., *Roberti Grosseteste Episcopi quondam Lincolniensis Epistolae*, Rolls Series, no. 25 (London: Longman, 1861), pp. 4–5. In addition, Grosseteste used analogues of sculptors and other craftsmen. On the centrality of imagination, see, for example, Leclercq, "The Love of Beauty as a Means and an Expression of the Love of Truth," pp. 69–72; and R. W. Southern, "Aspects of the European Tradition of Historical Writing, 4: The Sense of the Past," *Transactions of the Royal Historical Society*, 5th series, 23 (1973): 244. A helpful synthesis of doctrines about imagination in the twelfth and thirteenth centuries is in Douglas Kelly, *Medieval Imagination: Rhetoric and the Poetry of Courtly Love* (Madison: University of Wisconsin Press, 1978), esp. pp. 26–56. Kelly describes a movement from understanding to visualization of what is understood, "the artist's Image, projected as it

cycles of interplay between speculation and matter enrich the spiritual life, especially when the senses were "prone to many sorts of error" and were besides, "the windows of death," to be bolted shut with holy fear and love?[6]

At the very outset, two points must be emphasized: the variety of actions of which the imagination was thought capable, and the physical effects of imagination. As in so many other ways, Augustine of Hippo was a canonical authority on the imagination. He recognized that the imagination operated differently in people asleep and dreaming, in raging lunatics, and in ecstatics such as diviners and prophets. The imagination could join part of one memory image (for example, blackness) to part of another (for example, a swan) and from miscellaneous elements produce a composite image of something that never existed (a black swan). Moreover, the imagination could function independently of the physical actions of the body. Augustine frequently found that he had to read a page or a letter more than once because his mind wandered, even as his eyes were moving across the text. Nor were the effects of the imagination in its various modes limited to the mind. The Bible described how Jacob had propagated sheep of different colors by placing variegated rods for pregnant ewes to see at their watering troughs. Daily experience proved that the chameleon's body changed color according to what it saw; and that, as Jacob had shrewdly observed, what pregnant females saw left marks on the bodies of their offspring.[7] There were, to be sure, phantasms that worked in the minds of dreamers and lunatics, phantasms too intruded by the Devil to alarm or seduce the soul; but there were also authentic visions conveyed by God to delight the eyes of the spirit, and these could transform the soul and mark the body, indeed, loosen the tongue of the mute. The power of visual impressions on the soul—real or fancied—could be fatal. In Chaucer's words: "Lo which a greet thyng is affeccioun: / Men may dyen of imaginacioun, / So depe may impressioun be take."[8]

---

were into matter" (pp. xi–xii, 55), but I wish to indicate another kind of movement in which visualization comes *before* understanding. In a collection of rich and informative essays, Jacques Le Goff calls for "a history of the imagination," illustrating the kinds of subjects that should appear in such a history (*The Medieval Imagination*, trans. Arthur Goldhammer [Chicago: University of Chicago Press, 1988], pp. 4–5).

[6] *The Cosmographia of Bernardus Silvestris*, chap. 13; Wetherbee, trans., p. 122. *Vita S. Modani*, chap. 4; *Acta Sanctorum*, 1 Feb., p. 504, citing Jer. 9:21, a verse also quoted by Bernard of Clairvaux in his *Sermon on Conversion*, 6.11; Jean Leclercq and H. Rochais, eds., *Sermones*, in *S. Bernardi Opera*, vol. 4 (Rome: Editiones Cisterciensis, 1966), 1:85. Cf. Teresa of Ávila's complaint that her feeble imagination was an impediment to spiritual progress. *Autobiography*, chaps. 4, 40; E. Allison Peers, trans., *The Complete Works of Saint Teresa of Jesus* (London: Sheed and Ward, 1950) 1:81, 391–92.

[7] *De Trinitate*, 10.3.5, 11.4.7, 11.8.15, 11.10.17; *Corp. Christ., ser. lat.*, 50, pp. 317–18, 341–43, 351–52, 353–54.

[8] See Talbot, ed. and trans., *The Life of Christina of Markyate A Twelfth Century Recluse*,

Ideas about cognition turned, quite naturally, to sight and hearing, the two senses most readily employed in imaginative speculation, and to the instruments of visual and verbal images by which, through the superior judgment of reason, the outer and inner worlds were brought into correlation, or, rather, made parallel. Translation was the key to synesthesia.

As an intellectual enterprise, historical writing shared the fundamental hermeneutic gaps characteristic of all verbal discourse; there were disparities for the speaker (and, in reversed order, for the hearer) between things and perceptions, between perceptions and thoughts, and between thoughts and words. There were many events that one could understand better by seeing, as an eyewitness, than indirectly, by hearing the accounts of others.[9] As an extension of cult, historical writing participated in another range of hermeneutic gaps; for it dealt with things that could not be expressed in words and yet that could not be spoken of except in words.

Considering such matters, one could become entangled in words and kept by them from the realities that they purported to express. Ordinarily, when words were heard, the hearer's mind descended into its inner depths and imaged forth from it forms and things formed that corresponded with the things that the words had named. Thus, in portraying his subject's odor of holiness and elegance in gesture and speech, and the honor and splendor of his bearing, a biographer could say that such characteristics were better understood than said.[10] Many things could not be expressed by tongue or writing; many wonders could only be described by analogy— "as if angels," "as if deified."[11] This imaginative effort was inadequate most of all when spiritual or divine things were named.

As the example of the illiterate apostles demonstrated, to see, not to hear or to read, was to understand. No more than John the Divine's inward eyes were theirs so blinded that the signs of what they saw could not be formed in their spirits, or understanding of what had been seen, shine forth

---

chap. 75, p. 170. *Miracula Adalberonis Episcopi Wirziburgensis*, chap. 10; *MGH, SS* 12, p. 143. On Rupert of Deutz as "Bildvisionär," Wilhelm Kamlah, *Apokalypse und Geschichtstheologie: Die mittelalterliche Auslegung der Apokalypse vor Joachim von Fiore*, Historische Studien, Heft 285 (Berlin: Ebering, 1935), pp. 108, 113. Egid Beitz, *Rupertus von Deutz: Seine Werke und die bildende Kunst,* Veröffentlichungen des kölnischen Geschichtsvereins, no. 4 (Cologne: Verlag des kölnischen Geschichtsvereins, 1930), pp. 14–15. Geoffrey Chaucer, *Canterbury Tales*, "The Miller's Tale," lines 425–27.

[9] E.g., Gervasius of Canterbury, *Chronica*; William Stubbs, ed., *The Historical Works of Gervase of Canterbury*, Rolls Series, no. 73 (London: Longman, 1879), 1:27, on the architectural elements in Christ Church, Canterbury, reconstructed after a catastrophic fire: "Quae omnia visu melius quam auditu intelligere volenti patebunt."

[10] *Martyrium Arnoldi Archiepiscopi Magontini*; Johann Friedrich Böhmer, ed., *Fontes Rerum Germanicarum* (Stuttgart: Cotta, 1855), 3:282.

[11] E.g., *Translatio Godehardi Episcopi Hildesheimensis*, chaps. 1, 2; *MGH, SS* 12, p. 643. *Vita Adalberonis Episcopi Wirziburgensis*, chap. 13; *MGH, SS* 12, p. 135.

in their minds.[12] But what was possible for these "unlettered, ignorant men" was not possible to others. "Demons confess and fear our Lord, Jesus Christ, the crucified. Jews and false Christians do not acknowledge, but despise and mock him."[13] Did not the Jews and Pontius Pilate see the same man as the Apostles?

Yet, even for those who rightly discerned what they saw, there were barriers to understanding. To be sure, the words sent the mind inward, but there the eyes of the mind (whether analytic or recollective) could only be swallowed up in clouds; for things spiritual and divine had neither forms nor images, nor could progress in them be made through words or forms of words. The mouth was taught to speak the Lord's words and the heart, to consider them as often as a person wished. But however much a person desired it, understanding came, not through such indirect means as words and recollected images, but directly through the experience of the affects and the inward feeling of enlightened love.[14]

Thus, a second area of cognitive inconsistency opened, in addition to that in which historians felt a moral constraint to turn their eyes from the empty spectacles of this world. For, based though it was on memory, the figurative work of imagination obeyed its own laws, which were more esthetic than rational and which certainly were unfettered by the law of contradiction. The method of figuration purported to detect meanings hidden in events. But, equally, it cast a veil over historical texts in the deliberate effort to intimate by some suspicion that something was to be understood other than what was said. "By far the greatest proof of art," Quintilian wrote, "is given when one thing is intimated through another,"[15] repeating the sense of Aristotle's famous statement that the invention of metaphor was one of the greatest arts in poetry, and one that could not be learned from others for it was "an intuitive perception of the similarity in dissimilars" (*Rhetoric* 1459a).

In the effort to imply more than was said, plain speech was avoided in favor of obscurity; ornament, novelty, and variety were deployed to heighten the pleasure of discovery by making it difficult, and to magnify the importance of subjects that easy access would have made seem worthless. The emphases on obscurity and laborious discovery underscores the role of figuration as a digestive process, rather than as an expository contrivance, merely the arrangement of materials. For Augustine and for authors in centuries after him, imaginative figuration was "not a linguistic or

---

[12] Rupert of Deutz, *Commentum in Apocalypsim*, 1.1, 2.3, 6.10, 9.15; Migne *PL* 169:851, 852, 894, 1009, 1111, 1112.

[13] *Vita Norberti Magdeburgensis*, chap. 14; *MGH, SS* 12, p. 687.

[14] William of St-Thierry, *Speculum Fidei*, chaps. 74–77. See n. 170.

[15] Quintilian, *Institutes*, 9.2.92, 93.

textual phenomenon."[16] As the Father himself wrote: "There is no need for much controversy about the name of a thing when the thing itself is clear beyond any shadow of doubt."[17] Firmly ensconced in patristic methods of Scriptural exegesis, figuration was naturally found useful in other areas of historical inquiry, not least in those concerning recent events about which it was dangerous to speak plainly.[18] As a calculated device of indirect reference, it cultivated ambiguity and multiplied images.

How were these hermeneutic gaps, both unavoidable and contrived, to be bridged? What common term could allow translation between their segmented terms? One clue is given by a general preoccupation with beauty. Historical writers in the period under review valued rhetorical elegance and used such words as *decus* (glory or grace), *lepos* (charm), and *ornatus* (grandeur) to define stylistic beauty. They revised texts composed in earlier generations because, they judged, "moderns" had mastered a "more careful beauty" than the crude beauty attained in the past; they engaged in ambitious building schemes richly to adorn and beautify their monasteries and churches.[19] (As an experienced translator, Bede observed that Caedmon's verses could not be rendered into another language word for word "without losing their beauty and dignity."[20]) But their esthetics reached beyond style to another order of beauty. They wrote of the *decus* of faith and of virtue; of "the most beautiful perfection of the Church," preached by John the Baptist, spread by Christ through the world, and yearned for in its "most perfect glory (*decus*)" by believers still on earth.[21] Portents, symbolic associations, and liturgical practices that witnessed to the Church's perfection were also "beautiful."[22] In imitating the discipline of the primitive Church and holding firmly to the apostolic foundation of the faith, Bede wrote, he and his brethren also anticipated receiving the reward that the early Christians had received. They carried "in the present a most beautiful figure of future blessedness." Dying, he said, his soul desired to see Christ,

[16] Gerald L. Bruns, "The Problem of Figuration in Antiquity," in *Hermeneutics: Questions and Prospects*, ed. Gary Shapiro and Alan Sica (Amherst: University of Massachusetts Press, 1984), p. 158. I owe this reference to Professor Sica.

[17] *City of God*, 9.23; *Corp. Christ., ser. lat.*, 47, p. 270.

[18] Cf. Quintilian, *Institutes*, 9.2.65–66. Augustine, *De Doctrina Christiana*, 1.6.6; 2.6.7–8; *Corp. Christ., ser. lat.*, 32, pp. 9–10, 35–36.

[19] *Gesta Abbatum Gemblacensium*, chaps. 75, 76 (*De Anselmo Abbate*); *MGH, SS* 8, p. 551. Sigebert of Gembloux, *Gesta Abbatum Gemblacensium*, chaps. 29–30 (*De Olperto Abbate*); *MGH, SS* 8, p. 537. See below, n. 99.

[20] *Ecclesiastical History*, 4.24; Bertram Colgrave and R.A.B. Mynors, eds., *Bede's Ecclesiastical History of the English People* (Oxford: Clarendon, 1969), p. 416.

[21] Bede, *Hom.*, 2.19 (*In Vigilia Nativitatis S. Iohannis Baptistae*); *Corp. Christ., ser. lat.*, 122, pp. 326–27.

[22] E.g., Bede, *Hom.*, 1.12 (*In Theophania seu Epiphania Domini*), 1.17 (*Post Epiphaniam*), and 2.17 (*Dominica Pentecostes*); *Corp. Christ., ser. lat.*, 122, pp. 87, 123–24, 306.

his king, in his beauty.[23] Whatever other needs may have been satisfied by these ideals, the guiding principle was that of moral beauty; its corollary was that beauty inspires love.[24]

The esthetic familiar to historical writers in the period under review therefore encompassed rhetoric with the trope unnamed in rhetoric, by which a speaker said one thing so that another would be understood.[25] In some of his sayings, Christ himself had left gaps, or ellipses, so that one would have to listen for what was "beneath" the words; and, indeed, all the revelations of Scripture were composed on a principle of latency. "The Old Testament preached God the Father manifestly, but God the Son not so manifestly, but rather obscurely. The New Testament manifested God the Son, but covertly revealed and made known the deity of the Holy Spirit. Afterwards, the Holy Spirit was preached when it gave us a more open manifestation of its divinity."[26] The sense of words lay in a beauty testified to not only by verbal figuration, but also by nonverbal figures, through the whole range of imaginative arts employed in the Christian cult, not least of which were music, painting, and architecture. For the arts of the imagination were the media in which the mind multiplied its images, all alike witnesses to the same primal powers, all alike instruments of translation by which the heart could pass from experience of the beautiful to epiphanies of Beauty. Reading and understanding the Scriptures was only the beginning of the vision that would be perfected when the redeemed saw their Lord face to face.[27]

We must now turn directly to the cognitive exercise by which those instruments were deployed. Given the name—"transitions" (*transitus*)—that John Scotus Eriugena applied to these tools for moving through a segmented order from one figure to others, it is appropriate that the cognitive exercise employing them was translation. William of St-Thierry (ca. 1085–ca. 1148) observed: "Just as there [in Paradise] Christ will not be known as human powers allow, so also here, those desiring to know him above what he is as a man should not stick too much with words, but should pass by them, as by a boat, from faith to sight." Some German bishops, his contemporaries, acutely observed movement in the opposite direction, be-

[23] Cuthbert, *Epistola de obitu Bedae*, in Colgrave and Mynors, eds., p. 584. *Hom.*, 2.16 (*Post Ascensionem*); *Corp. Christ., ser. lat.*, 122, p. 300.

[24] Talbot, ed. and trans., *The Life of Christina of Markyate A Twelfth Century Recluse*, chaps. 70, 80; pp. 156, 186.

[25] Quintilian, *Institutes*, 9.2.65. Augustine, *De Doctrina Christiana*, 3.37.56; *Corp. Christ., ser. lat.*, 32, pp. 115–16.

[26] Rupert of Deutz, *Commentum in Apocalypsim*, 5.9; Migne *PL* 169:1004 (*subaudiendum*). Anselm of Havelberg, *Antikeimenon*, 1.6; Migne *PL* 188:1147–48 (*submonstravit et subinnuit*).

[27] Rupert of Deutz, *Commentum in Apocalypsim*, *ep. ad Fridericum Archiepiscopum Coloniensem*; Migne *PL* 169:826.

ginning with a picture, advancing from picture to written text, and from the text to a normative sanction for conduct prior to the text. (The bishops did not take account of the processes of imagination, to which William alluded.[28]) But synesthetic transition either from words to vision or from vision to words was more than the practical decipherment of cryptic words by emblematists or iconographers. It required direct physical experience, or discipline of the body, as well as intellectual abilities. Together with various branches of theology, kinesthetic aspects of ascetic discipline provided a "boat" by which one could oscillate between verbal and visual images, go beyond both kinds of images to affective response, and, finally, move from physical perception to spiritual epiphany. They included not only personal acts of mental contrition and physical mortification, but also collective liturgical acts performed in the midst of paintings that simulated the presence of Christ and the saints, and psalmody, to which invisible hosts of angels were thought to attend.

A recollective and mimetic phenomenon common to other societies was at work. Establishing the use of song in rituals to force "the imagination to work on certain lines," Bowra observed: "Primitive song takes its singers out of themselves by making them act a part, even if this is themselves as they have recently been or hope to be.... The words illuminate the action, and the action adds body to the words." As in the theater, performance of ritual song, normally associated with prayer, engaged the imagination "not so much pictorially but emotionally."[29] Ritual psalmody was, in effect, a complex means, not of decipherment, but of spiritual transport, giving coherence through rhythm and vigor to other sensory perceptions, notably visual and verbal ones. I shall illustrate this kinesthetic process chiefly with reference to the Fathers and the Venerable Bede.

The terms employed to express translation all imply transport, or spatial movement. "Interpretation" (*interpretatio*, from *inter-pretari*) denotes a mediation or brokerage between parties. An interpreter (*interpres*, from *inter-praesto*) was someone who stood or was present between other parties. Horace's *fidus interpres* was a "trustworthy middle-man."[30] Bede preferred other words that equally denoted spatial movement: translation (*translatio*, from *transfero*, to "hand over" or "carry across") and transfuse (*transfundo*, to pour from one container into another).[31] The spatial sense

[28] William of St-Thierry, *Speculum Fidei*, chap. 79; Davy, ed., cited n. 170, p. 88. Rahewin, *Gesta Friderici*, 3.17(16); *MGH*, *SSrrG*, p. 188.

[29] C. M. Bowra, *Primitive Song* (Cleveland, Ohio: World, 1962), pp. 29–30, 209.

[30] Horace, *Ars Poetica*, line 133.

[31] E.g., *Hom.*, 1.21 (*In Quadragesima*); *Corp. Christ.*, ser. lat., 122, p. 154. See the quite different senses of *translatio* used by Stephen G. Nichols, Jr., *Romanesque Signs: Early Medieval Narrative and Iconography* (New Haven, Conn.: Yale University Press, 1983), pp. 9 (a "prin-

was preserved in the literal meaning of the verb "*transferro*," as, for example when Augustine wrote about the "translations" of Enoch, Christ, and the whole temple (i.e., people) of God from earth to heaven,[32] and other authors wrote about "translations" of relics or bishops from one place to another. Verbal translations bridged cognitive space; when translators rendered sense for sense instead of word for word, they might also provide the means by which readers could negate emotional distance.

Plainly, cognitive and affective space belonged to orders different from physical existence and linear dimensions. They belonged to the order of time, inasmuch as their spiritual dimensions were measured by duration; to that of quantity, inasmuch as those dimensions were gauged by intensity; and to that of axiality, inasmuch as their relation to a common spiritual center and circumference was the measure. Augustine's celebrated discussions of memory and time in the *Confessions* served as a classic definition of these kinds of space. Augustine concluded that the memory was the "stomach," or the "treasury," of the mind, and that intellectual and affective life consisted fundamentally in the digestive process, by which the memory absorbed, associated, and distinguished its contents. Time itself was not the movement of bodies—sun, moon, and stars, a potter's wheel, or any other external event—but rather the inward "distention" or "stretching" of the mind around the object of its attention. Thus, "spaces of time" were not regular, abstract periods so much as they were events that occurred "in a place that is not a place" in the memory, events whose proportions were defined by quantity and axiality according to the singleness or multiplicity of love(s).[33] In the *Confessions*, Augustine took great pains to indicate how in those events words, "images of images,"[34] were referred to other nonverbal contents of the memory-stomach (including "images," or sensory impressions, and still other things present in the memory immediately and not indirectly, by images) to establish understanding. Among the defining referents were the "perturbations" of the soul: desire (*cupiditas*), joy (*laetitia*), fear (*metus*), and sadness (*tristitia*).[35]

Inasmuch as digesting sacred history was linguistic for Bede on the deep hermeneutic level of meaning, it was so by virtue of its analogue with linguistic translation, especially in these connotations of physical movement, "as by a boat," aimed at bridging the hermeneutic gap in the superficial level of verbal exchange.

---

ciple of continuity and change" relating human events to "divine intentionality") and 133 (a transfer of power, as in the well-known term *translatio imperii*).

[32] *City of God*, 15.19; *Corp. Christ., ser. lat.*, 48, pp. 481–82.

[33] *Confessions*, 10.8.12–10.14.22, 10.24.35, 11.23.29; *Corp. Christ., ser. lat.*, 27, pp. 161–66, 174–75, 208–14.

[34] *Confessions*, 10.15.23; *Corp. Christ., ser. lat.*, 27, p. 167.

[35] *Confessions*, 10.14.21–22; *Corp. Christ., ser. lat.*, 27, pp. 165–66.

Bede himself was at least trilingual. Like Archbishop Albinus of Canterbury, "he was so well instructed in the study of Scripture that he had no small mastery of Greek, while he understood Latin as completely as his native English language."[36] On Scriptural evidence, he believed that the peoples of the earth had originally spoken one language, but that in punishment of Babel's pride the primal unity was shattered into linguistic confusion.

The miracle at Pentecost, when, filled with the Holy Ghost, the Apostles spoke "with other tongues, as the Spirit gave them utterance . . . [and] every man heard them speak in his own language" (Acts 2:4–5), exemplified for him how the humility of the Church had restored the unity that Babel's pride had broken. But ambiguity in the biblical account left some doubt whether the miracle were one of speaking or of hearing, that is, whether the Apostles had spoken in diverse languages, or whether each listener heard, not in the language in which the Apostles proclaimed the wonders of God, but in his own. What was clear to Bede, however, was that the giving of the Holy Spirit at Pentecost, with its miracle of understanding, differed from the giving of the law to Moses on Mt. Sinai. For, on Sinai, the people stood, terrified, at a great distance while God, descending in fire, wrote the law on stone with his finger. At Pentecost, the Spirit entered the house where the Apostles were. Striking none with fear, it settled, in tongues of fire, on their heads, and wrote in their hearts. At least an implied distinction was present in his mind between human wisdom, which can be externally learned and taught, and the inward wisdom which God gave as he gave the gift of tongues.[37]

Bede's knowledge of history, and his own experience of five languages in the British Isles, including Latin, did not permit him to minimize the divisiveness of language as a multiplier of images. Indeed, it provided an apt illustration of his proposition that spiritual distance could be measured not by space so much as by disposition.[38] In recent times, King Egbert of

---

[36] *Ecclesiastical History*, 5.20; Colgrave and Mynors, eds., p. 530. On the general problem of linguistic divisions, see Bernhard Bischoff, "The Study of Foreign Languages in the Middle Ages," *Speculum* 36 (1961): 209–24.

[37] *Expositio Actuum Apostolorum*, 2.2–6. *Retractatio in Actus Apostolorum*, 2.2; M.L.W. Laistner, ed., *Bedae Venerabilis Expositio Actuum Apostolorum et Retractatio* (Cambridge, Mass.: Medieval Academy, 1939), pp. 15–16, 98–99. See Peter the Venerable's comment that Greek and Hebrew Scriptures should be read as complementing each other, not as differing, since "linguae tantum diversae sunt, sensus linguarum idem est. Sonus duplex est, intellectus unus est." *Adversus Iudeorum Inveteratam Duritiem*, chap. 2; *Corp. Christ., continuatio medievalis*, 58, p. 21.

[38] *Ecclesiastical History*, 1.1; Colgrave and Mynors, eds., p. 16. Bede recorded how Bishop Aiden of Lindisfarne had spoken in his native language in order not to be understood by King Oswine of Deira and his thanes; how King Oswiu of Northumbria, having lived in Ireland, became fluent in the languages of the Irish; how Bishop Cedd acted as interpreter at

Kent's project to have an Archbishop of Canterbury appointed who could preach to him and his people in their own language had been thwarted by papal act. Theodore of Tarsus, the Archbishop who was actually appointed, required the services of Benedict Biscop as translator. At about the same time, King Cenwealh of Wessex grew tired of hearing Bishop Agilbert's foreign speech and eventually provoked him to return to his native Gaul.[39] Together with these allusions to the most exalted levels of his society, Bede's account of Caedmon, the stablehand, Bede's own translation of the Gospel of John into Anglo-Saxon "for the utility of God's Church" and his reference to the use of paintings in his monastery for the benefit of the unlettered who "discerned the Lord's works through attentive study" of the pictures,[40] leave no doubt that Bede's daily environment was at least bilingual, and that many of the historical inquiries that he inventoried in his preface to the *Ecclesiastical History* were conducted not in Latin but in a vernacular tongue.

When Bede read varying translations of Scripture, he was instinctively aware of the processes of understanding that produced them; it says much about that awareness that Bede spoke of his own formal translations as being, not word-for-word, but according to the sense.[41] The distinction was rather more than the academic one between "literal" and "free" translations. For, retaining Augustine's distinction between the mnemonic, preconceptual "sense of the thing" and what the limits of one or another language allowed,[42] Bede was contrasting equivalence in form between words (an exercise in synonyms) with identity in substance of intent (an exercise in association).[43] Even more exactly, his emphasis was on identity in the act of mnemonic associating, rather than on the formal associations that the process eventually brought forth. As indicated earlier, the exercise of associating was affective as well as intellectual. But in spiritual matters, it

the Synod of Whitby; and how a letter from Abbot Ceolfrith of Jarrow to King Nechtan of the Picts had to be translated into Pictish. *Ecclesiastical History*, 3.14, 25; 5.21; Colgrave and Mynors, eds., pp. 258, 296, 298, 552. On the *lingua Latinorum* as a "principle of unity" in Bede's portrayal of the tribes about him as "the English people," see H.E.J. Cowdrey, "Bede and the 'English People,' " *Journal of Religious History* 11 (1980–81): 502–4.

[39] *Vitae Abbatum*, chap. 3; Charles Plummer, ed., *Venerabilis Bedae Historia Ecclesiastica . . .* (Oxford: Clarendon, 1886), 1:366–67. *Ecclesiastical History*, 3.7, 25; Colgrave and Mynors, eds., pp. 235, 300.

[40] *Ecclesiastical History*, 4.24 and Cuthbert, *Epistola de Obitu Bedae*; Colgrave and Mynors, eds., pp. 416, 582. *Hom.*, 1.13 (*S. Benedicti Biscopi*); *Corp. Christ.*, *ser. lat.*, 122, p. 93.

[41] *Ecclesiastical History*, 4.24 (on verses by Caedmon) and 5.24 (Bede's epilogue to the *History*, concerning the life and passion of St. Anastasius); Colgrave and Mynors, eds., pp. 416, 568.

[42] See above, nn. 16, 30.

[43] On the distinction between form and substance, see *Comm. on II. Peter 3*: 13; David Hurst, trans., *Bede the Venerable: Commentary on the Seven Catholic Epistles*, Cistercian Studies Series, no. 82 (Kalamazoo, Mich.: Cistercian Publications, 1985), p. 151.

transformed the soul more radically than the intellect. At its most exalted level, in the inward communion of Christ and the soul, it was the mutual assimilation of seer and seen.

In his commentaries, Bede frequently paused to remark on discrepancies among Scriptural translations. Yet, not only was he never troubled by them, but, like Augustine before him, he welcomed their diversity as opening multiple accesses to the hidden, but manifold, intent of Scripture.[44] His confidence that the discrepant forms of texts conveyed the identical substance derived ultimately from Bede's belief that all who proclaimed the word of God—whether authors of Scriptural texts or authentic exegetes— and all other faithful hearers of the Word understood in and through the same Spirit, and not by virtue of the fabrications of their own minds.

Bede had impeccable precedents for his emphasis, not on formal or literal equivalence, but on sense as the goal of the digestive process by which a translator moved from one set of mute letters on a page to another, maintaining identity of substance. St. Jerome had set down an extensive rationale for this point of view in his celebrated letter to Pammachius, *On the Best Form of Translation* (*Ep. 57, De Optimo Genere Interpretandi*). Jerome marshalled weighty historical precedents, both pagan and Christian, for his argument that one should translate "not word for word, but sense for sense," regardless of what had to be omitted, added, or changed, given the peculiarities of each language. The Father asserted that rhetorical devices (such as inversion of words for emphasis), cases, figures of thought as well as of speech, and vernacular expressions in one language were incommensurate with those in others. At the outset, Jerome appeared to make an exception for Scripture, "in which even the order of words is a mystery."[45] But as his argument unfolded, he took great pains to inventory discrepancies between quotations of Old Testament passages in the Gospels and in other New Testament texts and the original texts. He also displayed wide divergences between the Old Testament and the Septuagint translation, and between his own translation and other versions.

Jerome wrote that there was no loss in meaning if a word or two were added or subtracted. Confusions of names, misquotations, and misattributions were also evident in Scripture and in its translations. Evangelists and Apostles had sought the sense, not the words, he wrote, and they had not kept to the order of words when the matter at issue lay open to the understanding. To be sure, impious men had seized on the resulting discrepancies, accusing the translators of falsification. But, Jerome insisted, even though the Evangelists, the Septuagint, and Jerome's translation all

---

[44] See Augustine, *Confessions*, 12.24.33; *Corp. Christ., ser. lat.*, 27, pp. 233–34. Bede, e.g., *Comm. on James 4*: 6, 5: 20; *I. Peter 1*: 24–25, 3: 20; *II. Peter 2*: 4; and *I. John 2*: 27, 3: 4; Hurst, trans., pp. 50–51, 64, 80, 104, 136, 182, 187.

[45] Chap. 5; Migne *PL* 22:571–72.

conflicted, "the variety of discourses (*sermonum*) is harmonious in unity of spirit."

Lack of skill in words, the Father concluded, was not to be held against any Christian. He revered, he said, not verbose rusticity, but holy simplicity; and he invoked the authority of St. Paul, who said that he imitated the virtues of those in whom greatness of holiness excused simplicity of speech.[46] The truth of translation (*veritas interpretationis*) lay in preserving in one language the "beauty and elegance" (*decorem et elegantiam*) of things that were well said in another.[47] No less than Cicero, Christian translators like St. Hilary of Poitiers had achieved that end by right of conquest, not by servitude to the sleeping letter of the text; they transposed meanings as though they were captives.[48]

Bede's statement that he translated the sense and not the words of Caedmon's verses because their "beauty and dignity" (*decus et dignitas*) was lost in moving from one language to another echoes Jerome's words and sentiments. (Indeed, it would now appear that much was lost in the acts of translation by which the *Ecclesiastical History* itself was written.)[49] Bede's statement reflects an esthetic that required indeterminacy, that placed the sense of words not in their literal meanings but in the beauty that they disclosed, a beauty that could not be transferred to another language but that had to be built up anew in a parallel linguistic structure. The hermeneutic gap between languages was not negated. Instead, it was transcended through the ambiguities and approximations of indeterminate linguistic parallels; for by means of them translation opened a new access to the beauty, the sense, that the original had disclosed. The sense was reached not in repose but in the movement of affective transport. The basis of that transport, and indeed of the arts of imagination that it used, were sensory impressions. That is to say, the art of translation, and all its mimetic sister arts, began in kinesthetic experiences.

We may now place in a wider context the possibility and conditions of

[46] Chaps. 9–12; Migne *PL* 22:575–78.

[47] Chap. 5; Migne *PL* 22:571–72.

[48] Chap. 6; Migne *PL* 22:572.

[49] *Ecclesiastical History*, 4.24; Colgrave and Mynors, eds., p. 416. Walter Goffart has argued that Bede's major objective in writing the *Ecclesiastical History* was the establishment of York as a metropolitan see independent of Canterbury. His presentation of the case is a study in "reading between the lines" (p. 254), first as regards Bede's inclusions and exclusions, his silences, and his suppressions of authentic facts hostile to his cause (pp. 251–53, 315), and then regarding the relation of Bede's *History* to three works that according to Goffart served Bede as antecedents. His explanation of why Abbot Ceolfrid abdicated is another exercise in reading between the lines of Bede's *History of the Abbots* (pp. 279–80). Goffart does not venture into esthetics, but I should like to think that there is a point at which his acute textual study intersects with the argument set forth here.

digestive translation.[50] Bede lived and moved in, and took his being from, a cult that comprised an entire, magnificently articulated world of remembrance and imitation, a sacramental world. In Bede's day, the Iconoclastic Controversy had just begun. It ravaged Byzantium through the eighth and ninth centuries and excited commentaries on the religious use of images from scholars in Rome and Gaul. However, the fear of idolatry and consequently the option of iconoclasm had been present in Christianity from the beginning, even in the writings of scholars, including Augustine of Hippo, who delighted in the sense of vision, adorning and explaining their doctrines with metaphors of visual form, color, and light, and shrinking above all from temptations that arose from concupiscence of the eyes.

This constant in Christian tradition justifies stressing the place of the visual arts in the religious cult that Bede lived, and associating them with verbal arts in a single endeavor to pass from sensory experience to spiritual epiphany. The pictures that Benedict Biscop imported from Rome and hung in the churches of Wearmouth and Jarrow constituted a small part of the figurative representations in Bede's daily life. Fragments of comparable artifacts indicate that the vestments, liturgical vessels, and reliquaries lovingly recorded by Bede almost certainly carried iconic figures, and some still extant works of art that Bede mentioned do bear, or were known to have borne, images. This is true, for example, of St. Cuthbert's coffin, and of the great church at Hexham, built by Archbishop Wilfrid and decorated with painted and carved images, including scenes from sacred history that were outstanding for their quality and brilliant colors. Bede's friend and correspondent, Bishop Acca, made sumptuous additions of ornaments and liturgical furnishings to Hexham. And others mentioned by Bede or known to have moved in his circle also participated in the astonishing flowering of visual arts that occurred in Ireland and the British Isles at the end of the seventh and the beginning of the eighth century, and that employed imaginative synesthesia as did the art of verbal translation.

Illuminated manuscripts are some of the greatest surviving monuments of their work, objects of dazzling splendor, such as the Book of Lindisfarne, the Willibrord Gospels, and the Gospels of St. Chadd. The manuscripts imported by Benedict Biscop can be assumed to have been illuminated, and in Bede's day their Roman style exercised a powerful effect on the monks in the scriptorium of Wearmouth and Jarrow, who executed the magnificent Codex Amiatinus and its (now mostly lost) companion volumes. At the same time, the scriptorium had also mastered a Celtic style of illumination, represented in the Durham manuscript of Cassiodorus's

---

[50] On Bede's attention to fine and mechanical arts, see Hans-Joachim Diesner, "Das christliche Bildungsprogramm des Beda Venerabilis (672/73–735)," *Theologische Literaturzeitung* 106 (1981): 866.

commentary on the Psalms, for which according to tradition Bede himself was a calligrapher. It should be emphasized that, because such manuscripts were thought to have value beyond their material and esthetic ones, they were frequently bound in covers of gold and gems and kept as relics in shrines of precious metal. When, at his martyrdom, St. Boniface raised his book above his head against the falling sword, it was not only as an obstacle but also as a talisman.

Like reliquary cases containing sacred books, St. Cuthbert's coffin served as a shrine for a sacred talisman—in this instance, the saint's body—and that function was indicated by the figures carved into the wood. The coffin was not "a first-rate work of carpentry," and the carvings could be dismissed as "simply infantile." But the representations of Christ, evangelists, saints, and angels were by no means lightly chosen. "Indeed," one critic has concluded, "it is probable that prayer and art were here fused in a deeper, magical union. A litany is a means of invoking the help and protection of the saints. Evidently, it was in order to secure this protection for the precious relics that the monks of Lindisfarne cited the litanies on the panels of the coffin. But in conjuring up the heavenly guardians in visible form, they went beyond a mere recital of a prayer and brought about what must have seemed its instant and perpetual fulfillment." The cultic role of images in Bede's own life, and their role in warfare against demonic spirits, was in his mind when he recorded that Augustine of Canterbury and his companions in the re-Christianization of Britain arrived in Kent bearing before them a silver processional cross as a banner and an image of Christ, "painted on a tablet," and singing litanies as they approached a king and people "given over to the cult of demons."[51] Such litanies were designed to create a synesthetic context of images in which the yearning soul could translate physical experience into spiritual epiphany.

Bede's accounts of two separate visions of the next world suggest the process of cognition with which we are concerned. The recipient of each vision imperfectly understood what he had seen and received elucidation from a heavenly informant. Bede recreated the explanations in words, but one doubts that he believed that the carnal event of speaking and hearing actually occurred. For not only are there similarities between these two incidents and those of inward spiritual discourse in the "silences and secret things of contemplation,"[52] but both recipients were rapt from their bod-

---

[51] *Ecclesiastical History*, 1.25, 30 (on the consecration of pagan shrines as Christian churches); Colgrave and Mynors, eds., pp. 74, 107–8. On the appearance of Benedict Biscop's panel paintings, see C. R. Dodwell, *Anglo-Saxon Art: A New Persepective* (Ithaca, N.Y.: Cornell University Press, 1982), pp. 84–90. See also Ernst Kitzinger, "The Coffin-Reliquary," in *The Relics of St. Cuthbert*, ed. C. F. Battiscombe (Oxford: Oxford University Press, 1956), pp. 212, 280.

[52] *Ecclesiastical History*, 4.28; Colgrave and Mynors, eds., p. 434.

ies, one by death. Later the recipients described what they had seen and heard, just as visual testimony was given when a wound that had been secretly inflicted upon the disembodied soul of one of them later appeared openly on his body. They spoke of their experiences reluctantly, not to the frivolous or casual inquirer, but only to those who, smitten with terror of eternal suffering and hope of everlasting joys, approached them in penitence and wished to drink some advancement in piety from their words. Bede described with wonder the extremes of spiritual contrition and the physical austerities practiced by the two men after their experiences, and he reported that one of them, recounting his vision in the bitter cold of winter, sweated as though it were midsummer, "because of the immensity of what he remembered, whether fear or sweetness."[53]

It was significant that Bede used the digestive word "drink" to characterize the hearing of these accounts, for he wished to underscore the assimilation of the preverbal sense in the words by the hearers. He imagined a translation of sense into affects and finally, into action, an absorption of the sense into the person of the hearer.[54] But his account actually suggests a complex pattern of overlapping processes of translation: the one, for the visionaries, from the spiritual to the figurative levels; and the other for the hearers, who were already effectively disposed to absorb the meaning in the words, oscillating between the figurative and analogical levels, with hopes of ascending to the spiritual. Whether for the visionaries or for their hearers, the process began in recollection of sensory experience and in imagination, ending in mimesis. The hearers digested both visual and verbal memories into affective responses, not spiritual communications vouchsafed to the visionaries, but rather the words and lives of the men themselves.

The esthetic informing Bede's digestion of history did not acknowledge the work of art as something self-contained and self-explanatory. To the contrary, its coherence depended upon something quite outside itself. Reflecting its origin in hermeneutic gaps of language, it therefore permitted formal mnemonic expressions that were fragmented, whether in the pericopes of Scripture and Scriptural commentaries, or in the icons (or iconic paintings) of churches and manuscripts, or in the formally discontinuous anecdotes, documents, and miscellaneous dossiers of evidence that comprised historical accounts. The same fragmented, discontinuous effect later characterized the tropes out of which drama evolved, and which provided

---

[53] *Ecclesiastical History*, 3.19, 5.12; Colgrave and Mynors, eds., pp. 268–76, 488–98.

[54] Cf. *Comm. on I. Peter* 3: 21–22; Hurst, trans., p. 106. Bede also used the same word, "drink" (*haurire*) in the prayer concluding his history. *Ecclesiastical History*, 5.24; Colgrave and Mynors, eds., p. 570. There he prayed that Christ, who had granted him to drink the words of knowledge, would also grant him to go to Christ, the well-spring of all wisdom, and to appear before his face.

yet another kind of mimetic response. This was so, at least in part, because the beauty that works of art possessed lay not simply in their formal qualities as material objects, but in the viewer's ability to grasp them and the violence of sacred drama in a figurative way, notably as figures of coming beatitude or punishment. The object was to understand images, not only as manifestations but also as revelations. In the end, that rendering, whether of verbal or of visual forms, was an affective, indeed an erotic, translation of fear into the love that casts out fear, an affective transport or translation from violence into beauty that encompassed intellectual, psychological, and physical disciplines and all the arts.

That Bede's esthetic encompassed the translation of so many kinds of images, all of which appeared as fragments or manifestations of a preexistent unity, introduces an element of stochastic play. The stochastic element sprang from an assumed divergence between two kinds of wisdom. On the one hand, there beckoned "earthly wisdom which is poured indiscriminately into the hearts of men, and in which even wicked men, having no remorse for their crimes down to their last day, are often seen most splendidly to excel."[55] On the other, there called the wisdom infused into the elect by the Holy Spirit. The stochastic element, the element of risk, was heightened by the evidence of self-deception, which was part of the indeterminacy of esthetic translation. For, as Bede wrote, "many do not have charity and destroy the unity of the Church by their perverse teaching and nevertheless argue that they have the Holy Spirit in them."[56]

Bede's austere teachings on divine vengeance as a manifestation of beauty posited distributive justice, but his doctrine of election raised the possibility that human beings were played by the game of translation more than they were players in it. They were living stones built into the spiritual Temple, which was the body of Christ, resting on those who went before them and supporting those who came after. But stones that became leprous had to be removed, if they could not be cleansed.[57] When they spoke under divine inspiration, were not the prophets like those stones set into, or removed from, the walls, or, someone asked, like "a reed-pipe [which] receives the breath of the human mouth to make a sound, but nevertheless cannot itself understand the sound which it provides"? Bede dismissed this query as absurd. The prophets were seers because they saw the words spoken to them by the Holy Spirit; their minds grasped clearly the mysteries that visions inwardly disclosed to them, and they were able to express outwardly to others, in words chosen by themselves, what they had beheld in secret.[58]

[55] William of Malmesbury, *De Gestis Regum Anglorum*, 1.59, on Bede; Stubbs, ed., 1:64.

[56] *Comm. on I. John 3*: 24; Hurst, trans., p. 199.

[57] *Comm. on I. Peter 2*: 5; Hurst, trans., pp. 82–84.

[58] *Comm. on II. Peter 1*: 21; Hurst, trans., pp. 133–34.

And yet, this resounding affirmation of freedom did not evade either the stochastic, indeterminate quality of play in translation or the possibility that the prophets and their hearers, the elect, alike were played as reed pipes in the symphony of vengeance. This was true because of Bede's settled insistence that spiritual understanding was not verbal, that correct understanding was not possible without enlightenment by grace, and that even correct understanding was, not only an exercise of affective transport in the individual mind, but also a vast movement by which understanding passed across the centuries of sacred history, through stages of incompleteness as it was slowly translated from manifestation into revelation and finally into love.

The esthetic and erotic understanding just described was by no means unique to Bede, although he expressed and applied it in a distinctive fashion. My references to Augustine and Jerome point to its origins in the early centuries of the Church. With its figurative, analogical, and spiritual stages, with its crucial distinction between (prelinguistic) meaning and words, with its avoidance of the vicious circle by positing an incontrovertible distinction between the soul and Christ, and finally with its violence and eroticism, it long survived Bede. From the beginning, its locus was in the mnemonic and mimetic world of cult, and, paradoxically, the writing of history, itself mnemonic and mimetic, served the command of that cult to shun the vain spectacle of this perishing world. Early in the twelfth century, the austere Carthusian, Guigo (ca. 1083–1137), captured the prelinguistic character of translation that encompassed all the imaginative arts. He identified the point at which the hermeneutic circle of cult was thought to diverge from the vicious circle of idolatry. "Whatever form you enjoy," Guigo wrote, "is as though a male to your mind. For the mind yields and lies down beneath it; and it is not conformed and assimilated to you, but you, to it. And the image of the form remains impressed in your mind as though a statue in its own temple, and to it you immolate not a bullock, not a goat, but your rational soul and body, that is, your whole self, when you enjoy it."[59]

There is one further comment to be made on translation as a paradigm of the imaginative arts and how they were experienced and used. We have repeatedly underscored the observation that the play of the imagination between the lines of the text was encouraged by such factors as hermeneutic gaps, inexact parallels between visual and verbal arts, and narrative discontinuities created by the fascicle method of composition. Translation

---

[59] Guigo of La Grande Chartreuse, *Meditationes Guigonis Prioris Cartusiae: Le Recueil des pensées du B. Guigue*; André Wilmart, ed., Études de Philosophie médiévale, vol. 22 (Paris: Vrin, 1936), #249, p. 110. See also #333, p. 126, and below, n. 69. It is worth recalling the explicitly coital nature of some spiritual visions, as for example in Talbot, ed. and trans., *The Life of Christina of Markyate A Twelfth Century Recluse*, chap. 73, p. 168.

provided a vast space for imaginative play by virtue of its inexactitude. Writers recognized that the meaning of a text was changed in translation by gains and losses.[60] But this inescapable quandary of having to deform in order to create was not the only, or chief, reason for inexactitude.

There are many testimonies to the imperfect Latinity of lower clergy and great prelates, most surprisingly among the delegation of English bishops, accounted very eloquent and learned men, who were sent to the papal court to plead against Thomas à Becket. They only displayed, one and all, Latin bedecked with barbarism, solecism, and wrong metre.[61] Likewise, there are many examples of bishops who were totally unfamiliar with the vernacular languages of their sees, or whose facility with the vernacular limited them to the halting use of circumlocutions.[62] To be sure, instances are recorded in which sermons preached in one language were readily understood by listeners in another, and in which holiness likewise enabled simultaneous understanding between two persons who lacked a firm linguistic common ground.[63] But, in such analogues with the gift of tongues at Pentecost,[64] the intervening exercise of translation was evaded. The Devil, after all, could translate.[65]

The inexactitude of translation, together with its indeterminacy, returns us to the fact that all the imaginative arts betrayed those same characteris-

[60] See above, chap. 1, n. 23.

[61] Giraldus Cambrensis, *Gemma Ecclesiastica*, 2.36; J. S. Brewer, ed., *Giraldi Cambrensis Opera*, Rolls Series, no. 21 (London: Longman, 1862), 2:347. See also 2.35–37; ibid., pp. 341–57, and preface, pp. lxii–lxvi.

[62] On Albero of Trier, see above, chap. 1, n. 25. On the Norman bishops introduced after the conquest of England, see David J. Bernstein, *The Mystery of the Bayeux Tapestry* (Chicago: University of Chicago Press, 1986), p. 56. On the deliberate nomination in England and Wales of bishops who could not speak the vernacular, see Giraldus Cambrensis, *De Invectionibus*, 5.8; J. S. Brewer, ed., *Giraldi Cambrensis Opera*, Rolls Series, no. 21 (London: Longman, 1861), 1:133. Cf. the plight of Bishop William Longchamps of Ely, "who had no skill in the English language," when a band of English men and women captured him while he was attempting to escape from Dover disguised in women's clothes. Giraldus Cambrensis, *De Vita Galfridi Archiepiscopi Eboracensis*, 2.12; Brewer, ed., pp. 411–12.

[63] On the preaching of the second Crusade by Bernard of Clairvaux and of the third Crusade by Baldwin of Canterbury, see Giraldus Cambrensis, *De Rebus a se Gestis*, 2.18; James F. Dimock, ed., *Giraldi Cambrensis Opera*, Rolls Series, no. 21 (London: Longman, 1861), 1:75–76. On simultaneous understanding by a hermit to whom, in a miraculous vision, God gave the power to understand and be understood by others in Latin (but not mastery of syntax), see Giraldus Cambrensis, *De Rebus a se Gestis*, 3.2; ibid., pp. 89–91. On the simultaneous understanding brought about in answer to prayer between Margery Kempe and her German confessor in Rome, see B. A. Windeatt, trans., *The Book of Margery Kempe* (Harmondsworth, Eng.: Penguin, 1985), chap. 33, pp. 118–19.

[64] On Bede's discussion of whether the gift of tongues was actually a gift to the Apostles of speaking in unfamiliar languages or a gift to their auditors of understanding, each in his or her own language, what the Apostles were saying in theirs, see above, n. 37.

[65] *Vita Norberti Magdeburgensis*, chap. 10; *MGH, SS* 12, p. 680.

tics, especially as they multiplied images in different media, according to correspondingly different critical methods. The senses supplied data; the imagination worked its speculative transfigurations; the reason judged; the artist's hand performed. There is no need to extend the list of ways in which the indeterminacy, or impossibility, of translation between languages or imaginative arts made itself known. Enough has been said to establish the credentials of translation as an enterprise both of mimetic and of imaginative cognition, whether it operated in the sphere of language or, more broadly, in the critical transformation of verbal into visual images and of visual into verbal. Its possibilities and its limitations were alike essential to its power not only to convey, but also to multiply, images in different media almost indefinitely, supposing in them all that violence was a means of transfiguration into celestial beauty.

## CULT

In discussing cognition, we have cast some light on how criticism was thought to transform experience into information; and information, into epiphany. We must now go a step further in exploring what was meant when historical texts were considered "instruments of cognition." We must identify more closely the conditions that made it possible for the play of mind to move from cognition in general through multiple images to specific cognition of God. Those conditions existed in the character of historical writings as artifacts of religious cult. And yet, to speak of them is to consider what Gibbon denounced as the results of "ten centuries of anarchy and ignorance," a "progress of superstition" that was "rapid and universal." We shall be dealing with what Gibbon regarded as "the various, though incoherent, ornaments which were familiar to the experience, the learning, or the fancy" of the period.[66]

Religious cult was the prism through which historical writers contemplated power in its varied manifestations. Not only did it serve as a channel, and its guardians as ministrants, of divine power, but it also was seen to invest human beings with spiritual powers that could be exercised, for example, in chanting psalms or celebrating the Eucharist over wax images; in cursing one's enemies[67]; in exorcising demons that inhabited the temples

[66] *Decline and Fall of the Roman Empire* (New York: Modern Library, n.d.), chap. 38, 2:402, 419, 429. Certainly, cult was the matrix in which developed the "public narrative for which the term *saga* is not inappropriate," the common knowledge and report in which the personal utterance of an historial writer took shape. Spencer Cosmos, "Oral Tradition and Literary Convention in Bede's Life of St. Aiden," *Classical Folia* 31 (1977): 49, 63.

[67] Adam of Bremen, *Gesta Hammaburgensis Ecclesiae Pontificum*, 3.55(54); *MGH, SSrrG*, p. 200. Giraldus Cambrensis, *Gemma Ecclesiastica*, dist. 1, chap. 49; Brewer, ed., p. 137. Giraldus Cambrensis preserved another account that may likewise indicate a belief in sympathetic

and sculptures of pagans[68]; and in a wide array of miracles that restored the sick to wholeness and the dead to life. The cult set the rules of the game for imaginative play, providing rituals of honor and vengeance through which participants could not only re-enact, but also empathetically relive through each liturgical year the cycle of crime, revenge, and redemption that constituted sacred history. Bernard of Clairvaux implied some of this when he wrote of psalmody, "Singing must not empty the letter of its sense, but impregnate it."[69] And the theatrical affinities of the liturgy, with its tragic scenario of crime, punishment, and redemption, were by no means lost to participants. Those who recited tragedies in theaters, Honorius Augustodunensis wrote, represented the deeds of fighters to the people by their gestures. In the same way, he said, our tragic actor, the priest, represents by his gestures the battle of Christ to the Christian people in the theater of the Church.[70]

Thus far, our discussion of cognition has dealt chiefly with patterns of mental action. However, the acknowledgment that the senses provided the materials employed by the imagination in sympathetic magic points to another aspect of the subject, namely, the kinesthetic fact of ascetic discipline inculcated, enforced, and continually played out with the boundless ingenuity of liturgical arts. The authors and readers of our texts anticipated the exercise of divine power through the bodies of saints and the physical actions of ritual; and this expectation that the holy would be, and in some senses would have to be, manifested in the physical gesture was part of the expectation that readers would peruse texts with a kind of redactive criticism, editing them and seeking epiphanies between the lines.

We are therefore obliged to ask what marks of cult historical texts display as representations of power. One is the reverse of Gibbon's definition of ignorance. *Cognitio Dei et cultus*, the endeavors served by the righteous— which Gibbon regarded as "superstition"—were counterbalanced in the

---

magic. In his *Life* of Geoffrey of York, Giraldus reported that King Richard I was blocking the translation of his brother to the see of York, which their father, Henry II, had ordered on his deathbed. According to Giraldus, the reason for this was that Richard alleged that Geoffrey used to put a golden circlet on his head, saying "Would not this head be fit to bear the kingly crown?", and trample on a sheet of parchment bearing Richard's image, uttering the words, "Thus ought the most wicked king to be trodden under foot and made subject." *De Vita Galfridi Archiepiscopi Eboracensis*, 1.8; Brewer, ed., p. 379.

[68] E. g., Herbord, *Dialogus de Vita S. Ottonis Episcopi Babenbergensis*, 2.30; Jan Wikarjak, ed., Monumenta Poloniae Historica, n.s., vol. 7, fasc. 3 (Warsaw: Państwowe Wydawnictwo Naukowe, 1974), p. 121.

[69] Leclercq, "The Love of Beauty as a Means and an Expression of the Love of Truth," pp. 63–64 (quoting *ep. 98*. 2). See above, n. 59.

[70] Honorius Augustodunensis, *Gemma Animae*, 1.83; Migne *PL* 172:570. Honorius added a detailed list of analogies between events in the passion of Christ and liturgical actions. See ibid., 1.82, cols. 569–70, for a description of individual liturgical vestments as weapons or armor for spiritual warfare.

thinking of our authors by "ignorance of the Creator and worship of an insensate thing" (*ignorantia Creatoris et cultus rei insensibilis*), in other words, idolatry. At issue was the distinction between the humanity of believers and the animality of unbelievers. For "without knowledge of his Creator, every human being is an animal," on a level with mindless beasts of burden.[71] Historical study was an aid, or even a propaedeutic, to the study of sacred doctrine.[72]

It followed that historical writing was informed by the peculiar negation of time that figures in cult. One aspect of power in cult is that it draws into one focus the past, present, and future. It does this by prescribing formulae, calendars, and disciplines through which the devout relive past wonders, invoke present ones, and savor foretastes of those promised and yet to come. Consequently, in liturgical cycles epiphanies of power are experienced in patterns of recurrence. Events—even those widely separate in time and place—have typological rather than historical value. History thus becomes a structure of doctrinal precepts illustrated by examples,[73] whose real, typological coherence is disclosed, not to the eye that sees only the outward distinctions of phenomena, but rather to the vision enlightened by inward contemplation of spiritual unities.

Quite naturally, writers took the wheel as an emblem of this way of thinking about recurrence in the long course of human experience. The simplest use of the metaphor was the Wheel of Fortune, an image conveying the terrifying mutability of the world, which with its "astounding spin" could exalt to honor or hurl down to ignominy.[74] The difference between recurrence in the world and recurrence among the elect was marked by a more elaborate use of the metaphor to characterize, not the changefulness of Fortune, but the constancy of divine order in the midst of change. The Prophet Ezekiel's vision of a wheel inside a wheel invited scriptural interpreters to dwell upon the enigma of stability in change—and thereby to spring up, as Pope Gregory the Great wrote, from history into mystery.[75]

The double wheel represented Holy Scripture. For some, the wheel inside a wheel exemplified the principle that the New Testament was hidden by allegory in the Old, and that, whether latent in the pages of the Old or

---

[71] Ebo, *Vita S. Ottonis Episcopi Babenbergensis*, 2.11; Jan Wikarjak, ed., Monumenta Poloniae Historica, n.s., vol. 7, fasc. 3 (Warsaw: Państwowe Wydawnictwo Naukowe, 1969), p. 72.

[72] Cf. Giraldus Cambrensis, *Descriptio Kambriae*, pref. prima; Dimock, ed., p. 158: "In his [historical studies] itaque, tanto aedificio juvenilibus annis tuta struentes fundamenta, ad eximios tam maturae tam sacrae scientiae tractatus postmodum explicandos, maturiores annos, Deo duce, vitaque comite, reservavimus."

[73] E.g., Giraldus Cambrensis, *Gemma Ecclesiastica*, 1. proem; Brewer, ed., p. 6.

[74] E.g., Giraldus Cambrensis, *De Vita Galfridi Archiepiscopi Eboracensis*, 2.19; Brewer, ed., pp. 429–30. See below, n. 151.

[75] *Hom. in Ezechielem*, 1.6.15, 3; Migne PL 76:829.

revealed in its own, the New was called "the eternal Testament" because it expressed a changeless understanding. The double wheel turned but never retraced its tracks because, possessing the spiritual understanding of the Old Testament, the New moved toward the end of the world, while its immutable truths were continually imparted to believers.[76] Even exegetes long centuries after the Testaments were written said nothing new as long as they held to this inner unity.[77]

Others, looking to the end of the world, construed the inner wheel to represent "general history," including the historical accounts of the Old Testament, with the Gospels toward the center of the wheel, and the Apocalypse at its hub.[78]

To all exegetes, the metaphor of the double wheel, expressive as it was of recurrences in cult, gave assurance of stability in change as plainly as the metaphor of Fortune's Wheel exemplified the precept of universal ruin. For, throughout the ages, one and the same Spirit moved, raised, and set in place the prophet's wheels, which were fastened together and moved as one.[79]

The habit of organizing human experience typologically, by precept and example, was of a piece with the concept of sacred recurrence (but not repetition) represented in the metaphor of Ezekiel's double wheel. Both were essential to a discipline of empathetic participation by which readers projected themselves into the events of sacred history. Time for the righteous was conceived not so much as a straight line as a circle, in which all the blessed stood equidistant from Christ, their common center.[80] Indeed, it was possible to conceive of God, "in whom we live and move and have our being," regardless of time, as a sphere whose circumference was nowhere and whose center, everywhere. Insofar as historical writing in general was intended to serve the object of moral exemplarism—to induce readers to embrace the good and eschew the evil—it demanded that readers imagine themselves as characters in the text, as though in a drama, and experience vicariously the feelings and destinies of those characters.

Writers knew perfectly well that their works could fall into the hands of some, including great men, whom literature made sick, and who, when excellent books came their way, swiftly shut them up in cases, as though in

[76] Gregory the Great, *Hom. in Ezechielem*, 1.6.16, 12; 1.6.17, 17; Migne *PL* 76:834, 836–37.

[77] Rupert of Deutz, *Anulus*, bk. 3; Migne *PL* 170:597.

[78] Joachim of Fiore, *Enchiridion super Apocalypsim*; Edward K. Burger, ed. (Toronto: Pontifical Institute of Medieval Studies, 1986), pp. 10–12.

[79] John of Salisbury, *ep. 256*; W. J. Millor and C.N.L. Brooke, eds., *The Letters of John of Salisbury* (Oxford: Clarendon, 1979), 2:516.

[80] Gerhoch of Reichersberg, *Tractatus in Ps. 18*: 11 and *Tractatus in Ps. 45*: 6; Migne *PL* 193:930, 1575–76. *De Edificio Dei*, chap. 3; Migne *PL* 194:1203–4.

perpetual imprisonment.[81] By contrast, the affective response sought by writers presupposed that, even as they criticized redactively, readers would see themselves in the work as though in a mirror.[82] But the mirror of outer vision was of little or no account unless the mirror of the mind were cleansed and polished by the goading prick of conscience; unless the reading were informed with unction; diligence with piety; understanding with humility; and the whole study with divine grace.[83]

Commonly, reading included both solitary reflection (*meditatio*) and discourse with an interlocutor, a bantering of questions and answers with more than one other person (*collatio*).[84] The discipline of reading in this way, by empathetically re-creating or reliving events in the text, required both visual and verbal imagination. Thus, the monastic *lectio* proceeded from a book; prayer began with a picture; and contemplation, and its sweetness, flowed into the soul from both.[85] It was possible for verbal and visual images, and contemplative devotion, to converge at a single physical point, as when the devout wore away manuscript illuminations by repeatedly kissing them.[86] Yet, the general principle that the multiplication of images, acted upon by the imagination, was necessary for contemplative enlightenment appeared even in Bernard of Clairvaux's portrayal of mystic elevation. Faith comes by hearing, he wrote. But sight is the preparation for hearing; and hearing, a step by which one progresses from obedience to the glory of sight. Even when the mind was irradiated with divine light, it retained imaginary likenesses of lower things left by the senses that now conformed with divinely infused perceptions. Still present, still employed, at the moment of illumination, Bernard taught, those imaginary likenesses made the pure and dazzling beam of truth more bearable for the soul and easier to communicate.[87]

[81] Giraldus Cambrensis, *Descriptio Kambriae*, pref. secunda; Dimock, ed., p. 161. See also Margaret Rickert, *Painting in Britain: The Middle Ages* (Baltimore, Md.: Penguin, 1954), p. 217, on manuscripts that were kept under lock and key as treasure and used only on rare ceremonial occasions.

[82] E.g., William of Malmesbury, letter to Earl Robert, *De Gestis Regum Anglorum*, 3. *ad fin.*; Stubbs, ed., 2:355–56.

[83] Bonaventura, *Itinerarium Mentis ad Deum*, prol., in *Tria Opuscula*, 5th ed. (Rome: Quaracchi, 1938), p. 296.

[84] Edouard Jeauneau, "Jean de Salisbury et la lecture des philosophes," *Revue des Études Augustiniennes* 29 (1983): 146–49.

[85] Betrand of Pontigny, *Vita b. Edmundi Archiepiscopi Cantuariensis*, in Edmond Martène, ed., *Thesaurus novus Anecdotorum* (Paris: Delaulne, 1717), 3:1797.

[86] Reginald of Durham, *Libellus de admirandis beati Cuthberti Virtutibus*, chap. 76; James Raine, ed., Surtees Society, vol. 1 (London: Nichols, 1835), p. 160. Reginald of Durham, *Libellus de vita et miraculis S. Godrici, heremitae de Finchale*, chap. 102; J. Stevenson, ed., Surtees Society, vol. 20 (London: Nichols, 1847), p. 109.

[87] *Sermo 41*. 2.2–3.3. *Sermones super Cantica Canticorum*, 36–86; J. Leclercq, C. H. Talbot,

As we saw in discussing cognition, the synesthetic multiplication of images, through varieties of translation, was well recognized in doctrines about how the mind worked. There is no need to re-emphasize that aspect of our subject or to refer to the use of visual representations of sacred history, expanded by verbal explanations, as exemplars for action by living men and women.[88]

The greater point for us now is that the cult organized conscious control over the ensemble of imaginative arts, which trained the mind to read imaginatively between the lines, and that it thereby educated both artisans to work in methods calculated to produce specific esthetic epiphanies and audiences to respond in desired ways. The great task of the cult was to reform the soul. Given the function of the senses as messengers of the higher mental faculties, the essential preliminary of that task was to master, and coordinate, the kinesthetic tools of psychic reform. Thus, when historical authors in our period compared their texts with other arts—with painting, or theater, or music, for example—their analogies testified to the powers of cult in several aspects—to the artistic power to create forms in different media to make up one immense ideological context; to the psychological power to reform mind and heart through imagination; and to the social and political power to consume material resources in the conspicuous opulence of religious institutions as they were destroyed and rebuilt over and over again.[89]

In considering the interplay among imaginative arts in the service of cult, it is essential to remember that historical writers and their audiences were themselves practitioners, critics, and patrons of visual, performing, and literary arts (figure 3).[90] Testimonies exist to prelates, abbots, and bish-

---

and H. M. Rochais, eds., *S. Bernardi Opera* (Rome: Editiones Cistercienses, 1958), 2:29–30. On the rest of contemplation, see also *Vita Wicberti*, chap. 16; *MGH, SS* 8, p. 514.

[88] In 1111, for example, when Henry V had captured Pope Paschal II and was intent on extorting from him both the unction and coronation as emperor and a sanction of lay investiture, he is reported to have pointed to a painting of Jacob wrestling with an angel and quoted the words of Jacob, "I shall not let you go unless you bless me" (Gen. 32:26). Balderic, *Gesta Alberonis*, chap. 3; *MGH, SS* 8, p. 245.

[89] E.g., analogues with painting, Giraldus Cambrensis, *Descriptio Kambriae*, letter to Stephen Langton; Dimock, ed., p. 156. William of Tyre, *Chronicon*, pref.; *Corp. Christ.*, continuatio medievalis, 63A, p. 99. Giraldus Cambrensis, *De Vita Galfridi Archiepiscopi Eboracensis*, introitus secundus; Brewer, ed., p. 361. See also chap. 6, n. 80.

On theater, *Miracula S. Wicberti*, chap. 8; *MGH, SS* 8, p. 523: "Quam tragediam quia satis cantata est in mundi theatro hic referre supersedeo, cum proprium locum desideret eius plena relatio." See also chap. 7, n. 23.

On music, Herbert of Bosham, *Liber Melorum*, prol.; James Craigie Robertson, ed., *Materials for the Life of Thomas Becket Archbishop of Canterbury*, Rolls Series, no. 67 (London: Longman, 1877), 3:535.

[90] On Bede, Ordericus Vitalis, and Matthew Paris, see this chap., n. 50, and chap. 4, nn. 14–20. See also Goscelin of St. Bertin, a gifted musician, whom William of Malmesbury

ops, who themselves deployed the ensemble of imaginative arts in their pastoral care and rule. From one source, we hear of an abbot who was eminent in his skills as painter, sculptor, and goldsmith; from another, of an archbishop who had mastered the Liberal Arts and who had no superiors in painting, sculpture, chasing, and other manual arts.[91]

Bishop Otto of Bamberg (ca. 1062–1139) may stand as a specific example of this kind of ruler. Before he became bishop, as a relatively young man he served Emperor Henry IV as master of the works, overseeing the construction of Speier cathedral. As bishop, he constructed about twenty religious houses, some of which required elaborate architectural projects such as leveling hills and constructing water conduits (with lead wells). These he built according to elegant designs, adorned with paving, plaster ornamentation, paintings, and the like, and supplied with abundant and rich liturgical furniture. When he undertook his missionary journeys to Pomerania, he employed the same esthetic means to spiritual epiphany, destroying pagan temples and replacing them with handsome and well-supplied churches. He carried with him rich vestments and a store of luxurious fabrics, vessels made of precious metals, costly books, and a large inventory of other articles of great opulence (such as an ivory staff and embroidered stockings), with which he sought the favor of his intended converts and used in gift exchanges with great princes. Otto's biographers repeatedly witnessed to his skill in psalmody.[92]

Otto of Bamberg himself practiced a discipline of great physical and spiritual asceticism; in his missionary journeys, he was consumed by ardor for

ranked as a hagiographer second only to Bede. William of Malmesbury, *De Gestis Regum Anglorum*, 4.342; Stubbs, ed., 2:389. For the suggestion that Otto of Freising took a hand in designing illuminations for his *Chronicle*, see Walther Scheidig, *Der Miniaturenzyklus zur Weltchronik Ottos von Freising im Codex Jenensis Bose q. 6*, Studien zur deutschen Kunstgeschichte, Heft 257 (Strassburg: Heitz, 1928), pp. 41–42. Other examples follow in the text above. For a discussion of patrons who were also practicing artisans, see Joseph Neubner, *Die heiligen Handwerker in der Darstellung der Acta Sanctorum: Ein Beitrag zur christlichen Sozialgeschichte aus hagiographischen Quellen*, Münsterische Beiträge zur Theologie, Heft 4 (Münster: Aschendorf, 1929), esp. chaps. 4–5, pp. 158–205. See also pp. 143 and 168–70 (Bernward of Hildesheim), pp. 143, 167 (Tiemo of Salzburg), and p. 165 (Godehard of Hildesheim).

[91] Evert F. van der Grinten, *Elements of Art Historiography in Medieval Texts: An Analytical Study*, trans. D. Aalders (The Hague: Nijhoff, 1969), pp. 26–27. See Dodwell's reference to richly decorated manuscripts "associated with Thomas Becket and his secretary, Herbert Bosham." C. R. Dodwell, *Painting in Europe, 800 to 1200* (Baltimore, Md.: Penguin Books, 1971), p. 206.

[92] Ebo, *Vita S. Ottonis Episcopi Babenbergensis*, prol.; 1.4, 17, 18, 20, 21; 2.3, 15; 3.1, 3; Wikarjak, ed., pp. 7, 13–14, 31–42, 57–58, 79, 92–94, 99. Herbord, *Dialogus de Vita S. Ottonis Episcopi Babenbergensis*, 1.11–17, 21, 32, 38; 2.9, 11, 12, 17, 22, 24; 3.1, 8, 13, 14; Wikarjak, ed., pp. 12–18, 24–25, 34–35, 42–48, 77–79, 82, 90–91, 100, 106–7, 148, 162–63, 172–74.

*Figure 3.* Many patrons of art were themselves artists or artisans. This medallion from the Guthlac Roll represents St. Guthlac building his oratory with his own hands. The Guthlac Roll was made in England in the third quarter of the twelfth century. *British Library, Harley Roll Y.6.*

martyrdom. He restricted his diet to incredibly little, and, as bishop, never ate his fill, even of bread. He submitted to be lashed by priests until the blood flowed. On travels, while he himself walked with bleeding feet on frozen ground, he urged others to regard their own comfort. He toiled, a biographer observed, for the honor of Christ, the salvation of the people, and contempt of self.[93]

[93] Ebo, *Vita S. Ottonis Episcopi Babenbergensis*, 1.9, 16; Wikarjak, ed., pp. 21, 30. Herbord, *Dialogus de Vita S. Ottonis Episcopi Babenbergensis*, 1.28, 29; Wikarjak, ed., pp. 30–31.

His whole concern was to display "the glory and cult of Christ," to bring forth in the material world an "image and shadow" of liturgies in heaven. The monasteries, with all their beauties, were a designed and controlled environment for "holy lections, psalmody and prayers, masses and contemplation of divine things, fasts and vigils, and struggles against spiritual wickednesses, contrition of flesh and heart, almsgiving and abundant hospitality."[94] Others were quite able to contrast the glories with which he endowed the cult with the meanness and lack of beauty they found elsewhere. To them, the contrasting strains of his use of the arts and his ascetic rigor expressed the "splendor" of his virtues, the "elegance" of his ways (morum), his "elegant and urbane discipline."[95] But they also proclaimed nobility, glory, and honor in a worldly sense.

Even when they were found only implicitly between the lines, the epiphanies of art were necessarily epiphanies of destruction as well as of creation; to transform is also to destroy. Otto of Bamberg's asceticism indicates another gateway of destruction, not the ideological one visited upon pagan art, nor the practical one of reshaping materials to accommodate an as yet imaginary form, but rather a cultural one, in which the ascetic maker ironically denies his own creation. In the same way, as we saw at the outset, historical writers adverted to the events that they recounted as warnings to turn from "the perverse and useless things of mortals . . . [and] the gross emptiness of spectacles in this world" and to the hidden majesty of God.[96]

Inevitably, this ethos of ironic denial was sharpened by changes in esthetic taste and critical (or artistic) techniques that appeared to serve the purposes of spiritual reformation better than earlier ones. One style superseded another and caught the imagination better than the old. Thus, Archbishop Adalbert of Hamburg-Bremen (1043–72), striving to make all things new and to leave everywhere a monument to his own nobility, scorned the "golden mediocrity" of his predecessors. He tore down the cathedral that his immediate predecessor had just completed, together with the city walls and a monastery constructed of dressed stone that, by its beauty, refreshed all who saw it. Yet the expenses of his lavish building program added to heavy political debts and drove him to further destruction. In an hour, he melted down treasures that had accumulated over many generations in the church at Bremen. He would, he gloried, restore

---

[94] Ebo, *Vita S. Ottonis Episcopi Babenbergensis*, prol., 1.21, 3.1; Wikarjak, ed., pp. 2, 39–42, 91. Herbord, *Dialogus de Vita S. Ottonis Episcopi Babenbergensis*, 1.18; Wikarjak, ed., pp. 19–20.

[95] Ebo, *Vita S. Ottonis Episcopi Babenbergensis*, 1.16, 20; Wikarjak, ed., pp. 30, 37. Herbord, *Dialogus de Vita S. Ottonis Episcopi Babenbergensis*, 2.16, 3.30; Wikarjak, ed., pp. 88, 90, 193–94.

[96] See chap. 2, n. 11; chap. 5, n. 36; chap. 6, n. 57; chap. 7, n. 62.

it all ten times over, and replace in gold the church that his predecessors had built in silver.[97]

Destruction of works of art, and of whole complexes such as churches and monasteries regularly occurred, whether by accident (as by fire) or by design in acts of war, payments to military defenders, exactions of tribute by secular rulers, or plunder by ecclesiastical superiors. Books, including saints' lives and other histories, were among the treasures accumulated "for God's cult."[98] But the ascetic eye could see that these treasures and their creators were also liable to the universal mutability of earthly things.

A great lesson concerning power and the arts was thought to have been exhibited by the career of Archbishop Arnold of Mainz (1153–60). Arnold labored for the beauty of the Lord's house and such were his accomplishments that in conduct, beauty, adornment, and piety he seemed to have set up the throne of glory for himself in his see. A man of commanding presence and "most elegant form," he celebrated liturgies in vestments of the most precious fabrics, some woven in gold, whose workmanship surpassed the material. Such was this splendor when he presided in pontifical array that neither Melchizedek nor Solomon in all his glory could be compared with him. Yet Arnold's biographer studiously contrasted this happy state with the misery in which the Archbishop died, trapped alone by his enemies in a burning monastery, his body tormented and scorched by the blistering flames. With vivid detail, the biographer portrayed the holy martyr savagely pursued and killed by his hunters, and his body grotesquely mutilated by them and left naked and unburied for three days in the summer heat to be dishonored by the pestilent mob of Arnold's former flock.[99]

The author provided a clue to the object lesson drawn from the imaginative arts and their creators—to a culture of conspicuous waste—when he represented Arnold as crowned with martyrdom: "He approaches, a sacrifice and oblation, but also a holocaust. He approaches, a victim, the anointed priest. . . . He approaches, now reddened and scorched by unspeakable torment, and, soon after, in the joys of eternal life, washed with his own blood as a martyr and faithful witness, an unconquered soldier to be crowned forever by his King, Lord, and God, Christ Jesus."[100]

The cult of martyrs, forever triumphant with Christ over their enemies, was a definitive celebration of the double theme of honor and vengeance. The conspicuous waste of the imaginative arts in an ascetic ethos devoted

[97] Adam of Bremen, *Gesta Hammaburgensis Ecclesiae Pontificum*, 3.3, 9, 46(45); *MGH, SSrrG*, pp. 145–46, 150, 189.

[98] E.g., the inventory in *Gesta Abbatum Gemblacensium* (*De Olperte Abbate*), chaps. 41–44; *MGH, SS* 8, pp. 540–41.

[99] *Vita Arnoldi Archiepiscopi Mogontini*; Philipp Jaffé, ed., *Monumenta Mogontina*, Bibliotheca Rerum Germanicarum, vol. 3 (reprint, Aalen: Scientia, 1964), pp. 619–21, 663–74.

[100] Ibid., p. 667.

to that cult becomes comprehensible, as a display of political power, as proof of the transience of all earthly things, and as sacrifice.

In our discussion of cognition, we found that the processes of thought, which began with the senses, were considered to be negated and completed by divine inspiration. The discussion of the imaginative arts, which addressed the senses, has similarly brought us to a paradoxical negation and completion. For the works of art with which ascetic communities enveloped themselves and informed their minds and hearts—"great and noble edifices"—were also offerings of charity, works by which their makers and patrons sought to prepare palaces for themselves in heaven.[101] This sense of sacrifice returns us to the *motifs* of divine honor and vengeance as a manifestation of beauty, and of violence as a means of transformation into beauty; it is surely part of what historical writers implied between the lines when they described their works as offerings presented from their neediness, as the widow cast her two mites into the almsbox of the Lord (Mark 12:41–44).[102]

The dramatic portrayal of Arnold's death, complete with elaborate set speeches and prayers (which no human being could have heard) ascribed to the solitary and hunted Archbishop in his last moments, leads us to another conclusion. We have maintained that readers were expected to complete texts for themselves by a form of redactive criticism, one which also might involve empathetic participation in the drama of the events portrayed. The process of cognition that we have described required imaginative visualization as a means of empathetic participation in the gaps between the fragments that constituted the text. It required poetic play.

In an apparition, two young men brought a crown to Christina of Markyate from "the Son of the Most High King." She was astonished at its splendor, but the angelic messengers assured her: "You wonder at the beauty and workmanship, but you would by no means be wonderstruck if you knew the technique [*artem*] of the craftsman." The same distinction had been drawn by the Prophet Isaiah (44:11–20), when he distinguished between the worshipper of an idol and the metalsmith and carpenter who made it, taking part of a tree to make a fire for baking bread or roasting meat, and another part of the same wood to carve an idol "according to the beauty of a man." It had been part of the antipagan argument of early Christians, who pointed to the discrepancy between the awe paid to idols and the mechanical skills by which their armatures were constructed and their surfaces molded and cast. Here we encounter the effects of a similar

---

[101] Cf. Matthew Paris, *Chronica majora* (a. 1254); Henry Richards Luard, ed., *Matthaei Parisiensis, Monachi Sancti Albani, Chronica Majora*, Rolls Series, no. 57 (London: Longman, 1880), 5:454–55.

[102] E.g., Giraldus Cambrensis, *Gemma Ecclesiastica*, 1. proem. ante rem., J. S. Brewer, ed., pp. 4–5. William of Newburgh, *Historia Rerum Anglicarum*, 1. proem; Richard Howlett, ed., p. 18.

distinction in the minds of authors, many of whom were themselves artists, between their materials, the desired effects of their works on the imagination, and the techniques (or art) required to stimulate imaginative play in the spaces of the text.[103]

Reading history therefore became an event by which what happened in the theater of the world, in all its grandeur and terror, was recreated and restored to wholeness in the theater of the mind. Arnold's biographer testified to this discipline of imaginative re-enactment of one violent event when he called the Archbishop's death a "wretched spectacle."[104] Henry of Livonia's account of the conversion of Estonia contains an anecdote that illustrates the concept of history as a theater of dread. During the winter of 1205–6, Henry reported, the Germans decided to perform a play so that the pagans could learn the rudiments of the Christian faith by visual experience. An interpreter carefully explained the enactments to recent converts and those who were still pagans. However, when the moment came to perform a battle between Gideon and the Philistines, the Estonians mistook art for life and fled in terror. Henry added that they were calmed and regathered to see the rest of the play in peace.[105]

The pagans' consternation may have amused their German hosts, but as we have seen in western European culture itself, the object of writing and reading history as spectacle was precisely to transport the audience from part to whole, from image to epiphany, by stirring up feelings of love, pity, and fear. Such indeed was the method of reading that the Germans employed in the theaters of their minds for their own conversion from worldly to spiritual things; they planned to recreate, in a theater of flesh and blood, the same method for the conversion of the Estonians. In either case, the epiphany of esthetic closure was not in the text but in the playing of the reader's (or viewer's) mind. There is indeed an analogue with theater as late as the sixteenth century, when a play could be written by a number of authors, each contributing a different scene without consistency in the *dramatis personae* or even in the development of plot. There too "the effect of the play was the combined effect of the single scenes," as combined by the imagination of the audience at work between the scenes.[106]

---

[103] Talbot, ed., *The Life of Christina of Markyate A Recluse of the Twelfth Century*, chap. 52, p. 128. That the play need not be good humored is demonstrated by Geoffrey of Monmouth's "teasing abuse" and insults. Valerie I. J. Flint, "The *Historia Regum Britanniae* of Geoffrey of Monmouth: Parody and Its Purpose. A Suggestion," *Speculum* 54 (1979): 452–59. See also Ray's suggestion that, in the *Historia Pontificalis*, John of Salisbury highlighted the ridiculous and inept for the amusement of Peter of Celle. Ray, "Rhetorical Scepticism and Verisimilar Narrative in John of Salisbury's *Historia Pontificalis*," pp. 88–90.

[104] *Vita Arnoldi Archiepiscopi Mogontini*; Philipp Jaffé, ed., p. 668. See chap. 5, nn. 37, 46; chap. 6, after n. 74; chap. 7, nn. 23, 46.

[105] *Chronicon Lyvoniae*, 3.9.14; *MGH, SS* 23, p. 252.

[106] See Levin L. Schücking, *Character Problems in Shakespeare's Plays: A Guide to the Better Understanding of the Dramatist* (New York: Holt, 1922), p. 113.

## John of Salisbury

We have now indicated some characteristics that historical writings in the period under review had as artifacts of cult. We have traced the transmutation of experience through criticism into information, and we have observed the further passage from information in the words of the text to epiphany between the lines. We have found that the imaginative, synesthetic multiplication of images, especially visual and verbal ones (enhanced by the powerful psychological discipline of psalmody), was essential to this way of thinking, and indeed that through a fusion of violence and beauty it established an interplay among the arts of imagination, including historical writing.

The period under review produced no works on the philosophy of history, or on historical understanding in the abstract. Thus, unified schemata on those subjects, such as the one just presented, are attempts to establish a coherence that is nowhere explicitly stated. Substantiation can come only from testing the schemata against actual historical texts of the period. We shall do this in a later section. There was, however, one author whose writings covered such a range of philosophical and historical subjects that he did address the coherence among the imaginative arts that we have been discussing, although his comments were set forth in bits and pieces, and by no means systematically.

That writer was John of Salisbury, and we may sum up our comments thus far by referring to his writings as intermediate between the implied evidence that is most common and the systematic expositions that we lack.

John of Salisbury has been acclaimed as a paragon of "medieval humanism" and "the most notable representative of that revival of learning which gave the title of 'medieval renaissance' to the twelfth century."[107] Although his reputation as a historical writer depends on a small proportion of his oeuvre,[108] historical argumentation runs throughout his major writings (the *Policraticus* and the *Metalogicon*) and the collection of 325 letters unevenly spanning his career. And yet in all his works, from the universal history that he left as hardly more than a collection of episodes, to his biographies of Anselm of Canterbury and Thomas à Becket, to his other treatises and letters, the characteristics of "medieval humanism" that he displayed included unreliable chronology, confused arrangement of mate-

[107] Hans Liebeschütz, *Mediaeval Humanism in the Life and Writings of John of Salisbury*, Studies of the Warburg Institute, vol. 17 (London: Warburg Institute, 1950), pp. 116–17. C.N.L. Brooke, Introduction to W. J. Millor, H. E. Butler, and C.N.L. Brooke, eds., *The Letters of John of Salisbury* (London: Nelson, 1955), 1:lvi. See also Marjorie Chibnall, "John of Salisbury as Historian," in *The World of John of Salisbury*, ed. Michael Wilks (Oxford: Blackwell, 1984), pp. 169–77.

[108] Johannes Spörl, *Grundformen hochmittelalterlicher Geschichtsanschauung: Studien zum Weltbild der Geschichtsschreiber des 12. Jahrhunderts* (Munich: Hueber, 1935), p. 79.

rials, polemical argumentation, inaccurate and biased observation, and lack of system. In some instances, he plainly falsified, or fabricated, evidence, following Quintilian's justification of lying in a good cause.[109]

What we have called the atomistic, or fascicle, method of composition was John's norm. He retained fragments, one editor commented, "while surrendering to chaos and confusion any more sustained sequence of events."[110] He continually interrupted the logical sequence of his own thought. John was, another scholar observed, "more interested in stories drawn from his library than in the straightforward exposition of ideas."[111]

Even in political thought, where he achieved special distinction because of the *Policraticus*, his intellectual disposition kept him from recognizing the importance of constitutional changes in his day and confined him to discourse made up of an accretion of antiquarian anecdotes and metaphors.[112] It may be true that John was the only philosopher who, in the wake of the Aristotelian revival of his day and early scholasticism, was able to frame a historical conception of the world (*Weltbild*).[113] But, for him, the information at hand was composed of disconnected bundles of information. In much the same way, he considered his *Historia Pontificalis* the continuation of a chronicle by Sigebert of Gembloux, and his memoirs of Anselm and Becket elements in dossiers made up of other writings by and about them.[114] In his correspondence, he frequently wrote in the same way, making up packets of documents (*fasciculi litterarum*) from which recipients could piece together their own connective links, adding to the

---

[109] Ibid., p. 88. Liebeschütz, *Mediaeval Humanism in the Life and Writings of John of Salisbury*, pp. 97–98. Georg Miczka, *Das Bild der Kirche bei Johannes von Salisbury*, Bonner historische Forschungen, Bd. 34 (Bonn: Röhrscheid, 1970), p. 53. Ray, "Rhetorical Scepticism and Verisimilar Narrative in John of Salisbury's *Historia Pontificalis*," pp. 83, 84, 86, 89, 91. See also John O. Ward, "Some Principles of Rhetorical Historiography in the Twelfth Century," in *Classical Rhetoric and Medieval Historiography*, ed. Ernst Breisach (Kalamazoo, Mich.: Medieval Institute, 1985), pp. 107–11.

[110] Brooke, Introduction to *The Letters of John of Salisbury*, 1:lvi.

[111] Liebeschütz, *Medieval Humanism in the Life and Writings of John of Salisbury*, pp. 116–17.

[112] Liebeschütz, *Medieval Humanism in the Life and Writings of John of Salisbury*, pp. 97, 116–17.

[113] Spörl, *Grundformen*, pp. 73, 79. But cf. ibid., p. 92: John had no fixed *schema* in mind. "Für ihn ist Geschichte ein freies Spiel der Kräfte."

[114] See *Historia Pontificalis*, prol., Marjorie Chibnall, ed., *John of Salisbury's Memoirs of the Papal Court* (London: Nelson, 1956), pp. 2–3. *Vita Sancti Anselmi*, prol.; Migne *PL* 199:1009. *Vita Sancti Thomae Cantuariensis*, prol.; Migne *PL* 190:196. R. W. Southern, *Saint Anselm and His Biographer: A Study of Monastic Life and Thought, 1059–c. 1130* (Cambridge: Cambridge University Press, 1963), pp. 217, 338. Beryl Smalley, *The Becket Conflict and the Schools: A Study of Intellectuals in Politics* (Oxford: Blackwell, 1973), p. 107. Smalley considered John's reference to other works an acknowledgment that "hagiography did not suit [his] talents," rather than a considered method of composition.

written materials what John had entrusted verbally to his messengers.[115] In the *Metalogicon*, he referred to the fascicle method, mixing ancient with modern testimonies to refresh the reader,[116] and, in transmitting the *Policraticus* to his friend, Peter of Celle, he specifically indicated the kind of reading that the "fascicle method" was intended to provoke, a form of "redactive criticism."[117]

Because John considered historical writing part of his endeavors as a philosopher, his lack of system in historical writings requires some comment, for it casts some light both on how he regarded the enterprise of philosophy and on what lessons he thought a philosopher could distill from human experience. John was convinced that few could glimpse "knowledge of the true, love of the good, and worship of God," and that the fewest of the few, the elect, could persevere in their calling until death.[118]

Convinced of the wisdom of the few and the ignorance of the many,[119] he refused to follow where in Antiquity elitism had led Stoics and Cynics, namely, to the goal of *apatheia*, or emotionless virtue. To the contrary, he argued, the more the suffering the greater the virtue, if only the cause were right.[120] To illustrate how Christ inflicted pain to cure and killed to vivify, he drew on various analogues: sons flogged by their fathers; servants by their masters; followers disciplined by teachers; and the sick cauterized or cut by physicians.[121] Sanctification came through the affects, not through *apatheia*; but of course this grace was limited to the wise few whom the worldly considered mad but who, in fact, looked down from the height of virtue on the theater of the world and, scorning the play of Fortune, were impervious to all its vanities and lunacies. What they saw enacted was a

---

[115] E.g., *epp. 12, 204, 218, 298, 304*; Millor, Butler, and Brooke, eds., 1:19; Millor and Brooke, eds., 2:304, 368, 696, 722.

[116] *Metalogicon*, prol.; Clement C. J. Webb, ed., *Ioannis Saresberiensis Episcopi Carnotensis Metalogicon Libri IIII* (Oxford: Clarendon, 1929), pp. 3–4.

[117] *Ep. 111*; Millor, Butler, and Brooke, eds., 1:182: "Edidi librum de curialium nugis et vestigiis philosophorum, qui michi a vestro placebit aut displicebit arbitrio. Incultus est, et ex edicto meo, a vobis amicis desiderat emendari."

[118] *Metalogicon*, prol.; Webb, ed., pp. 4–5. *Ep. 203*; Millor and Brooke, eds., 2:300. Thus, even though John held that logic was the servant of physics and ethics, while ethics served no other branch of philosophical inquiry, he still recognized the privileged position of "l'idéal évangélique" as distinct from the "maximes de la sagesse antique." For example, he regarded charity as the supreme virtue. Jeaneau, "Jean de Salisbury et la lecture des philosophes," pp. 150–51.

[119] *Ep. 209*; Millor and Brooke, eds., 2:316.

[120] Cf. his uses of the axiom that the cause, not death, made a martyr. *Ep. 305*; Millor and Brooke, eds., 2:727. John's *bête-noir*, Gilbert Foliot, quoted the same axiom, *ep. 170 (Multiplicem nobis)*, in Z. N. Brooke, Adrian Morey, and C.N.L. Brooke eds., *The Letters and Charters of Gilbert Foliot* (Cambridge: Cambridge University Press, 1967), p. 239.

[121] *Ep. 276*; Millor and Brooke, eds., 2:584. Cf. *ep. 194*; Millor and Brooke, eds., 2:270.

farce (or, perhaps, on second thought, a tragedy) played out before the eyes of God, his angels, and the wise few, the spectators of these circus games.[122]

From time to time, John prepared theatrical effects for readers of his works. One very notable example of this technique occurs in his description of Becket's martyrdom—that *"stupendum et miserabile spectaculum"*— when he turned from narration in the third person to direct discourse, a dramatic dialogue between Becket and his assassins.[123]

True to rhetorical tradition, John mistrusted words. Philosophy or its end, wisdom, he wrote, sought after things, not words,[124] but it did in fact deal in the medium of words. Thus, sophistry was able to flourish as a technique in deceiving with false images[125]; great scholars, including Abelard and Gilbert of Poitiers, were tangled in serious difficulties by the interpretations that their disciples, torturing the letter, placed on their doctrines.[126] Words were like leaves in the wind, but John discountenanced the arrogant waywardness of those who made the Church's judicial powers a laughingstock and considered the law of God, on which those powers were based, no more than words.[127]

Patently, written words were silent. The task of the interpreter was to interrogate them, to find out what was hidden in them, as Christ was hidden in the words of Scripture, to open up the letter as though it were a shell and disclose the meaning inside.[128] One of John's fixed principles was that an interpreter was obliged to seek the original meaning of the author who wrote the words, rather than the meaning that, in the interpreter's judgment, they made.[129] Yet, he knew how difficult this recovery was, even

---

[122] *Policraticus*, 3.8, 9; Clement C. J. Webb, ed., *Ioannis Saresberiensis episcopi Carnotensis Policratici . . . Libri VIII*, 2 vols. (Oxford: Clarendon, 1919), 1:192, 199. Cf. *ep. 311*; Millor and Brooke, eds., 2:760: ". . . spectaculum facti sumus Deo et hominibus et angelis et persecutorum Christi canticum tota die," an allusion to 1 Cor. 4:9. See also chap. 7, n. 23.

[123] *Vita Sancti Thomae Cantuariensis*; Migne *PL* 190:204–6. John employed the same change to dialogue in recounting Becket's death to John of Poitiers, *ep. 305*; Millor and Brooke, eds., 2:730. The two texts have strong affinities. See also the use of direct discourse for theatrical effect in the *Historia Pontificalis*, chaps. 2, 6, 8, 10–11, 37, 40, 41, 42; pp. 7–8, 12–13, 18, 22–25, 74, 79, 81–82, 84–85.

[124] *Metalogicon*, 1.6; Webb, ed., p. 21.

[125] *Metalogicon*, 4.22; Webb, ed., p. 188.

[126] *Metalogicon*, 2.17; Webb, ed., pp. 91–92. *Historia Pontificalis*, chap. 10; Chibnall, ed., p. 22.

[127] *Ep. 187*; Millor and Brooke, eds., 2:248. On John's "ambivalent" attitude toward rhetoric, acknowledging its benign and its treacherous powers, see Ray, "Rhetorical Scepticism and Verisimilar Narrative in John of Salisbury's *Historia Pontificalis*," pp. 63, 67–68. On classical antecedents for this attitude, see Ray, ibid., p. 67 and Nancy F. Partner, "The New Cornificius: Medieval History and the Artifice of Words," in *Classical Rhetoric and Medieval Historiography*, ed. Ernst Breisach, pp. 22–23.

[128] *Policraticus*, 7.12, 13; Webb, ed., 2:137–38, 144–45, 147.

[129] *Epp. 248, 253*; Millor and Brooke, eds., 2:500, 510. Matthew of Vendôme, *Ars Versifi-*

when it was not deliberately thwarted by the fraudulent and arbitrary twisting of words.[130] For it was surely presumptuous, a use of vain imaginings, for one person to try to unfold the hiddenness of another's mind, since God alone could judge the human heart.[131] At any rate, the essential thing was not who the author was, but what he wrote.[132] Experience taught John that translation of texts from one language into another was very prone to put barriers of many kinds between interpreters and author's meanings.[133]

But what of Scripture, written by one author, the Holy Spirit? In ferreting out the mind of that author, who could claim to have been made an interpreter of heavenly things, unless, perhaps, Christ dwelt in his heart?[134]

Thus, there was a distinction between interpretation, the wrestling with words, and understanding, the apprehension of things latent in them. Bernard of Clairvaux was so steeped in Scripture, John wrote, that he made its words his own in everyday conversation as well as in his public addresses and writings. But Bernard's assimilation of what was authentic in Scripture was demonstrated not by his vocabulary but by his manner of life and his devotion. Plainly, his life and works showed forth the fourfold fruit of contemplation: abasement of self, charity toward one's neighbor, contempt of the world, and love of God.[135] To be sure, authors calculated how most effectively to capture the attention of particular audiences. Yet among the responses that the wise, like Bernard, sought to arouse as they matched rhetoric to audience were affective ones of tears and prayer, including, notably, intercessory prayer for the authors themselves.[136]

John's concept of actual events as spectacle, generally of violence, and of historical writing as depiction to be enacted in the theater of the mind suggests how he solved the predicament of linguistic indeterminacy. It also goes far toward explaining how he could expect readers to find unity in the fascicles and fragments of his historical texts. The key was likeness (*similitudo*). The basic act of knowing was a movement from something known to something unknown, establishing likeness in the gap between them.

---

catoria (*The Art of the Versemaker*), 1.115; Roger P. Parr, trans. (Milwaukee, Wis.: Marquette University Press, 1981), p. 58.

[130] *Ep. 187*; Millor and Brooke, eds., 2:232.

[131] *Ep. 301*; Millor and Brooke, eds., 2:708.

[132] *Policraticus*, 8. prol.; Webb, ed., 2:226–27.

[133] *Metalogicon*, 4.6; Webb, ed., p. 171. *Historia Pontificalis*, chaps. 24, 25; Chibnall, ed., pp. 55, 56, 58.

[134] *Epp. 194, 209*; Millor and Brooke, eds., 2:273, 332–34. *Policraticus*, 2.26; Webb, ed., 1:139–40.

[135] *Historia Pontificalis*, chap. 12; Chibnall, ed., pp. 26–27. *Policraticus*, 3.2; Webb, ed., 2:175.

[136] *Policraticus*, 1.4; 8.12; Webb, ed., 1:31–35, 2:315–16. *Epp. 209, 304*; Millor and Brooke, eds., 2:324–26, 724. *Vita Sancti Anselmi*, chap. 18; Migne *PL* 199:1040. *Vita Sancti Thomae Cantuariensis*; Migne *PL* 190:208. *Metalogicon*, prol., 4.42; Webb, ed., pp. 4–5, 219.

Figures of speech—metaphor, metanomia, synedoche, and simile—were instruments for this transference, or "translation," in language,[137] but ideas about comparable mimetic translations enabled John to explain how the soul played among all the imaginative arts.

John shared the common opinion that human nature, in all individuals, was one and uniform.[138] The distinguishing characteristic of humanity was to be conscious of its capacities for reason and feeling (*ratio et passibilitas*),[139] and yet the soul, unable to see either itself or God directly, was prone to wander from God, ignorant of its origin and powers.[140]

If the essentials of human existence could not be known directly, they had to be apprehended indirectly. John conceived an elaborate hierarchy, a series of stages of cognition, by which the soul passed from the data of bodily senses to wisdom. Imagination was the first act of the soul, the first movement after the reception of sensory data, and the necessary preliminary of all the rest. In the same way, all speculation, being inductive, presupposed the senses.[141] All the arts were brought about by the same inductive process, as the mind registered disconnected sensory data and accumulated in the stomach of memory the occurrence of many things often repeated. From that accumulation of many experiences, reason framed rules. From the body of rules, the intellect established an art, prescribing the things to be done by the art. Intellect was the highest human faculty, beholding all that was human, and having before itself the divine causes of things. However, for some, intellect was surpassed by wisdom, a power not of nature but of grace, which, in the truly wise, completed and presided over the entire cognitive process. Inasmuch as the fear of the Lord was the beginning of wisdom, imagination, at the beginning of the process—the fear-ridden imagination of punishment—was directly related to the power of wisdom at the process's end to see the invisible things of God that the created world manifested. Through these epiphanies, the soul became more at one with God through the unity of love.[142]

---

[137] *Metalogicon*, 1.19; 3.1, 7, 8; Webb, ed., pp. 46, 121, 146, 148. Concerning John's reliance on translations of Greek philosophical texts, see Jeauneau, "Jean de Salisbury et la lecture des philosophes," pp. 162–64, 168–73.

[138] *Metalogicon*, 1.1; Webb, ed., p. 6.

[139] *Metalogicon*, 4.33; Webb, ed., pp. 201–2.

[140] *Metalogicon*, 4.9, 20; Webb, ed., pp. 175, 186.

[141] *Metalogicon*, 4.8; Webb, ed., p. 173.

[142] *Metalogicon*, 4.8–11, 17–19; Webb, ed., pp. 173–77, 182–85. On "la conviction que toutes les disciplines sont solidaire, liées entre elles (*connexae*) par des liens inextricables," see Jeauneau, "Jean de Salisbury et la lecture des philosophes," p. 155. On Hugh of St. Victor's similar idea that "all the arts go through the same stages of growth, and their development has the same general chronological pattern as the restoration of man's spiritual nature," see R. W. Southern, "Aspects of the European Tradition of Historical Writing, 2: Hugh of St. Victor and the Idea of Historical Development," *Transactions of the Royal Historical Society*,

For John, to imagine was specifically to visualize. Images were laid up in the treasure chest of memory, to be kept and frequently ruminated upon. When the mind wished images, imagination was born, working by a process of comparison not unlike the method of *diacrisis* (or distinction) used by grammarians who were broadly and thoroughly educated in various disciplines. The grammarians' method so provoked visualization that it was called "*illustratio*" (illustration) or "*picturatio*" (picturing). By it, they took the raw matter of history, argument, or fable, or any other matter, and worked it over with such varied critical discipline and grace of composition and embellishment that their finished works could be seen as an image, a sampler perhaps, of all the arts.[143]

John did not relate the memory, the supplier of images for imagination, to the noblest part of the body when he described it as a stomach. But its fundamental part in the process of cognition justified the analogy, inasmuch as the stomach in the body had the same office digesting miscellaneous foods for general nourishment as the prince in the body politic.[144]

We can now locate historical writing in the general process of thought as John portrayed it. Historiography was the deliberate creation of memory, filled perhaps with images that, however ill-assorted and mismatched, opened through their likenesses (including foreign ones) a multitude of speculative doors. As an artificial memory (considered a stomach or treasure chest) a text provided—as did the mind's recollective faculty—materials to be acted upon by reason and, supremely, by the wisdom that came only through the infusion of divine grace.

John certainly recognized that if imagination were not rightly governed by the higher powers of the soul, it could produce great mischief in the making and reading of history. Such activities as idolatry and witchcraft were synonyms for ecclesiastical disobedience.[145] When misdirected by delusions, an assembly of prelates could prove itself a theatrical mis-en-scène rather than the image of a venerable council.[146] Of course, worldly courtiers and clerics alike, immersing themselves in luxurious diversions served up by mimes, actors, craftsmen of various sorts, and musicians, not to men-

---

5th series, 21 (1971): 171. Some such convictions help explain the blurred line between history and fiction as described, for example, by Flint, "The *Historia Regum Britanniae* of Geoffrey of Monmouth: Parody and Its Purpose. A Suggestion," pp. 447–49.

[143] *Metalogicon*, 1.24; Webb, ed., p. 54.

[144] *Policraticus*, 6.25; Webb, ed., 2:72. See Cary J. Nederman, "The Physiological Significance of the Organic Metaphor in John of Salisbury's *Policraticus*," *History of Political Thought* 8 (1987): 211–23, although the article does not consider the metaphor as John ascribed it to Pope Hadrian IV, to which I am referring.

[145] *Epp. 82, 187, 217, 244, 248, 281*; Millor, Butler, and Brooke, eds., 1:128; Millor and Brooke, eds., 2:232, 366, 484, 500, 616. See also John's references to the anti-pope, Victor IV, as an idol set up and worshipped by Frederick Barbarossa. *Ep. 124*; Millor and Brooke, eds., 1:211, 213.

[146] *Ep. 124*; Millor, Butler, and Brooke, eds., 1:212.

tion women, could pass over into the terrible desert of moral forgetfulness, like one captivated by the vanity of plays in a theater. For them, death entered through the windows of the eyes.[147]

But such was not the spectacle played out before God, the angels, and the wise few, or the "imagination of punishment" that was the first step toward wisdom. Such also were not the results of historical inquiry that John sought when he began his chronicle with "the Son of the inviolate Virgin, who in the beginning was the Word," hoping through God's help to disclose the invisible things of God through things that were made, and, by the examples of reward and punishment in his pages, to stir up his readers to be more scrupulous in fear of the Lord and cultivation of justice.[148]

Like the other historians with whose writings we are concerned, John of Salisbury viewed epiphanies of power through the faceted prism of a cult of sacred violence. Cult supplied the precepts by which the mind drew unity out of fragments. John, too, refracted those epiphanies doubly, through the facets of opulence and asceticism. Toward the end of his career, he found in the martyred Thomas à Becket an incarnation of this interplay of critical norms. Although the fashion of his people required the Archbishop's house to be nobly furnished with precious utensils and various implements, he despised wealth and its display as though it were dung. Dressed in costly raiment, he was a pauper in spirit; joyful of countenance, he was contrite in heart; amidst the splendor of his table, he practiced abstinence.[149] Always, his holy death lay before him.

This double cultic vision of opulence and asceticism may well have contributed to the atomistic effect of John's segmented "fascicle" method of composition. With its association of all the imaginative arts in one family of cognition and its technique of accumulating examples illustrative of moral precepts, it did indeed encourage a fragmentary structure of discourse and intuitive association, rather than straightforward narration and analysis.

However, just as thought about cognition yielded a diagram of how the mind had to establish coherence among the fragments of sensory images, so too cult supplied ways of thinking that juxtaposed incommensurables in an invisible unity. The most evident traces of that unity, hidden between the lines, are the objectives that John hoped to achieve by historical reflection: among them, the didactic purpose of moral reform (or conversion), and the polemical—indeed, political—object of celebrating exemplars of righteousness (notably Anselm and Becket) brought into conflict against their kings by their warfare against the dark errors of infidelity.[150]

---

[147] *Policraticus*, 7.17; 8.6, 12, 14; Webb, ed., 2:160, 250, 309, 328.

[148] *Historia Pontificalis*, prol.; Chibnall, ed., pp. 3–4.

[149] *Vita Sancti Thomae Cantuariensis*; Migne *PL* 190:198.

[150] *Vita Sancti Anselmi*, prol.; Migne *PL* 199:1009.

Cult gave John the circumstances in which he lived and wrote, the sense that violence and beauty were in identifiable ways synonymous, and motives for historical study. It also provided a concept of time that sanctioned an atomistic structure of discourse, even while it provided multiple levels of association. Of course, John knew a repertoire of chronological times—those dates that came from the creation, those from the incarnation of Christ, and those from the foundation of Rome. There was also dating by regnal years among others. His allusion to Ezekiel's wheel inside a wheel, and his abundant references to Fortune's capricious Wheel demonstrate that he was also aware that, in any event, mixed times could converge (figure 4).[151]

These metaphors expressed an imaginative play—play in movement, not over and done with—that combined segmented, dissimilar elements. They took account of some relations (for example, typological ones) that stood outside of time. They also took account of events that occurred in time but that were not necessarily related by temporal sequence. For example, the norms of equity were changeless. But the times were very different for a creditor and a debtor as they awaited nonsequentially the same event: the repayment of a loan.[152] In their meditations, saints, like prophets, had seen past and future at the same instant and absent things as though they were present.[153] Even while to some it might appear that, in persecution, they had fallen victim to the play of wanton Fortune, they knew that persecution was a season of purging, testing, and enlightenment. As the prophet's wheel foreshadowed in its multiple act of turning and advancing yet remaining ever stable, the end of conflict would crown them with an imper-

---

[151] On Ezekiel's wheels, see above, nn. 75–79. On Fortuna's Wheel, see (e.g.) *ep. 31*; Millor, Butler, and Brooke, eds., 1:49. John's writings are full of references to Fortune's savagery, rages, jealousy, and capricious, random play. See *Metalogicon*, 3.10; Webb, ed., p. 161. *Policraticus*, 1.13; 2.2, 22; 3.6, 8, 14; 5.4, 11, 17; 6.1, 3, 4, 14; 7. prol., 19; 8.4, 12; Webb, ed., 1:61, 69, 129, 185, 191–93, 224, 292–93, 331, 365; 2:5, 13, 15, 38, 90–93, 179, 240, 308. *Epp. 13, 17, 21, 27, 28, 31, 32, 96, 97, 124, 144, 161, 165, 192, 193, 194, 199, 202, 212, 247, 253, 256, 288, 292, 305*; Millor and Brooke, eds., 1:21–22, 29, 31, 33, 44, 45–46, 49, 52, 53, 148–49, 149–50, 205; 2:32, 78, 88, 264, 266, 270, 286, 298, 344, 496, 510, 518, 636, 666, 728. A striking illumination from the thirteenth century represents a combination of Fortune's Wheel with Christ's. Paralleling Ezekiel's vision of a wheel inside a wheel, the wheels are concentric, that of Fortune being inside that of Christ, with a representation of the Blessed Virgin and John adoring the Lamb of God at their common center. See Richard Georg Salomon, ed., *Opicinus de Canistris: Weltbild und Bekenntnisse eines avignonesischen Klerikers des 14. Jahrhunderts*, Studies of the Warburg Institute (London: Warburg Institute, 1936), vol. 1, pp. 310–11; vol. 2, plate 72. I was led to this illumination by Elaine Beretz, "Fortune Denied: The Theology against Chance at Saint-Etienne, Beauvais" (Ph.D. diss., Yale University, 1989), pp. 206–8. I am grateful to Ms. Beretz for the reference.

[152] See chap. 7, after n. 46. *Ep. 287*; Millor and Brooke, eds., 2:634.

[153] *Vita Sancti Anselmi Cantuariensis*, chap. 3; Migne *PL* 199:1013.

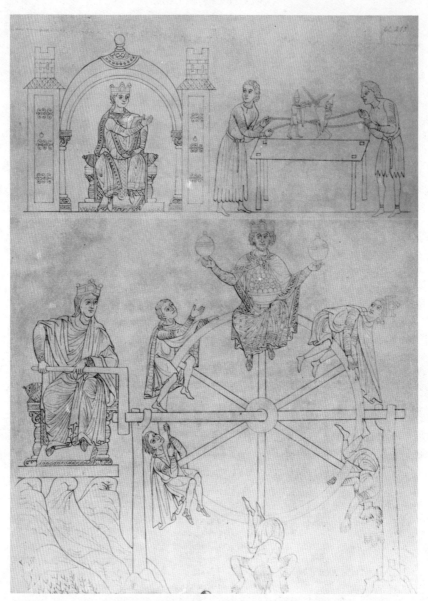

*Figure 4.* Two illuminations from Abbess Herrad of Hohenburg's *Hortus Deliciarum* represent, side by side, the twelfth-century fascination with spectacle and the dramatic turns of Fortune. In the top register, the artist depicted King Solomon watching a puppet play; in the lower one, Fortune cranking her Wheel. *Plates from A. Straub and G. Keller,* Herrade de Landsberg, Hortus Deliciarum. *Strasbourg, 1879–99. Princeton University Library.*

ishable crown.[154] Before the mind of God, all events were present from the beginning; the future ones were not absent, nor did the past slip away. To be sure, there were occasions when Christ appeared to be sleeping and the order of the prophet's wheel to have been supplanted by the terrifying caprice of Fortune's. Yet even then what occurred in the passage of time was what had been decreed by God and had until that time remained latent in preceding events, for "nothing is hidden that will not be revealed."[155]

Plainly, only a varied figure could convey the character of times playing together in any event.[156] For, true to Augustine's definition of time as distention of the mind,[157] John's varied times reflected diverse frames of mind. The times were mixed for creditor and debtor because they anticipated repayment with different feelings. The contemporary rulers, whom John regarded as re-personifications of wicked Scriptural rulers because of their intrusions into Church affairs, did not measure their reigns as he did.[158] Heretics were blind to what John considered their historical roles as the forerunners of Antichrist, if not the Antichrist in person,[159] and Becket's enemies certainly did not associate his cognitive time with Christ's, as did John, nor theirs with Satan's ministers of wickedness.[160]

Not every one could detect the spectacle of history in the violent confusion of events, just as not every priest standing at the altar could behold the Passion as though Christ were physically present.[161] Only the wise few in whom Christ made his dwelling could see the invisible things of God through the things that were made and therefore correctly discern the times. Advancing in knowing and worshipping God, they saw a unifying pattern behind the apparently disorderly events of the world: the pattern of retributive justice. Out of love, God purged the wrongs of his errant children by flagellating them.[162] John had heard of cruel and inhumane surgeons, but the chastisement that God visited upon his chosen ones recalled merciful physicians, who inflicted pain to heal.[163] God inflicted this form of vengeance as a merciful father to chasten and, finally, to crown his chil-

---

[154] *Ep. 298*; Millor and Brooke, eds., 2:696. Cf. *Policraticus*, 3.8; Webb, ed., 1:191.

[155] *Metalogicon*, 3.4; 4.37; Webb, ed., pp. 136, 208–9. *Ep. 305*; Millor and Brooke, eds., 2:730. On Christ sleeping, *Policraticus*, 8.23; Webb, ed., 2:406–7 and *Metalogicon*, 4.42; Webb, ed., pp. 217–19. Christ awakened, *ep. 251*; Millor and Brooke, eds., 2:506.

[156] Cf. *Policraticus*, 3.8; Webb, ed., 1:191: "Varia figura temporum actuum quaedam varietas est."

[157] See above, after n. 32.

[158] *Policraticus*, 8.22; Webb, ed., 2:398–99.

[159] *Ep. 234*; Millor and Brooke, eds., 2:429.

[160] E.g., *epp. 230, 305*; Millor and Brooke, eds., 2:414, 728.

[161] *Vita Sancti Thomae Cantuariensis*; Migne *PL* 190:198.

[162] *Ep. 195*; Millor and Brooke, eds., 2:276.

[163] *Epp. 221, 238, 267, 276*; Millor and Brooke, eds., 2:380, 452, 540, 584.

dren, drawing them purged from his crucible.[164] But heavy retribution awaited those who dishonored Christ, for God would not cede his glory to another by withholding punishment from them. If he did not cast them down into poverty and shame in this life, he would surely visit upon them a miraculous vengeance (*ultio miraculosa*) in the day of his wrath.[165] Vengeance upon them befitted God and profited the Church, and it encouraged the just to rejoice in their warfare for its vindication of God's glory. They washed their hands in the blood of sinners.[166]

Certain of the pattern of honor and vengeance, of beauty being realized through violence and conveyed by cult, John built into his ideas of history the conventional glorification of martyrdom. We encounter a similar device in the biographer of Arnold of Mainz. It was no dishonor to be overwhelmed by Antichrists, false prophets, and other ministers of Satan in this world. For by the persecution, ignominy, and death that they inflicted on the righteous, they conferred the imperishable glory of martyrdom on their victims and the infamy of eternal death upon themselves. Imitating Christ in obedience to the shame of the Cross, saintly martyrs offered themselves as sacrifices, none in a more Christ-like fashion than Becket, whose body was slain and whose blood shed at the very altar where he had daily offered the Eucharistic sacrifice. Becket's sacrifice, like Christ's, brought about both propitiation and punishment. "But who of the faithful," John asked, "may dare doubt that God will either convert or grind into dust the authors and perpetrators of so great a sacrilege?"[167] Who indeed could doubt that the martyrs too would come in glory, heralded by the sound of priestly trumpets, at that moment near at hand when Christ entered in triumph the Kingdom gained with his own blood?[168] The coherence of all history turned on that sacrifice and that triumph. The power of history to amuse, enlighten, and convert depended on the ability of readers to see themselves playing roles in the spaces between the lines of the texts, to relive with ardor, pity, and dread the events recounted.

. . .

We have now examined some propositions of unity that lay behind the extremely segmented and fragmentary historical texts of John of Salisbury. We have found that they confirm the observations that we had earlier abstracted from a wide variety of historical writers. They illustrate the importance of the imagination, particularly the imagination at play in the gaps

[164] *Ep. 239*; Millor and Brooke, eds., 2:455. Cf. *ep. 197*; ibid., p. 280.
[165] *Epp. 189, 193, 239, 307*; Millor and Brooke, eds., 2:254, 256, 268, 454, 744.
[166] *Ep. 310*; Millor and Brooke, eds., 2:756.
[167] *Ep. 305*; Millor and Brooke, eds., 2:730.
[168] *Ep. 242*; Millor and Brooke, eds., 2:472.

between the episodes and fascicles that comprise the text. They indicate the importance of the multiplication of images—especially visual and verbal ones—that entitled historical thinking to be counted among the imaginative arts, in part by drawing upon their methods of criticism. These images also established a particularly direct kinship between historical imagination and theater. The propositions that we have examined underscore the importance of cult in supplying the unwritten, imaginative coherence that evoked epiphanies between the lines of the text, the characteristic fusion of violence and beauty at the sacrificial heart of the cult, and the vital role of affective responses—especially those of love, pity, and terror—in achieving the task of edification and conversion that historical writers set for themselves. Such was the whole purpose of teaching by examples intended to attract or repel. Finally, these propositions leave no alternative to John's assertion that the ways of imaginative thinking expressed in our texts did not belong to the ignorant multitude. Philosophy, he wrote, is content with few judges and she disdains to commit the soundness (*sinceritatem*) of her work to vulgar criticism.[169]

Enough has now been said to suggest how in the minds of our authors experience was digested by criticism into information, and information employed as a stepping stone to epiphany for some but not for all. The signifying function of words hinged on the imagination. Casting words about ourselves, William of St-Thierry wrote, we become enveloped in them and kept by them from the divine reality that cannot be expressed in words. For the function of words is to image forth forms in the thought of the speaker or hearer. When these forms and the things formed are in the world, words draw the mind outside itself to the things of which they are signs. However, when they are signs of things spiritual and divine, they send us inward. Since there can be neither forms nor images of such things, the mind becomes ensnared in its own imaginations. The blinding flash of divinity itself is needed to free cognition of the faith from the vanity of imagination.[170] It remains to demonstrate ways in which the central role of visual imagination left traces in some historical texts and to suggest how, in time, visualization lapsed as a precondition of historical thought.

[169] *Ep. 209*; Millor and Brooke, eds., 2:316.
[170] William of St-Thierry, *Speculum Fidei*, chaps. 74–77, in *Deux Traités sur la foi: Le miroir de la foi, l'énigme de la foi*, ed. M.-M. Davy (Paris: Vrin, 1959), 86–88. See nn. 14, 87.

## Chapter 4

# FROM ONE RENAISSANCE TO ANOTHER

THE PREMISE that historical writing was an instrument of cognition depended on abstract ideas about cognition. Those ideas concerned the process of coming to know, rather than particular things that were known. The difference in literary form between historical texts of the twelfth century and those of the fifteenth and later indicates a profound change, not only in style, but also, at a far deeper level, in the ways in which the conditions, possibilities, and limits of cognition were conceived. I have two tasks in this chapter. The first is to trace some lines of continuity in modes of representation and in the ideas of cognition that they presupposed, from the twelfth to the fourteenth century. Consequently, my second task is to indicate a few reasons why works of the twelfth-century "Renaissance" and its aftermath ceased to be regarded as possible instruments of cognition in the Renaissance of the fourteenth and fifteenth centuries. Throughout, I shall have to take into account the close relationship of beauty and violence that was central to the imaginative arts. I shall begin with two chronicles, those written at the monastery of St-Évroul, in Normandy, by Ordericus Vitalis (1075–ca. 1142) and, at the monastery of St. Albans, in England by Matthew Paris (1200–1259).

### ORDERICUS VITALIS AND MATTHEW PARIS

Taken as wholes, the chronicles of Ordericus Vitalis and Matthew Paris appear to be undigested accumulations of notes, documents, and memoirs. They are indeed to be counted among those works in which the author disrupts every possible continuity, leaving the reader to complete the work, narratives, or clusters of narratives, that, in fact, "aim, not at illumination, but at obscurity and dissimulation."[1] The amorphous flow of events did remind Ordericus and Matthew of the shapeless rush of storm or river.[2]

---

[1] Paul Ricoeur, *Time and Narrative*, trans. Kathleen McLaughlin and David Pellauer (Chicago: University of Chicago Press, 1984), 1:75 (referring to Frank Kermode), 77.

[2] For the metaphor of an ocean storm, see Ordericus, *Ecclesiastical History*, 8.13; Marjorie Chibnall, ed. and trans., *The Ecclesiastical History of Ordericus Vitalis*, 6 vols. (Oxford: Oxford University Press, 1968–80), 4:212. For uses of the metaphor of a river, or stream of time, see Ordericus, *Ecclesiastical History*, 6.8; Chibnall, ed., 3:262. Matthew Paris, *Chronica majora* (a. 1247); Henry Richards Luard, ed., *Matthaei Parisiensis, Monachi Sancti Albani, Chronica Majora*, 7 vols., Rolls Series, no. 57 (London: Longman, 1872–83), 4:605.

Yet the question remains: Were the discontinuities of their texts the result of inadvertence and want of ability, or (as is true of such modern writers as James Joyce and Roland Barthes) of deliberate esthetic choice, perhaps of art imitating nature? Let us review the evidence, turning first to the manifest discontinuities in the chronicles.

Bede's *Ecclesiastical History* also consisted of a very miscellaneous compilation of materials. But his general theme of conversion under the aegis of the Roman church was pervasive enough to sustain a general coherence, sharpened, perhaps, by unstated but still driving aspirations. However, Ordericus more than once confessed that he could find no overarching direction or meaning in his own work. He could not, he wrote, consider divine judgment or expose the hidden causes of things, but only set down the course of events for posterity. Each of those who came after, he wrote, would have to choose what was useful in the text, according to the divine inspiration vouchsafed to that person. Obedient to the commands of his monastic superiors, Ordericus said, he wrote chiefly to avoid the spiritual dangers of idleness, expecting that another, more clear-sighted than he and more potent in interpreting events, would in time assimilate Ordericus's materials, and those of other writers, into yet another chronicle, more effective than his predecessors' in teaching those who came after him.[3] Even this deferral of understanding to the future is absent from the "undisciplined and unsystematic" accretions of Matthew Paris.[4]

Bede conceived his *Ecclesiastical History* as the work of one theme—how Christianity, once accepted in the British Isles, was rejected and recovered—a reductive theme that he illustrated with accounts of how those through whom the grace of the Gospel spread had lived and died, down to

---

[3] On Bede, see Walter Goffart, *The Narrators of Barbarian History (A.D. 550–800): Jordanes, Gregory of Tours, Bede, and Paul the Deacon* (Princeton, N.J.: Princeton University Press, 1988), pp. 17 ("Bede is known to have a plot."), 249–50, 325–27. Cf. Ordericus Vitalis, *Ecclesiastical History*, 5.1, 6.1; Chibnall, ed., 3:8, 214. Marjorie Chibnall, *The World of Orderic Vitalis* (Oxford: Clarendon, 1984), pp. 214–15. Nancy F. Partner's judgment is that ". . . the mass of [Ordericus's] material, arranged with evident difficulty into chronological sequence, uncontrollably shapeless, tends to drown out any particular impression . . . His history, like that of so many of his contemporaries, is full of good things—but the structure of the edifice, which Tacitus' friends found so boring to discuss, is hopelessly lost." "The New Cornificius: Medieval History and the Artifice of Words," in *Classical Rhetoric and Medieval Historiography*, ed. Ernst Breisach, Studies in Medieval Culture, no. 19 (Kalamazoo, Mich.: Medieval Institute, 1985), p. 15. See also Robert W. Hanning, *The Vision of History in Early Britain: From Gildas to Geoffrey of Monmouth* (New York: Columbia University Press, 1966), pp. 63–90.

[4] Richard Vaughan, *Matthew Paris*, Cambridge Studies in Medieval Life and Thought, n.s., no. 6 (Cambridge: Cambridge University Press, 1958), p. 130. Cf. Antonia Gransden's reference to Matthew Paris's "almost uncontrollable amount of data," in *Historical Writing in England, c. 550 to c. 1307* (Ithaca, N.Y.: Cornell University Press, 1974), p. 363.

his own day.[5] In a sense, his *History* is a sequential album of such illustrations.

It was no longer possible for Ordericus and Matthew Paris to reduce history to the theme of conversion. Bede had been able to identify the Roman communion and obedience (especially in Benedictine monasticism) with conversion to righteousness. By their days, the frontier of Christianization had moved far from the lands of central interest to the two chronicles. It had for them become synonymous, not so much with conversion as with wars to wreak vengeance upon the enemies of Christ and to purify the holy places that infidels had profaned.[6]

Likewise, it had become difficult to identify righteousness with institutional obedience. Hierarchic disputes of the eleventh and twelfth centuries, culminating in the papal schism of 1131–38, punctuate Ordericus's pages. Ordericus lamented that, while God had worked miracles through the saints in earlier times and books recorded their glory and wonderful signs, the prelates of his own day fell short in holiness, and had nothing to offer historians except their litigious wranglings, their fascination with worldly pomp and riches, and the frenzied madness of vices characteristic of men given over to carnal loves.[7] Matthew's tirades against the avarice of the papal court give an even sharper measure of the change from Bede's concept of the Church in time. It would have been inconceivable for Bede to denounce the Roman Curia, as Matthew did, for "confounding piety with impiety, having laid aside her shame, as a vulgar, brazen harlot available to all for hire, staining the purity of England by its contagion," and kindling the wrath of God against itself.[8]

Otto of Freising, Hugh of St. Victor, Joachim of Fiore and others built complaints such as these into broad and powerful themes of impending apocalypse. The association of ecclesiastical abuse with the advent of Antichrist and the Last Times certainly occurred to Ordericus and Matthew. Yet, unlike other writers of their generations, they did not seize upon that association as an organizing principle that could counteract the centrifugal effects of their historical perspectives.

Execution contributed to the diffuseness of the two chronicles as much as the absence of theme. By contrast with Bede, Ordericus Vitalis and Matthew Paris undertook universal chronicles beginning at the Creation, and they attached their own accounts to works by earlier writers, which they edited and adapted in various ways. Ordericus acknowledged his appro-

---

[5] Cf. *Ecclesiastical History*, pref.; Bertram Colgrave and R.A.B. Mynors, eds., *Bede's Ecclesiastical History of the English People* (Oxford: Clarendon, 1969), pp. 4, 6.

[6] Ordericus, *Ecclesiastical History*, 9.1; Chibnall, ed., 5:4. Matthew Paris, *Chronica majora* (*a.* 1248); Luard, ed., 5:24.

[7] *Ecclesiastical History*, 5.1, 6.1; Chibnall, ed., 3:8, 214.

[8] *Chronica majora* (*a.* 1241); Luard, ed., 4:100.

priation of William of Jumièges' (fl. 1070) chronicle, but Matthew Paris appropriated that by Roger of Wendover (d. 1236) without a word. As Ordericus's deference to the understanding of some later and wiser scholar indicates, he, at least, expected his work to be similarly adapted and expanded piecemeal. Thus, execution gave the chronicles the nature of a diffuse informational flow.

What evidence, then, do they display of esthetic strategy? There is, first of all, the evidence of probability. It is unlikely that Ordericus and Matthew could have excluded esthetic judgment from works that occupied them for decades and that constituted primary achievements of their monastic careers. Like Bede, they passed their lives in surroundings of great and calculated beauty, in buildings recently constructed and among treasures collected within living memory. With the austerity of the early Cistercians, Ordericus's contemporary, Bernard of Clairvaux, dismissed the pleasures of visual images as impediments to affective devotion.[9] But the cult to which Ordericus and Matthew were consecrated obliged them to worship God in beauty accessible to the senses as well as in the immaterial beauty of holiness. They recorded mutilation of sacred images as a rebuke to God by his people, as a blasphemy of the infidel, or as a sign of apostasy calling forth vengeance through the offended image.[10] Cult made it possible, not only to recognize Christ and his saints, in apparitions, from their images,[11] but also in imagination to pass from image to epiphany.

The intended beneficiaries of these chronicles were such as could believe that writing history was a way to purify the soul from sin, at least by averting the temptations that lurked in idleness.[12] They believed that meditation on history had a part in restoring the soul as the image of God, an image-likeness that sin deformed. But they were also, not infrequently, men who

---

[9] Apologia, 12.28; J. Leclercq and H. M. Rochais, eds., S. Bernardi Opera (Rome: Editiones Cistercienses, 1963), 3:104.

[10] E.g., Ordericus, Ecclesiastical History, 8.11; Chibnall, ed., 4:194. Matthew Paris, Chronica majora (a. 1249); Luard, ed., 5:66. For practices similarly involving the ritual abasement of relics (chiefly in the eleventh and twelfth centuries), see Patrick Geary, "L'humiliation des saints," trans., Manon Waller, Annales, Économies, Sociétés, Civilisations 34 (1979): 27–42. Ekkehard of Aura recorded that, when crusaders reached Nicaea and the neighboring regions, they were stupefied by the "miserable spectacle" of pictures in churches and oratories on which the Islamic conquerors had mutilated the noses, ears, hands, and feet. Chronicon (a. 1099); MGH, SS 6, p. 212.

[11] E.g., Giraldus Cambrensis, Expugnatio Hibernica, dist. 2, chap. 30 ("Visio et Visionis Exposicio"); A. B. Scott and F. X. Martin, eds. and trans. (Dublin: Royal Irish Academy, 1978), p. 212. See Robert Bartlett, Gerald of Wales, 1146–1223 (Oxford: Clarendon, 1982), especially concerning Giraldus as a "comparative philologist," pp. 208–10. I am obliged to Ms. Jane Chamberlain for the reference to Giraldus. Cf. the celebrated story that Constantine the Great recognized the two men who had appeared to him in a vision when Pope Silvester I showed him an icon of Sts. Peter and Paul. Donatio Constantini, chaps. 6–8.

[12] Ecclesiastical History, 5.1; Chibnall, ed., 3:4.

had mastered several arts—a skilled lector and cantor, for example, who was also a preeminent calligrapher and illuminator, or another brother who was eloquent in speech and skilled in many arts, such as carving, metalworking, and calligraphy, and who "forced the novices to read and sing well, using words and whips." Such men practiced and taught their arts as spiritual exercises for the same reasons as histories were written and read: to enhance virtue and evade vice; and to make themselves and others instant in prayers and vigils, zealous in fasts and other ascetic torments of the flesh, and severe towards trangressions of the monastic rule,[13] all for the sake of restoring the image in the soul.

Ordericus and Matthew were both connoisseurs of art and skilled artists themselves. Ordericus was a master calligrapher whose work can still be seen in ornamented and illuminated manuscripts. His chronicle continually praises "noble" buildings, resplendent in their "astonishing workmanship" and "surpassing beauty."[14] He marvelled at costly liturgical vestments and ornaments. He delighted in the sweetness of choral music, and in the poems of Hildebert of Le Mans, valued "above gold and topaz," and in the songs of warriors.[15]

Matthew Paris, too, was a calligrapher, and he also "had such skill in the working of gold and silver and other metals, and in painting pictures, that it is thought that there has been no equal to him since [his day] in the Latin world."[16] Matthew himself owned works of art, some of which he may have made.[17] He inventoried the rings and jewels belonging to the monastery of St. Albans; he provided lists of paintings executed there in his

[13] Ordericus, *Ecclesiastical History*, 3; 8; Chibnall, ed., 2:86, 106; 4:330. Chibnall, *The World of Orderic Vitalis*, p. 71.

[14] *Ecclesiastical History*, 8.8, 27; 11.30; Chibnall, ed., 4:170, 330; 6:138. Some gauge of the cost of individual works is given by Ordericus's report that a penitent Peter of Maule made restitution to the priory of Maule by giving a year's grape harvest to the Virgin "for purchasing a statue." *Ecclesiastical History*, 5; Chibnall, ed., 3:200. Obviously, I have concluded that Ordericus's thinking was formed, not only by verbal imagination, or "textuality" (as Brian Stock cogently maintains in *The Implications of Literacy: Written Language and Models of Interpretation in the Eleventh and Twelfth Centuries* [Princeton, N.J.: Princeton University Press, 1983], pp. 75–76), but also by visual imagination.

[15] *Ecclesiastical History*, 3; 4; 6.3; 10.8; Chibnall, ed., 2:108, 352, 354; 3:218; 5:236.

[16] Vaughan, *Matthew Paris*, p. 19, quoting Matthew's continuator, Thomas Walsingham (ca. 1400). Nancy F. Partner has argued that Matthew was motivated by "narrow parochial loyalties and dim spirituality," and that, by assiduous dedication to self-interest, he freed himself "from the self-denying discipline of a deeply felt monastic vocation, if [he] had ever experienced one." *Serious Entertainments: The Writing of History in Twelfth-Century England* (Chicago: University of Chicago Press, 1977), pp. 154–55. Much in Matthew's writings indicates deficiency in the supreme monastic virtue, charity, but there is evidence that he retained an emotional commitment, not only to his community, but also to the discipline and ritual of monasticism, which, of course, encompassed the literary, visual, and performing arts.

[17] Vaughan, *Matthew Paris*, p. 18.

day, especially those by Richard the Painter (ca. 1241–50) and "the incomparable painter and sculptor," Walter of Colchester.[18] He took special note of the devotional paintings that St. Edmund Rich, Archbishop of Canterbury, used to carry with him, or reliquary shrines and other liturgical furniture, as well as architectural structures, windows, ornamental sculpture, and panelled ceilings. He adorned his own writings, including the *Chronica Majora*, with ornaments and illuminations.[19]

The words "*elegans*," "*eleganter*," and "*elegantia*," were favorites of Ordericus and Matthew, and it is clear that they pronounced those words with artistic understanding and esthetic discernment. They may well have wondered, with another monk, whether sculptors and painters of sacred images gained by their work some special reward from God.[20]

The evidence of artistic license is plain in the selection and deployment of evidence; the authors intended to represent, not to document. Ordericus's purposeful manipulation of evidence generally appeared at the source, in selection and exclusion, rather than in falsification. His omissions concerning women, the Jews of Rouen, popular advocates of religious reform, events in the great world of politics, and anything to do with Germany have a programmatic character.[21] By contrast, Matthew "is basically unreliable as a historical source." He had "something of the forger in him."[22] By carelessness and calculation, he occasionally altered documents incorporated in his chronicle. His vehement biases, including a global xenophobia, profoundly warped his judgment. When he undertook a rescension of earlier segments, modifying his intemperate judgments of the great and powerful, he is known to have replaced some accounts with "apparently fictitious" entries.[23] He openly and frequently acknowledged the suppression of evidence. "Lest truth give birth to enemies (which often happens),"

[18] Vaughan, *Matthew Paris*, pp. 186–87, 209, 211, 234. See also the biographies of John I, the twenty-first abbot of St. Albans, and William of Trumpington, the twenty-second, in Richard Vaughan, ed. and trans., *Chronicles of Matthew Paris: Monastic Life in the Thirteenth Century* (New York: St. Martin's Press, 1984), pp. 24–25, 47, 49.

[19] E.g., *Chronica majora* (*a.* 1244); Luard, ed., 4:324. On Matthew's own paintings, Vaughan, *Matthew Paris*, pp. 205–34 (chap. 11; "Matthew Paris the Artist"), and Gransden, *Historical Writing in England, c. 550 to c. 1307*, pp. 362–66, 376. See now the comprehensive study by Suzanne Lewis, *The Art of Matthew Paris in the "Chronica Majora,"* California Studies in the History of Art, no. 21 (Berkeley: University of California Press, 1987), demonstrating Matthew's integration of verbal and visual components.

[20] Caesarius of Heisterbach, *Dialogus Miraculorum*, 8.23; Joseph Strange, ed. (Cologne: Heberle, 1851), 2:100.

[21] *Ecclesiastical History*; Chibnall, ed., 6:xix. Chibnall, *The World of Orderic Vitalis*, pp. 155, 158, 164, 190, 193, 198. See also his suppression of information concerning the worldly, self-indulgent pleasures pursued by Bishop Gilbert Maminot of Lisieux because Gilbert had ordained him subdeacon. *Ecclesiastical History*, 5.3; Chibnall, ed., 3:20.

[22] Vaughan, *Matthew Paris*, p. 134.

[23] Vaughan, *Matthew Paris*, pp. 130–31, 143, 151–52, 198.

he wrote in a celebrated aside, "these things, though true and manifest, must be veiled with dissimulation, for the state of historical writers is hard. If they tell the truth, they provoke men; and, if they commit falsehoods to writing, God, who separates speakers of truth from flatterers, does not countenance them."[24]

The method of composition by accumulation indicates how they wished to use this license. In fact, it was a common method of exegesis, in which witness was joined to witness. Like most exegetes, Bede believed that this method of collation and expansion clarified Scriptural texts, and he described his history as having been drawn "not from any one authority, but from the faithful telling of countless witnesses."[25] Formless repetitiveness did not diminish the beauty of exposition. Rather, it emphasized the beauty of precepts that were demonstrated in so many varied ways. There was no need to be content with one instance when many were ready to be gathered.

That the works appear ill-digested and, at points, undigested, miscellanies is due in part to the fact that they are compilations, or collections, rather than treatises. However, their very disorderliness recalls the parallel that, in the period under review and for centuries after, works of art were collected and treasured along with vast arrays of mismatched curiosities or "marvels."[26] Ordericus mentioned a jumbled array at the court of William the Conqueror, including the horns of wild oxen cased with precious metal at both ends among the garments woven and encrusted with gold, and vessels of gold and silver, and, in a great treasure intended for St-Évroul, apart from precious vestments and a silver chalice, an elephant's tusk and the claw of a griffin.[27] The segmented accounts in these chronicles and the

[24] *Chronica majora* (*a*. 1254); Luard, ed., 5:469–70.

[25] *Comm. on I. John 3:* 1; David Hurst, trans., *Bede the Venerable: Commentary on the Seven Catholic Epistles* (Kalamazoo, Mich.: Cistercian Publications, 1985), p. 184. *Ecclesiastical History*, pref.; Colgrave and Mynors, eds., p. 6, where Bede stated that he had written about Cuthbert "ea quae certissima fidelium virorum adtestatione per me cognoscere potui. . . ."

[26] On the persistence of this attitude toward collection in later centuries, see Julius Schlosser, *Kunst-und Wunderkammern: Ein Beitrag zur Geschichte des Sammelwesens* (reprint, Braunschweig: Klinkhardt und Biermann, 1978).

[27] *Ecclesiastical History*, 3; 4; Chibnall, ed., 2:60, 62, 198. According to Herbord's biography of Bishop Otto of Bamberg, the pagan temples at Stettin contained similar ornaments among its treasures. Herbord recorded that the Slavs had deposited in the temples "horns of wild bulls [or bison] covered with gold and encrusted with gems, some for use as drinking cups and others as musical instruments." Herbord, *Dialogus de Vita S. Ottonis Episcopi Babenbergensis*, 2.32; Jan Wikarjak, ed., Monumenta Poloniae Historica, n.s., vol. 7, fasc. 3 (Warsaw: Państwowe Wydawnictwo Naukowe, 1974), pp. 260–62. See also William of Poitiers, *Gesta Guillelmi Ducis Normannorum et Regis Anglorum*, pt. 2, chap. 44; Raymonde Foreville, ed., Les classiques de l'histoire de France au Moyen Âge, vol. 23 (Paris: "Les belles lettres," 1952; p. 123. After mentioning the robes of William the Conqueror's entourage, woven and encrusted with gold, and vessels of silver and gold—incredible in number and beauty—Wil-

treasures alike were hoards meant to surprise, amuse, and awe the spectator. They displayed beauty not only by their costliness, variety, and novelty
but also by their aggregate, labyrinthine mass, capable indeed of many different arrangements. The coherence and discrimination by which they
were accumulated generally had little to do with whether or how they were
eventually sorted out.

We are prepared to find traces of an esthetic program, not in formal
structure so much as in the methods employed to reach the heart through
the imagination. Like Bede, Ordericus and Matthew lived in multilingual
worlds. With all its illusions and indeterminacies, translation was part of
their daily lives as a linguistic strategy, and also as a cognitive one by which
experience could be rendered into information, and information into empathetic participation in the actions portrayed. Dramatic catharsis was one
goal of teaching by historical example, and translation, as rendering, was
the strategy of achieving it. Thus, the repetitiveness of examples inculcat-
ing fear, pity, and love drew upon the esthetics that prescribed emulating
purity of soul, and that held up as models of ascetic piety those who fled
from the world, even in the midst of it, the martyrs above all and those
who like them suffered and were persecuted. Thus, among his contemporaries, Matthew singled out for particular admiration Archbishop Edmund
Rich (ca. 1175–1240, a prelate whose devotional use of icons Matthew
also noted). Rich commanded the xenophobic Matthew's admiration both
for political and for ascetic reasons. He had resisted the intrusion of foreigners into the English church. In return, he had suffered humiliation and
defeat by King and Pope, but he had won ascetic glory equally through
victory over self. That victory, for Matthew, was symbolized by a hairshirt
that the Archbishop wore day and night, ingeniously plaited and tied to
give the flesh no surcease from its torture.[28]

Above all, the beauty of holiness drew Ordericus and Matthew repeatedly to the theme of honor and vengeance. Their thinking was shaped by
the conviction that beauty was manifested as justice. Throughout, Ordericus was guided by his assumption that God, the righteous judge, saw all,
and would repay each person as he deserved, leaving no wrong unpunished
here or in the world to come. The object of historical writing was to educate the human race by recording and holding up for meditation how the
great had been cast down and the humble exalted, the reprobate damned
and the just saved, so that mankind might ever fear God's judgment and

---

liam continued: "His tantum ex poculis coenaculum ingens bibebat, aut cornibus bubalinis
metallo decoratis eodem circa extremitates utrasque."

[28] *Chronica majora* (*a.* 1244); Luard, ed., 4:328–29. Concerning the effects of the Archbishop's mortifications on his body, *Chronica majora* (*a.* 1240); Luard, ed., 4:74. Matthew
described another hairshirt worn, with iron hoops, by Bishop Richard de la Wyche of Chich-
ester, *Chronica majora* (*a.* 1253); Luard, ed., 5:380.

love his rule, avoiding the sin of disobedience and offering up what faithful bondservants owe their lord.[29]

Ordericus's accumulated witnesses testified to the symmetrical opposition of holiness and piety, in which justice was balanced off by injustice (or tyranny), humility by pride, mercy by cruelty (or anger), charity by avarice (or envy), fame (*memoria perennis*) by infamy, and zeal and vigilance (*studium sanctitatis*) by lust and sloth.[30] These and other parallels likewise expressive of holiness and impiety were timeless, just as the envy impelling Ordericus's contemporaries, so Ordericus judged, was the same that expelled Adam from Paradise.[31]

Portraying God as "the Lord of vengeance,"[32] Matthew Paris too found that retribution gave history its dominant and ever repeated theme, both in God's government of the world and in the emotions prompting human actions. Centuries earlier, Augustine had drawn this universal connection when he characterized anger as lust for revenge. An irate scribe, he wrote, could smash a stylus or reed that wrote badly. "Even this," Augustine continued, "quite irrational though it is, is still lust for revenge and is, so to speak, a kind of shadow of [universal] retribution, that those who do evil should suffer evil."[33]

As they reflected on this theme in various elaborations, Ordericus and Matthew detected a marked difference between the random turmoil of human events and the inexorable pattern of God's rule. The demarcation between the areas ruled by wisdom and by Fortune latent in Bede's work is explicit in their writings. Both authors repeatedly employed the metaphor of Fortune's Wheel to portray the instability of mortal life, the swiftness with which the world's pomp and glory passed away as though the flower of grass, and the retributive truth of Christ's words: "With whatsoever measure ye meet out, it shall be measured to you in return" (Luke 6:38). Human actions were the sport of Fortune, spinning her wheel or casting her dice with ravenous caprice that expressed the bestiality of human nature and the tendency of human wills always to sink into wickedness. In a more sinister way, Ordericus believed that the avenging Fury's violent rage, daily claiming new victims, belonged to the play and sport with which Satan tricked mortals out of Paradise.[34]

[29] *Ecclesiastical History*, 4; 6.10; Chibnall, ed., 2:318, 320, 350; 3:360.

[30] Ibid., 2:244, 246.

[31] Ibid., 2:64.

[32] E.g., *Chronica majora* (*a.* 1250), "*ultionum Dominus*" and (*a.* 1255), "*Deus Dominus ultionum*"; Luard, ed., 5:124, 536.

[33] *City of God*, 14.15; *Corp. Christ., ser. lat.*, 48, p. 438.

[34] *Ecclesiastical History*, 4; 11; Chibnall, ed., 2:246; 6:10. For the metaphor of the Wheel of Fortune, see Ordericus, *Eccclesiastical History*, 7.5, 12.19, 13.43; Chibnall, ed., 4:14; 6:242, 544. For Matthew Paris's references to the Wheel of Fortune, see *Chronica majora* (*aa.* 1240, 1241, 1247, 1255); Luard, ed., 4:72, 162, 601; 5:531. For references to the sport of For-

In their esthetic appeal to terror, pity, and love, Ordericus and Matthew contrasted Fortune and wisdom, the torrent of instability into which vengeance plunged the world with the constancy and order of God's justice. For Ordericus, Satan was the trickster whose invisible hand played with human lives. Matthew denied that God played tricks or trifled. He reworded a verse of Ovid so as to say that divine power "rages" (*saevit*) in human affairs, and not, as Ovid had written, that it "plays" (*ludit*) in them.[35]

Yet no one could penetrate the immensity of the depths of God's wisdom. His judgments were a "great abyss" and all the more to be feared for their hiddenness. If He were not sporting with human affairs, it was difficult to avoid the conclusion that, even though their wickedness blinded them to the fact, sinners were hopelessly trapped, like a fish in a net or a bird in a snare; for human intent was bound to fail if it ran counter to what, in his providence, God had ordained.[36] This was the esthetic truth to which the masses of witnesses accumulated by Ordericus and Matthew testified. Meditation on how it was continually revealed through the years was intended, by sympathetic imagination, to produce a spiritual catharsis in the reader, stimulating pity for those upon whom vengeance had fallen, love of God, and fear of his inescapable judgment.

The motif of play and the possibility that human beings were trapped in (or played by) a game recalls Bede's esthetic paradigm. Enough has been said to indicate that, despite the unsystematic and miscellaneous character of their chronicles, Ordericus and Matthew did submit their materials to a process of digestion, and that process resembles Bede's in some essential details. Their works are montages, joining witness to witness. But they are

---

tune, *Chronica majora* (*aa.* 1241, 1248); Luard, ed., 4:137, 5:13. For the metaphor of Fortune casting dice, *Chronica majora* (*a.* 1244); Luard, ed., 4:245. For the metaphor of a flower of grass, Ordericus, *Ecclesiastical History*, 4; 7.16; Chibnall, ed., 2:318, 4:109. See also chap. 3, n. 151; chap. 5, n. 28; chap. 7, n. 83.

[35] *Chronica majora* (*aa.* 1244, 1248); Luard, ed., 4:311 (adapting Ovid, *Ep. ex Pont.* 4.3.49), 5:4 ("Non enim Deus calumpniosus vel cavillosus.") The author of the *Vita Adalberonis Episcopi Wirziburgensis*, by contrast, did not hesitate to combine Ovid's verse (with *ludit*) with Scriptural citations to illustrate how God chose the elect. Prol., *MGH*, *SS* 12, p. 129. See also Hans-Eberhard Hilpert, "Zu den Prophetien im Geschichtswerk des Matthaeus Paris," *Deutsches Archiv* 41 (1985): esp. 180 (Matthew typically referred prophetic texts to the past, not to the future) and 185: "Es wäre trotzdem falsch, daraus zu folgern, Matthaeus' Geschichtsauffassung wäre in unserem Sinne rational gewesen. Sein Glauben an alle Arten von wundersamen Vorzeichen, vor allem in der Natur, erscheint oft ganz naiv. Sogar zur Wahrsagerei scheint er einen Hang gehabt zu haben, nicht für die grossen politischen Ereignisse, sondern für das individuelle Ergehen."

[36] Ordericus, *Ecclesiastical History*, 3; 4; 12.26, 45; Chibnall, ed., 2:276; 6:302, 368. See also *Ecclesiastical History*, 6.1; 9.1, 14; Chibnall, ed., 3:214; 5:4, 282. Matthew Paris, *Chronica majora* (*a.* 1236); Luard, ed., 3:350–51 (on why God permitted the Saracens to be seduced by Mohammed's errors).

neither self-contained nor self-explanatory. Employing a highly eclectic technique of montage and assuming points of reference outside their texts, Ordericus and Matthew aimed at the reader's esthetic—indeed, visual—recreation, not of events only, but of the cathartic responses provoked by those events, chiefly fear, pity, and love. The object of those responses was an inward beauty of virtue that could be known only when it was digested, not into texts or formal knowledge, but using them as means into life and practice. Thus, the process of digestion was kinesthetic as well as esthetic; its kinesthetic aspects were rooted in the monastic discipline of spiritual contrition and physical mortification, and in its multiplication of verbal and visual images in the enactments of ritual.

Digesting history for them was, therefore, an ensemble technique of cognition. By it mnemonic images were multiplied in different media (chiefly, visual, tactile, and auditory), each complementing deficiencies of the others and being completed by the mimetic imagination of the viewer, reader, or hearer. The multiplication of images intensified the inadequacy of each medium to convey the whole story, the gaps that it left to be filled in. But, in the gaps created by the deficiencies of the media, the esthetic imagination set to work, translating experience into information, and information into spiritual epiphanies. The imagination did not rest in contemplation of one image, but constantly played among many, in the repertoires of all the arts.

## A NUCLEAR WAY OF SEEING

How can we explain the power of narrative to convince? In the twelfth century, criticism was, as ever, a medium of discovery. But the guiding principles of criticism, as we have thus far recovered them, are strikingly unlike those that have been familiar since the fifteenth century. They identified imagination with visualization. Consequently, by contrast with post-Renaissance criticism—which, though mimetic, gave pride of place to verbal culture—we have to deal with a way of seeing or, at least, a perspective in the strict, visual sense. If any such mimetic way of seeing were common to the imaginative arts—to what has been called a tradition of "symbolic synesthesia" (chap. 2, n. 56)—we should certainly be able to find traces of it in the visual arts as well as in historical writing. It is essential to emphasize that not all the modes of understanding demonstrated in our materials were linguistic, and therefore that understanding was not by any means identical with such exclusively linguistic activities as explanation and interpretation. The modern equation between understanding and interpretation does not exhaust the hermeneutic programs in these materials. What does the evidence disclose?

The perspective that we have identified is capable of being linear, that is, of following a straight line of vision. However, given its lapses, odd con-

gruences, and confusions of temporal sequence, it is also capable of counterlinearity or even nonlinearity. One might be inclined to think that writers and artists were playing with multiple perspectives, as indeed artists did
combine varied scenes and perspectives in the same painting, and Scriptural commentators built up structures of multiple meaning (which is also
to say, of visual associations in the minds of readers). While they ex-
pounded variety as a characteristic of beauty, and thus an esthetic norm, all
twelfth-century writers on beauty and order presupposed unity in diversity. Therefore, they experienced some overarching way of seeing prior to
the various perspectives that they expressed. That way of seeing was mimetic. Evidently that substratum, that critical means of discovery, was
what vanished in the fifteenth century. It was replaced by an esthetic of
paintings limited to individual subjects, unambiguous and static in their
own three-dimensional spaces. It was well suited to ways of thinking that
united past, present, and future in a timeless unity of prophecy and fulfillment. By the fifteenth century, it was supplanted by a sense of time that
excluded reckoning *tempi* by multiple relationships and applied a single
reckoning by chronological sequence.[37] A great change had occurred in
what was required for narrative to be convincing.

My argument is that the mimetic way of seeing, which encompassed
multiple points of view, was not a linear perspective. It was, instead, a circular—or, more properly, a nuclear—one that permitted the kinds of segmentation, linearity, counterlinearity, and non-linearity that we have encountered. It was the kind of perspective that one can still experience while
scanning a frieze, as one's eye, with its limited focal point, darts from place
to place, from side to side. It was most likely a souvenir of much earlier
days, when the visual memory was adapted, not only to the fixed image of
the codex, but also the moving band of the scroll.[38]

In an attenuated form, the visual mimesis associated with the scroll long
survived the common use of the scroll itself. Its disappearance begins to be
evident in Gothic art; by the sixteenth century, the esthetic of the scroll
had become quite alien. But I believe that its presence in the twelfth century can be demonstrated, not only from historical writings, but also from
evidence of the visual arts.

That this way of seeing was, precisely speaking, nuclear is indicated by
what we have already said concerning the "fascicle" method of composition. As we have demonstrated with regard to historical writing, works

[37] See Donald J. Wilcox, *The Measure of Times Past: Pre-Newtonian Chronologies and the
Rhetoric of Relative Time* (Chicago: University of Chicago Press, 1987), pp. 137–48, 152. On
the multiplicity of *tempi*, see below, chap. 7.

[38] The nuclear perspective was by no means limited to Europe before 1200. See Rudolf
Arnheim, *The Power of the Center: A Study of Composition in the Visual Arts* (Berkeley: University of California Press, 1988).

were composed as anecdotes, short narratives, or clusters of narratives. There was a designed incompleteness in the structure of works as albums made of fascicles, or nuclei which enabled viewers or readers to break components of a work apart and reassemble (or "reconceptualize") them, perhaps with other materials, in quite a different order.

More needs to be said, however, to indicate that the perspective in question was circular as well as nuclear. We have already encountered the wheel as a dominant paradigm of change, whether in the crazy spin of Fortune's Wheel, or in the concentric wheels of Ezekiel, interpreted as representing prophecy and fulfillment. Not surprisingly, there were corresponding paradigms in ideas about thought itself.

. . .

Of all the esthetic values that we have examined, the most difficult to grasp is surely the principle of "discoordination," which, as Meyer Schapiro defined it, was "a grouping or division such that corresponding sets of elements include parts, relations, or properties which negate that correspondence."[39] This disruptive principle added to delight in variety, detail, and exoticism, ran directly counter to the classical unities, whether as actually nurtured in Antiquity or as reinterpreted in the fifteenth century. Nothing could have been more opposed to the requirement that narrative, to be convincing, had to be consecutive. The disruption of organic unity was heightened by the fact that separate elements in a given work of art were frequently complete in themselves, set on their own individual axes.[40] Yet, contemporary writers continually referred to the visual realism of paintings and witnessed to the power of such works of art to engage the mind and soul.

Twelfth-century viewers saw something in the works that Renaissance humanists and their successors missed. What made it possible to discern unity in diversity? The cornerstone of that discernment was the conviction that wholeness—envisioned as circularity—prevailed in the created world, and that the methods of knowing, as well as the objects of knowledge, described a vast circle of perfection. No doubt other considerations were also in play when an illuminator represented Philosophy at the hub of a wheel comprised of the Liberal Arts. But it would be wrong to overlook the circularity that came from the assumption that all rivulets of wisdom sprang from the same source, an assumption that encased the ancient con-

[39] Meyer Schapiro, "The Sculptures of Souillac," in *Romanesque Art* (New York: Braziller, 1977), p. 104.

[40] Meyer Schapiro, "On the Aesthetic Attitude in Romanesque Art," in *Romanesque Art*, pp. 4, 8, 10, 16–20.

cept of a circle of knowledge (or encyclopedia).[41] Did not monks tonsure their heads in a circular fashion to symbolize the virtue that adorned thought, trimming the hairs that remained to the same length as a sign that the harmony of love (*caritas*) consummated all the virtues?[42] The God in whom all lived and moved and had their being was Alpha and Omega. The perfect roundness of the physical world—the heavens and the earth—circumscribed a cross, which was formed by the intersection of its equal longitude and latitude, demarking the four parts of the world which Christ saved by his Cross.[43] The Cross itself was seen as a round object when represented under the figure of the mystic winepress. And yet, as we shall see, the circle became a principle of discoordination.

Thus, when a contemporary scholar detects a "cruciform semiosis" (or organizing principle) in twelfth-century narrative, he has identified an important figure of thought, one that is both cruciform and circular. Indeed, the "circular progression" that he has identified was at work, not only in the narrative of the Crucifixion, "from divine to human [and] from human to divine," but also in narratives of human events.[44] It was present in the sense of history that located Christ's first preaching his doctrine among the Jews and his consummation of it among them at the end of the world[45] in crucifixes and paintings that, while made as biaxial compositions, yet described cycles of events at the outer extremities, whether on plaques on the arms of a cross or as continuous strips of illustrations encircling the borders of a page, rounding the composition as the rim of a hemisphere (figure 5).[46]

Detached from the specific symbolism of the cross, or of cruciform organization, the circular perspective is commonly implied in illuminations that represent actions or groups in lines that, to an eye accustomed to

[41] Rosalie Green et al., eds., *Herrad of Hohenbourg: Hortus Deliciarum*, 2 vols., Studies of the Warburg Institute, vol. 36 (London: Warburg Institute, 1979). See illustration no. 33, in 1:104 and 2:571. On the circle of knowledge, e.g., Gregory Thaumaturgos, *Panegyric on Origen*, chap. 15.

[42] *Hortus Deliciarum*, text no. 679, 2:312, quoting Honorius of Autun's *Gemma Animae*. The text continues: "Quod autem barba radimus, inberbes pueros similamus, quos si humilitate imitabimus, angelis, qui semper juvenili etate florent, equabimur."

[43] The circularity of the Cross took another form in Alcuin's "strange vision of the world as an enclosure (like a sheepfold) encircled by Christ's blood." Schapiro, "Two Romanesque Drawings in Auxerre and Some Iconographic Problems," in *Romanesque Art*, p. 309, citing the *Vita Alcuini*; Migne *PL* 100:96.

[44] Stephen G. Nichols, Jr., *Romanesque Signs: Early Medieval Narrative and Iconography* (New Haven, Conn.: Yale University Press, 1983), pp. 104–17, 120, 127.

[45] *Hortus Deliciarum*, text no. 790, 2:382.

[46] For an example of an illumination of this sort, see Meyer Schapiro, "Two Romanesque Drawings in Auxerre and Some Iconographic Problems," in *Romanesque Art*, pp. 306–27. I am obliged to Dr. Adelaide Bennett for this reference.

*Figure 5.* The composition of this magnificent book cover, one of many treasures made for Abbess Theophanu of Essen (1039–56) is an example of how on a rectangular object the elements of cross and border could be used to serve a circular perspective. *Essen, Domschatz. Photograph courtesy of Herr Prälat STD Alfred Pothmann, Kustos, Domschatzkammer Essen.*

three-dimensional representations, seem flat.[47] In the same way, it was in the habit of interpreting events as figural, or typological, repetitions of incidents in Scripture or of ever-recurrent episodes in the conflict of virtues against vices. In the circularity of mutual reflection, the deeds of earlier people were figures of what later people did. Mimesis, enforced by the exegetical technique of discerning "dissimilar likeness and like dissimilitude," sustained the assumption of a prevalent and informing circularity in the cosmos and in history.[48]

Thus, even images that were not circular by design and that were not on round surfaces (such as bowls or transept vaults) were imagined as if they were circular. We have repeatedly encountered the assumption that the spectator (or reader) completed the composition and, consequently, that the focal points of compositions were in the minds of the viewers. The "fascicles" were arranged so that spectators could enter and explore the spaces between them. This expansion of the work of art made mimetic criticism a medium of discovery. The circular perspective placed spectators at the center of the work of art, or, in other words, encircled them with a frieze ever revolving before their minds' eyes. How was it possible for a circular, or nuclear, perspective to become a means of discoordination?

Some visual evidence of this way of seeing exists in the strip-illuminations frequent in manuscripts prior to the thirteenth century. These illuminations resemble comic strips in that they are serial pictures, frequently with captions, sometimes with discourse and stage directions. Although they may illustrate an adjacent text, they may, like other kinds of illumination, exist "entirely independent of the accompanying text."[49] They were capable of being arranged in single-page compositions of two or more strips, or in serial strips that extended over several pages and strongly resemble scrolls.

Augustine of Hippo lived and worked in a world familiar both with codices and with scrolls; not long after his time scrolls ceased to figure in the reader's normal day. It might therefore seem unlikely that the way of

[47] For example, *Hortus Deliciarum*, illustrations 60 (Israelites dancing around the Golden Calf) and 63 (Moses' Tabernacle, surrounded by a frieze of Israelites) and 2:74, 80. In an anthologized text, Herrad recorded another intended three-dimensionality of two-dimensional representation. Haloes of saints were represented as circles around the heads of saints, according to the text, not only to indicate that they enjoyed the light of eternal splendor with which they were crowned, but also because, being painted in the shape of a round shield, the haloes designated the divine protection that guarded them as with a shield. Text no. 789, 2:379.

[48] For the phrase "*similitudo dissimilis et dissimilitudo similis*," see Rupert of Deutz, *Commentum in Apocalypsim*, 12.21; Migne *PL* 169:1202.

[49] Schapiro, "On the Aesthetic Attitude in Romanesque Art," in *Romanesque Art*, p. 7, referring specifically to a twelfth-century Cistercian copy of works by Pope Gregory the Great.

*Figure 6*. This medallion from the Guthlac Roll represents donors at the altar-reli-
quary of Crowland Abbey. The rolls on which their donations are recorded strikingly express the visual distinction between codex-reading and roll- (or scroll-)
reading. The donors, represented here as contemporaries, lived between the eighth
and the twelfth centuries. The bound, recumbent figure at the right, with a green
demon leaving his mouth, records a miraculous cure at Guthlac's tomb. *British
Library, Harley Roll Y.6*.

seeing conditioned by the scroll survived the demise of the scroll itself. And
still, there are symptoms of that survival, attenuated perhaps, yet distinct.

One symptom is the frequency of the scroll (or roll) in the visual arts.
One can not discount the effect of ancient exemplars or the force of convention on painters and carvers; nor can one set aside the purely decorative
effect of the scroll as a ribbon, binding elements of a composition together.
Yet, the ubiquity of the scroll in eleventh and twelfth-century visual arts is
striking. The Bury St. Edmunds Cross and one medallion from the Guthlac
Roll (figure 6) showing benefactors unfurling their charters at St. Guthlac's tomb are thickets of scrolls (or rolls). In some representations, artists

correctly included the spindles or tabs at each end of the scroll.[50] Not uncommonly, codices and scrolls appear together in the same representation.

A more telling symptom is the actual use of rolls. Unlike a scroll (*volumen*), a roll (*rotula*) moves from top to bottom, rather than from side to side. Yet, both display the essential difference from the codex that the movement of the eye proceeds along a continuous strip, rather than, as in codices, being sharply framed by the isolated, and isolating, contours of the page. Indeed, the processual movement in scanning a roll from top to bottom is, if anything, more pronounced than that in perusing a scroll. For, since texts on scrolls were written in columns, the eye moved both from one side to another, along the band, and also up and down the individual columns.

A word specifically about illuminations may be in order. The visual image formed in the memory by a codex is very different from that formed by scrolls. The image of the codex is sharply framed; that of the scroll is processual, as columns run in sequence. The introduction of the codex initiated a fundamental change in the character of book illuminations, and thus, in the interplay of picture and text. Conservatism prevailed in the early decades of the codex. Just as, after the invention of printing, books were made to look like manuscripts, so too, in the early decades of the codex, copyists mimetically reproduced in a different format the columnar arrangement of the scrolls and some dominant characteristics of scroll illumination. But, in time, the format and the materials used in producing codices led to a decided change, which has been called the emancipation of the miniature from the text.[51]

The sheets and gatherings of the codex made cross-referencing far easier than it was in the scroll. Finding a reference point in a scroll could require winding through a length of material between 20 feet and 70 feet long. (Egyptian scrolls 130 feet long have been preserved, and a scroll 300 feet long, containing the entire text of Thucydides's *History*, is recorded.)[52] For this reason, it was essential for pictures in a scroll to be adjacent to the texts

---

[50] E.g., the illumination at the beginning of the Gospel of Matthew in the Carilef Bible (1088–96), now in the Cathedral Library, Durham (Durham. Lib. Cathedral, k. II. 4. fol. 87vo.), and an illumination showing a scroll held by the hand of God descending to St. Benedict in an early eleventh-century Psalter from Canterbury, now in the British Library (Arundel 155. fol. 133r). On the use of scrolls in eleventh and twelfth-century illuminations, see Schapiro, "Two Romanesque Drawings in Auxerre and Some Iconographic Problems," in *Romanesque Art*, pp. 306–8, 310. Schapiro especially identifies the scroll (together with the eagle) as an emblem of John the Evangelist. I am obliged to Dr. Lois Drewer for identifying manuscripts mentioned in this chapter.

[51] Kurt Weitzmann, *Illustrations in Roll and Codex: A Study of the Origin and Method of Text Illustration*, 2d ed. (Princeton, N.J.: Princeton University Press, 1970), p. 89.

[52] David Diringer, *The Hand-Produced Book* (London: Hutchinson's Scientific and Technical Publications, 1953), pp. 129–30. Mr. William Mitchell kindly directed me to this book.

that they illustrated, or to be squarely in the midst of those passages. Illustrations in codices could be detached from their reference points in the text and gathered together at some other convenient place. Large frontispieces, detached from the text, became possible to a degree that the format of the scroll excluded by its consecutive run of columns. Moreover, the toughness of vellum membranes and the fact that, as pages, they were not subject to the stress of being rolled, made possible the use of heavier, and thus more brittle, paints and modelings than could be used on scrolls. Characteristically, scroll illuminations depended for survival on being executed in light pen-and-wash drawings.

Thus, in codices, illustrations could become independent of the text. Backgrounds and frames were introduced, isolating the miniature from the text, even when it was not placed in a separate section of illustrations.[53] Pictures could be used to decorate a codex as well as, or instead of, interpreting the sense of the words. But the separation of miniature from text by a frame need not destroy the central, or nuclear, perspective.[54] And, in fact, the use of rolls and the copying of scroll illuminations continued in the eleventh and twelfth centuries as parts of the bookmaker's craft.

In the eleventh century, the integration of pictures with text characteristic of scrolls continued in the liturgical roll. That the integration was intended, at least in some cases, for viewers is indicated by the fact that some illuminations were made upside down in the text so that the audience, standing in front of the lector, could see them as he read. This highly specialized form of book, in its several varieties, was largely limited to southern Italy, although it would be peremptory to dismiss the effect that the use of such rolls at major religious centers, Monte Cassino not least among them, may have had on visitors from beyond the Alps.[55] Far more numerous were rolls of prayer, necrology, and genealogy, and a species of official record so common that in England it was placed under the responsibility of a Master of the Rolls.

Although (even taking liturgical rolls into account) illuminated rolls were uncommon,[56] ancient texts and illuminations, taken from scrolls,

[53] Weitzmann, *Illustrations in Roll and Codex*, pp. 69, 72, 83, 89, 93, 97. See also Kurt Weitzmann, "Book Illustrations of the Fourth Century: Tradition and Innovation," in *Studies in Classical and Byzantine Manuscript Illumination*, ed. Herbert L. Kessler (Chicago: University of Chicago Press, 1971), pp. 97, 124, and idem, "Illustrated Rolls and Codices in Greco-Roman Antiquity," in *The Book through Five Thousand Years*, ed. Hendrik D. L. Vervliet (New York: Phaidon, 1972), pp. 165–66, 172–74.

[54] See Arnheim, *The Power of the Center*, chap. 4 ("Limits and Frames"), pp. 51–71.

[55] C. R. Dodwell, *Painting in Europe, 800 to 1200*, The Pelican History of Art (Baltimore, Md.: Penguin Books, 1971), pp. 127–29.

[56] The Guthlac Roll is a notable rarity. Margaret Rickert, *Painting in Britain: The Middle Ages*, The Pelican History of Art (Baltimore, Md.: Penguin, 1954), p. 96: "The form of the Guthlac Roll is almost unique in late medieval manuscripts, that is, the rotulus or roll, rather

continued to be made. To be sure, the transmission between ancient scrolls and eleventh- or twelfth-century codices may have been indirect, through a chain of intervening codices. However, the introduction of heavy paints in manuscript illumination had by no means driven out the use of the lighter materials employed in the pen-and-wash method. Reinforced by continuity of method, copies in codex form preserved the characteristic integration of pictures and text—a method used in late Antiquity for continuous narrative—that had existed in the prototype scrolls.[57]

Hardly any historical writings are illuminated richly enough to provide evidence of a circular (or wraparound) perspective inculcated, so to speak, by thinking in scrolls. To be sure, the Bayeux Tapestry, as a vast frieze, illustrates the visual effects of that perspective (figure 7); so does an earlier document (1015–22), the bronze column of Bishop Bernward of Hildesheim, a small counterpart of Trajan's column, portraying scenes from the life of Christ. But among historical writings, the illustrations surviving for Otto of Freising's *Chronicle* are unusual. (Similar illuminations occur in a number of south German manuscripts attributed to the "Regensburg school" of the late twelfth century. A particularly celebrated example is a German translation of *The Song of Roland*, now in the library of Heidelberg University [Codex Pal. Germ. 112].)

Like illustrations for scrolls, these illuminations for the *Chronicle* were executed in the light materials of the pen-and-wash method. Their relation to the text represents a hybrid of scroll and codex. For, while they are set apart from the surrounding text by frames, those frames are not thick, colored borders segregating visual from verbal elements. Instead, they are verses, the letters of which easily blend into the text, just as the spaces between their letters and words blend into the blank grounds of the pictures. Likewise, the degree of substantive integration between pictures and text is hybrid. For while the general subjects of pictures and surrounding text correspond, extreme divergences occur. At some points, the illumination, the caption, and Otto's text go their separate ways. At others, two of the elements coincide. At still others, Otto's text is so general that the illu-

---

than the codex or book form." See also George Warner, *The Guthlac Roll: Scenes from the Life of St. Guthlac of Crowland by a Twelfth-Century Artist. Reproduced from Harley Roll Y.6 in the British Museum* (Oxford: Roxburghe Club, 1928). The Roll (about 9 feet, 6½ inches long) contains no text and six rows of three medallions each. The first part of the Roll, which may have contained a text and additional medallions, is lost.

[57] Examples are the twelfth-century copies of the Utrecht Psalter (from Canterbury, now in the British Library [Harley 603]; Bibliothèque Nationale [MS. Lat. 8846]); the Eadwini Psalter, now in Trinity College, Cambridge (R. 17.1); a copy of the comedies of Terence (from St. Albans, now in the Bodleian Library [Auct. F. 2. 13]); and two copies of Prudentius's *Psychomachia* (now in the British Library [MS. Add. 24199] and in Corpus Christi Library, Cambridge [CCC. 23]). I am obliged to Dr. Adelaide Bennett for the observation about the continuity of pen-and-wash techniques.

*Figure 7*. The wraparound frieze perspective is suggested in this sketch of how the Bayeux Tapestry could have looked displayed in Dover Priory. The simulation is the work of Dr. Barnett Miller, imposed on an engraving from T. H. Turner, *Some Account of Domestic Architecture in England from the Conquest to the End of the Thirteenth Century* (Oxford, 1851). *The Plate is here reproduced by the kindness of Dr. Miller and of John Calmann & King, Ltd.*

mination, in its concreteness, constitutes a separate composition. There are, finally instances in which Otto's text, the metrical caption, and the illustration form a coordinated unit.[58]

For our purposes, the telling fact, the clue to the role of nuclear perspective as a tool of discoordination, is the degree to which the illuminations were organized by strips as visual nuclei. Some illuminations appear alone.[59] But the vast majority are arranged in two or three strips, or regis-

[58] Walther Scheidig, *Der Miniaturenzyklus zur Weltchronik Ottos von Freising im Codex Jenensis Bose q. 6*, Studien zur deutschen Kunstgeschichte, Heft 257 (Strassburg: Heitz, 1928), pp. 7, 8, 9, 11, 12, 13, 17, 18, 20, 21, 26, 28, 33–34, 35, 38, 41–42.

[59] Scheidig, *Der Miniaturenzyklus zur Weltchronik Ottos von Freising*, pp. 28, 29, 33, 32, 34.

ters, on one page. Generally, each strip depicts one scene, but in several instances a strip was divided into two scenes. Thus, two pages display as many as five scenes each. The order of the strips indicates that they, and their metrical captions, were intended to be studied from top to bottom and, when appropriate, from left to right in a ribbon sequence. Their nuclear arrangement indicates that they could also be studied as fascicles, in any order, broken apart like the enamelled plaques of a cross and reassembled in the album of the viewer's imagination.

For a more complete illustration of the nuclear perspective as a tool of discoordination, we must turn to a work that can not be called a historical writing in the strict sense, despite its preoccupation with sacred history: the *Hortus Deliciarum*. This manuscript was compiled at the convent of St. Odile, in Alsace, toward the end of the twelfth century (ca. 1176–96). Although it was destroyed in 1870, during a bombardment of Strassburg, careful descriptions of its contents and drawings of its illuminations had been made earlier in the nineteenth century. Using these materials, scholars have reconstructed, with some gaps, its organization and contents. Chiefly the creation of the Abbess Herrad, it consisted of at least 342 leaves. The manuscript included a wide variety of written materials (1165 texts in all). Most of them were excerpts from treatises on theology, ascetic discipline, and Church order. Compositions in verse, some by Herrad herself, were also included. Musical notations and marginal directions and commentaries added to the variety of the work. Although the citations include selections from several eminent twelfth-century writers, there are few references to ecclesiastical history after the age of the Apostles, and none to the periods after that of the Church Fathers.

The great glory of the *Hortus* was certainly its opulent program of illumination, which produced no fewer than 136 large pictures and forty or so other pictures and diagrams. Particularly in view of the fact that the manuscript was added to at various times, one might very well assume that the work of writing and illuminating was done partly or entirely in a scriptorium at St. Odile's. Nuns elsewhere were recognized for their skill in producing luxurious manuscripts. But it is not possible to determine the scriptorium where, or the gender of the scribes by whom, the *Hortus* was made.[60]

Often called an encyclopedia, the compilation was intended to be an anthology in the literal sense. Herrad wrote that she had worked like a bee, collecting into one book honey from varied blossoms of sacred and philo-

---

[60] Green et al., eds., *Hortus Deliciarum*, 1:1, 31. On Herrad as an illustration of educational achievements of twelfth-century women, see Joan M. Ferrante, "The Education of Women in the Middle Ages in Theory, Fact, and Fantasy," in *Beyond Their Sex: Learned Women of the European Past*, ed. Patricia H. Labalme (New York: New York University Press, 1980), p. 16.

sophical literature. She had, she said, prepared a "garden of delights" in which those in her convent "could take some eager pleasure in the collected flowers of texts."[61]

By using the term "garden of delights," Herrad consciously drew an analogy between her book and Paradise, the eternal *"hortus deliciarum."*[62] But, with the age-old metaphors of bee and variegated flowers (or anthology), she also testified to the discontinuous nature of the work. Certainly the materials follow a distinct organization into eight parts.[63] Scholars differ on the degree to which they detect the dominance of order over miscellany.[64] The scholar who, above all, undertook the reconstruction of the *Hortus*, specifically argued that, informed by an architectonic design, the work was not a "scrapbook."[65]

However, it certainly has discontinuous features of an album. Not only may Herrad have continued the work of her predecessor, the Abbess Rilinda, but the enterprise of compilation continued through Herrad's life and perhaps after her death.[66] Intermittent alterations intruded many irregularities. At least twenty percent of the manuscript leaves are "half-size or smaller" insertions.[67] New sequences of texts and violations of original juxtapositions of texts and pictures were imposed by interpolation. Moreover, great numbers of glosses and notes, many in German, were added in the margins and between the lines of the texts. The character of the *Hortus* as an album composed of fascicles liable to imaginative revision is underscored by the fact that the leaves of the manuscript remained unbound, contained in a vellum wrapper, until the sixteenth century.

Herrad knew the doctrine that Christ suffered five wounds in order to redeem the bodily senses which the Devil had ensnared.[68] Presumably, even before the Crucifixion, the senses had served laudable purposes. Even then,

[61] *Hortus Deliciarum*, text no. 2, 2:4.

[62] *Hortus Deliciarum*, text no. 773, 2:374.

[63] Creation (folios 1v–17r); sacred history from Adam and Eve to the Patriarchs (folios 17r–36v); Christology (folios 36v–167v); the Apostolic Church (folios 167v–199r); Virtues and Vices (folios 199v–220v); Ecclesiology (folios 221r–240v); Apocalypse (folios 240v–263v); and Faith and Order (folios 264v–320v). See Bischoff's division of the work into four parts: Old Testament, New Testament, Church and Last Times. *Hortus Deliciarum*, 1:41. On Green's characterization of it as a "great triptych," ibid., p. 25.

[64] Cames, Bischoff, and Curschmann argue for extreme eclecticism or even the absence of system. Green maintains that meticulous planning prevailed. Gérard Cames, *Allégories et symboles dans l'Hortus deliciarum* (Leiden: Brill, 1971), p. 127. Bischoff, Curschmann, and Green in *Hortus Deliciarum*, 1:22, 24, 36, 42–43, 73–74 (specifically on the use of German in the glosses). See also Dodwell, *Painting in Europe, 800 to 1200*, p. 172, on "the grandeur of the conception of the whole."

[65] Green, in *Hortus Deliciarum*, 1:22.

[66] Green, in *Hortus Deliciarum*, 1:25.

[67] Evans, in *Hortus Deliciarum*, 1:3. See also Green, ibid., p. 17.

[68] *Hortus Deliciarum*, text no. 319, 2:139.

paintings served as the books of the laity, adornments of houses, and devices for recalling the lives of earlier people to memory. Moses introduced sculpture into churches; Solomon, painting.[69] At any rate, Herrad evidently considered variety a mode a beauty, above all the kind of variety that produced a "multitude of pictures," such as adorned the veil of Moses's tabernacle, woven as it was with images of every flower that earth engendered and with such other pictures of animals as artists (*pictores*) could find room for.[70] But how were the pictures to be seen to moral effect, just as vividly, for example, as the righteous would see the wicked in their eternal torment in order to rejoice all the more in their own deliverance?[71]

A clue is given in Herrad's conventional advice to her nuns that they ceaselessly "unroll" or "turn" (*volvere*) the book in their hearts.[72] Another is the frequency with which scrolls (or rolls) appear in her illuminations. These reflect conventions of Byzantine and Latin art, especially in representations of Christ holding a scroll.[73] They also express a way of seeing that witnessed to the cosmic order, depicted in numerous circular illuminations in Herrad's book, to the correspondence between the order of the world (the macrocosm) and that of the human body (the microcosm); to a concept of the circle of knowledge expressed in Herrad's "wheel" of Philosophy and the Liberal Arts (see figure 9); to a paradigm of change set forth in her picture of Fortune's Wheel (see figure 4); to a visualization of Christ's Cross as a circular winepress (see figure 12); and, finally, to the dramatic vision of the apocalyptic day of wrath when the sun would turn black, and the moon become as blood, and "the heaven depart as a scroll when it is rolled up together" (Rev. 6:12–14; see figure 8). The perspective that governed these illuminations is also represented in a strip of vellum decorated with scenes from the career of John the Baptist. This strip painting was executed in the same scriptorium as the *Hortus Deliciarum*. Although one scholar considered it a roll made for private devotions, it now has been identified as a *flabellum*, a circular fan made as a liturgical ornament. Its interest for us is that it is as much as study in nuclear perspective as a roll (or scroll) might be.[74]

---

[69] *Hortus Deliciarum*, text no. 789, 2:379.

[70] *Hortus Deliciarum*, text no. 157, 2:75. See also inscriptions on illustration no. 96. Ibid., 1:129 on the *"pulchra varietas"* of Zechariah's vision.

[71] *Hortus Deliciarum*, text no. 876, 2:438.

[72] *Hortus Deliciarum*, text no. 1, 2:3. See also Gerhoch of Reichersberg, *Tractatus in Ps. 64*, pref. *B*; *MGH, Ldl* 3, p. 439: "Nam, si revolvantur antiqua Romanorum pontificum scripta, nusquam in eis reperitur hoc nomen. . . ." This usage is frequent in Peter the Venerable's treatise against the Jews. *Adversus Iudeorum Inveteratam Duritiem*, chaps. 2, 4, 5. *Corp. Christ., continuatio medievalis*, 58, pp. 31, 120, 175.

[73] E.g., illuminations no. 118, 160, 217, 305. See the representation of the flying scroll (*volumen volans*) in Zechariah's vision. Illumination no. 96. *Hortus Deliciarum*, 2:107.

[74] Rosalie B. Green, "The Flabellum of Hohenbourg," *Art Bulletin* 33 (1951): 153–55.

The most knowledgeable of all critics considered that ". . . the usual movement [of the eye] in the *Hortus Deliciarum* is left-to-right . . ."—in other words, a "reading-order."[75] But this characterization omits, in any event, the important movement from top to bottom. It also conspicuously omits the "unrolling" or "turning" motion required by individual minia-tures composed in a circular mode, and by many of the strip illuminations. Among the latter, two illustrate varieties of the nuclear perspective and its discoordinating effects particularly well. They also underscore the associa-tion between violence and beauty characteristic of the period.

The first is the warfare of Virtues and Vices (folios 199v–204r). Here the strip illuminations are arranged in quasi-symmetry on facing pages. There are three tiers of illuminations on each page except the last two. Of these, the left page displays a medallion representing the chariot of Avarice and (below) a row of three Vices led by Blasphemy, brandishing spears to the right. The facing page shows a medallion portraying the chariot of Mercy, beneath which stands a row of eight Virtues, led by Fortitude, withstanding the assault from the left. An inscription inserted at the bot-tom of the page to the right of the Virtues marks the "end of the conflict of Virtues and Vices fighting invisibly within souls" (folio 203v). The other verbal segments of the illustrations, as they have been reconstructed, were limited to dramatic stage directions, short statements identifying ac-tions.

We shall return to the perplexing fact that, in the present arrangement, the battle recommences after what should have been the final encounter, between Generosity, on the one side, and Avarice and Rapine, on the other, which precedes the large medallions. As the strips have been recon-structed, the medallions and their pendants end the sequence of strips that begins with the top register on folio 199v, Pride's assault on Humility (fo-lio 200r). These two strips carry the eye across from left page to right page. But the eye must move back to the extreme left; for Humility's defeat of Pride occurs in the middle strip on folio 199v. This zig-zag movement continues through three duels to the bottom of the pages. The duel of Wrath and Patience is begun and ended in the facing top tiers of folios 200v and 201r. But the zig-zag movement resumes in the second tiers with the conflict of Envy and Charity, ending, in the bottom tier, with the vic-tory of Sobriety over Gluttony. The conflicts of Vainglory and Prudence, and of Falsehood and Justice, resume the zig-zag order on folios 201v and 202r.

At this point, the visual narrative changes, together with the arrange-ment of illuminations. Now, instead of passing through a series of two- or three-scene episodes described by confrontations on facing pages, the nar-

75 Green, in *Hortus Deliciarum*, 1:135, 148.

rative shifts to a more complex account. With her soft blandishments, Luxury accosts the Virtues, scattering violets from her wagon. Brandishing the standard of the Cross, Temperance so frightens Luxury's horses that they overturn her wagon, and Temperance crushes her to death under a millstone symbolizing Christ. Avarice gathers up Luxury's spoils. Born of Avarice, Rapine joins in the plunder. But Generosity strips Avarice and pierces her to the heart, distributing the pillage to the poor. The arrangement of the illuminations for this segment leads the eye from left (folio 201v, bottom tier) to right (folio 202r, bottom tier), then down the three strips on folio 202v, up to the top of the facing page (folio 203r) and down its three strips. The series ends with a return to quasi-symmetry in the two medallions and the assault of Blasphemy against Fortitude, previously described.

Scanning this sequence of illuminations requires several movements, all of which are varieties of a continuous, scrolling action. The curious resumption of conflict, between Blasphemy and Fortitude, beneath the medallions, leads to a further consideration. The medallions resemble the large illuminations with which scrolls frequently began. It is possible that, working from an ancient prototype, or from an intervening copy, the illuminator of the *Hortus* transposed the medallions and the assault of Blasphemy against Fortitude from the beginning to the end of the fascicle. Some such transposition is also indicated, not only by the exceptionally ornate conclusion that the medallions and their pendants make for the Psychomachia, but also by the abruptness with which the cycle begins, with the duel of Pride against Humility (folios 199v and 200r). The elaborate medallions with the assault of Blasphemy against Fortitude would have been an appropriate prologue to the rest of the conflict, beginning with the duel of Pride against Humility. If this were the original form of the Psychomachia, the initial asymmetry between the chariot of Avarice and that of Mercy would form a narrative circle with the concluding struggle of Avarice against Generosity. Despite their placement in the codex, the medallions with their pendants, even in the present arrangement, could be taken as the beginning, as well as the end, of the nucleus of a narrative cycle.

The codex form also obscures the nuclear organization of the second set of miniatures, an elaborate portrayal of the Last Judgment (figure 8). Folios 251v and 253r, which were intended to face each other, formed the nucleus of this representation, which then moved outward toward the front of the codex with representations of the saved, and toward the back with representations of the damned. The sequence on beatitude ended with a great portrayal of the Celestial Court (folio 244r, now very imperfectly known); that on damnation, with a corresponding miniature of Hell (folio 255r). Possibly the text on six cities—the angelic city, the city of the

*Figure 8.* The use of the wraparound perspective is indicated by these tiers of strip illuminations from the Last Judgment sequence in Herrad of Hohenburg's *Hortus Deliciarum*. The focus of attention is Christ enthroned, represented on a facing page. Notice the visual play of representing a Scriptural text that speaks of the heavens as a scroll (Rev. 6:14) in this scroll-composition. On iconographic irregularity in this illumination See chap. 4, n. 77. *Plate from A. Straub and G. Keller*, Herade de Landsberg, Hortus Deliciarum. *Strasbourg, 1879–99. Princeton University Library.*

world, Jerusalem, Babylon, Hell, and Paradise—was intended as a colophon for the entire composition (folio 256r).

Stretching over pages organized into strip illuminations and concluding with full-page miniatures, this elaborate work is certainly a "polyptych."[76] However, in the absence of any method of foldout presentation, the order of the illuminations is also recognizable as that of an encircling frieze, moving symmetrically to right and left. Adapted to the format of the codex, it also required a darting movement from top to bottom and across folios.[77]

The illustrations of the conflict of Virtues and Vices were set forth without accompanying texts, apart from identifying captions which, apparently, were written directly on the pictures. The elaborate Last Judgment cycle also appears to have been designed as a pictorial section, with captions identifying figures. The later interpolation of short leaves with sometimes extensive excerpts broke up the pictorial sequence and made it difficult to achieve the visual sweep originally intended. The two cycles therefore stand in visual contrast with some other sections of the manuscript in which a close interplay exists between texts and illuminations,[78] and in even sharper contrast with sections that were illustrated lightly or not at all.[79] Yet, as unusual as they were in their extent, they elaborated in the form of friezes the same nuclear perspective that characterized the circular representations of order in the cosmos, in the subjects of learning, in sacramental life, and even in the destructive play of Fortune. They also indicate a disjunctive, nonlinear perspective from which the purely literary sections could be read and visualized.

As Herrad's manuscript demonstrates, the nuclear perspective enabled authors to deploy a multiplicity of detail radiating from narrative centers. Used repeatedly in the framework of a large collection of fascicles, such as the *Hortus Deliciarum* or the historical writings with which we are primarily concerned, it served the principle of discoordination. Yet, even so large

---

[76] *Hortus Deliciarum*, 1:217.

[77] An aberration has certainly occurred in illumination no. 325 (folio 251r), where the proper order from right to left has been reversed. (It begins from right with hermits and anchorites and ends at left with martyrs.) The order of dignity, and symmetry with illumination no. 335 is thereby violated. (On a parallel reversal, see illumination no. 63, *Hortus Deliciarum*, 1:116.) It is impossible to determine whether this were an error of the illuminator of the *Hortus* in following a Byzantine model, or a confusion that entered with the nineteenth-century tracings on which the reconstruction depends. (Cf. *Hortus Deliciarum*, 1:161, on "a problem in copying, rather than in composing.") Numerous other illuminations in the manuscript present comparable puzzles. In the "frieze" of the Last Judgment, a second irregularity is present on folio 251r, where the river of life (balancing the river of fire on folio 253r) is recorded only as a set of dotted lines between the second and third tier of strips, cut off from its origin, the throne of Christ.

[78] On illumination no. 286, see *Hortus Deliciarum*, 1:197.

[79] E.g., the concluding section on Faith and Order (folios 264r–320v) does not appear to have been illustrated.

and variegated an album as the *Hortus*, comprising many nuclei, presupposed a single, invisible nucleus outside the work: the spectator's eye. Herrad's reference to "unrolling" the anthology by readers was at one with her description of how she had assembled it, moving as a bee from flower to flower and composing what she gathered into a sweet honeycomb. Readers too in unrolling her compilation would refresh their souls as they fed on its honeyed drops.[80] Projected from the spectator's point of view, the convictions that there was beauty in intricate variety and unity in multiplicity brought all events and all possible events into wholes that were visualized as cycles, or as circles within circles, turned upon each other like the spirals of a scroll.

As applied in the *Hortus Deliciarum*, the principle of discoordination that we have been examining offered many options. These appear, not only in manuscripts, but in other kinds of artistic expression, in fresco cycles, for example, some of which set forth episodes in regular chronological sequence, while others present disjunctive arrangements of narrative elements.

It should be noted, if only briefly, that the sacred theater unrolling before the spectator played the same drama of honor and vengeance, and enacted the same association of violence and beauty, characteristic of the historical writings with which we are chiefly concerned. The eight general subjects to which Herrad devoted the "fascicles" of her compilation were variations on those themes. Honor and vengeance came to vivid expression in the illustrations of the conflict between Virtues and Vices and those of the Last Judgment. The power that those motives exerted achieved full expression in the gruesome portrayals of how the Virtues eradicated the Vices; the Virtues were graphically represented as women in conflict against women, of good women beheading, crushing, and spearing evil.

. . .

The way of seeing that we have described, common in the tenth and eleventh centuries, was becoming old-fashioned by Herrad's day. The change appears "in the interiors of churches of the thirteenth century [where] there is a greater uniformity of parts, an approach to the Renaissance, at the expense of that exuberant fantasy which delights us in Romanesque art."[81]

The same tendency appeared in painting, where the rule of multiple perspectives and figures on different axes in individual paintings was gradually

---

[80] *Hortus Deliciarum*, text no. 2, 2:4. See Arnheim, *The Power of the Center*, chap. 3 ("The Viewer as a Center"), pp. 36–50.

[81] Schapiro, "On the Aesthetic Attitude in Romanesque Art," in *Romanesque Art*, pp. 5–6.

excluded. Little by little, the polyptych, divided as it was into little panels, gave way by the late fourteenth century to the painting conceived as "a single pictorial field."[82] The assumption of beauty in intricate variety and unity in multiplicity lost its dominance. This change naturally militated against nuclear organization. A simultaneous change militated against circularity, namely, the development of three-dimensionality, or vanishing-point perspective. In the twelfth century, figures defined space. They were often depicted on blank surfaces with neither background nor foreground. Figures were dominant; however, by the fifteenth century, the development of vanishing-point perspective, with the dramatic evocation of foreground, middle distance, and background, integrated figures into a self-contained pictorial space. "Space now contains the objects by which formerly it was created."[83]

Evidently, the old nuclear perspective did not suddenly and completely end. Cimabue continued, occasionally, to represent multiple perspectives, and, as we shall see, the nuclear organization continued to be used from time to time as a narrative device in literature. However, the change was definite. And this is indicated by the fact that strip paintings, a genre from Antiquity until the twelfth century, ceased to be made. It is also indicated by the attenuation of the scroll in paintings. As we have seen, the scroll served as an important emblem in the twelfth century, and occasionally (as in the Bury St. Edmunds Cross, Figure 1) as a key compositional element. After the twelfth century, scrolls appear in isolated compositions.[84] But such instances are rare. By and large, the scroll survived in an attenuated way as a decorative convention; an emblem of the angel of the Annunciation, of John the Baptist, and of St. Jerome; and a simple captioning device, sometimes displayed by fatuous *putti* (Figures 9, 10).[85]

[82] Jacob Burckhardt, *The Altarpiece in Renaissance Italy*, ed. and trans. Peter Humfrey (Cambridge: Cambridge University Press, 1988), p. 55.

[83] John White, *The Birth and Rebirth of Pictorial Space*, 3d ed. (Cambridge, Mass: Harvard University Press, 1987), pp. 123, 167. David Wilkins ascribes the growth of pictorial realism in religious art in some measure to "the Franciscan religious revolution of the thirteenth century." David Wilkins, "The Meaning of Space in Fourteenth-Century Tuscan Painting," in *By Things Seen: Reference and Recognition in Medieval Thought*, ed. David L. Jeffrey (Ottawa: The University of Ottawa Press, 1979), pp. 117–18.

[84] E.g., the Tres Belles Heures (ca. 1400), Brussels, Bibliothèque Nationale, MS 11060–61, p. 11, representing the Madonna and Child. The child writes on an extensive scroll as he suckles.

[85] On Giotto's use of scrolls to break through the picture plane, see Wilkins, "The Meaning of Space in Fourteenth-Century Tuscan Painting," p. 113. The visual experience of scroll painting had periodic revivals. For example, one notes a broadside advertising a mid-nineteenth-century panorama of Bunyan's *Pilgrim's Progress*, displaying life-size figures on two rolls of canvas, nine feet wide and one-quarter of a mile long. According to the broadside, "The canvas alone weighs half a ton!" The panorama was taken on the road as a kind of silent

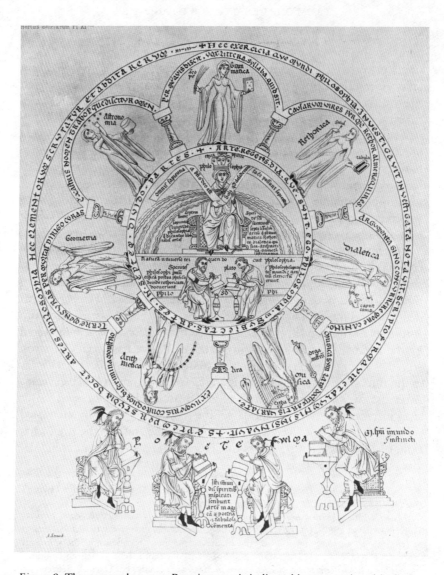

*Figure 9*. The caesura between Renaissances is indicated by comparing this depiction of the Liberal Arts with that in figure 10. Here, an illuminator of Herrad of Hohenburg's *Hortus Deliciarum* (ca. 1180) applies circular perspective. Philosophy is enthroned, encircled by the Arts. The picture also demonstrates the use of scrolls as fundamental elements in composition. Short texts are integrated into the illumination, although longer supporting texts did appear on adjacent pages. *A. Straub and G. Keller*, Herrade de Landsberg, Hortus Deliciarum. *Strasbourg, 1879–99. Princeton University Library.*

*Figure 10.* This illustration (ca. 1465) portrays Philosophy introducing the Liberal Arts to Boethius. By contrast with the illumination in figure 9, this painting is entirely devoid of circular perspective, and the scrolls have been diminished to purely emblematic functions. Further, the illumination has been thoroughly subordinated to the text (the Latin original and a French translation of Boethius's *Consolation of Philosophy*) and divided from it by a frame. *The Pierpont Morgan Library, New York. M. 222 F.*

## CHAUCER

A number of careful studies indicate that the esthetic we have been considering resonates in Chaucer's works, which were at least as far as Dante's from the monastic cult in which it had been formed and nurtured. Chaucer's sense that beauty embraced the ugly, the irregular, and the ridiculous, and his use of incongruity as a principle of composition, as well as one of humor, indicate his affinity to the esthetic of what Bernard of Clairvaux had called "deformed beauty" (*deformis formositas*).[86] As an assiduous translator of works originally written in Latin, French, Anglo-Norman, and Italian, and an adept in moving among English dialects, Chaucer had mastered translation as a cognitive and as an affective strategy. The characters that he portrayed and his comments about his own works make it plain that he wrote for an audience in which such experience was not uncommon. The use of devices to fragment narrative, as well as the techniques of episodic compilation (as in the *Canterbury Tales*) carved out hermeneutic gaps between the fragments or tableaux comparable with those between accounts in historical works or between Dante's relief panels. Filling those gaps is the task of readers; it is left to their powers of imaginative recreation to multiply verbal and visual images in such a way as to make poetry "a mode of vision."[87] Such was the essence of the esthetic that we have been exploring, one that came through motion and not repose, and, specifically, through "psychological movement" in the viewer or hearer.[88]

The inadequacy occasionally confessed by Chaucer's narrators signals the space where this dramatic enactment occurs, where the reader supplies what the narrator left unsaid or found unsayable. As in the esthetic exemplified by historical writers considered earlier, the gap between the fragments said and the wholeness unsaid defines two dimensions: the first, an evident one of turbulent and aimless change, where Fortune reigns; and the second, one of obscure order, or pilgrimage.[89]

This distinction is especially evident in the works, notably *Troilus and Criseyde* and *The Knight's Tale*, in which Chaucer reflected upon history, or, more exactly, on pagan Antiquity. For there, in Chaucer's mind, the

---

theatrical performance in New Jersey and New York. New Jersey Collection; Alexander Library; Rutgers, the State University of New Jersey.

[86] See Przemysław Mroczkowski, "Mediaeval Art and Aesthetics in *The Canterbury Tales*," *Speculum* 33 (1958): 219–20.

[87] Winthrop Wetherbee, *Chaucer and the Poets: An Essay on Troilus and Criseyde* (Ithaca, N.Y.: Cornell University Press, 1984), p. 243. See V. A. Kolve, *Chaucer and the Imagery of Narrative: The First Five Canterbury Tales* (Stanford, Calif.: Stanford University Press, 1984), pp. 9, 30, 42, 59–60, 185.

[88] Mroczkowski, "Mediaeval Art and Aesthetics in *The Canterbury Tales*," p. 218.

[89] Wetherbee, *Chaucer and the Poets*, pp. 200–201. Cf. Kolve, *Chaucer and the Imagery of Narrative*, pp. 165–68, on the cycle of life.

ordering principles revealed in Christian doctrine exert no influence on a "world view" that, being entirely secular, was fundamentally incoherent, and that, lacking the revealed truth of Christian doctrine, labored under defective spiritual discernment, however compelling they found the fragment of truth available to them.[90] And yet doctrine was a means, rather than an end. The difference between pagan and Christian was not one of formal doctrine, but rather one of emotional direction that authentic doctrine made possible. For attentive Christian readers, love guided the way through "patterns of allusion" in poetry and in the world to the realities that they signified; love broke through the linguistic barriers of rhetoric that were intellectual to spiritual apprehension that was purely esthetic; and finally, in that apprehension, love disclosed the kinship of poetry and history. Thus, in a way entirely reminiscent of the twelfth century, Chaucer was both artist and moralist. His stance was distant from that of his contemporary, Boccaccio, but near Pope Innocent III's, whose treatise *On the Misery of the Human Condition* he professed to have translated.[91]

*Troilus and Criseyde* illustrates this continuity particularly well. It is a virtuoso example of translation, as rendering, according to the principle of *sensus, non verba*. Though based on Boccaccio's *Filostrato*, fully two-thirds of the poem is Chaucer's independent composition. For all his revisions and expansion, *Troilus and Criseyde* remains a collection, or montage, of scenes illustrating the presence in human affairs of two spheres: the one governed by Fortune's ever-turning Wheel, the sphere of tragic mutability; and the other, conformed to principles of divine order and harmony. As in the historical texts that we have considered, the spheres of Fortune and wisdom confront each other for the esthetic objective of contrast, and perhaps also to excite the cathartic responses of pity, fear, and love. Without intruding Christian elements into the pre-Christian texture of his story, Chaucer yet revealed in his epilogue that the second sphere, of happiness or beatitude, was dominated by the redemptive sacrifice of Christ.

For our purposes, the salient facts are that translation characterized both the method of composition and the cognitive—which is also to say the affective—strategies of *Troilus and Criseyde*, and that Chaucer deployed it through the fascicle, or montage, technique of composition. The poem is

---

[90] Wetherbee, *Chaucer and the Poets*, pp. 157, 235. George Kane, *The Liberating Truth: The Concept of Integrity in Chaucer's Writings*, The John Coffin Memorial Lecture, 1979 (London: Athlone Press, 1979), p. 11.

[91] Wetherbee, *Chaucer and the Poets*, pp. 17, 46–47, 85, 126, 223, 238. Kane, *The Liberating Truth*, pp. 10, 14. Concerning twelfth-century writers, see also Partner, *Serious Entertainments*, p. 211: "History participated in the fashions and techniques of fictional narrative to the extent that historians were able to imitate the stylistic elements of 'high' literature; nothing in an historian's education or cultural milieu would have prompted him to think that history needed a new and different set of techniques or forms."

an essay on the urgency and danger of rendering verbal and visual images into stimuli of the affects.

Throughout, Chaucer represented verbal images as more treacherous than visual. Troilus is the victim of "double wordes slye, / Swiche as men clepen a word with two visages" (5.898–99). But visual images could also deceive. Troilus's love for Criseyde results from a carnal vision. He sees her. Sight quickens desire and affection. A fixed and deep sensory impression sinks into his heart. He contemplates her figure in the mirror of his mind. This vision, at the beginning of the story, proved to Troilus that love dwelt "within subtile stemes" of the eyes (lines 295–98, 302–5, 365–66). But precipitating lust, it plunged Troilus into the anguished "pleye," or game, with Criseyde, in which he eventually was thrown from Fortune's Wheel to destruction. Such was the outcome of his translation of sensory experience into information, and of information into epiphany.

Yet, another, and greater, epiphanic translation was in store for Troilus. In falling and in dying, he passed from the servitude that he had seen in "blunde lust" to the freedom of spiritual sight and love. Chaucer balanced the carnal vision of Criseyde, at the beginning of his poem, with the spiritual vision of harmony opened to Troilus's soul when it rose from earth "to the holughnesse of the eighte spher" (5.1809), contrasting the woe of this transient world with the "pleyn felicite that is in hevene above," on which we should cast "al oure heart" (5.1818–25). Whether in carnal or in spiritual imagination, the rendering of images into epiphanies is exactly the "casting" of the heart.

Finally, *Troilus and Criseyde*, like the other works considered in this essay, gave honor and vengeance a primary role in that erotic translation. Like them, *Troilus* distinguishes between the vengeance that upholds honor in Fortune's sphere and the vengeance that in secret ways exacts retribution for injuries to divine honor. What sets *Troilus* apart from the earlier texts is Chaucer's sense that Troilus's wrathful thirst for vengeance against Diomede for Criseyde's betrayal of him, leading to his own death, proved to be the means by which he fell victim to the Greeks in their quest to avenge the ravishing of Helen. This portrayal of a noble character destroyed by its own defect marked the revival of the tragic sense. The secularization of an ill-starred love was one step away from explaining human experience by retributive theology, and toward discerning in it only the play of its own inner forces, a stochastic, self-explanatory, and self-generating game.

This departure from norms current in the twelfth century is complete in Shakespeare's *Troilus and Cressida*. Hector, not Troilus, was the noble character destroyed by a tragic flaw, in this case, by mercy; but suffering led neither Hector nor any other character to wisdom or redemption. Shakespeare's play is a portrayal of lechery and war, of an entire world destroyed in consequence of lust. There is no hint of an eternal beauty transcending the earthly, of carnal experience elevated into spiritual epiphany. While Chaucer concluded his poem with a redemptive apotheosis of Troilus and a confession of his own faith in Christ, Shakespeare's last word was Pandarus's cynical bequest to the audience of the diseases, the fruits of lechery, that were killing him.

At a deep level, therefore, Chaucer, like Dante, was a beneficiary, not only of "scholastic Latin culture,"[92] but of monastic culture extending beyond Bede to the patristic age. His retelling, in the Prioress's tale, of the story of Jewish ritual murder of Christian boys, connects him with darker elements of that culture, represented by the Bury St. Edmund's Cross and Matthew Paris's parallel accounts. But in its darkness and in its splendor, it was a culture that steadfastly affirmed poetry and history as cognate ways of seeing discourse through the eyes of the heart, and of reshaping the heart through the imagination.

## A CHANGE IN COGNITION

Whatever similarities there may have been between Chaucer's narrative strategies and those of twelfth-century writers, a watershed in imaginative thinking divided the two epochs. Likewise, there are similarities between Giotto's methods of representation and twelfth-century paintings, not least of which is the use of several perspectives and lighting illusions in the same composition. However, one has only to compare the nuclear strip paintings of the twelfth century (of which the *Hortus Deliciarum* presented some paramount exemples) with the illuminations of Chaucer's *Canterbury Tales* in the Ellesmere manuscript to establish the measure of change. By contrast with the frieze-like compositions of the earlier period, the miniatures in the Ellesmere manuscript were framing devices for the text. Elaborate floral borders were drawn around three edges of the page; and, at the beginning of each tale, the illuminator(s) intended to insert a portrait of the teller, as an index marker. (This plan was not completed.)

Not only did the text entirely dominate the illustrative program, but the use of heavy borders isolating page from page and the reduction of the function of miniatures to marginal reference points actually worked against the composite wholeness of which the fascicle technique was possible. There is no trace of the late Antique sense, fully accomplished in scrolls

---

[92] David Burnley, *A Guide to Chaucer's Language* (Norman: University of Oklahoma Press, 1983), p. 225. On the distinction between "a distinctive 'Renaissance' quality" in Boccaccio's *Il Filostrato*, Chaucer's model, and the "classicism" which Chaucer substituted for it in *Troilus*, see A. J. Minnis, *Chaucer and Pagan Antiquity*, Chaucer Studies, vol. 8 (Cambridge: D. H. Brewer, 1982), p. 61.

and conserved, after a fashion in codices, that miniatures and text formed a continuous narrative.

Let us take stock. Our evidence thus far has demonstrated that, for historical writers and their audiences in our period, the art of understanding (or hermeneutics) was a branch of esthetics. As instruments of cognition, historical texts aimed both at general cognition and at the particular version denoted by John of Salisbury's term "*cognitio Dei et cultus*." Thus, the objects of the cognitive exercise could be mnemonic (recording the memory of persons and events) or hedonic (giving pleasure); but, beyond these, there was always the greater mimetic purpose of moral conversion, served when history taught by precept and example. The dominant precepts that we have discovered are those of honor and vengeance, especially as worked out in God's dealings with a world still cursed by its own disobedience. Cognition worked by an ensemble technique in which the mind drew on its experience of all the arts of imagination. A text set the imagination running into the labyrinth of associations, digesting sensory data left by experience into information, exploring even dead ends for the joy of it, and, as readers projected themselves and their feelings into the action related, digesting information into epiphany.

Writing and reading historical texts was therefore a matter of expanding the context—first, with regard to cognition, by associating the data of history with data provided by other imaginative arts; and, second, with regard to cult, by the ensemble technique of association provided authors and readers in the environment (most often monastic) in which they passed their daily lives. Incompleteness was essential to the associative play of the imagination. Each of the arts was characterized by the deficiencies of the medium that it used. We have stressed the deficiency of literature in the inability of words to convey the actual presence of the things that they name. More broadly, we have concluded that historical writers employed methods of composition that were designed to leave their works incomplete in themselves and required imaginative expansion. Thus, they made up their texts in segmented fascicles, or montages, or depicted their works as parts of wider fascicles (as John of Salisbury did his *Lives* of Anselm and Becket), leaving spaces between the lines where the imagination of readers could constitute the connective tissues.

The process of digestion presupposed served a beauty that was, certainly, defined by the classic canons of wholeness (*integritas*), proportion (*proportio*), and clarity (*claritas*). But wholeness induced radical fragmentation of narrative and a mélange of genres in individual works.[93] Corre-

---

[93] Franz-Josef Schmale, *Funktion und Formen mittelalterlicher Geschichtsschreibung: Eine Einführung* (Darmstadt: Wissenschaftliche Buchgesellschaft, 1985), pp. 105–23. Chibnall, *The World of Orderic Vitalis*, p. 215.

spondingly, proportion (understood as the relation of parts to the whole), allowed not composition but accretion of segments. Clarity encouraged eloquence through the obscurity of figuration, an ornamented style that left the real message unsaid in what was said, latent and "to be discovered by the penetration of the hearer."[94] Even the plain style of history, unplumbed by the ornate techniques of allegorical inquiry, did not escape this hiddenness; for as Bede, the most direct of medieval historical writers, commented, "through history, history is figuratively represented."[95] This obscure clarity required a continual translation (or rendering) of visual and verbal images into affective stimuli such as is common to all poetic undertakings, history, and fiction. Thus, extracting the unsaid from the said, Bede compared his work with that of a sculptor, as he carved an allegorical sense out of the historical text of Samuel.[96] The reasons why the historical writings of the twelfth century no longer readily served as instruments of cognition in the fourteenth lie in the complete reinterpretation of the norms of wholeness, proportion, and clarity. The issue is not the contrast between nonesthetic forms of composition in the earlier period and esthetic forms in the later, but rather the unintelligibility of twelfth-century literary esthetics to its lineal descendent.

Indirectly, therefore, our discussion has a bearing on the continuing debate between those who contend that understanding is primarily verbal, or discursive, and those who hold that understanding is fundamentally visual. Under the persuasion in modern hermeneutics that all understanding is linguistic, recent studies of hermeneutic strategies in medieval historical writings have accentuated rhetorical analysis, particularly regarding tropes. However, the problematic of cult and figuration extends beyond the reach of rhetoric as normally defined. Furthermore, the proposition that all understanding is linguistic invites a tautology. To be circumscribed by "the structure of discourse" means that, even if there is some reality outside language, we may be "sealed in a linguistic house of mirrors." Equivocal arguments have been advanced asserting that, while a tautology is involved in the "thesis that temporality is brought to language to the extent that language configures and refigures temporal experience," the circularity is or can be that of "an endless spiral," rather than that of a vicious circle.[97]

[94] Quintilian, *Institutes*, 9.2.65.

[95] *De Schematibus et Tropis*, 2.2; *Corp. Christ., ser. lat.*, 123A, p. 166: "Per historiam namque historia figuratur."

[96] *In Primam Partem Samuhelis, Libri III*, prol.; *Corp. Christ., ser. lat.*, 119, p. 2.

[97] Nancy F. Partner, "Making Up Lost Time: Writing on the Writing of History," *Speculum* 61 (1986): 95. See also Nancy S. Struever, "Historical Discourse," in *Handbook of Discourse Analysis*, ed. Teun A. van Dijk (London: Academic Press, 1985), 1:249: "Words make history." I am obliged to Professor Alan Sica for drawing my attention to Struever's article. Brian Stock has lent his support to this position in his book, *The Implications of Literacy*, e.g., pp. 455–56: "Interpretive models evolved from texts, whether disseminated by verbal or written

Writers between Antiquity and the Renaissance of the fourteenth and fifteenth centuries were acute enough to detect the danger of circularity that inhered in identifying understanding as linguistic. Defenders of orthodox doctrine mordantly accused heretics of walking into the trap, imposing fabrications of their own minds on the sense of Scripture and thus engaging in idolatrous self-worship—confusing, in fact, *verba* for *sensus*. Correspondingly, for writers in the period under review, the distinction between understanding and interpretation (or explanation), effaced in modern hermeneutics, remained vivid. For them, obscurity could be part of eloquence, and understanding, not discourse so much as vision. By the sixteenth century, a distinct change had occurred in the tradition of "symbolic synesthesia."

This part of our discussion cannot be concluded without some attempt to explain how recent scholars, learned, perceptive, and rigorous as they are, have given so little weight to the digestive process that guided Bede and other monastic writers in the shaping of their histories. How has it been possible to assert that all historical writing, including theirs, is formed by rhetorical methods, rather than by esthetic ones which posited the multiplication of verbal and visual images and the translation of those images into cathartic stimuli of the emotions?

The answer appears to lie in the traditions of historical writing and, particularly, in the fundamental insistence of Renaissance authors that history was a literary study, a branch of rhetoric. Digesting history came to be seen as a philological endeavor, consisting of decipherment, interpretation, and explanation. Evidence was appraised with reference to its own medium, genre, and epoch. The object was archaeological reconstruction. By contrast, in the process that I have described, digesting history was a speculative endeavor, consisting of figural, analogic, and spiritual stages. Evidence was appraised with reference to materials of quite disparate origins and natures. The object was esthetic reliving, or epiphany. While reason could guide archaeological reconstruction, the speculative faculty of imagination had to be brought into play to achieve epiphany.

In the tasks of decipherment, interpretation, and explanation, translation assumed quite a different character from the one that it displayed in works that I have considered above. Understanding did come to be increasingly linguistic, more and more indistinguishable from explanation and interpretation. This was due, in part, to the removal of the writing and the consumption of historical works from the environment of cult. The social classes in which Renaissance scholars lived, and for which they

---

means, were increasingly called upon to provide explanations for behavioral patterns" to the point at which texts structured experience. Stock contends that the structure of experience by texts was possible because of the formation of "textual communities" within existing institutions. See also Ricoeur, *Time and Narrative*, 1:71–72.

wrote, were multilingual, but for them translation had ceased to be an affective strategy in daily life. It remained a cognitive strategy for undertakings of a linguistic nature. The center of gravity of historical writing was removed from cult, and from places and professions consecrated to cult, where linguistic translation had been twinned with affective transport, and minds schooled in mimesis had been required by the daily practice of cult to play among the images of the arts as though they constituted a unified field.

The conception of historical writing as a rhetorical enterprise brought with it an emphasis on style—that is, on the manner of expression and the form of organization—frequently with a discount on substance. The adaptation of classical norms led to an insistence on integrity, proportion, and clarity within the work itself, and, correspondingly, to a movement away from the mismatched compilation of the chronicle to unities that could be achieved in a monograph. A sense of kinship between history and poetry survived, but in a different key. For in the Renaissance it reenforced the accent on the wholeness in the text rather than in the spaces between its segments; it now provided its own license for omissions, inclusions, and even inventions to enhance the cogency of visible form.

As the esthetic values of a text were raised from the depths of the gaps created by the montage, or fascicle, method of composition to the surface of the written word, the room for esthetic translation constricted. Decipherment and interpretation, analysis of the material text, replaced the preverbal and previsual exercise of imaginative digesting. Texts could be read, noted, and learned, but there was no need inwardly to digest them, to absorb their unspoken coherences and take them to heart. Understanding and explanation were equated, two aspects of the same philological, and specifically grammatical, exercise. The *sensus* of a word was its signification, including metaphorical cross-references, and not as Augustine had defined it, the unspoken and unspeakable perception, beyond the finitude of any language.[98] Thus conceived, the *sensus*, restrictively defined as meaning, was derived from a word's setting in a text, and from the linguistic usage of the age as demonstrated by other contemporary documents. Philology demonstrated that the grammatical situation, the applicability of words, varied as did social situations in communities, e.g., the applicability of laws. Anachronism strongly indicated inauthenticity, and, thus, with regard to *sensus*, distinct limits were set to the possibility of common understanding across the ages.

Philological decipherment and interpretation further limited the scope of affective translation as the enterprises of history and faith diverged ever more widely. The introduction of textual criticism in Biblical scholarship

[98] Chap. 3, n. 16 and after n. 32.

excluded Scriptural exegesis both from translations and from interpretation built up by the accumulation of witnesses. For, philologists contended, any representations of Scripture other than the original text were deceptive refractions of the light in the original. The imagined spiritual unity in the texts of Scripture was decomposed by rejecting allegorical resolutions to seeming conflicts and absurdities in the texts, and by an insistence on the ways in which diverse material methods and circumstances had differently shaped the composition of each Scriptural text. Finally, the privileged status of Scripture was discounted when pagan sources were employed to test the veracity of Scriptural narratives. The interpretation of Scripture was equivalent to that of Aristotle's writings, or of nature. Thus, the affective transport of love—"believing in" Christ—that Bede and his monastic followers considered essential to perception of the truth in Scripture became irrelevant, as did even the belief of which demons were capable. History retained its mnemonic character. But authors rarely expressed the conviction that history also had a mnemonic call from within the text that the mimetic response of its readers completed. It was no longer a component in a sacramental world.

The divergence of history from faith had consequences not only for interpretation, or for textual analysis of Scripture, but also for all branches of historical explanation. Of those consequences, one of the chief was certainly a conviction that human experience had no meaning or direction outside itself. The familiar paradox of hiddenness continued, with its dyad of appearance and reality. But the hidden causes of history predominately referred to human calculation, artifices, and passions, to the imperceptible convergence of destinies, or to a chain, probable or not, of accidents. Continuity was sought within change, not outside it, and the processes of change were considered to be moved by impersonal forces, described either in mechanistic (causal) or organic (developmental or evolutionary) terms. Events followed an indefinite sequence, perhaps cyclical, with no evident direction or goal. Thus, canons of historical explanation, like those of decipherment and interpretation, militated against affective translation from data to epiphany as a method of digesting history, and it had no place for the erotic character that had demanded the inward digestion of experience, first, into information and, second, into epiphany.

The shift of history's purpose from esthetic reliving to archaeological reconstruction limited, where it did not exclude, affective translation. Furthermore, monastic writers before the Renaissance had lived in an environment which disciplined them to play with images, rendering verbal ones into visual and vice versa. This it did not only because the multiplication of verbal and visual images constituted the physical context of architecture, ornament, and theological discourse, but also because that very multiplication was internalized by the training of monks to be proficient judges and workers of the arts, and by the kinesthetic discipline of ritual and asceticism, not the least powerful component of which was psalmody. Serving fundamental emotions of love and fear, ritual and asceticism combined, not to detach viewers or readers from the work of art, but to immerse them directly in the realities expressed through images in different media, which were unified in a single dramatic enactment. Changes during the Renaissance greatly reduced the frequency, among writers and readers of history, of this acquired expectation of synesthetic immersion, through love, pity, and fear, in another reality.

The militance of monastic writers derived in some measure from a sanctification of vengeance infused with eroticism. This volatile ideal, fusing beauty with violence, was inculcated, celebrated, and enacted in daily liturgy and affirmed by comprehensive systems of theology. During the Renaissance, the fusion of vengeance and eroticism was solemnized in tragedy, but, in many areas, it ceased to be a norm of life. The detachment of historical writing from cult coincided with the discovery of previously unknown cultures and the inception of the comparative study of religion with its corollary, historical relativism. Interpenetration of the spheres of Fortune and wisdom became tenuous. It became possible to understand that the lessons about honor and retributive justice taught in Scripture and sanctified in cult was one of the thousands of associations that human beings fabricated about God in an attempt to identify the divine with their own vicious passions, masking inhuman vengeance with the name of justice. At the same time, the growth of the state, with its intended monopoly over violence, reduced the legal status that society accorded private vengeance. "Revenge," Bacon wrote, "is a kind of wild justice, which the more a man's nature runs to, the more ought law to weed it out" (*Essay of Religion*). A corollary had to be the possibility of detaching beauty from violence.

The examples of Dante and Chaucer demonstrate that this esthetic could indeed persist outside monastic institutions, but not that it could so persist when the configurations of hermeneutic gaps at the core of historical discourse had fundamentally altered. Yet such a radical change did occur. With rhetoric came logic, and the rules of logic excluded kinds of association that esthetics had allowed. Association by likeness, contiguity, and contrast persisted, yet with the narrowed scope of logical consistency, which was obedient to the law of contradiction. Association by likeness excluded what was foreign or unlike from the equation. Recast to serve causal explanation, association by contiguity attended to spatial and temporal relationships, descriptive of the chain of cause and effect and of organic connections, rather than affective contiguity transcending space and time. Governed by the law of contradiction, association by contrast allowed only association by mutual repellence or opposition. It excluded antipathies that reverberated in one another as a single discordant harmony.

For reasons such as these, and for many others, a cloud of forgetfulness passed over the esthetic method examined in this essay. On the further side of its passage stood St. Thomas Aquinas, serene in his acceptance of translations as authentic expressions of Scripture and ancient Greek philosophy; on the other, Erasmus, with his insistence on casting aside translation and returning to texts as their authors left them. Changes in Renaissance esthetic thickened the impenetrability of the cloud. Ignorance permitted Giorgio Vasari (1511–71) to write that Cimabue (fl. 1300) had begun the practice of introducing verbal captions into paintings. This, he wrote, Cimabue had done in a small tempera painting of the Crucifixion, in which angels held scrolls inscribed with Christ's words to the Virgin (*Mulier, ecce filius tuus*) and to John (*Ecce, mater tua*), and Scripture's commmentary on these words (*Ex illa hora accepit eam discipulus in suam*). Unaware as he evidently was of the long centuries before Cimabue in which verbal and visual images had been juxtaposed, Vasari set forth an explanation that displayed a corresponding ignorance of the esthetic that justified the practice. Cimabue, he wrote, had hit upon this "idiosyncratic and novel" device of aiding art with words so as to clarify (*esprimere*) his conception (*concetto*).[99]

Considering that Cimabue had imposed the scroll-borne words on his design as labels, rather than integrating them into it, Vasari had lost sight of the synesthetic association of verbal and visual images in a single oscillating rhythm that had been familiar in the centuries before Cimabue. The stylized abstraction of late medieval paintings seemed to him unable to arouse the dramatic immediacy of paintings in the style favored by Vasari. The same loss of an earlier sense of dramatic presence is evident in the criticism of medieval altarpieces by Vasari and other Renaissance artists because of their multiplicity of scenes, divided by elaborate frames. The collection, or compilation, of scenes repelled the artists of the sixteenth century, with their commitment to single images, rather than to field images united by the play of imagination. Their esthetic demanded repose at a single point, not movement.

On the further side of the artistic cloud of forgetfulness, Dante stood before the relief panels, hearing Virgil admonish him, "Do not set your mind on one place only."[100] On the other side, ever denouncing medieval art as destructive of beauty, Vasari climaxed his career as an iconoclast by demolishing the existing interior of Santa Croce in Florence and consign-

---

[99] *Le Opere di Giorgio Vasari*; Gaetano Milanesi, ed. (Florence: Sansoni, 1906), 1:255.
[100] Dante, *Purgatorio*, canto 10, line 46.

ing the great altarpiece by Dante's contemporary, Ugolino di Nerio, to the oubliette where long after it was dismembered, out of sight and mind.[101]

Occasionally, working within but against their own tradition, historians in the present day may still glimpse contours that the humanists' cloud of unknowing concealed.

[101] On Vasari's demolitions in Santa Maria Novella and Santa Croce, see Marcia B. Hall, *Renovation and Counter-Reformation: Vasari and Duke Cosimo in Sta Maria Novella and Sta Croce, 1565–1577* (Oxford: Clarendon, 1979), p. 18 (a reference to Ugolino's altarpiece of ca. 1330) and throughout.

## PART II

# Reading between the Lines

## Chapter 5

# THE KINGDOM OF GOD: A SILENCE OF INTUITION

THUS FAR, we have identified a few guidelines that governed historical writing as an art of the imagination. Like any compositions, the works with which we are concerned depended on exclusion as well as inclusion, but even what was included has appeared shapeless to modern scholars. There is little regard for narrative unity, no organic wholeness. At some times, one encounters gaps in a narrative; at others, a concatenation of narratives. To lay hands on the thinking behind the montage effect of these texts, we must turn from the words to the silences between the words, understanding, to be sure, that silences arise for different reasons. We shall explore three. One, about the Kingdom of God, arose through intuitive awe; another, about women, through familiarity; and a third, about time, through complexity.

As we begin to recover elements of a violent esthetic from between the lines of histories, we turn above all to the designation that, our authors believed, set them apart from the world and that proclaimed their present allegiance and future destination. They were, they said, citizens of the Kingdom of God.

For Christian interpreters, the Kingdom of God has always been a subject of great difficulty. In this essay, I shall consider how it was understood by some German writers in the eleventh and twelfth centuries. My first task must be to affirm that the hermeneutic tradition in which those writers worked was one of predicament, rather than of solution, and that it arose from difficulties in harmonizing Scripture. It will become evident that, in reconstructing their predicament, we shall be concerned with ways of thinking that made the texts thinkable, but that, with time, fell into the silent spaces between the lines.

The range and importance of historical views among twelfth-century writers is indicated by a statement of Friedrich Heer: "The emergence of figures such as Rupert of Deutz, Hugh of St. Victor, Anselm of Havelberg, Otto of Freising, Hildegard of Bingen, Ekbert of Schönau, Gerhoch of Reichersberg, and finally of Joachim of Flora is a phenomenon unparalleled until we reach the pullulating abundance of the last days of the Empire, the epoch of Goethe, Schelling, Hegel, and Hölderlin."[1] But in what regard was the intellectual legacy of these writers predicamental?

We are confronting a chain of hermeneutic silences, for the silences that we are to study concerning the Kingdom of God in twelfth-century texts mirror silences that the authors of those texts found in the Scriptures themselves. The predicaments that twelfth-century writers encountered arose from regard for Scripture as the oracle of divine wisdom and, in some sense, the master plan for history. But the Kingdom of God was not a common subject in all Scriptural texts, particularly those of the New Testament. Texts of Scripture concerning God's Kingdom disagreed; and interpreters believed that the words of Scripture meant more, and something other, than they said. Such were the origins of the predicamental tradition concerning the Kingdom of God.

Leaving aside the books of the Old Testament and Apocrypha (and, as already stated, the Apocalypse), the idea of a divine Kingdom is dominant only in the Gospels of Matthew, Mark, and Luke. There are only two references in the Gospel of John, and a handful scattered through the other letters and books of the New Testament. Different terms were used. The Gospel of Matthew refers predominantly to the Kingdom of heaven, whereas those of Mark and Luke witness to the Kingdom of God. Reinforced by anagogical references in the Psalms, other New Testament texts attest to a City of God, named Jerusalem. There was a Gospel of the Kingdom, which had to be preached, but it conveyed mysteries which Christ spoke in parables, open to those whose eyes saw and whose ears heard, but closed to those who, seeing, did not see and, hearing, did not hear, nor did they understand. That Gospel of mysteries came, not to the natural man, but to those who were born again (John 3:3). For, as Paul wrote, the Kingdom of God was not in word, but in power (1 Cor. 4:20).

As interpreters read and collated the texts of Scripture, they found difficulties other than terminology. The Kingdom of God was "not meat and drink" (Rom. 14:17), but it was "the marriage supper of the Lamb" (Rev. 19:9. See also Mark 14:25 and Luke 14:15; 22:18, 30). The Kingdom of God was not of this world (John 18:16), and yet Scripture demonstrated to some "under the Christian name, that the kingdom of Christ will come on earth, and that, with the saints blissfully ruling with him there in the earthly Jerusalem, after a thousand years, Satan will be done away with and then finally cast down, and the saints taken up into the heavenly kingdom."[2] The Gospels witnessed that even among those closest to Jesus, and taught directly by him, some believed that his Kingdom would come on

---

[1] Friedrich Heer, *The Holy Roman Empire*, trans. Janet Sondheimer (London: Weidenfeld and Nicolson, 1968), p. 88. I should like to thank Professor Mark Toulouse for suggesting the subject of this chapter to me.

[2] Otto of Freising, *Chronicon*, 8.26; *MGH*, *SSrrG*, pp. 431–32.

earth. Was it not in this sense that the Kingdom of God had been taken from the reprobate Jews and "given to a nation bringing forth the fruits thereof" (Matt. 21:42–43)? Finally, the Kingdom of God was present, but not yet come. "The kingdom of God is within you" (Luke 17:21). "Now is come salvation, and strength, and the kingdom of our God" (Rev. 12:10). But it was also "near," "at hand," "not far." The Son of man was yet to be seen "coming in his kingdom," "coming in clouds of heaven with power and great glory" (Matt. 16:28, 24:30).

Evidently, the Kingdom of God made sense in a portrayal of human life as conflict—conflict against objective enemies and against the imperfections in human nature itself. The Kingdom of God required the kingdom of Satan (or Antichrist) for its own definition, much as good was rendered comprehensible by evil. But Scriptures introduced a wide range of alternative ways to interpret the conflict and eventual triumph of God's City.

Christian exegetes delighted in harmonizing discordant texts, but disagreements of this magnitude presented hurdles that not even the most powerful could leap. The literalism of the Jews, dispersed into exile after the earthly kingdom was taken from them, was a great caution against equating the Kingdom of God with any existing historical institution, including the hierarchic Church. While other writers ignored that warning, Augustine took it to heart. The Kingdom of God, he wrote, would come at the end of this earthly pilgrimage. Its historical anticipation, the City of God, existed in all the ambiguity of the conversion process, a *civitas permixta*, comprised of good and evil and, even so, not conterminous with the hierarchic Church, since it excluded professed Christians who were actually reprobate and included unbelievers still to be converted. The mystery of God's City on earth comprised also the mystery of iniquity.[3] Thus, even though Augustine placed the City of God in its conflict with the city of man, at the dramatic center of history, his refusal to identify the cities with actual institutions, and specific events as fulfilling prophecies about those cities, left the Kingdom of God a tool of hermeneutic confusion rather than of explanation. A hermeneutic gap existed between the Kingdom as historical fact and the Kingdom as spiritual *figura*.

Such was the legacy that writers in the eleventh and twelfth centuries received and transmitted. They had no doubt that the Kingdom of God actually existed. They repeated Boethius's representation of God as ruler of the cosmos.[4] Coronation rituals portrayed secular princes in the likeness of God, the King of kings, and, acknowledging Christ's character as priest, the imperial *ordo* prescribed that the Pope make the emperor a cleric, robing

---

[3] Gerhart B. Ladner, *The Idea of Reform* (New York: Harper, 1967), pp. 278–79.

[4] Cosmas of Prague, *Chronica Boemorum*, 2.4, 3.60; *MGH, SSrrG*, pp. 89, 238.

him with clerical vestments.[5] Other rituals likewise duplicated celestial archetypes. Suger's remark that, at the consecration of St. Denis the celebrants appear to be a heavenly, rather than a human, chorus performing a divine and not a human office,[6] was anticipated by the grandiose architectural and liturgical program of Archbishop Adalbert, in Bremen: "He sought out everything great, everything wondrous, everything glorious in divine and human things, and, for that reason, he is said to have delighted in the smoke of aromatic spices and the flash of lights, and the resonating thunder of deep voices. He drew all these appointments from reading the Old Testament, where the majesty of the Lord appeared on Mount Sinai. And he was accustomed to do many other things out of the ordinary to modern people who were ignorant of Scriptures, although he did nothing without authority of the Scriptures."[7] After the restoration of the church at Jerusalem (ca. 1104), the Archangel Gabriel was said, on good authority, to have delivered a letter sent by Christ to that Church and, through it, to all churches, a letter that brought menacing threats to prevaricators and comfort to the pious.[8]

To be sure, the predicament of the Kingdom of God presented one face to the writers in question; it presents quite another to us. To us, reading texts of the eleventh and twelfth centuries, an age of apocalyptic speculation, the predicament is one of silence. Confident as they were of the Kingdom of God's reality, writers seldom employed it as a device of historical explanation or, indeed, even mentioned it. To be sure, Adam of Bremen recorded that Archbishop Adalbert, in his grandiose enterprises, wished to regain "a golden age, driving all workers of iniquity from the city of God." He designated some psalms to be recited to invoke vengeance against the church's enemies. But the reforms launched under this identification of God's City with a historical institution led to grief. Adalbert's episcopal enemies expelled him from the imperial court "as if he were a magician and a seducer," and eventually his own people in Bremen hissed at him as they did at heretics.[9]

Of all the writers under consideration, Otto of Freising confronted the problem of literalism most directly. Reading prophecies of Ezekiel and Isa-

---

[5] Reinhard Elze, ed., *Ordines Coronationis Imperialis; MGH, Fontes Iuris Germanici Antiqui*, pp. 25, 31, 40, 46.

[6] Suger, *De Consecratione*, chap. 6. Erwin Panofsky, ed., *Abbot Suger on the Abbey Church of St.-Denis and Its Art Treasures*, 2d ed. (Princeton, N.J.: Princeton University Press, 1979), p. 114.

[7] Adam of Bremen, *Gesta Hammaburgensis Ecclesiae Pontificum*, 3.27(26); *MGH, SSrrG*, p. 170.

[8] Ekkehard of Aura, *Chronicon (a. 1104); MGH, SS* 6, p. 267.

[9] Adam of Bremen, *Gesta Hammaburgensis Ecclesiae Pontificum*, 3.47 (46), 55(54), 63(62); *MGH, SSrrG*, pp. 190–91, 200, 208–9.

iah literally, he wrote, the Jews thought that, at the advent of their Messiah, the earthly Jerusalem would be restored with great glory, and that they would be rich, ruling with him there, in the delights of all earthly glory. Nominal Christians who believed in the millennial rule of the saints followed in the Jewish error of literalism.[10]

There were, Otto held, three correct ways of understanding "the city or Kingdom of Christ": the present or future state of the Church on earth, including both good and evil; its state in heaven, keeping only the good in the glory of its heavenly bosom; and its state after the fullness of the nations had entered it, that is, "when all Israel shall be saved" (Rom. 12:25–26).[11] At different points in his *Chronicle*, Otto employed each of these figurative identifications, but, as so often, multiple meanings were not conducive to clarity. When he turned to the apocalyptic descent of the holy City from heaven, Otto found himself dealing with "a mystical and profound matter" that, he said, far exceeded his ability. Adverting to Augustine's interpretation, Otto embraced with the veneration due a holy secret what the Father had said, but he admitted that he did not fully understand what his solution had been.[12] In fact, only the last book of Otto's *Chronicle* (Book 8) deals precisely with the "city or Kingdom of Christ." The irregular and inconsistent allusions scattered throughout the earlier books do not establish any narrative cohesion, although Otto himself referred to all the previous sections as a prologue to the last book.[13]

Writing about Pope Gregory VII's excommunication of King Henry IV, Otto violated the principle against identifying prophecies of the Kingdom with specific events. The Church, he wrote, was the great stone, uncut by hands, in Daniel's prophecy, and Gregory's anathema against Henry had shattered the clay feet of the iron statue representing the Roman Empire. But Otto also had to record the kind of quandary to which such identifications could lead. Great evils, he wrote, had followed Gregory's blow. Rome had been besieged, taken, and laid waste. Pope had been raised up against pope; king, against king. Gregory himself, who excelled all bishops and Roman pontiffs in zeal and authority, had died in exile.[14]

The lack of attention paid to the Kingdom of God in historical writings is surprising in an age of intense apocalyptic speculation; the narrative difficulties into which Otto falteringly stumbled are a sign of the great divide between historical and apocalyptic speculation. The reasons for our predicament—the relative silence in texts concerning the Kingdom of God—is

[10] *Chronicon*, 8.26; *MGH, SSrrG*, pp. 431–32.
[11] *Chronicon*, 8. prol.; *MGH, SSrrG*, p. 390.
[12] *Chronicon*, 8. 26; *MGH, SSrrG*, pp. 433–34.
[13] *Chronicon*, 8. prol; *MGH, SSrrG*, p. 393.
[14] *Chronicon*, 6.36; *MGH, SSrrG*, pp. 305–6.

rooted in the predicament that faced writers in the eleventh and twelfth centuries. Here, I can only recall some dominant pieces in their puzzle.

First and foremost were difficulties in interpreting the highly discrepant Scriptural references to the Kingdom of God, and in applying them to contemporary circumstances. The general difficulty in equating prophecies of the Kingdom with events, the multiplicity of meanings attached to the Kingdom, and difficulties inherent in Scriptural texts (especially those read in the light of apocalypticism) kept Otto of Freising as thoroughly as they had kept Augustine from bridging the hermeneutic gap between the Kingdom of God as historical fact and as spiritual *figura*. The conflict between the city of truth and the city of perversity could be employed to represent, in an episodic fashion, antipathies in human existence and the great dramatic themes of mercy and vengeance, but not to construct a coherent narrative of events. Possibly for this reason, Otto himself entirely abandoned the two cities as an organizing principle when he undertook his later work, *The Deeds of Frederick*.

We are confronting a familiar difficulty: the perception of silence in the letter of a text when there may be none in the unspoken message between the lines of the text. This distinction between the letter and the space between the lines makes it possible for one reader to see less in a text than is there, and another to see more. For the one who sees less than is there, what is absent is simply absent. For the one who sees more, what is evidently absent may be, not only conspicuous, but actually present by its absence, just as, in so many instances, the eye and the memory insist on seeing what is palpably not there. Let me now suggest some lines of association that may lie behind the silence of our texts concerning the Kingdom of God. I shall deal with two varieties of association. The first is sacramental.

The Kingdom (or City) of God was understood as an incarnational (and therefore sacramental) bonding, outside the limits of history. Both Otto of Freising and Gerhoch of Reichersberg elucidated this essential premise by adverting to Psalm 121:3: "Jerusalem is built as a city that partakes of the same center" (*cuius participatio in idipsum*). This city, Otto commented, is built not in our fashion or with our stones, but by divine power and out of the elect, its living stones. "How," he asked, "will its participation be in the same (*in idipsum*), without any division (*caesura*) remaining?" The stones, he answered, partake of him who said, "I am who am," and, "He who is, sent me to you." All partake of the identity of him who remains eternally, changelessly, always in one and the same mode; divine contemplation makes all adhere *in idipsum*.[15] The *idipsum* constituting the city was

---

[15] *Chronicon*, 8.36; *MGH*, *SSrrG*, pp. 433, 435.

God. Gerhoch visualized the city as a building erected on a round foundation, in which all points were equidistant from the center, drawn back as one to the invisible point of unity.[16]

By introducing a further association between the city of God and the "temple wondrous in equity," Gerhoch made the incarnational and sacramental implication explicit. For, he wrote, the temple was the Lord's body (cf. John 2:21), which, by its superabundant equity, suffices to abolish the iniquities in us all, giving satisfaction to the Father by perfect thanksgiving through the saving sacrifice of his body and blood.[17]

Quite naturally, writers turned to the Eucharist as a point at which the Kingdom of God became historical, at which, as Hildegard of Bingen wrote, "the majesty of God shows its power most fully."[18] It was a temporal manifestation of "the heavenly Easter where [the elect would] eat with the Lamb of 'the unleavened bread of sincerity and truth.' "[19] But, Gerhoch wrote, wicked priests and bishops, laboring to rebuild Babylon within the walls of Jerusalem, did not partake of the Lamb's marrow and fatness, although they offered the sacrifice and became participants of his body and blood.[20] Even those who approached the banquet of the altar, that heavenly table, and felt themselves "fattened at that table on the flesh of the immaculate Lamb, Jesus Christ, and inebriated with the cup of his sacrosanct blood," and who knew that Christ, the King, supped with them on the sweetness of their spiritual progress, knew that in the profound and unsearchable judgments of God they had reason to fear the sentence, "Many are called, but few are chosen" (Matt. 22:14).[21] In psalmody, too, the pious had a foretaste of the sweetness of their celestial homeland.[22]

More than any act other than the Eucharist, martyrdom rendered God's Kingdom incarnate. "The city or empire of Christ" spread from Judaea to all peoples through the efforts of the "architects and princes of that city," the Apostles "who attacked the world, not with weapons, but, far more effectively, with the word of God, and, more brilliantly than the Romans, triumphed over the whole world, not with the blood of others, but with

[16] *Liber de Edificio Dei*, chaps. 1, 3; Migne *PL* 194:1195–97, 1203. *Tractatus in Ps. 45*: 6; Migne *PL* 193:1575–76.

[17] *Tractatus in Ps. 64*, chaps. 81–84, 88–89; Migne *PL* 194:58–59, 61–62.

[18] *Scivias*, visio 2.6:10; *Corp. christ., continuatio medievalis*, 43, p. 239.

[19] Adam of Bremen, *Gesta Hammaburgensis Ecclesiae Pontificum*, 2.82(78); *MGH, SSrrG*, p. 141.

[20] *Tractatus in Ps. 64*, chap. 171; Migne *PL* 194:114.

[21] Hermannus quondam Judaeus, *Opusculum de Conversione Sua*, chap. 21; *MGH*, Quellen zur Geistesgeschichte, 4:125–27.

[22] Otto of Freising, *Chronicon*, 7.35; *MGH, SSrrG*, p. 372. Hildegard of Bingen, *Scivias*, visio 3.12:11; *Corp. christ., continuatio medievalis*, 43A, pp. 630–31.

their own."[23] Modern heroes of the faith also offered themselves as sacrifices and oblations.[24]

Helmold observed the precise connection with the Eucharist. A priest, he wrote, received a premonition when he saw the species of flesh and blood in the chalice at the elevation. His bishop recognized that as a sign of much tribulation and bloodshed for the Christian people; for "as often as the blood of martyrs is poured out, Christ is crucified again in his members."[25] Assailed by Slavs on his first missionary journey, Bishop Otto of Bamberg rebuked the loving disciples who had saved him, taking on their bodies the blows intended for him. "With joyful spirit and cheerful countenance," he had gone into the mêlée hoping to be called to receive the crown of martyrdom. He had been struck down into the mire. When he pulled himself up, he raised his hands to heaven, giving thanks that, though he had not been slaughtered, he had at least been worthy to receive one blow in God's name.[26] No less ready than before for martyrdom, he departed on his second missionary journey immediately after blessing the chrism and celebrating the Eucharist, "fasting and shod with sandals as he had been, standing at the altar."[27]

As historical fact, the Kingdom of God, even in its eschatological versions, belonged to incarnational theology, not to the sphere of temporal events. The temporal sphere was far from sacrosanct; it was governed by the Wheel of Fortune, and the dimension governed by Fortune could be thought of quite apart from that ruled by divine wisdom.[28] In another land, John of Salisbury commented that almost everything done in the teeming throngs of worldly people was more like a comedy than a real event (res gesta). Apart from the saving remnant of 7,000, reserved by the Lord to himself, the whole world appeared to act out a comic mime. On

[23] Otto of Freising, Chronicon, 3.14; MGH, SSrrG, pp. 150–51.

[24] E.g., Martyrium Arnoldi Archiepiscopi Magontini; Johann Friedrich Böhmer, ed., Fontes Rerum Germanicarum (Stuttgart: Cotta, 1855) 3:318.

[25] Helmold, Cronica Slavorum, 2.109; MGH, SSrrG, p. 215.

[26] Herbord, Dialogus de Vita S. Ottonis Episcopi Babenbergensis, 2.24, 25; Jan Wikarjak, ed., Monumenta Poloniae Historica, n.s., vol. 7, fasc. 3 (Warsaw: Państwowe Wydawnictwo Naukowe, 1974), pp. 107–10. S. Ottonis Episcopi Babenbergensis Vita Prieflingensis, 2.6; Jan Wikarjak, ed., Monumenta Poloniae Historica, n.s., vol. 7, fasc. 1 (Warsaw: Państwowe Wydawnictwo Naukowe, 1966), p. 36.

[27] Ebo, Vita S. Ottonis Episcopi Babenbergensis, 3.3; Jan Wikarjak, ed., Monumenta Poloniae Historica, n.s., vol. 7, fasc. 2 (Warsaw: Państwowe Wydawnictwo Naukowe, 1969), p. 98.

[28] See Cosmas of Prague, Chronica Boemorum, 2.10; 3.29, 36; MGH, SSrrG, pp. 97, 199, 208. Cf. Helmold, Cronica Slavorum, 2.101; MGH, SSrrG, p. 199: "impetum faventis fortunae . . . Domino scilicet favente." On a smiling, or (benevolently) laughing Fortune, see C. H. Talbot, ed. and trans., The Life of Christina of Markyate A Twelfth Century Recluse (Oxford: Clarendon, 1959), chap. 55, p. 134. For a thirteenth-century artist's incorporation of Fortune's Wheel in the circle of Christ's providence, see chap. 3, n. 151.

reflection, he considered that, since all that was sweet in this world eventually turned bitter, and joy always into sorrow, tragedy was more like the lives of men than comedy. Fortune encompassed both, and John quoted sardonic lines of Petronius that, he held, illustrated the theater of this vast, amazing, and unspeakable tragedy or comedy, where Fortune ruled: "A blind cast of a lot overturns the ridiculous labors of men; / Our ages are a joke and a sport for the gods." He carefully noted that arguing that all fell subject to the play of Fortune did not exclude the Aristotelian regress of all things to God, the first cause.[29]

In a similar vein, Otto of Freising discarded the Kingdom of God as a leitmotiv when he turned from the *Chronicle* to the *Deeds of Frederick*, explaining that he had cast the earlier work as a tragedy, not with regard to the order of events so much as with regard to their misery. He had done so, he wrote, because of his own somber cast of mind, which events since Frederick Barbarossa's accession had turned to gladness. Fortune, he added, had not yet turned her frown toward Frederick.[30]

Certainly, it was possible to reconcile the spheres of Fortune and wisdom, but with a terrible equation between might and right. Count Guido of Biandrate is said to have made this equation during Frederick Barbarossa's siege of Milan in 1158. "But, of course," he said, "Fortune rules in every matter. 'She honors and abases,' as it is said, 'acccording to caprice, rather than true deserts.' This Fortune [of ours] has changed a little; for she is changeable, and what is constant about her is that she is volatile and by no means lasting. Let us go with the Wheel. Perhaps the one who is now cast down to the dust will again be swept up on high to the stars. For it is a most valid law absolutely binding on wild beasts as on human beings, that the weaker yield to the more powerful, and that victory obeys those

[29] *Policraticus*, 3.8; Clement C. J. Webb, ed. (Oxford: Clarendon, 1909), 1:190–96. See also the figure of speech used by Lambert of Hersfeld, *Annales* (*a.* 1075); *MGH, SSrrG*, p. 233 (concerning the war of the Saxons and Thuringians against King Henry IV): "Sed plebs omnem spem suam ab armis ad preces verterat; quae si non proficerent, incunctanter animo fixerat omnia feda etiam atque crudelia pocius tolerare quam se certamini committere et ancipitem fortunae aleam, quam semel infausta congressione experta fuisset, denuo temptare." See also chap. 3, n. 151; chap. 4, n. 34; chap. 7, n. 83.

[30] *Chronicon, ep. ad Fridericum*; *MGH, SSrrG*, pp. 2–3. *Gesta Friderici*, prol.; *MGH, SSrrG*, p. 11. See also *Chronicon*, 1. prol.; *MGH, SSrrG*, p. 7, referring to early Christian histories "in quibus non tam historias quam erumpnosas mortalium calamitatum tragedias prudens lector invenire poterit." Cosmas of Prague, *Chronica Boemorum*, 3.24; *MGH, SSrrG*, p. 193: ". . . sed ne videamur velut hyrcino cantu explicuisse tragediam, redeamus, unde paulo digressi sumus, ad chronicam." See also Rupert of Deutz, *Commentum in Apocalypsim*, 10.17; Migne *PL* 169:1133: "Pleni sunt libri, imo satiata jam sunt theatra orbis terrarum regum tragoediis. . . ." See also ibid., 4.7, col. 955. Rupert referred frequently to *spectacula* in his commentary on the Apocalypse: 3. prol.; 6.11; 7.12; 8.13; 10.17, 18; Migne *PL* 169:903, 1031, 1045, 1050, 1054, 1073.

who are mighty in arms. Further, 'he who resists power resists the ordinance of God.' "[31]

To speak in this fashion—and much more as John of Salisbury and Otto had done—is to suggest that the Kingdom of God as a historical fact was nothing more than a rhetorical figure, to be employed or left aside at the judgment of the writer acting as artist. As I move toward the end of my hermeneutic argument, I want to stress the fact that the writers in question deliberately omitted the Kingdom of God as a major interpretive device. Their choice, and its deliberate nature, is indicated by their awareness that historical writing was, like any art, subject to the will of the artist.

There are, indeed, ample witnesses to artistic license in historical writings of the eleventh and twelfth centuries. It was safer, one author wrote, to narrate a dream that no one had witnessed than to write the deeds of contemporaries. And although Otto of Freising contended that it was better to fall into the hands of men by writing unpleasant truths than to retouch the facts (as an artist repaints color over a besmudged face in a painting), the reverse was evidently possible.[32] In the *Deeds of Frederick*, Otto himself demonstrated how thoroughly he could restore a darkened face by recasting the disastrous reign of his kinsman, Conrad III, as a triumph; Otto's objective was to glorify the dynasty to which he belonged and to vindicate its accession to the imperial office. Helmold carefully inventoried the reasons why historians might not provide accurate representations of events, and concluded by comparing the portrayal of human actions with carving the most intricate sculptures (*subtilissimis celaturis*). In both cases, he wrote, clearly grasping for an exception to his list of errors, it was necessary for there to be some reflective insight that neither favor, hatred, nor fear could deflect from the way of truth.[33] But Helmold knew that perspective was entirely in the eye of the beholder, just as light is hateful to sick eyes not because of the fault of the light, but because of the sickness of the eyes.[34] From their perspectives, skeptical readers might judge even histories written with the most scrupulous attention to authenticity to be fiction, having come through Virgil's gate of ivory.[35]

The profligate destruction and reconstruction of the age gave abundant

[31] Rahewin, *Gesta Friderici*, 3.46; *MGHSSrrG*, p. 220.

[32] Cosmas of Prague, *Chronica Boemorum*, 3. apologia; *MGH, SSrrG*, p. 160. Otto of Freising, *Chronicon, ep. ad Reginaldum*; *MGH, SSrrG*, p. 5. See chap. 1, n. 5; chap. 5, nn. 23–49; chap. 6, n. 2; chap. 7, nn. 11–22.

[33] *Cronica Slavorum*, 2.96; *MGH, SSrrG*, pp. 188–89.

[34] *Cronica Slavorum*, 2.96; *MGH, SSrrG*, p. 189.

[35] Adam of Bremen, *Gesta Hammaburgensis Ecclesiae Pontificum*, prol.; *MGH, SSrrG*, pp. 2–3.

evidence of art's power to destroy old representations of the Kingdom of God and to replace them with entirely new ones. Archbishop Adalbert's vaunting projects of destruction and rebuilding were a case in point; these enterprises, together with his territorial expansion, required him to break up earlier works of art to pay the bills. The works that he sent to the melting pot included two crosses and a chalice, all studded with precious stones, weighing altogether twenty marks of gold. Grieving at the sacrilege that he was forced to perform, the smith charged with melting them said in confidence that when he broke them up, he heard at the stroke of his mallet a sound as though the voice of a weeping child.[36]

But the bearing of art on the hermeneutic gap between the Kingdom of God as historical fact and as spiritual figure does not come from the power of the artist to turn the same event, at will, into comedy or tragedy, or even in imagination to body "forth / the forms of things unknown . . . and give to airy nothing / a local habitation and a name."[37] Art does elucidate that gap by its deficiencies. Theories about the respective deficiencies of various arts—literature, painting, and sculpture, for example—were not developed in the eleventh and twelfth centuries. But the deficiencies of words were a topos of rhetoric and part of the practical experiences of daily life. It was clear that some persons were so striking in appearance that no artisan carv-

[36] *Gesta Hammaburgensis Ecclesiae Pontificum*, 3.46(45); *MGH, SSrrG*, pp. 189–90. A continuator of Florence of Worcester similarly recounts that a massive silver crucifix, given by King Canute a century before its destruction, emitted a dreadful, thundering groan "as though from heaven" when the fire engulfing the church consumed it. *Chronicon ex chronicis, continuatio*; Benjamin Thorpe, ed. (London: English Historical Society, 1849), 2:133.

Adalbert of Hamburg-Bremen's demolition was a purposeful one, in the same category as the ravages of papal legates (in 1157) described by Rahewin. *Gesta Friderici*, 3.11; *MGH, SSrrG*, pp. 178–79: "Porro quia multa paria litterarum apud eos reperta sunt et scedulae sigillatae ad arbitrium eorum adhuc scribendae, quibus, sicut hactenus consuetudinis eorum fuit, per singulas aecclesias Teutonici regni conceptum iniquitatis suae virus respergere, altaria denudare, vasa domus Dei asportare, cruces excoriare nitebantur, ne ultra procedendi facultas eis daretur, eadem qua venerant via ad Urbem eos redire fecimus." There were also pious demolitions, such as the one instituted by Abbot Godehard of Hersfeld, who gave great numbers of precious objects to the poor, including the metal extracted by melting down two hundred golden stoles, and the destruction of St. Adalbert's original tomb prior to the translation of his relics. Lambert of Hersfeld, *Institutio Herveldensis Ecclesiae*; *MGH, SSrrG*, p. 349. Cosmas of Prague, *Chronica Boemorum*, 2.4; *MGH, SSrrG*, p. 88. Writers were perfectly familiar with impious destruction, such as the Saracens' mutilation of sacred icons at Nicaea, which, as Ekkehard of Aura reported, crusaders viewed with sorrow, and the destruction of churches by raging mobs. Ekkehard of Aura, *Chronicon* (a. 1099); *MGH, SS* 6, p. 212. Lambert of Hersfeld, *Annales* (a. 1074); *MGH, SSrrG*, pp. 184 (Harzburg), 188–89 (Cologne). See also chap. 1, n. 6; chap. 3, after n. 89; chap. 6, n. 57; chap. 7, n. 64.

[37] *A Midsummer Night's Dream*, 5.1. See also chap. 3, n. 104; chap. 6, n. 77; chap. 7, nn. 23, 46; below, n. 46.

ing white ivory and no painter of murals could express them;[38] some events likewise eluded the written word and had to be seen to be believed.[39]

Deficiencies of media did not inhibit representations of the Kingdom of God in the visual arts (including architecture), liturgy, or theology. But, in historical writings, the deficiencies of medium were amplified by deficiencies of genre. In his erratic effort to sustain the theme of the two cities, Otto of Freising repeatedly oscillated between his theological speculations and the "order of history,"[40] perhaps an allusion to what I have identified as the disjunction between the spheres of Fortune and wisdom. He thought it necessary to anticipate critics who would attempt to deny the utility of his work by arguing that he had unworthily mingled difficult and hidden evidence from Scripture with historical accounts of evils.[41] Cosmas of Prague, who never discussed the City of God, evaded the whole issue of a mixed genre. He had written down his "senile ravings," he said, as a pleasant pastime for Severus, provost at Melnik. Severus, he said, would never find anything so laughable as his history, with its grammatical slips, but whether the book pleased or displeased him it should not be shown to a third set of eyes.[42]

Yet Cosmas's preface to another recipient, Master Gervasius, indicates with how many a large grain of salt these comments should be taken. There, anticipating a wider audience, he asked Gervasius to gird up the loins of his mind, to take scraper, chalk, and pen in hand, erasing what was excessive and adding what was needed.[43] Otto, too, had asked a recipient of his *Chronicle* to supply what had been left out, correct what had been ill said, and delete what was superfluous, but Otto further justified the suppression of evidence so that great matters should not be made to appear contemptible by being spread out to the common view.[44]

The works of Otto and Cosmas thus share a common feature: a studied incompleteness. This calculated deficiency of the genre is consistently witnessed to by historical writers in the period under review, and it distin-

---

[38] Cosmas of Prague, *Chronica Boemorum*, 3.24; *MGH, SSrrG*, p. 193. Among the deficiencies of words was certainly their inability to convince. See, for example, Adam of Bremen's description of the pagans paying no attention whatever to Archbishop Adalbert's "declamatory" sermons against their debaucheries and sexual offenses contrary to nature. *Gesta Hammaburgensis Ecclesiae Pontificum*, 3.56(55); *MGH, SSrrG*, pp. 201–2.

[39] Adam of Bremen, *Gesta Hammaburgensis Ecclesiae Pontificum*, 3.34(33); *MGH, SSrrG*, p. 176.

[40] Otto of Freising, *Chronicon*, 3.16, 6. prol.; *MGH, SSrrG*, pp. 155, 261.

[41] E.g., *Chronicon*, 8. prol.; *MGH, SSrrG*, pp. 392–93.

[42] Cosmas of Prague, *Chronica Boemorum, ep. ad Severum; MGH, SSrrG*, pp. 1–2.

[43] Cosmas of Prague, *Chronica Boemorum, ep. ad Gervasium; MGH, SSrrG*, p. 3. See also Cosmas's *proemium ad Clementem*; ibid., p. 81.

[44] *Chronicon*, 8.35; *MGH, SSrrG*, pp. 456–57. On historians' awareness and intention of writing for very small audiences, see chap. 7, nn. 49–60.

guishes their works from works in other artistic media and genres. The crucial fact was that a historical work was portrayed as part of a continuing composition in which the reader became both audience and coauthor, rather than as a work that a single writer made complete and self-explanatory. Readers too were expected to exercise artistic license through redactive criticism. Part of that license was association by implied contrast, as, for example, when narrative portrayal of the sport of Fortune implied by contrast the unportrayed rule of wisdom. The audience's expansion of the text by such associations is an essential piece in our hermeneutic puzzle.

I return to the predicament of how the Kingdom of God could be both conspicuous and present in the unspoken message by virtue of its absence from the written text. It is worth stressing that the works were written and intended to be read as artifacts of a religious cult that centered on the violent ritual death of one man at the hands of other men. Thus, they belonged to the universe of cult that also included the verbal and visual arts, including liturgy, that did represent the Kingdom of God. Even when writers did not cast their works in a mixed genre, as Otto of Freising did, the anticipated audience included readers who, in simplicity, sifted through the secrets of Scripture, gathering knowledge of kings, prophets, and battles from the beginning of the world to the praise of virtue and the abomination of vice; and a second body of readers, who, on account of their great zeal in writing, renounced the hurly-burly of affairs, and pursued the way of wisdom in the secret leisure of contemplation stretching the apex of their minds toward the invisible things of God, laboring beyond their powers in their desire to draw near to those mysteries.[45] A third kind of reader is represented by Frederick Barbarossa's esteemed counsellor and warlord, Bishop Eberhard of Bamberg, whose acute practical judgment and diligence made him famous through many lands. His zeal for delving into the sense of Scripture and for discourse on learned questions so grasped his attention that he was able to meditate earnestly upon them even at the very moment when he had to reckon with the shifting anxieties of military command in the thick of battle.[46]

Reverberating through the theater of cult in their daily liturgies, contemplations, and Eucharists, the Kingdom of God was present to them and they to it in a space created by the incompleteness of the historical text. Silence, darkness, and the unspoken in the said are the workshops of the redactive imagination. History is both a mimetic and a mnemonic enterprise. Far from excluding affective and pathetic fallacies, readers of the works in question cultivated them as mnemonic ways to kindle their own

[45] Helmold, *Cronicon Slavorum, ep. ad canonicos*; *MGH, SSrrG*, p. 1.

[46] Rahewin, *Gesta Friderici*, 4.32(29); *MGH, SSrrG*, pp. 274–75. See chap. 3, n. 104; chap. 6, n. 34; chap. 7, nn. 23, 46; above, n. 37.

passions as they performed the roles prescribed to relive the sufferings, temptations, and triumphant deaths of Christ and his saints, and to partake of their blessedness. In the process, they contrasted the meaningless sport of Fortune with the signifying decrees of wisdom. For through habitual discipline of empathy they learned by example more readily than by word.[47] The discipline of reading Scripture as though it were a mirror encouraged the belief that, in other modes of discourse too, one could be transfigured, as actors were, into the personae of the people in the text.[48] Thus, inflamed by empathetic participation, their living experience of sacrifice in the unspoken message of the text closed the hermeneutic gap between the Kingdom of God as fact and as figure.

. . .

The subject of the Kingdom of God presented considerable difficulties in the passage from criticism to epiphany. The Kingdom was a holy secret, not accessible to all by reading the letter of Scripture, and applying words of Scripture concerning the Kingdom to historical events and institutions was highly problematic. The reason was not simply the difficulty of portraying dramatically something that was both "at hand" and "not yet." Instead, it was that the mysteries of the Kingdom were not accessible to the natural man. Scripture yielded parables teaching its concealment, except to eyes enlightened by grace, and at the times appointed for them to see. In the dimension of history, even the Church was not the Kingdom of God, but a mixed city. And all promoters of dissent and reform alleged that Babylon was being rebuilt within the walls of Jerusalem, perhaps even by the chosen and consecrated rulers of the Church.

To mitigate these hermeneutic difficulties, writers brought critical techniques of Scriptural exegesis to bear, including the search for multiple meanings and the drawing of figural analogies. Yet, it was commonly understood that no amount of effort by the author could lead to epiphany in this matter. The experience of epiphanies of the Kingdom of God occurred in history, but they were not of history. They derived from redactive criticism by readers and hearers, whose intuition of the holy was opened by grace, whether through spiritual enlightenment, or through the sacraments which re-enacted violence, or through vicarious participation in sacrificial martyrdoms recorded in histories.

One function of historical writings was to open vicarious experience of the holy to such readers as were able to achieve it, to disclose to them how

[47] Hermannus quondam Judaeus, *Opusculum de Conversione Sua*, chap. 5; *MGH*, Quellen zur Geistesgeschichte, 4:87.

[48] Cf. Hermannus quondam Judaeus, *Opusculum de Conversione Sua*, chap. 16; *MGH*, Quellen zur Geistesgeschichte, 4:114.

those who participated in the holy were immune to the turmoil of Fortune, which constituted the historical drama, whether comedy or tragedy, of this world. Historical writers, therefore, employed the deficiencies of their medium (words) and genre to stimulate the speculative, mimetic play of imagination in the hermeneutic gaps of their texts, to arouse feelings of dread, pity, and love, and, in this way, to invite their readers to pass from redactive criticism, through silence, to epiphany between the lines.

## Chapter 6

# THE HERMENEUTIC ROLE OF WOMEN: A SILENCE OF COMPREHENSION

HISTORICAL texts of the eleventh and twelfth centuries are, on the whole, accumulations of anecdotes. They lack the fundamental elements of narrative wholeness—a beginning, middle, and end—and they flagrantly defy the canons of proportion and clarity. And yet I have argued in this study concerning the Kingdom of God, their segmented and directionless mode of discourse was possible because it was, for the authors and the intended readers, informed by a general esthetic, namely, an esthetic of cult, which presupposed much that was unsaid in the said, including an acceptance of violence (beginning with sacrifice) as a medium of beauty. We have established that something is said in the spaces between the lines. But what principles of hermeneutic exclusion and inclusion governed that esthetic? (I say "hermeneutic," rather than "narrative," because my chief interest is in ways of understanding that were prior to narrative.) "For you know," Otto of Freising wrote to Rainald of Dassel, "that all doctrine consists in two things: in avoidance (*fuga*) and in acceptance (*electione*)."[1]

I have made a beginning with our discussion of the Kingdom of God, which is a subject that could be apprehended but not comprehended. Now, I propose to go further in the attempt to retrieve some of those principles from the silences between the lines. Unlike the Kingdom of God, the subject of women was one that twelfth-century writers believed that they could comprehend all too well. Their silences concerning the City of God may have derived from their conviction that it was a holy secret, known by intuition and sought in epiphany, but that concerning women assuredly derived from a comprehension that impaired epiphany of the Kingdom.

---

[1] *Chronicon, ep. ad Reginaldum*; *MGH, SSrrG*, p. 4. See also John of Salisbury, *Metalogicon*, 3.6; Clement C. J. Webb, ed., *Ioannis Saresberiensis Episcopi Carnotensis Metalogicon Libri IIII* (Oxford: Clarendon, 1929), p. 145 (concerning Aristotle's *Topics*): "Et quia solum accidens ad comparationem venit, tertius comparabilium vim aperit, et insistens nature accidentium que sit eligendi aut fugiendi ratio, et in ipsis eligendis que preeligenda, et in fugiendis que pre ceteris fugienda regulariter monstrat." A general discussion is to be found in Alphons Lhotsky, "Fuga und Electio," in Alphons Lhotsky, *Aufsätze und Vorträge: Europäisches Mittelalter. Das Land Österreich* (Munich: Oldenbourg, 1970), 1:82–91. I am obliged to Professor Jo Ann McNamara for encouraging me to write this essay.

Evidently, retrieval of this sort has small expectations when the silence comes about from an esthetic judgment that excludes all inquiry. The deeds of the craven, Otto of Freising wrote, should be buried in silence, or, if they were drawn forth into the light of day, they should be used as examples to inspire terror. But this was only one reason for excluding peoples and events from recorded history. "The perfidious city of faithless Jews and Gentiles still remains," Otto wrote on another occasion, drawing a contrast with the City of Christ, "but, by comparison with the more noble kingdoms held by our people, hardly any things done by them in their realms (vile as they are before God and the world) are found to be worthy of writing down or of commending to posterity." Why did Christian authors write about the Jews? Peter the Venerable, abbot of the great monastery of Cluny, spoke of the Jewish people when he said: "I am drawing the terrible beast out of its lair to exhibit it in the theater of the whole world, to make it an object of ridicule in the sight of all peoples."[2] The historylessness of Jews and Muslims (not to mention heretics and lower social orders) is a silence in which nothing is said. But, as I have argued, the silence concerning the Kingdom of God is, in fact, a testimony to the context of cult in which the histories were written and were expected to be read. Historians' portrayals of the sphere governed by the random, meaningless sport of Fortune in fragmentary tableaux were intended to evoke, by associations of likeness, contiguity, and contrast, the realm governed by divine wisdom as it was expressed and experienced in cult. The silence concerning women is also instructive, but rather more complex than that concerning the Kingdom of God. For it required the deliberate suppression of evidence that was neither repellant to good morals, nor hostile to Christian faith, nor yet witness to the existence of social orders so low as to be beneath what was assumed to be the dignity of history; rather, it required suppression of evidence about people who belonged to the pith and life's blood of the dominant orders in Christian society. A key to the sacrificial center where violence fused with beauty was that a man must be ritually killed by men.

My task is twofold. In the first section of this essay, I shall describe the kinds of information about women that historical writers permitted to escape through their hermeneutic screen, an indication of the vast body of information that was suppressed. In the second section, I shall suggest the hermeneutic principles that dictated suppression. In this way, we may be able to recover some understanding of the game that both the suppressed and the suppressors played.

---

[2] *Gesta Friderici*, prol.; *MGH, SSrrG*, p. 9. *Chronicon*, 5. prol.; *MGH, SSrrG*, p. 228. Peter the Venerable, *Adversus Iudeorum Inveteratam Duritiem*, chap. 5; *Corp. Christ., continuatio medievalis*, 58, p. 125. See also chap. 1, n. 5; chap. 2, n. 5; chap. 5, nn. 23–32; chap. 7, nn. 11–22.

## TRACES OF A SUPPRESSED WORLD

First, I turn to the words that by their presence indicate what is absent. It must be said at the outset that the authors under review moved in a world in which women held power, the means of violence, over men, whether as abbesses, or territorial rulers, or the greatest princes of their day (figure 11).[3] Scholars who entered the orbit of Pope Eugenius III, such as Gerhoch of Reichersberg and Anselm of Havelberg, not to mention the Pope's fellow-Cistercian, Otto of Freising, must have known as well as John of Salisbury how greatly that Pontiff revered Hildegard of Bingen as a person to whom God had revealed new and wondrous things, while the Pope said that he could only use ineptly the key of knowledge that had been entrusted to him.[4] At a less exalted social level, women worked as merchants,

---

[3] E.g., when a young man, Otto of Bamberg served as the "Joseph" of an abbess's household in Regensburg. Ebo, *Vita S. Ottonis Episcopi Babenbergensis*, 1.3; Jan Wikarjak, ed., Monumenta Poloniae Historica, n.s., vol. 7, fasc. 2 (Warsaw: Państwowe Wydawnictwo Naukowe, 1969). p. 12. Cosmas of Prague believed that Mathilda of Tuscany could enthrone or depose more than 120 bishops. *Chronica Boemorum*, 2. 31; *MGH, SSrrG*, p. 126. A Bohemian magnate, fleeing into Poland, was made a knight of the Lady Judith, wife of Duke Wladislav. Cosmas of Prague, *Chronica Boemorum*, 2.41; *MGH, SSrrG*, p. 144.

See chap. 1, nn. 39–43; chap. 2, nn. 28–29, 37–43, 48, 49; below, n. 48. Also consult Shulamith Shahar, "De quelques aspects de la femme dans la pensée et la communauté religieuses au XIIe et XIIIe siècles," *Revue de l'histoire des religions* 185 (1974): esp. 32–41, concerning Abelard's doctrine on the nobility of women contrasted with Heloise's attitude of self-accusation. Yet Abelard also insisted that, according to Scripture, men must not be subject to women. For the patristic background, see, in general, Joyce E. Salisbury, "The Latin Doctors of the Church on Sexuality," *Journal of Medieval History* 12 (1986): esp. 280, 282–84.

There were many reasons for disapproving the power that women exerted in eleventh- and twelfth-century society. See, for example, Sigebert of Gembloux's disapproval of the sequence of four marriages that made Osburga the ancestress of almost the entire nobility of Lotharingia. *Vita Wicberti*, chap. 1; *MGH, SS* 8, p. 508. However, one must also remember Giraldus Cambrensis's explanation that women exerted power over men for the same reason that female hawks were stronger than male hawks, namely, that they excelled in violence and malice. *Topographia Hiberniae*, dist. 1, chap. 12; James F. Dimock, ed., *Giraldi Cambrensis Opera*, Rolls Series, no. 21 (London: Longman, 1867), 5:36. See chap. 2, n. 31.

The circumstances, therefore, are quite different from the argument by Linda Nochlin that there have been no great women artists in modern European culture because women were excluded from institutions and positions that would have enabled them to shape collective esthetic norms. "Why Have There Been No Great Women Artists?," *Art News* 69 (1971): 22–39, 67–71. Cf. Elizabeth Alford and Ingrid Stadler, "A Discussion of Linda Nochlin's Essay, 'Why Have There Been No Great Women Artists?,' " in *Contemporary Art and its Philosophical Problems*, ed. Ingrid Stadler (Buffalo, N.Y.: Prometheus Books, 1987), pp. 45–59.

[4] John of Salisbury, *ep. 185*; W. J. Millor and C.N.L. Brooke, eds., *The Letters of John of Salisbury* (Oxford: Clarendon, 1979), 2:224. See also the letter of Eugenius III to Hildegard; Migne *PL* 197:145. On the acknowledgment by Eugenius of Hildegard's authority at a synod in Trier, Barbara Newman, *Saint Hildegard of Bingen: Symphonia* (Ithaca, N.Y.: Cornell University Press, 1988), p. 4.

*Figure 11.* The status of women as rulers of men is represented in this medallion from the Guthlac Roll, which depicts Guthlac's admission to Repton, a double monastery for men and women governed by the Abbess Elfrida. *British Library, Harley Roll Y. 6.*

and some were esteemed for their shrewdness in business, although they ran the risk of being suspect as having the power to divine by dreams or to traduce the spirits of others.[5] Like almost any other circumstance, the subjection of men to the direction of women in circumstances of violence

[5] E.g., C. H. Talbot, ed. and trans., *The Life of Christina of Markyate A Twelfth Century Recluse* (Oxford: Clarendon, 1959), chaps. 20, 76; pp. 66, 68, 172. It was a tribute to Christina's practical acumen that her father entrusted the keys of his treasure chest to her, even while he was trying to subvert her vows of chastity and force her into marriage. Ibid., chap. 33, p. 92. On the power of her example of holiness to draw men into the monastic life, see ibid., chap. 50, p. 126.

could be, and was, opportunistically advanced to justify revolt. Yet the fact itself was quite normal in the government of ecclesiastical and secular institutions.

In the world of historical writers of the twelfth century, vengeance was a dominant motive. When women appear in their pages, they are generally portrayed as seeking vengeance, rather than exacting it.[6] However, traces of a different reality glimmered through the veil of words when Cosmas of Prague recorded that the Dowager Duchess Judith of Bohemia, having been exiled by her son, could only avenge the wrong done her by marrying King Peter of Hungary. The sway that the Countess Mathilda held over northern Italy, and the revolt raised against the Emperor Henry V by a sister of Lothar of Supplinburg, Duke of Saxony, are other indications of how great women were fully able to play the game of vengeance.[7]

Seen against this background of fact, the artful silences of our texts indicate that the mnemonic, or documentary, function of history was not paramount for their authors. We know that women participated in great and dramatic events, but we are often told this in passing to illustrate something else. For example, when Lambert of Hersfeld wished to underscore the extreme difficulty of Henry IV's desperate passage through the Alps to Canossa in dead of winter, the chronicler described the Queen and other women in Henry's entourage being drawn over ice and snow in the skins of oxen. Many, Lambert added, died; many fell ill; few reached Italy unscathed.[8] Nor, in fact, were women excluded from the world of cult. The sight of women approaching the altar of the cathedral at Metz to leave offerings of incense was so common that an enterprising cleric used that disguise to place papal letters of interdict on the altar. No one noticed until he cast his disguise aside, and amidst pandemonium, raced away on horseback.[9]

[6] E.g., Cosmas of Prague, *Chronica Boemorum*, 2.17; *MGH, SSrrG*, p. 109. Cf. the dispute over whether Henry II of England commanded that his granddaughters' eyes be put out. Antonia Gransden, *Historical Writing in England, c. 550 to c. 1307* (Ithaca, N.Y.: Cornell University Press, 1974), p. 199. See David J. Bernstein, *The Mystery of the Bayeux Tapestry* (Chicago: University of Chicago Press, 1986), pp. 158–59 ("Blinding as a Norman Punishment").

[7] *Chronica Boemorum*, 2.17; *MGH, SSrrG*, p. 108. Ekkehard of Aura, *Chronicon* (a. 1123); *MGH, SS* 6, p. 261.

[8] Lambert of Hersfeld, *Annales* (a. 1077); *MGH, SSrrG*, p. 287. Cf. also Rahewin's brief allusions to the vital part taken by the Empress Beatrice in Frederick Barbarossa's Italian campaigns. *Gesta Friderici*, 3.47(41), 4.28(26), 4.46(38), 4.54(45); *MGH, SSrrG*, pp. 222, 272, 285–86, 292.

[9] Balderic, *Gesta Alberonis*, chap. 4; *MGH, SS* 8, p. 246. By contrast the *Life* of Christina of Markyate attests that it was extraordinary for women to approach the altar. Talbot, ed. and trans., chap. 77, p. 176. Clearly a master of disguise, Albero masqueraded as a servant in Rome to hide himself beneath the table of the Emperor Henry V, changing his costume and begriming his face, hair, and beard. *Gesta Alberonis*, chap. 5; *MGH, SS* 8, p. 246. See also the

Concerning women, some information is suppressed; in the suppression, other information is given. As did not happen in regard to historyless Jews, heretics, and servile orders, something was said in the silences that illuminated the assumptions underlying the modeling process—the hermeneutic method—by which the texts were formed. The complexities hinge on three conditions. Of these, the greatest, and most imponderable, is the virtually complete lack of women authors in the western historical tradition from classical Antiquity until modern times. The fact that all the histories here under review were written by men can, therefore, be explained only partially with reference to Christian prohibitions against women in the magistracy of the Church. It calls for wider study in the context of the classical tradition as a whole.[10] I can only address the taboo against female historians indirectly; the burden of my comments must deal with the two other conditions that make our study complex: what is said and what is not said.

. . .

Although women are conspicuous by their absence from the ranks of historians, works of art, some of which we shall examine, provided many indications that women were interested in history and indeed that, as patrons, copyists, or artisans, they produced historical works. How did women regard themselves as actors in history? This must be my first question in exploring what is said. Fortunately, the dearth of materials is not complete. By indirection, the *Hortus Deliciarum*, which yielded examples of the nuclear perspective (chap. 4), also sheds some light on ways in which one learned woman, the Abbess Herrad of St. Odile's, understood the historical achievements of women.

---

attempt by William Longchamps, bishop of Ely and chancellor of England, to escape from Dover in women's clothes. His disguise compounded the ignominy of his capture as portrayed by Giraldus Cambrensis, but part of his humiliation was also that women detected and removed his disguise. Giraldus's celebrated misogyny is evident in his portrayal. *De Vita Galfridi Archiepiscopi Eboracensis*, 2.12; J. S. Brewer, ed., *Giraldi Cambrensis Opera*, Rolls Series, no. 21 (London: Longman, 1873), 4:410–11. In Byzantium, the usurper Theophilus Eroticus, was also humiliated (*inter alia*) by being "dressed in women's clothes and paraded through the Hippodrome." Michael McCormick, *Eternal Victory: Triumphal Rulership in Late Antiquity, Byzantium and the Early Medieval West* (Cambridge: Cambridge University Press, 1986), p. 179. Christina of Markyate escaped from her father by disguising herself as a man. Talbot, ed., *The Life of Christina of Markyate A Twelfth Century Recluse*, chap. 33, p. 90.

[10] See above, chap. 2, n. 51. The absence of women from the ranks of historical writers is evident, for example, in Peter Dronke, *Women Writers of the Middle Ages: A Critical Study of Texts from Perpetua (†203) to Marguerite Poreta (†1310)* (Cambridge: Cambridge University Press, 1984). Dronke's consideration of Hrotsvitha of Gandersheim's *Gesta Ottonis* is instructive in the emphasis placed by Hrotsvitha on her "womanly nature" as a disqualification for the historical work that she had undertaken (ibid., pp. 75–77, 296–97).

I recognize the singular character of the *Hortus*. Destroyed and known only through transcripts, tracings, and skillful reconstruction, it comprises a literary and artistic category of its own. Furthermore, it corresponds with the demands of a patron or of patrons who had in view the specific responsibilities of an abbess and the needs of a particular community, quite apart from the unknown personal motives that inspired the production of so unusual and opulent a work.

As we observed, the historical sections of the *Hortus* are chiefly based on Scripture; a few texts derive from the age of the Church Fathers. There is nothing to indicate a conception of continuous development, of change and continuity in human experience generally or in the history of the Church, extending from the Creation until Herrad's day. Yet Herrad brought a wealth of learning to bear. Nearly fifty literary works are quoted, many extensively. They include Scriptural commentaries, ascetic treatises, historical texts, religious poetry (some by Herrad herself), and other genres. Ivo of Chartres represents canon law. And one is struck by the fact that Herrad's library included not only antiquarian books, but also writings by such contemporary authors as Peter Lombard, Rupert of Deutz, Peter Comestor, Bernard of Clairvaux, and Honorius Augustodunensis, not to mention the poetry of Hildebert of Le Mans and Petrus Pictor. The presence of musical notations testifies to another kind of erudition, and the abundance of German glosses interpolated in Latin passages from the beginning of the work to the end leaves no doubt of the bilingual character of Herrad and of the community that she wished to edify with her "useful book." Certainly, the illuminations for which the *Hortus* is most celebrated give evidence of the visual erudition at St. Odile's, everywhere informed by Byzantine as well as by Latin prototypes. Throughout this vast essay of compilation, one finds a highly idiosyncratic and educated originality at work, expressed now in the illustration of an extracanonical text reporting an act of the Apostle Paul (illustration no. 256), now in a set of miniatures portraying the legend of Ulysses and the Sirens for which there are no known precedents (illustrations nos. 297–99).

The critical intellect organizing these literary and visual materials did not stop with texts. For, reflecting criticism of morals in the Church common in her day, Herrad included bitter verses against contemporary prelates, new successors of Judas, she wrote, who sell Christ, and of the new Marthas, who contemplate coins and wealth and scornfully trample on Christ's gold.[11] Nor did the confusion of secular and religious modes of life by

[11] Rosalie Green et al., eds., *Herrad of Hohenbourg: Hortus Deliciarum*, 2 vols. Studies of the Warburg Institute, vol. 36 (London: Warburg Institute, 1979), text no. 816, 2:400.

some children of the Church escape censure.[12] In her sense of ascetic reform, as in other regards, Herrad applied to herself the same Scriptural verses that Gerhoch of Reichersberg employed to claim the inspiration of the Holy Spirit, a swiftly moving pen.[13]

Herrad, however, had reasons that Gerhoch did not for paying particular attention to women and to subjects of interest to women. Thus, an exceptionally rich block of texts is devoted to the Blessed Virgin's role in the life and mission of Christ, and another, in the section on Faith and Order, is given over to subjects pertaining to marriage and the family. The great illumination with which the manuscript ends, a two-page, anachronistic representation of the founding of St. Odile's in the presence of Christ and of the members of the community in Herrad's day, asserts the central theme of virginity, which runs throughout the work, expressing itself in self-identification of Herrad with the virginity of Christ, of the Blessed Virgin, and of John the Divine, the latter two of whom are portrayed in an unprecedented miniature as patrons of virgins.[14] It did not escape Herrad, in arranging texts on the Song of Solomon, that the bed on which Solomon slept represented the womb of the Virgin in which the infant Christ was sheltered (text no. 711). A perhaps ambivalent sense of the power of renunciation marks her comment that the nun's black habit symbolized "contempt for the embraces of men."[15]

Yet, amidst the opulence that she commanded and the learning that instructed her mind, and despite the self-confidence represented in the whole enterprise of the *Hortus*, Herrad expressed quite another attitude toward femininity. In her texts, she found strong negations. If Sarah had given birth to a daughter, instead of a son, the lineage of God's Mother would not have been so distinguished as it was. Why should the pain of circumcision be visited upon males, when women were more to be punished for sin than they? Bodies of those violently killed should not be carried into churches lest the pavement be polluted by their blood. For the same reason, the bodies of women who died in childbirth should not be brought to the church for burial. In her illumination of four elect men and four elect women in their beatitude, Herrad chose to balance the "perpetual youth" of the men with the "eternal beauty" of the women. Yet, she also knew that Moses had been overpowered and brought into disobedience by the beauty of an Ethiopian princess, and her miniatures of Ulysses and the

---

[12] Ibid., text no. 1155, 2:492.

[13] Ibid., text no. 1162, 2:506. See also the colophon in illustration no. 346, 1:227: "Dictat namque sic utrumque cito scribens calamus, Spiritus sanctus."

[14] Ibid., text no. 1, 2:2.

[15] Ibid., illustration no. 235, 1:182.

Sirens vividly set forth the ruin that lurked for men beneath the allures of women.[16]

Women figure in many illuminations, chiefly in those of Scriptural passages, such as the encounters between Jesus and the Samaritan woman and, again, with the woman caught in adultery. Great figures of the Old Testament—Judith, Esther, the Queen of Sheba—appear in her pages, together with the apocalyptic women of John's revelation, the Whore of Babylon and the Woman clothed with the Sun. Yet, in the majority of illuminations depicting men and women, the female figures are fewer than the male, and they appear at the outer edges of illuminations or at the back, in positions of subordination and deference. (This literal marginalization is particularly striking in the representation of the Crucifixion as the mystic winepress [illustration no. 307, figure 12 in this book].) No women are identifiable in the cluster of the saved in Abraham's bosom (illustration no. 344).

Thus, Herrad's originality did not shake off the authority of artistic conventions. But those conventions and the mentalities that they served combined to produce an exceptional program of violence in the hands of women. To be sure, in most cases, the warrant for this program exists in the texts of Scripture itself—in the story of Esther and the hanging of Haman, and in that of Judith's decapitation of Holophernes (itself a story of a man destroyed by a woman's deceptive beauty) and transportation of her grim trophy to be exhibited on the city walls. The illuminations, however, display a particular fascination with violent conflict. And the beheadings, stabbings, and mutilations represented as male activity in such episodes as the stories of David and Joshua, or the massacre of the innocents and the parable of the wicked steward, reappear with all explicitness in the illumination of the conflict of Virtues and Vices depicted as women in battle array. Here, the repertoire of slaughter is enlarged by suicide. In this regard, Herrad's work provides an analogy with Hildegard of Bingen's preoccupation with "the theme of war in Heaven, God against Lucifer," which relentless conflict she grasped as "the universe's primal threat."

As an essay on holy love, the *Hortus* expresses the erotic aspect of violence. A report of another woman of the era epitomizes this facet of the quest for holiness. Praying for her friend, Christina of Markyate was asked by God whether she would wish her friend to endure the pangs of death for God. With all the power of her ardent love, she exclaimed that she would, and that if it were God's evident will she would even sacrifice him

---

[16] On circumcision, ibid., text no. 130, 2:59. On Sarah, text no. 300, 2:128; on pollution of churches by bloodshed, text no. 790, 2:384; on the miniature of the elect men and women, illustration no. 342, 1:223; on Moses and the Ethiopian princess, text no. 145, 2:68; on the miniatures of Ulysses and the Sirens, illustrations nos. 297–99, 2:365–66.

*Figure 12*. The iconographic marginalization of women appears in Herrad of Hohenburg's representation of Heaven as Christ's mystic winepress. See also figure 8.
*A. Straub and G. Keller*, Herrade de Landsberg, Hortus Deliciarum. *Strasbourg,
1879–99. Princeton University Library.*

with her own hands, as Abraham had intended to sacrifice Isaac.[17] In this
case, the fact that Christina's gender denied her the sacrificial powers of the
priesthood may have added to her vehemence.

Enough has been said to indicate the complexity with which Herrad

[17] See chap. 2, n. 31, and above, after n. 10. On Hildegard of Bingen, Dronke, *Women
Writers of the Middle Ages: A Critical Study of Texts from Perpetua (†203) to Marguerite Porete
(†1310)*, p. 184. Talbot ed., *The Life of Christina of Markyate A Twelfth Century Recluse*, chap.
79, p. 180.

regarded the historical role of women, including herself. Of course, we have only fragments of her concepts in our hands, and they were, to be sure, the convictions of one woman. Is there evidence to enlarge our picture, to establish how general this complex attitude may have been and whether it figured also in the thinking of men?

. . .

I turn to another visual image, contemporary with the historical texts under review, but from another land: the Bayeux "Tapestry." The "Tapestry," commemorating William the Conqueror's defeat of Harold in the Battle of Hastings, was probably made for William's half-brother, Bishop Odo of Bayeux, between 1066 and 1082.[18] A great ribbon of embroidered linen, it stretches, in its present state, just over 230 feet; it is 19¾ inches wide. Apart from nearly 800 other representations of trees, ships, buildings, and animals, it displays 626 human figures, of which four are women. Of the four, one, a nude, appears in a threateningly amorous scene with a male nude in the border. The other three appear, rather inconspicuously, among the hundreds of figures in the "Tapestry's" main frieze. Two of them are incidental figures: a shrouded, mourning woman at the foot of King Edward's deathbed; and a woman fleeing with a child from a burning house. Neither of these is named. The third female figure, Aelfgyva, appears as a major figure in a scene with a "cleric," whose gesture toward Aelfygva's face may have something to do with the echoing gesture made by a distinctly priapic male nude in the border. But the inscription for this scene is incomplete. The characters and the event are otherwise unknown and, to some, "it contributes nothing to the story, except a moment of confusion."[19]

Parallels with written texts are notable. Beyond the fragmentary, episodic presentation of material, there is the address to the visual imagination, direct in the "Tapestry" and indirect in the theatrical presentations of histories "in the mode of tragedy" or as dramatic songs (*carmina*).[20]

Moreover, the "Tapestry" and the texts under review alike display general characteristics: selectivity that omitted much; and an abruptly frag-

[18] On "the Tapestry's singular method of narration," see Bernstein, *The Mystery of the Bayeux Tapestry*, p. 90, and "the integration of text and image," p. 146. For an alternate view of the origins and intent of the Tapestry, and an argument that it failed to satisfy the purposes for which it was commissioned (a failure that contributed to its survival), see Bernard S. Bachrach, "Some Observations on the Bayeux Tapestry," *Cithara* 27 (1987): 5–28.

[19] Norman Denny and Josephine Filmer-Sankey, *The Bayeux Tapestry: The Story of the Norman Conquest* (London: Collins, 1966), introduction *ad fin.*, n.p.

[20] E.g., Otto of Freising, *Chronicon*, *ep. ad Fridericum*, 6.31; *MGH*, *SSrrG*, pp. 2–3, 297. Otto of Freising, *Gesta Friderici*, 1.47; *MGH*, *SSrrG*, p. 65. Cosmas of Prague, *Chronica Boemorum*, 2.51; *MGH*, *SSrrG*, p. 159.

mentary narrative mode that presupposed a coherent order of visualization in the mind of artist and viewers. The actual omission and inclusion of women also betray patterns of thought common to them all. The contrast between the paucity of women and the abundance of horses in the "Tapestry" is striking, especially because the "Tapestry" portrays such a wealth of episodes running through the spectrum of social activity from menial tasks of cooking and serving a banquet to rituals of state, in some of which, at any rate, women might have been expected to appear. A woman is portrayed at Edward the Confessor's deathbed, but not in his funeral train or in the throng rapt in wonder at the comet associated with his death. A woman is portrayed as a victim of war, but not in any scenes of provisioning or transport, or as a denizen of the castles, manors, palaces, cities, and towns represented. Aelfgyva, the only female either named or assigned a major part in any episode, would seem, given the balanced gestures of the priapic nude in the border and the cleric touching her face, to have been an actor in a sexual interlude associated with the Norman Conquest, but it is a matter of debate whether that incident can be identified from extant documents.[21] Indeed, by its impenetrability, the Aelfgyva scene underscores what is true of all the episodes included, namely, that understanding the content of each scene, and the narrative interconnections of all scenes, depended, not on the work of art, but on the viewer's powers of visualization and association.

Finally, two additional points deserve emphasis. First, all three of the female figures in the frieze are highly stylized and repeat stock figures derived from the art of late Antiquity and perpetuated in early medieval book illuminations. They do not betray the kind of individuality expressed, for example, in the distinctive coiffures of Anglo-Saxon and Norman warriors. Second, while the "Tapestry" may have been designed by a man, it was assuredly executed by women, and women were among its intended viewers. Women created and received the representation of a past from which women had been expunged, except as rare and stereotyped abstractions. The evidence of the Bayeux Tapestry leads one naturally to ask why women were included at all in the visualization of history.

Evidently, the designer of the Bayeux "Tapestry" was guided by two main functions of historical thought: the mnemonic and the mimetic. Just as evidently, something persuaded him to apply them in a minimalist fashion to women, by comparison with their application to men, to details of armor and shipbuilding, and even to the favorite steeds of princes. By the

---

[21] Bernstein represents the position of indeterminacy. *The Mystery of the Bayeux Tapestry*, pp. 19, 30. However, J. Bard McNulty argues that Aelfgyva was the wife of King Canute, whose deceptions formed part of the network of legalisms on the basis of which William the Conqueror eventually claimed the throne of England. J. Bard McNulty, "The Lady Aelfgyva in the Bayeux Tapestry," *Speculum* 55 (1980): esp. 666–67.

"mimetic" function, I mean both the representation of events "as in a mirror" before the eyes of spectators, and the presentation of exemplary models to posterity for emulation. Indeed, there were severe limits to the mimetic functions that historical portrayals of women could serve in texts of a warrior society, and even of branches of such a society devoted to ascetic spirituality. The "woman's heart" was a synonym for cowardliness, an unpardonable reproach among warriors. Women asked for vengeance rather than wreaking it; they wept in disaster; they sat in lamentation among feeble old men.[22] I shall return to the esthetic barrier between men and women. For the moment, however, enough has been suggested to indicate that some function was prior to the mnemonic and mimetic ones and governed them.

. . .

From a different country, the historical texts under review display the same traits of selection and exposition that I have identified in the Bayeux "Tapestry." In them, too, references to women are fewer than those to men; they generally appear as parenthetic asides, frequently in dependent clauses. Portrayals of women (as distinct from references) are very few. On the whole, they correspond to the three categories noted in the Bayeux "Tapestry": women as victims of atrocities (in war or otherwise); as members of the entourages of great men; and as participants in some action possible because of sexuality (for example, marriage and procreation). Again, the minimalist application to women of history's mnemonic and mimetic functions witnesses to another prior and determining function. In their diversity and volume, the written texts are able to elucidate better than the "Tapestry" the strategies of acceptance and avoidance that entered into their modeling process.

One very obvious feature of the texts is that individual judgment by a given author determined the place of women in his history. If one departs from the assertion that nothing is more impure than stained menstrual pads, which contaminate whatever they touch, one's conclusions are nec-

---

[22] Helmold, *Cronica Slavorum*, 1.35, 67, 88(87); *MGH, SSrrG*, pp. 70, 127, 172. Cosmas of Prague, *Chronica Boemorum*, 2.17, 3.36; *MGH, SSrrG*, pp. 109, 208. Rahewin, *Gesta Friderici*, 3.42(38); *MGH, SSrrG*, p. 216. See also n. 93. Cf. below, n. 31, on the "manly heart" in women. The stereotype of womanly weakness and timidity characterized even works that praised women. For example, Talbot, ed. and trans., *The Life of Christina of Markyate A Twelfth Century Recluse*, chaps. 21, 78; pp. 68, 178. Cf., ibid., chaps. 34 (Christina is disguised as a man), 44, pp. 90, 114, where the author admonishes Christina to manliness, or praises her for that quality. In ibid., chap. 43, p. 114, where a would-be seducer has exhibited himself nude to Christina: "Unde nonnunquam virum illam non feminam esse dicebat quem virago virtute virili predita recte effeminatum appellare poterat."

essarily limited.[23] Idiosyncracy of choice is particularly evident when one compares the portions of the *Deeds of Frederick* written by Otto of Freising with those by Rahewin. Rahewin had taken down Otto's earlier history, the *Chronicle*, from his very mouth.[24] He collaborated with the Bishop in digesting materials for, and in writing early portions of, the *Deeds of Frederick*, which Otto himself at his death and Frederick Barbarossa thereafter entrusted to him for completion.[25] Yet, Rahewin's abandonment of the pattern of interpolating philosophical interludes, which Otto announced in his prologue and pursued in the first Book of the *Deeds*, was only one indication that his notion of how to shape the material at hand fundamentally differed from the Bishop's. His fascination with atrocities of war was another indication of how widely his temperament varied from Otto's. The place which he assigned women in the panorama of history was yet a third.

Otto completed the first Book. He may have drafted the second without completing it. Book I is punctuated with frequent references to dynastic marriages and their ensuing pedigrees, and with a few incidental allusions to important political or ceremonial actions performed by women. Although Book II records the marriage of Frederick with Beatrice of Burgundy and an anecdote recounting how in distant centuries Lombard women had masqueraded as soldiers, it also displays a sharp decline in frequency of references to women. Such references as there are continue to be extremely rare in the concluding two books, which are thought to have been composed by Rahewin alone. There, they consist of a commemorative passage on Otto of Freising's family (4.14[14]); three allusions to Beatrice's part in Frederick Barbarossa's Italian campaigns (3.47[41], 4.46[38], 4.54[45]); an anecdote concerning the discovery by a Byzantine Empress of a plot to murder her husband (3.54[47]); and several comments on the sufferings of women in Frederick's wars (3.42[38], 4.71[61], 4.72[62]). It is significant of Rahewin's thinking that, when commenting on the barbarism of the Slavs (3.1), he omitted allegations of sexual license, concubinage, the abortion of illegitimate children, and female infanticide, which occur in other texts on the subject.[26]

The decisive character of individual judgment is underscored by com-

---

[23] Rupert of Deutz, *Commentum in Apocalypsim*, 4.6; Migne *PL* 169: 952.

[24] Otto of Freising, *Chronicon, ep. ad Fridericum*; *MGH, SSrrG*, p. 3.

[25] Rahewin, *Gesta Friderici*, 3. prol.; *MGH, SSrrG*, p. 162.

[26] On the abortion of illegitimate children, Cosmas of Prague, *Chronica Boemorum*, 2.4; *MGH, SSrrG*, p. 86. On female infanticide, Ebo, *Vita S. Ottonis Episcopi Babenbergensis*, 2.12; Wikarjak, ed., p. 74. Herbord, *Dialogus de Vita S. Ottonis Episcopi Babenbergensis*, 2.18, 33; Jan Wikarjak, ed., Monumenta Poloniae Historica, n.s. vol. 7, fasc. 3 (Warsaw: Państwowe Wydawnictwo Naukowe, 1974), pp. 95, 126. See also Adam of Breman's inventory of pagan depravities, including drunkenness, contentiousness, bloody brawling, adultery, incest, and other impurities beyond the limits of nature. *Gesta Hammaburgensis Ecclesiae Pontificum*, 3.56(55); *MGH, SSrrG*, pp. 201–2.

paring Rahewin's nearly womanless world with the world according to Cosmas of Prague. Unlike the other writers in our sample, Cosmas was married, a sign of the slowness and incompleteness with which the Gregorian norm of clerical celibacy was imposed; it appears that he and his wife had children. The daily experience of family life in conjunction with clerical duties may well have colored his historical writing.[27] His first chapters are a myth of Bohemia's origins. Although he invoked a founding father, Boemus, he portrayed a woman, the seeress (*phitonissa*) Lubossa, as the creatrix of the civil and political order, and a tribe of women "like Amazons" as the primordial inhabitants of the region where at Lubossa's prophetic direction Prague was built. Cosmas dramatically portrayed opposition provoked against the regiment of women by the fact that Lubossa and her sisters governed through magical powers, and by the ill-tempered insistence that, since women were long on hair and short on understanding, it was better for a man to die than to be ruled by a woman.[28] Using the conventional association of *virtus* with *vir*, Cosmas described how Lubossa yielded to the request of her people for a duke, and how, married to him, she placed her powers at his service in bridling a wild people to the rule of law.[29] "And from that time forth, after the death of the Prince, Lubossa, our women were under the power of men."[30]

Throughout the balance of his history, Cosmas frequently referred to women, indeed, far more frequently than his contemporary historians. The fascinating ambivalence of women's innate power and social subordination, set forth in his mythic account of origins, also informs many of his

[27] See Josef Hemmerle, "Cosmas von Prag," in *Lebensbilder zur Geschichte der böhmischen Länder*, ed. Ferdinand Seibt (Munich: Oldenbourg, 1981), 4:35–36. I am obliged to Ms. Phyllis Jestice for drawing my attention to this article.

[28] *Chronica Boemorum*, 1.4; *MGH, SSrrG*, pp. 11–13. The three sisters are identified as *phitonissa*, *venefica*, and *malefica*. Ibid., p. 13. In his encounters with the pagan Pomeranians, Otto of Bamberg denounced the heathenism in the professional activities of a "*phitonissa*." Ebo, *Vita S. Ottonis Episcopi Babenbergensis*, 2.12; Wikarjak, ed., p. 75. See also Adam of Bremen's comment that "mulier spiritum habens Phitonis" prophesied Archbishop Adalbert's death. *Gesta Hammaburgensis Ecclesiae Pontificum* 3.64(63); *MGH, SSrrG*, p. 210. Although magical powers or powers of second sight were not infrequently attributed to women, it is worth remembering that Frederick Barbarossa commanded a male magician and poisoner to be crucified. Rahewin, *Gesta Friderici*, 4.45; *MGH, SSrrG*, p. 285. Cf. the account of the crucifixion of a Christian by pagans in Ebo's *Vita S. Ottonis Episcopi Babenbergensis*, 3.6; Wikarjak, ed., p. 105. The indignity of being restrained by womanly power was resented not only by some of Cosmas's mythic Bohemians, but also by Adam of Bremen's German magnates during the regency of the Empress Agnes. *Gesta Hammaburgensis Ecclesiae Pontificum*, 3.34(33); *MGH, SSrrG*, p. 176.

[29] *Chronica Boemorum*, 1.8; *MGH, SSrrG*, p. 18.

[30] *Chronica Boemorum*, 1.9; *MGH, SSrrG*, p. 21. See Vladimir Karbusický, *Anfänge der historischen Überlieferung in Böhmen: Ein Beitrag zum vergleichenden Studium der mittelalterlichen Sängerepen*, Ostmitteleuropa in Vergangenheit und Gegenwart, no. 18 (Vienna: Böhlau, 1980), pp. 93–136.

vignettes. Sometimes they are redolent with irony, as in the account of an abbess whose satiric ingenuity was rewarded with exile. Sometimes they are pervaded with triumph, as in the story of the Countess Mathilda of Tuscany, a woman of manly action, who had the power to elect and enthrone, or to expel 120 bishops, and who, preserving her celibacy through the sudden and astonishing impotence of her bridegroom, cast the man out with contempt and curses.[31] In his day, one chronicler wrote, just as no woman was wealthier or more famous than Mathilda, so also no one at all in the laity was more outstanding in virtues and religion.[32] And yet, Cosmas' story of Mathilda, compelled to marry by her princes' desire that she produce an heir and in the event disowning her bridegroom, is an ironic pendant to the myth of Lubossa, compelled to marry by the Bohemians' desire for a duke and to live as an example to women thereafter in subjection to her husband.

(Parenthetically, I must note that Cosmas was writing about Mathilda's second marriage and that her earlier marital arrangements had given her political enemies cause for reflection. She was first married to Gozilo, the diminutive, humpbacked Duke of Lorraine, one of the greatest princes of his age. Then, Mathilda had adopted a kind of widowhood, separated from her husband by the Alps, except for one conjugal visit which she made each year, and for Gozilo's expeditions into Italy every third or fourth year. While her admirers drew analogies between Mathilda and Deborah, the Old Testamental judge, this marital separation and Mathilda's devotion to Pope Gregory VII gave her enemies and those who wished to depose Gregory occasion to charge that Mathilda had relaxed her celibacy in the Pope's arms.[33])

Even in Cosmas's *Chronicle*, women are subordinate actors. The characterizations observed in the Bayeux "Tapestry" and in Rahewin's portions of the *Deeds of Frederick* dominate: women as victims of atrocities, as satellites of great men, and as (at least prospective) objects of lust and agents of procreation. Rahewin, Cosmas, and the authors between the extremes represented by them applied, each in his own way, the same strategies of inclusion and avoidance, always keenly aware of the plasticity that historical writings shared with other arts, and always imagining their readers in the act of visualization.

Thus, allowing for the idiosyncratic choices of authors, it is possible to

---

[31] *Chronica Boemorum*, 2.14, 31–33; *MGH, SSrrG*, pp. 104–5, 126–30. Sophia, the daughter of King Bela of Hungary, refused to leave the convent of Admont and return to secular life. According to Herbord, she did so "corpore femineo viriles animos [*and* virili mente] gerens." *Dialogus de Vita S. Ottonis Episcopi Babenbergensis*, 1.38; Wikarjak, ed., pp. 47–48. See above, n. 22, on the "womanly heart" in men.

[32] Ekkehard of Aura, *Chronicon* (*a.* 1115); *MGH, SS* 6, p. 249.

[33] Lambert of Hersfeld, *Annales* (*a.* 1077); *MGH, SSrrG*, pp. 287–88.

detect a recurrent pattern of inclusion. Numerous subordinate themes occur. Exoticism is one: the entrancing and bizarre exoticism of women gifted in magical arts, of women in the alps of Norway and Sweden who grew beards, and of Amazons, to be mentioned with other monsters of distant lands such as cynocephali, cannibals, cyclops, and a human species having only one foot.[34] Women were also adduced in a figurative mode, as personifications of the Church (or of some particular church), of Rome, "the mother of Empire," or the menacingly capricious lady, Fortuna, who presided over human events, and her sister, Bellona, the goddess of war.[35] References to unsavory sexual practices among the barbarians served both fascination with the exotic and the need to sharpen ethnic identities, xenophobic attitudes that existing also among Christians found one expression when Duke Zpitignev commanded the expulsion from Bohemia of all Germans, including the dowager duchess, his mother, within three days.[36]

Exoticism, symbolism, ethnic identity—all these were less pervasive reasons for inclusion than the roles that most acutely illustrated the meaningless play of Fortune in the events of this world: procreation and suffering. To be sure, these roles had their counterweight in others that witnessed to the order of divine wisdom, transcending Fortune, roles exemplified by the saintly patronesses commemorated by Adam for bestowing their wealth upon the church at Bremen; by the devout women who served Vicelin of Oldenburg and Otto of Bamberg and sustained them in their missions, and to whom for their faithfulness visions and miracles were vouchsafed; by martyrs like St. Afra, who converted from her life of sin and through torments and crown of everlasting glory gave witness to sinners of God's grace; and St. Theodosia, who died for defending the veneration of sacred images and at whose tomb in Constantinople Otto of Freising (as he said in a rare autobiographical note) witnessed miraculous cures,[37] and above all the Blessed Virgin, the exemplar par excellence of purity and obedience. But, necessarily, the roles testifying to the sphere of wisdom, like those witnessing to the spin of deceptive Fortune's Wheel,[38] were not personal

---

[34] Adam of Bremen, *Gesta Hammaburgensis Ecclesiae Pontificum*, 4.19, 25, 32(31); *MGH, SSrrG*, pp. 246–48, 256–57, 265–67. See also chap. 3, n. 104; chap. 5, nn. 37, 48; chap. 7, nn. 23, 46.

[35] E.g., Cosmas of Prague, *Chronica Boemorum*, 3.7; *MGH, SSrrG*, p. 168 ("sponsa eius et mater ecclesia"). Helmold, *Cronica Slavorum, ep. ad canonicos*; *MGH, SSrrG*, p. 1 (the Church, Lübeck). Adam of Bremen, *Gesta Hammaburgensis Ecclesiae Pontificum*, 3.26(25). *MGH, SSrrG*, p. 168 (the church at Hamburg). Helmold, *Cronica Slavorum*, 1.28(30), 80(79); *MGH, SSrrG*, pp. 57, 151–52 (Rome, mother of Empire). Cosmas of Prague, *Chronicon Boemorum*, 2.10; *MGH, SSrrG*, pp. 96–97 (Fortuna and Bellona; references to Fortuna are numerous).

[36] Cosmas of Prague, *Chronica Boemorum*, 2.14; *MGH, SSrrG*, pp. 103–4.

[37] *Chronicon*, 3.43 (Afra), 5.18 (Theodosia); *MGH, SSrrG*, pp. 177–78, 247–48.

[38] Cosmas of Prague, *Chronica Boemorum*, 2.44; *MGH, SSrrG*, p. 151.

but abstract and characterless paradigms of subordination or of the idea that all were eventually victims.

Some traces of the strategy of avoiding women led further, beyond the limited mnemonic and mimetic functions served by inclusion. Comments on learning and play are particularly instructive. Quite naturally, the scholarly authors of the histories under review memorialized the erudite accomplishments of their subjects. They wrote about princes who knew letters, practiced psalmody, and excelled in eloquence,[39] about prelates (some of whom, born princes, had been educated at their parents' courts) whose amazing skill in the Liberal Arts served them well as "ruminators," teachers, and interpreters of Scripture,[40] and about lesser clerics who were at home in philosophy and imbued with eloquence.[41] They extolled the learning of those to whom they dedicated their works, and, using the rhetorical device of antiphrasis to convey the opposite of what was said, they drew attention to their own rhetorical skill and knowledge of classical literature (witnessed by quotations and allusions) by proclaiming their own ignorance, ineptitude, and (in the case of Cosmas of Prague) senile dementia.[42] They deplored the ignorance and indiscipline of clerics who, abandoning their cultic duties, went drinking in taverns and meandering at large through houses and public squares and gave themselves over to vanities or, in their crudeness and ignorance, continued to serve in choir, wearing laymen's clothes, living like headless monsters or bestial centaurs.[43] To speak of learning, of course, is to speak of the esthetic network of unseen associations, through allegory and symbols, that encompassed the verbal, visual, and performing arts in a single cult of sacrifice.

The authors give little evidence that women entered this esthetic world, where a man was repeatedly killed by men. "Ritual is nothing more than the regular exercise of 'good' violence," and the supreme acts of ritual violence were restricted to men. And yet women did move through the same worlds of cult and court as they.[44] Formal prohibitions, such as that for-

---

[39] Helmold, *Cronica Slavorum*, 1.32(33); *MGH, SSrrG*, p. 65. Cosmas of Prague, *Chronica Boemorum*, 2.16, 19; *MGH, SSrrG*, pp. 107, 111. See also Ekkehard of Aura's epitaph on Cuono, son of Otto of Nordheim, Duke of Bavaria. *Chronicon* (*a.* 1103); *MGH, SS* 6, p. 225.

[40] E.g., Cosmas of Prague, *Chronica Boemorum*, 1.31; 2.26, 42; *MGH, SSrrG*, pp. 56, 119, 147.

[41] E.g., Cosmas of Prague, *Chronica Boemorum*, 2.28, 29; *MGH, SSrrG*, p. 123.

[42] Cosmas of Prague, *Chronica Boemorum, prol. ad Severum*, 3.59; *MGH, SSrrG*, pp. 1–2, 237.

[43] Helmold, *Cronica Slavorum*, 1.44; *MGH, SSrrG*, p. 88. Cosmas of Prague, *Chronica Boemorum*, 2.26; *MGH, SSrrG*, p. 119.

[44] René Girard, *Violence and the Sacred*, trans. Patrick Gregory (Baltimore, Md.: Johns Hopkins University Press, 1977), p. 37. See Joan M. Ferrante, "The Education of Women in the Middle Ages in Theory, Fact, and Fantasy," in *Beyond Their Sex: Learned Women of the European Past*, ed. Patricia H. Labalme (New York: New York University Press, 1980), with

bidding Gilbertine nuns the use of Latin, except on rare occasions, were
unusual. France, the magnet for men who aspired to be learned, attracted
Cosmas of Prague and Otto of Freising, not to mention among many others Vicelin of Oldenburg, a figure of apostolic magnitude in Helmold's
account.[45] Indeed, going to France to study was so commonly accepted a
practice that a young Jew in Cologne, teetering on the edge of conversion,
used it as an excuse to delay the marriage that had been arranged for him.[46]
There, Heloise and Marie de France were hardly isolated in their erudition.
John of Salisbury, praising Lisieux for its teachers, "divine" in their eloquence, observed that Orléans was even more fortunate; for its ordinary
citizens were born eloquent, and common usage imbued young and old,
men and women, with refinement of speech.[47] Both wives of Henry I, of
England, were celebrated for their learning; they made the Angevin court,
in England or on the continent, a glittering center for scholars, poets, and
musicians.[48] Baudry of Bourgueil portrayed the private chamber of Hen-

---

particular sections on Heloise, Hildegard of Bingen, and Marie de France, pp. 19–34. On
the general acknowledgment of Hildegard of Bingen as *magistra*, see ibid., pp. 24–25.

[45] See the imposing list compiled by Peter Classen of twelfth-century German prelates who
studied in France, in "Zur Geschichte der Frühscholastik in Österreich und Bayern," *Mitteilungen des Instituts für österreichische Geschichtsforschung* 67 (1959): 251. Mr. Bruce Brasington
kindly led me to this article. For Otto of Freising's itinerary in France, see Leopold Josef Grill,
"Das Itinerar Ottos von Freising," in *Festschrift Friedrich Hausmann*, ed. Herwig Ebner (Graz:
Akademische Druck und Verlagsanstalt, 1977), pp. 154–55, 173, 177.

On the Gilbertines, *Institutiones ad Moniales Ordinis Pertinentes*, chap. 25; William Dugdale, ed., *Monasticon Anglicanum* (London: Longman, 1830), vol. 6, pt. 2, p. *lxxxii. Cf. the
instance in which a male anchorite spoke to Christina of Markyate "anglico sermone," although she was evidently able to read the Psalter in Latin. Talbot, ed. and trans., *The Life of
Christina of Markyate A Twelfth Century Recluse*, chap. 41, p. 106. For a general prohibition
against the use of the vernacular by men, see Anselm of Havelberg, *Liber de Ordine Canonicorum*, chap. 18; Migne *PL* 188:1106. On Hildegard of Bingen's bilingualism, Dronke,
*Women Writers of the Middle Ages: A Critical Study of Texts from Perpetua (†203) to Marguerite
Porete (†1310)*, p. 167.

Concerning a parallel instance, the rarity of examples of women's literary activity in the late
Roman world, see Elizabeth A. Clark, "Faltonia Betitia Proba and Her Virgilian Poem: The
Christian Matron as Artist," in *Ascetic Piety and Women's Faith: Essays on Late Ancient Christianity* (Lewiston, N.Y.: Edwin Mellen Press, 1986), pp. 124–47, esp. pp. 134–38, on the
pejorative treatment of Eve.

[46] Hermannus quondam Judaeus, *Opusculum de Conversione Sua*, chap. 10; *MGH*, Quellen
zur Geistesgeschichte, 4:98–99.

[47] *Ep. 110*, W. J. Millor, H. E. Butler, and C.N.L. Brooke, eds., *The Letters of John of Salisbury* (London: Nelson, 1955), 1:176.

[48] Mathilda of Scotland and Adelaide of Brabant. Joachim Bumke, *Mäzene im Mittelalter:
Die Gönner und Auftraggeber der höfischen Literatur in Deutschland, 1150–1300* (Munich:
Beck, 1979), pp. 234–35, referring to these queens as Margaret and Adeliza. The interests
represented were patently historical. See also Karl Leyser, "Frederick Barbarossa, Henry II
and the Hand of St. James," *English Historical Review* 90 (1975): 491. Leyser concludes that
after the death of Henry V of Germany, the Empress Mathilda returned to England with a

ry's sister, Adèle of Blois, as a miracle of learned invention, with its tapestries worked in scenes from sacred and profane history, its ceiling painted with constellations and zodiacal signs, its floor tesselated in a lifelike image of the sea and water creatures, and its bed adorned with statues representing Philosophy and the seven Liberal Arts. It was a complete representation of the cosmos that enveloped the person in the bed, even as the artistic ensemble had unfolded from her will. As the mere names of Eleanor of Aquitaine and her daughters, Marie of Champagne and Alice of Blois indicate, the role that great and powerful women assumed as models of intellectual refinement and fosterers of learning and the arts continued in the land that, above all others, attracted German scholars.

In Germany, the Angevin paradigm reproduced itself at the court of Henry the Lion, Duke of Saxony, whose wife, Mathilda, the daughter of Henry II and Eleanor of Aquitaine, established her own credentials as patroness of artists and poets.[49] Works by Hildegard of Bingen display an astonishing range of learning and literary refinement, and the poems of German troubadours presuppose an acutely discerning audience of women as well as men. Here and there, a learned nun emerges from the shards of a lost world, but seldom without difficulties such as, for example, attend the accounts of Diemont of Wessobrun, who is said to have copied fifty volumes during her career of forty years.[50]

Particles of knowledge can also be recovered concerning the women's convent at Admont, part of a double monastic community in the diocese of Salzburg. Such was its glory, within twenty years of its foundation in

---

great treasure. "Very likely the empress's haul included the autograph copy of a chronicle written for her husband. The manuscript with a picture of their wedding feast in 1114 is now in Corpus Christi College, Cambridge." See below, n. 70.

In his misogyny, Giraldus Cambrensis established a link between women and the arts at a lower social level. Concerning priests who cohabited with women, he contended that the women would, as housekeepers, light the priest's fires and extinguish their virtues. "Mulier enim, ut delicatas coenas et obsonia taceam, ad singulas nundinas caudatas in longum tunicas pulverem trahentes et terram verrentes, pretiosasque vestes quibus non illi solum sed multis placeat, extorquebit; palefridum quoque insignem, sensim et suaviter ambulantem, phaleris et sella deauratis picturis et sculpturis variis ad delicias ornatum." *Gemma Ecclesiastica*, dist. 2, chap. 22; J. S. Brewer, ed., *Giraldi Cambrensis Opera*, Rolls Series, no. 21 (London: Longman, 1862), 2:277. The long trailing dresses of precious fabric and the painted and carved saddles at this social level are worth remembering for comparison with the *objets de luxe* that, as we shall see, were sought after at a more exalted one. See chap. 1, nn. 39–43; chap. 2, nn. 28–29, 37–43, 48, 49; above, n. 3.

[49] Bumke, *Mäzene im Mittelalter*, p. 236. Wilhelm Kellermann, "Bertran de Born und Herzogin Mathilde von Sachsen," in *Études de civilisation médiévale (IXe–XII siècles): Mélanges offerts à Edmonde-René Labande* (Poitiers: C.É.S.C.M., 1974), pp. 452–55.

[50] Raymund Kottje, "Klosterbibliotheken und monastische Kultur in der zweiten Hälfte des 11. Jahrhunderts," *Zeitschrift für Kirchengeschichte*, 80 (1969): 151. *Mittelalterliche Bibliothekskataloge Deutschlands und der Schweiz*, Bd. 3, Teil 1 (Bistum Augsburg) (Munich: Beck, 1932), nos. 60–62, pp. 178–85. I owe these references also to Mr. Bruce Brasington.

1120, that King Bela of Hungary permitted Sophia, his only daughter, to enter the convent (1139), and sent with her all her regalia, "her entire chapel," which presumably included books together with the recorded treasures—relics, vestments, implements of gold and silver, other supplies (including beasts of burden), and, moreover, gold and silver beyond any calculation. A generation later (ca. 1165), the abbot of Admont considered the nuns so "wonderfully literate and practiced in knowledge of sacred Scripture" that on feast days when he could not be present with them he permitted some among the nuns to exhort the others. They were skilled in recording oral discourses directly or from memory, in transcribing texts from writing tablets to manuscripts, and in preparing manuscripts.[51]

In the thirteenth century, Vincent of Beauvais recognized the education of women as a subject of discourse. Yet, even he considered it to be an exercise in moral rather than intellectual formation, designed to inculcate, among other virtues, modesty and fear of men. Prayer and psalmody were major components in Vincent's curriculum for women; the slight, and disapproving attention that he gave to play is notable. (Psalmody, like the regular use of Latin, was forbidden Gilbertine nuns.[52])

The Psalter was a cornerstone of such education as women received. When the child, Bardo, who later became Archbishop of Mainz, was put out to a nurse to teach him his letters, his parents sought a woman named

---

[51] On Sophia, Herbord, *Dialogus de Vita S. Ottonis Episcopi Babenbergensis*, 1.38; Wikarjak, ed., pp. 42–48. Herbord continues to record that later, when Sophia's brother, Geza II, became king, he attempted to coerce her from the cloister. This attempt ended in failure, and the King's envoys left in Admont the precious vestments in purple, adorned with jewels, in which they had hoped to robe her when she reentered the world. On the learning of nuns at Admont, Jakob Wichner, *Kloster Admont und seine Beziehungen zur Wissenschaft und zum Unterricht* (Graz: privately printed, 1892), pp. 16–18. See also Gerlinde Möser-Mersky, *Mittelalterliche Bibliothekskataloge Österreichs*, Bd. 3: *Steiermark* (Graz: Böhlau, 1961), p. 3. I am obliged to Mr. Bruce Brasington for these references to Wichner and Möser-Mersky.

[52] Rosemary Barton Tobin, *Vincent of Beauvais' "De Eruditione Filiorum Nobilium": The Education of Women* (New York: Peter Lang, 1984), pp. 33, 71, 79, 90–91, 143. On the Gilbertines, *Institutiones ad Moniales Ordinis Pertinentes*, chap. 20; Dugdale, ed., p. *lxxx. See also n. 45, concerning the prohibition against Gilbertine nuns using Latin, and n. 83, on the second Lateran Council's prohibition of mixed choirs. On bilingualism at Herrad's convent of St. Odile, as demonstrated in the *Hortus Deliciarum*, see above, chap. 4 after n. 67. Christina of Markyate apparently read, sang, and meditated on the Psalms in Latin, though she conversed with her spiritual mentor in English. Talbot, ed. and trans., *The Life of Christina of Markyate A Twelfth Century Recluse*, chaps. 37, 41; pp. 98, 106.

It is interesting to compare the illiteracy produced by the education of Princess Amalia Gallitzin (1748–1806). She was sent to school in Breslau from early childhood until she was eight or nine years old. There she learned music, but she was not trained to read or write. Afterwards, for eighteen months she attended a French school in Berlin, where she was taught to dance and to converse in French. She also learned the rudiments of ancient mythology. When she returned to her parents' home, she took fright at her own illiteracy and taught herself to read.

Benedicta, who taught him the entire Psalter. As Archbishop, Bardo, in tender gratitude, took Benedicta into his care, becoming, his biographer wrote, the nurse of his nurse. Only small glimmers of the education of women appear, quite incidentally, in our texts. Much as Guibert of Nogent's widowed mother retained a master to teach him, the mother of Thietmar, provost of Hamburg, sought out a master to "imbue him with the divine cult and sacred letters."[53] Cosmas recorded a sister of Duke Boleslaus II, late in the ninth century, who, "schooled in sacred letters" and consecrated abbess by Pope John VIII, established the convent of St. George in Prague, and Judith, an eleventh-century duchess of Bohemia, whose parents sent her to a religious house to learn the Psalter.[54] Helmold likewise recalled a woman in the tenth century, daughter of the ruler of a Slavonic tribe and niece of a bishop of Oldenburg, who was "schooled in sacred letters" at an early age and made abbess at Mecklenburg.[55]

Other whispers of such learning survive in the citations of Virgil and Lucan with which an unnamed abbess adorned ironic, mocking verses that she cast into the teeth of a young prince, in the churches and monuments built and adorned by abbesses and other pious women,[56] and in Adam of Bremen's loving recollection of some works of art that the lady Emma, Bremen's great benefactress, had given that church: two crosses of gold set with gems, and an altar and a chalice brilliant with gold and encrusted with precious stones, all of which contained by weight twenty marks of gold.[57]

---

[53] As an example of the general knowledge of the Psalter, see the *Vita Norberti Magdeburgensis*, chap. 10; *MGH, SS* 12, p. 680. A demon possessing a girl taunted Norbert by uttering the *Song of Songs*, first in Latin and then in French and German translations, although, "dum sana esset, nichil nisi psalterium didicerat." On Bardo of Mainz (980–1051), see the *Vita Sancti Bardonis Archiepiscopi Magontini Prolixior*, chap. 1; Johann Friedrich Böhmer, ed., *Fontes Rerum Germanicarum* (Stuttgart: Cotta, 1855), 3:218. Similarly, an "unlearned" anchoress used the Psalter to teach the young Hildegard to read and chant. Newman, *Saint Hildegard of Bingen: Symphonia*, p. 1. Helmold, *Cronica Slavorum*, 1. 44; MGH SSrrG, p. 88. Helmold's account of how Vicelin was mocked by a priest at the castle of Everstein may indicate an educational experiment encouraged by Vicelin's patroness that failed. *Cronica Slavorum*, 1.42; *MGH, SSrrG*, pp. 84–85.

[54] Cosmas of Prague, *Chronica Boemorum*, 1.22, 40; *MGH, SSrrG*, pp. 42, 73.

[55] Helmold, *Cronica Slavorum*, 1.13; *MGH, SSrrG*, p. 26.

[56] Cosmas of Prague, *Chronica Boemorum*, 2.14; 3.11, 13; *MGH, SSrrG*, pp. 103, 171, 173. Two other women builders were Gerberga II, the abbess of Gandersheim (ca. 1000), who splendidly rebuilt her convent's church, and the Countess Richelda of Hainault (ca. 1070), who built the castle of Bellemont, with all its fortifications, and in the castle, a chapel, which she amply endowed with all necessary things. Wolfer, *Vita Godehardi*, chap. 21; *MGH, SS* 11, p. 182. Giselbert, *Chronicon Hanoniense*; *MGH, SS* 21, p. 493.

[57] Adam of Bremen, *Gesta Hammaburgensium Ecclesiae Pontificum*, 3.46(45); *MGH, SSrrG*, pp. 189–90. Adam had heard that when these treasures were broken up at the command of Archbishop Adalbert, the jewels extracted from the crosses were given to harlots. See the description of St. Edith's construction and adornment of a church at Wilton in the late tenth century, as recalled in the eleventh century. Goscelin, *Vita S. Edithae*, André Wilmart, ed., in

Indeed, even though much has perished, the vestiges of a lost world deliver the names of many princesses and abbesses who were great patronesses and commanded the work of the most expert artisans.[58]

The nuns of St. George's in Prague evidently contributed learning and opulent materials as well as manual dexterity to the making of the "worthy *ornamenta*" for the ministry of the altar that Bishop Henry of Olmütz commissioned from them as a gift for Pope Eugenius III. Their "trained and skillful hands" zealously completed the garniture and sent it to the Pope after the Bishop's death. Other texts indicate that the Pope's brief words of thanks signify a gift that included "whatever things were necessary to sacred offices," perhaps books as well as pontifical insignia such as a crozier and pectoral cross, candlesticks and vessels in precious metals, and a comprehensive inventory of vestments, from liturgical sandals to miter in gold, silver, silk, and jewels. The nuns at St. George's thus mastered not only the wealth devoted to a gift that even Eugenius, accustomed to magnificent display, considered notable, but also the iconographic knowledge and technical skills required to execute the lavish and diverse ensemble.[59]

---

*Analecta Bollandiana* 56 (1938): 5–101, 265–307. Edith commanded Benno of Trier, one of the priests assigned to educate her, to paint murals, and thus "totam vero basilicam tam solaria quam parietes omni colore pictura per manum artificiosi Benne decoravit, passionis dominice monumenta, ut in corde depinxerat, imaginata exposuit" (p. 87). See also the verses (met. 8, p. 89), celebrating the sumptuous materials, the vast number of figures in the decorative program, and the light that beamed through the sapphire blue glass.

[58] I shall take my references chiefly from Peter Lasko, *Ars Sacra, 800–1200* (Harmondsworth, Eng.: Penguin, 1972). Beginning in the tenth century, one can identify the Abbess Adelheid of Quedlinburg (and three other convents), a granddaughter of the Emperor Otto I, and her sister, the Abbess Mathilda of Essen (Lasko, p. 82). From the early eleventh century, the names of the Abbesses Judith of Ringelheim (sister of the great patron, Bishop Bernward of Hildesheim), Uta of Niedermünster, and Theophanu of Essen are known, together with that of the Empress Kunegunde (Lasko, pp. 117, 131–32, 136–37). From the twelfth century, one knows the Abbess Agnes of Quedlinburg, the Duchess Mathilda of Saxony and Bavaria, and the Empress Beatrice, wife of Frederick Barbarossa and co-donor with him of many treasures to the church at Aachen, including its celebrated chandelier (Lasko, pp. 79, 204, 207, 216, 218). Conrad of Hirsau compiled his *Speculum Virginum* on commission from an Abbess Theodora. C. R. Dodwell, *Painting in Europe, 800 to 1200* (Baltimore, Md.: Penguin Books, 1971), p. 172. Naturally, one should add the name of Hildegard of Bingen's male scribe, Volmar, who is represented with his patroness in the celebrated Lucca manuscript of her *Liber Divinorum Operum* (Lucca, Bibliotheca Statale MS. 1942).

[59] Eugenius III, *ep. 444*; Migne *PL* 180:1470. On the sumptuous fabrics in the papal travelling equipment in 1147/8, see Ernald, *Vita Bernardi*, 2.22; *MGH, SS* 26, p. 109. John of Salisbury recalled that Eugenius had the bed for Louis VII of France and Eleanor of Aquitaine adorned "de suo preciosissimis vestibus" as part of his effort to reconcile them. *Historia Pontificalis*, chap. 29; Marjorie Chibnall, ed., *John of Salisbury's Memoirs of the Papal Court* (London: Nelson, 1956), p. 61. That *ornamenta* could designate fabrics and other treasures is indicated by Frederick Barbarossa's description to Eugenius III of his royal coronation in Aachen. He was anointed and enthroned, and then, "nos vero in multiplicibus regiae dignitatis ornamentis, quibus partim per laicorum principum obsequia, partim per venerandas

Education was described as a form of play,[60] and the strategy of exclusion, marked in regard to the esthetic world of knowledge, was total in the sphere of play, whether sacred or profane. Describing the translation of the relics of St. Adalbert, which occurred in 1039, Cosmas of Prague repeated the order of procession. With the clergy and all the inhabitants of Prague (*universa plebs*) attending, Duke Bracizlaus I and Bishop Severus took first place, carrying the Martyr's relics on their shoulders. They were followed by abbots bearing the relics of Adalbert's five companions; then, by arch-priests with the body of his brother, Gaudentius of Gnesen; twelve priests struggling to bear a cross which Duke Mesco had given (and which was three times his own weight in gold); bearers of three great figured tablets of gold, set with gems, which normally adorned the altar where Adalbert's body rested; and, finally, an immense throng of noblemen fettered with manacles and collars of iron.[61] The absence of women, even of great ladies and abbesses, from this account of the procession is arresting, particularly since in another passage Cosmas reported that Duke Bracizlaus II was welcomed into Prague by mixed choirs of girls and youths.[62]

Associated with childhood, the word "play" was sometimes used to excuse or diminish the importance of an action. Perhaps this trivialization was appropriate when in the Crusader kingdom of Jerusalem noble youths affected the sport of driving nails through their own hands and arms. However, at least in one instance, the parents of boys below the age of puberty who were being held as hostages urged, and gave gifts to insure, that their sons be allowed to practice their childish games with their peers.

---

pontificum benedictiones vestiti sumus, regium animum induimus. . . .' "; Migne *PL* 180:1637. When he founded the monastery of Admont, Archbishop Gebhard of Salzburg (1060–88), sent "ornamenta complura auro, argento et serico valde preciosa, vestimenta scilicet sacerdotalia, libros, calices et queque divinis ministeriis necessaria." Gerlinde Möser-Mersky, *Mittelalterliche Bibliothekskataloge Österreichs*, Bd. 3: *Steiermark* (Graz: Böhlau, 1961), p. 1. An extensive inventory of "ornatus pontificalis apparatus" occurs in a diploma of Bishop Werner of Münster (1137), in Heinrich August Erhard, *Regesta Historiae Westfaliae*, Bd. 2 (Münster: Regensberg, 1851), p. 22. One indication of the magnificence with which Eugenius was surrounded occurs in Bernard of Clairvaux's reference to humility: "Nulla splendidior gemma, in omni praecipue ornatu Summi Pontificis." *De Consideratione*, 2.6.13; J. Leclercq and H. M. Rochais, eds., *S. Bernardi Opera* (Rome: Editiones Cistercienses, 1963), 3:421. See chap. 7, nn. 67, 78.

[60] Cosmas of Prague applied the same classical tag, "lusisti satis," to the study of grammar and dialectic and to wenching and feasting. *Chronica Boemorum* 1.9, 3.59; *MGH, SSrrG*, pp. 21, 237. See also Lambert of Hersfeld's comment on Archbishop Anno of Cologne, *Annales* (*a.* 1075); *MGH, SSrrG*, p. 242: "Is in Babenbergensi aecclesia in ludo tam divinarum quam secularium litterarum enutritus. . . ." Cf. Helmold, *Cronica Slavorum*, 1.42; *MGH, SSrrG*, p. 85, concerning the young Vicelin: "Non hunc ludi, non epulae cepto proposito detraxerant, quin aut legeret aut dictaret vel certe scriberet."

[61] Cosmas of Prague, *Chronica Boemorum*, 2.5; *MGH, SSrrG*, p. 90.

[62] Cosmas of Prague, *Chronica Boemorum*, 2.50; *MGH, SSrrG*, p. 157.

It was important for them to avoid the uncertainties of leisure and the tedium of captivity; their tender years required such nurture. It was considered unusual when the young St. Vicelin abandoned games and feasts to devote himself to study. John of Salisbury recalled how, in Antiquity, Rome's young men had prepared themselves by playing imaginary war games to triumph over actual adversities, games that their twelfth-century counterparts had every reason to know could be fatal.[63]

I have found no references to the importance of play in the nurture of girls, and much the same asymmetry characterizes data about the games of later years. Our texts allude to a diverse repertory of forms of adult play. In some, the comic shades into the sardonic or the grotesque, as in the savage bludgeoning that Bishop Jaromir-Gebehard of Prague and his attendants laughingly inflicted on the Bishop John,[64] or the atrocities of war described by Rahewin as games—a man whose hands and feet had been hacked away forced to crawl through the streets as a laughingstock, or the ballgame played by Barbarossa's soldiers in full view of the walls of Crema with the severed heads of Cremese soldiers.[65] Mockery of a captive made to sing for his life, the jokes and pranks regularly heaped upon the insane, and a woman's (imputed) contrivance of public humiliation to make her

[63] William of Tyre, *Chronicon*, 21.1; *Corp. Christ., continuatio mediaevalis*, 63A, p. 961. Lambert of Hersfeld, *Annales* (*a.* 1076). *MGH, SSrrG*, p. 274. Helmold, *Cronica Slavorum*, 1.42; *MGH, SSrrG*, p. 85. Compare, with Vicelin's aversion to play, Bernard of Clairvaux's comment on St. Malachy. *Vita Sancti Malachiae*, 1.1; Leclercq and Rochais, eds., *S. Bernardi Opera*, 3:310: "Non impatiens magisterii, non fugitans disciplinae, non lectionis fastidiens, non ludorum denique appetens, quod vel maxime illa aetas dulce ac familiare habere solet." John of Salisbury, *Metalogicon*, 3.10; Webb, ed., p. 162. For one example of fatalities that occurred "militiam ludendo," see Franciscus Salesius Schmitt, "Neue und alte Hildebrand-anekdoten aus den *Dicta Anselmi*," *Studi Gregoriani* 5 (1956): 14. See also, concerning the revolt in Cologne against Archbishop Anno, Lambert of Hersfeld, *Annales* (*a.* 1074); *MGH, SSrrG*, p. 189: "Econtra hi qui obsidebantur nunc supplicando, nunc pollicendo, quod diligentissime quesitum, si inveniretur, ipsis tradituri essent, callide ludebant operam perurgentium, usquequo archiepiscopum longius evectum atque in tuta iam loca progressum esse arbitrarentur."

[64] Cosmas of Prague, *Chronica Boemorum*, 2.27; *MGH, SSrrG*, pp. 120–22.

[65] Rahewin, *Gesta Friderici*, 4.55(45), 69(59); *MGH, SSrrG*, pp. 293, 315. The Cremese responded in kind, dismembering some of their captives in full view on the walls and hanging others in chains from the walls. Becker comments that the details that Rahewin supplied concerning the atrocities at Crema provide a surprising contrast with his generally sparse method of description. Dietrich Becker, *Die Belagerung von Crema bei Rahwin, im Ligurinus und im Carmen de gestis Frederici I. imperatoris in Lombardia. Untersuchungen zur literarischen Form staufischer Geschichtsschreibung* (Mannheim: N.p., 1975), pp. 201–3. See also Ekkehard of Aura, *Chronicon* (*a.* 1106). *MGH, SS* 6, p. 236: "Igitur mense Iunio iam fere mediante, rex Heinricus [IV] cum exercitu copioso, id est 20 milibus, Coloniam Agrippinam obsedit; sed cum esset, ut dictum est, multum per omnem modum munita, tres aut quattuor inibi ebdomadas casso pene labore consumpsit, excepto quod, ut fieri solet, iuventus, utpote morae impatiens, nonunquam pro muris concurrens, ludo crudeli fugat alterutrum vel sternit."

bridegroom the butt of ribald humor were all in the acknowledged repertoire of play.[66]

Generally in passing references, our texts represent many more benign
forms of play, such as gambling, splashing and swimming in a river,[67] "profane tricks,"[68] banqueting,[69] theater including minstrelsy and panto-
mime,[70] and hunting.[71] Princely entertainments called forth consummate
pleasure, "unending sports."[72] Apart from the imputation of rendering her
husband impotent by magical charms, which the Countess Mathilda dis-
proved by exhibiting herself on an elevated platform, naked as she came
from her mother's womb,[73] women enter none of these descriptions of
play, grotesque or benign, in which violence is persistent.

The esthetic exclusion of women from histories therefore corresponds
with the absence of women from play and, more precisely, from forms of
play that were essential to forming and exhibiting male identity and to
establishing relations among men. Thus, we return to the actors in the
continual, reciprocating cycles of honor and revenge. Anthropological
studies of what some have called "the male esthetic" and others "the poetics

[66] Cosmas of Prague, *Chronica Boemorum*, 1.38, 2.32; *MGH, SSrrG*, pp. 70, 129. Rahewin,
*Gesta Friderici*, 4.43(36); *MGH, SSrrG*, p. 283.

[67] On gambling, see chap. 1, n. 39; chap. 7, n. 37. On swimming, see Cosmas of Prague,
*Chronica Boemorum*, 2.43; *MGH, SSrrG*, p. 149.

[68] Cosmas of Prague, *Chronica Boemorum*, 3.1; *MGH, SSrrG*, p. 161.

[69] Helmold, *Chronica Slavorum*, 1.42; *MGH, SSrrG*, p. 85. Adam of Bremen, *Gesta Hammaburgensis Ecclesiae Pontificum*, 3.39(38); *MGH, SSrrG*, pp. 181–83.

[70] Adam of Bremen, *Gesta Hammaburgensis Ecclesiae Pontificum*, 3.39(38); *MGH, SSrrG*,
pp. 181–83. Cf. Cosmas of Prague, *Chronica Boemorum*, 3.1; *MGH, SSrrG*, p. 161 (on semi-
pagan dramatizations). To illustrate the splendor of the marriage between Henry V of Germany and Mathilda of England, Ekkehard of Aura wrote: "Dona autem, quae diversi reges
atque innumerabiles primates domno imperatori in ipsis nuptiis miserunt, vel quae ipse im-
perator ex se innumerabili multitudini ioculatorum et istrionum atque diverso generi diver-
sarum gentium distribuit, quemadmodum nullus camerarius ipsius vel qui recepit vel qui
distribuit potuit numerare, ita nullus eiusdem imperatoris chronographus potuit litteris com-
prehendere." *Chronicon* (a. 1114); *MGH, SS* 6, p. 248. See above, n. 48.

[71] See the wonderstruck description given by Rahewin of the hunting park created by Frederick Barbarossa. *Gesta Friderici*, 4.86; *MGH, SSrrG*, pp. 344–45, and also on Frederick's love
of hunting, pp. 343–44. The contrast between the games of boys and the conflicts of men
suggests a trivializing of play (*Gesta Friderici*, 2.35, p. 144: " 'Ludus,' ait, 'hic puerorum, non
virorum videtur concertatio.' "), but compare Rahewin's comment on Frederick as a hunter
(*Gesta Friderici*, 4.86, p. 344): "Cum ludendum est, regiam tantisper sequestrat severitatem,
eiusque temperamenti est, ut sit remissio non vicians, austeritas non cruentans." See also
Adam of Bremen's description of the mayhem and unnatural practices induced by drunkenness among the unconverted Scandinavian peoples. *Gesta Hammaburgensis Ecclesiae Pontificum*, 3.56(55); *MGH, SSrrG*, p. 201: "Nam contentiones et pugnas, oblocutiones et blas-
phemias et quaecumque maiora scelera commiserint in ebrietate, in crastinum illi pro ludo
habent."

[72] Cosmas, *Chronica Boemorum*, 3.23; *MGH, SSrrG*, p. 190.

[73] Cosmas, *Chronica Boemorum*, 2.32; *MGH, SSrrG*, p. 129.

of manhood"[74] provide instructive parallels with other societies organized by the principle of male dominance and motivated by desire of honor and fear of humiliation.

In them, as in the society with which we are concerned, the essential fact was that honor was continually at risk. Consequently, each player in the game of honor was always vulnerable, always in need of estimable allies. The simulated battles of sport, such as gambling and athletic contests, and actual combat were means by which each player demonstrated the virtues of manhood and thereby his power to smite enemies with fear. Thus, he manifested his worthiness as an ally against common enemies in the struggle of men against men. The virtues noted by anthropologists include many of those that we have considered as spiritual virtues, including strength, wit, self-control, and courage. They entailed contempt for self, as far as self could be touched by pain, danger, and death itself, and contempt also for the judgment of the many when honor was at stake. As in ascetic discipline, acknowledgment of fear by warriors was fundamental to the glory of triumphing over immense odds and, in that unequal struggle, perfecting the "moral purity" demanded by love of honor, the purity of "masculine excellence" that engaged and strengthened the adherence of allies. As in ascetic disciplines, there was an idealization of nobility and of hardship as an enobling school.[75]

As in the theater—whether on the stage or in that ascetic amphitheater where "we are made a spectacle unto the world, and to angels, and to men" (1 Cor. 4:9)—the performance of manly deeds was for an audience. Here, the audience consisted chiefly of other players in the game of honor and retaliation. To be sure, women could observe the play, and mockery by them was among the worst humiliations that could befall a man. But, sweet as their praise might be to the victors, yet sweeter was the praise of worthy foes and allies who had been proven free of the corrosive weakness of women, those whom one counted as brothers in risk.

It is worth recalling the shreds of information, again ambivalent, provided by Herrad's *Hortus Deliciarum*. To be sure, fascination with play is indicated by an unprecedented representation of a marionette show of warriors before Solomon. But severe disapproval is also obvious in the statement that the "vanity of vanities" is designated by this "play of monstrosities," and, moreover, in the spin of Fortune's Wheel, represented below it. In fact, the play before Solomon and Fortune's Wheel, the demons

[74] The phrase, "the male esthetic," occurs in Robert and Janice A. Keefe, *Walter Pater and the Gods of Disorder* (Athens: Ohio University Press, 1988), p. 106. Michael Herzfeld, *The Poetics of Manhood: Contest and Identity in a Cretan Mountain Village* (Princeton, N.J.: Princeton University Press, 1985), p. 188: "the arts of manhood."

[75] Herzfeld, *The Poetics of Manhood: Contest and Identity in a Cretan Mountain Village*, pp. 131, 253, 255.

playing around the Ladder of Virtues and toppling unsteady souls, and the Sirens luring Ulysses and his men to their ruin all "admonish us to contempt of the world and love of Christ."[76] The whole inventory of play—feasts, drinking bouts, buffooneries, hostile pranks, and the like—into which irreligious clerics were drawn with lascivious youths, Herrad recorded, had reduced the kingdom to turmoil and deserved reprobation. The lowest of the low were jesters, who had no hope of salvation, since their whole intent was to be ministers of Satan, and actors who, like jesters, practiced transvestism, women dressing as men, and men, as women.[77] Yet the play of war is everywhere in Herrad's pages, and seldom more vividly portrayed than in the conflict of Virtues and Vices, violence of women allied against women mirroring that normally exercised in battle between cohorts of men.

## ESTHETIC RATIONALES FOR SUPPRESSION

We have established the obvious: the exclusion of women from the performance of sacrifice, the cult's focal act of violence, and thus exclusion from historical accounts of persons and classes privileged to enact that sacrifice. We now turn from what was suppressed to the reasons for suppression. The point of departure for this part of our discussion must be the intended theatrical character of histories.

We have emphasized the value placed on visual realism in the representational and performing arts, and in historical writing (chap. 2, n. 54). We now expand that observation. Historical writings were considered verbal counterparts of the works of painters who portrayed great deeds on sepulchral monuments. Some conceived a goal of vividness far greater than monuments could give.[78] One author wrote that, true to ancient models, he wanted to simulate the art of poets and, using the skill of historians, to renew past events through a narrative so knowing and vividly representational that readers could see them before their very eyes.[79] Yet, if readers

---

[76] Illustrations nos. 294, 299; 1:200, 202.

[77] Text nos. 635, 1155; 2:305, 492.

[78] Helmold, *Cronica Slavorum*, 2.100; *MGH, SSrrG*, p. 198. See also *Vita Godefridi Comitis Capenbergensis*, prol.; *MGH, SS* 12, p. 515.

[79] Balderic, *Gesta Alberonis*, chap. 16; *MGH, SS* 8, p. 252, aspiring to parity with Virgil, Statius, Livy, and Josephus. Citing Quintilian, John of Salisbury used allusions to painting to express the same thought. *Metalogicon*, 1.24; Webb, ed., p. 54. See the related statements by Otto of Freising. *Chronicon*, 8.20; *MGH, SSrrG*, p. 423: "Ponamus ante oculos illud tempus [the Last Judgment] quasi presens omnesque imperatorum seu regum civitatis illius [Babylon] ordines considerantes in persona omnium. . . ." *Chronicon*, 8.22, 8.33, p. 452: "Si reges vel imperatores terrenos in gloria sua fluxa et transitoria cum admiratione et quadam hilaritate videmus, quam inestimabili gaudio suffusos, ineffabili mentis iubilo repletos estimabimus, qui regem regum, creatorem universorum, in decore suo et gloria incomparabili et inmare-

or hearers were to have the impression of seeing the events portrayed, authors too had to write "with such unity of order and elegance of style as if [they] had seen them with [their] own eyes. . . . For this reason [the author being, or assuming the stance of, an eyewitness] we are used to calling a written text 'history' from *hysteron*, which in Greek means 'to see.' "[80]

When he observed this connection between seeing events and writing history, Rahewin noted that authors could achieve the illusion of being eyewitnesses only at the cost of recounting a few events out of the many that had occurred. And other authors, drawing further analogies between historical writing and the visual and performing arts, likewise emphasized the plasticity of materials as writers carved them into texts by selective inclusion and omission. Swayed by love or hope of favor, by hatred or fear, one of them noted, those there were few indeed among delineators of histories who paid to events the debt of an entirely faithful description; many were those who called light darkness and night, day.[81]

The sequestration of women from our accounts testifies to an esthetic attitude that molded the texts more, almost certainly, than the events recorded. It was common for ascetic writers, by the very act of denunciation, to document behavior that they condemned. Thus, when Gerhoch of Reichersberg railed against clergy bringing their women with them to theatrical performances in churches,[82] and when the Second Lateran Council (1139) forbade nuns to sing in the same choirs as monks (canon 27),[83] they testified that the mingling in play of which they disapproved actually occurred. However, there was also a range of attitudes that governed the inclusion of historical materials, which for example made it possible for Cosmas of Prague to delete all women from the translation of St. Adalbert's relics, even while recalling that mixed choirs greeted Duke Bra-

---

scibili caelesti angelorum et hominum stipatum milicia videbunt?" On painting, see also chap. 3, n. 86. See also chap. 2, n. 54; chap. 7, n. 27.

[80] Rahewin, *Gesta Friderici*, 2.41(26); *MGH, SSrrG*, p. 150.

[81] Helmold, *Cronica Slavorum*, 2. pref. 96; *MGH, SSrrG*, pp. 188–89.

[82] *De Investigatione Antichristi*, 1.5; *MGH, Ldl* 3, p. 315.

[83] Karl Joseph von Hefele and Henri Leclercq, *Histoire des Conciles* (Paris: Letouzey et Ané, 1912), vol. 5, pt. 1, p. 733. On Gerhoch's judgment that male and female voices should not be mixed because they could not sound the same tone, see *Exposit. in Cant. Moysis*, 1.20; Migne *PL* 194:1026. See the *Tractatus de Ordine Vitae*, 2.9; Migne *PL* 184:566: "Vox ipsa non remissa, non fracta, nihil femineum sonans (qualem multi gravitatis specie simulare consueverunt), sed formam quamdam et regulam ac succum virilem reservans. Hoc est enim pulchritudinem vivendi tenere, convenientia cuique sexui et personae reddere." This passage follows obloquies on the *sodomitica libido* and on those who love and praise handsome men (*homines*) because of their physical beauty and despise the deformed (2.8–9, col. 565). See below, n. 117. See also the prohibition against psalmody by the Gilbertine nuns, above n. 45. Anselm of Havelberg approved mixed choruses. *Liber de Ordine Canonicorum*, chap. 8; Migne *PL* 188:1101. Christina of Markyate heard a heavenly choir composed of men and virgins. Talbot, ed. and trans., *The Life of Christina of Markyate A Twelfth Century Recluse*, chap. 38, pp. 98, 100.

cizlaus II on his ceremonial entrance into Prague; and some in the same range of attitudes led Rahewin to select as a sign of impending disaster—together with apparitions of monsters by night, and wild beasts ranging through church buildings—a procession of boys and girls through the midst of the city, burlesquing authentic litanies with their pranks.[84]

At issue, regardless of facts, were the limits of empathy. A consequence of play is its power, through empathy, to bring about an exchange of personae by the players, the transformation of one person into another. For this reason, in religious devotions and liturgy where the human joins with the divine, "the concept of play merges quite naturally with that of holiness."[85] Yet for the authors of the historical texts under review, the demarcation between man and woman was at least as sharp as that between Christian and pagan. The character of history as visualization coincides with this division. In his panegyric on the spiritual awakening of his day as the harbinger of a new, resplendent age of holiness, Otto of Freising mentioned women only by way of emphasizing the sternness with which male religious avoided their presence.[86] The ascetic writers of our texts venerated figures like Bishop Lievizo of Bremen, whose chastity was so great that he rarely allowed himself to be seen by women, and the five saintly martyrs of Poland, St. Adalbert's disciples, to whom "the face of woman was execrable."[87] St. Ansgar's memory was venerated centuries after his death, in part for the exhortation he addressed to nuns, extolling their physical virginity yet deploring the tendency of many to be harlots in their minds.[88]

Reinforced by the Gregorian Reform's loathing of clerical marriage as

---

[84] Rahewin, *Gesta Friderici*, 4.16(13); *MGH, SSrrG*, p. 255.

[85] Johan Huizinga, *Homo Ludens: A Study of the Play Element in Culture* (Boston: Beacon, 1962), p. 25.

[86] *Chronicon*, 7.35; *MGH, SSrrG*, pp. 370–71. The *Life* of Christina of Markyate preserves an instance in which the habitual avoidance of the sight of a woman was divinely subverted, with the result that Christina and the hermit Roger became one heart and one soul in charity, and did not fear to live together in the same dwelling. Talbot, ed. and trans., *The Life of Christiana of Markyate A Twelfth Century Recluse*, chap. 38, pp. 100, 102.

[87] Adam of Bremen, *Gesta Hammaburgensis Ecclesiae Pontificum*, 2.29(27); *MGH, SSrrG*, p. 90. Cosmas of Prague, *Chronica Boemorum*, 1.38; *MGH, SSrrG*, p. 69.

Cf. Otto of Bamberg's act of piety in lifting and burying with his own hands the decaying corpse of a woman (whom he recognized as his sister because she was a daughter of Adam and of the Church): "I carry dead a woman whom, when she was alive, I ought to have shuddered to look upon." Herbord, *Dialogus de Vita S. Ottonis Episcopi Babenbergensis*, 1.32; Wikarjak, ed., p. 35. Herbord also portrayed Otto as Martha because of his ministrations and hospitality. *Dialogus de Vita S. Ottonis Episcopi Babenbergensis*, 1.41, 42; Wikarjak, ed., pp. 50, 52. Yet Otto discharged priestly and episcopal functions that brought him into dealings with women, as when he bestowed the monastic veil on Hildegard of Bingen. The sequestration of Gilbertine canons and nuns was so strict that at the Eucharist recipient and ministrant could not see each other. *Acta Sanctorum*, 4 Feb., 1:573.

[88] Adam of Bremen, *Gesta Hammaburgensis Ecclesiae Pontificum*, 1.44(46); *MGH, SSrrG*, p. 46.

"abominable" (*nefanda*),[89] this ancient aversion of celibate men to the company of women also distinguished the piety of male saints in later centuries, including, most profoundly, that of St. Francis of Assisi. In the celebrated temptation of his youth, St. Thomas Aquinas glimpsed a "most beautiful, impudent girl, as though a serpent with a human face." Ever after, he avoided the sight of women (unless constrained by need or utility), just as human beings keep their distance from vipers.[90] With such ideals in mind, historical writers turned repeatedly to the sexual promiscuity of the pagans, their concubinage, incest, fornication, and other practices that the writers regarded as contrary to nature. Otto of Bamberg represented both his own chastity and the dawning of a new age when, baptizing the Pomeranians, he not only divided the children, men, and women into separate groups, but also draped curtains in a circle around the font to screen the neophyte, naked in the baptismal font, from the baptizing priests. "The priest, standing at the screen, heard rather than saw that someone was in the water and, opening the curtain a narrow space," he immersed and anointed the baptisand's head and imposed a white robe.[91]

Confusion of gender roles was mistrusted or condemned. For example, in Normandy austere clerics attacked the effeminacy of the long hair and elaborate, trailing garments affected by knights,[92] and in England the Cistercian, Ailred of Rievaulx, condemned the theatricality of male singers in choir who set aside the vigor of the masculine voice in favor of the delicacies of the feminine and, with artifice, twisted and contorted their tones to suit. Using terms borrowed from St. Cyprian, Gerhoch of Reichersberg inveighed against men who "degraded" their virility to perform roles of women in the theater, "as though they were ashamed to be men."[93] (Many passages in John of Salisbury's writings likewise witness to his contempt for effeminacy.[94])

[89] See Adam of Bremen, *Gesta Hammaburgensis Ecclesiae Pontificum*, 3.30(29); *MGH*, *SSrrG*, p. 172.

[90] Bernard Gui, *Vita S. Thomae Aquinatis*, chap. 7; in D. Prümmer, ed., *Fontes Vitae S. Thomae Aquinatis* (Toulouse: Ed. Privat, Bibliopolam, 1929), fasc. 3, pp. 174–75.

[91] Herbord, *Dialogus de Vita S. Ottonis Episcopi Babenbergensis*, 2. 16. Wikarjak, ed., p. 89.

[92] E.g., Ordericus Vitalis, *Historia Ecclesiastica*, 8.10; Marjorie Chibnall, ed. and trans., *The Ecclesiastical History of Ordericus Vitalis* (Oxford: Clarendon, 1973), 4:188.

[93] *Speculum Charitatis*, chap. 23; Migne *PL* 195:571. *De Investigatione Antichristi*, 1.5; *MGH*, *Ldl* 3, p. 316. Cf. Cyprian, *ep. 1*; 8; Migne *PL* 2:215: ". . . quisquis virum in feminam magis fregerit." The same phrase occurs in a sermon of Maximus of Turin. On this passage, and on the late Antique observances in which transvestism and animal disguise featured, together with some medieval sequels, see Dieter Harmening, *Superstitio: Überlieferungs- und theoriegeschichtliche Untersuchungen zur kirchlich-theologischen Aberglaubensliteratur des Mittelalters* (Berlin: Erich Schmidt, 1979), pp. 138–43.

[94] E.g., John of Salisbury, *Policraticus*, 5.10, 6.14, 8.6; Clement C. J. Webb, ed., *Ioannis Saresberiensis Episcopi Carnotensis . . . Policratici . . . Libri VIII* (Oxford: Clarendon, 1909),

I have already spoken about the limited mimetic functions that historical representations of women were permitted to have for men. These few additional references illustrate a fundamental barrier to all play, including that of mimesis. Although Otto forbade Pomeranian mothers to continue their practice of female infanticide, on the argument that God created both male and female, and although his disciples believed that he loved them "with a maternal, rather than a paternal, love," neither his preaching nor his conduct modified the segregation of gender that blocked the translation of personae between men and women.[95] The same lack of confusion can be understood in praise of women for acting in a manly fashion, or for possessing "manly spirit and masculine virtue."[96]

I do not wish to discount the effect of misogyny on the segregation with which we are concerned. A collection of proverbs from the Middle Ages generally illustrates how commonly women were associated with anger, levity, deceit (including vice masked by beauty), and malice. Proverbs concerning men are more diverse in reference to virtues, stages of life, and kinds of action.[97] The authors of our texts were certainly not immune to the common and persistent attitudes that gave rise to these proverbs. Yet it must also be evident that the texts under review lack the ironies, tirades, and even the theological orientations of frank misogyny. In his account of how the human condition descended into misery, Otto of Freising omitted all mention of Eve,[98] and the only contrast that I have found between the

---

1:329; 2:39–40, 250. See also *ep. 206*, in Millor and Brooke, eds., *The Letters of John of Salisbury*, 2:308: "Illuc [in heaven] voluptas mollis et effeminata non habebit accessum, ubi carnem in veritate naturae permanentem spiritulis implebit vigor et exultatio angelica permulcebit."

Giraldus Cambrensis did not intend to witness to the credit of William Longchamps, Bishop of Ely, when he reported that the great prelate returned to her mother, as virginal as she had come to him, a girl who had been offered to him disguised as a boy. *De Vita Galfridi Archiepiscopi Eboracensis*, 2.12; Brewer, ed., pp. 411–12. See also 2.19; ibid., p. 429.

[95] Ebo, *Vita S. Ottonis Episcopi Babenbergensis*, 3.19; Wikarjak, ed., p. 128. Herbord, *Dialogus de Vita S. Ottonis Episcopi Babenbergensis*, 2.18; Wikarjak, ed., p. 95. See also Ekkehard of Aura's reference to Godfrey of Bouillon: ". . . populo Dei, quem paterna sollicitudine curabat, materna pietate fovebat. . . ." *Chronicon (a.* 1100); *MGH, SS* 6, p. 219. See also Rupert of Deutz, *Commentum in Apocalypsim*, 1.1; Migne *PL* 169:838: ". . . quia in illa tali genitura, beatae apostolorum animae, quasi matres exstiterunt, quippe quae morienti Domino Jesu Christo, donec resurgeret, materno affectu condoluerunt."

[96] E.g., above, nn. 22, 31. Lambert of Hersfeld, *Vita Lulli*, chap. 2; *MGH, SSrrG*, p. 309. Cunihild, the mother of St. Lull, was "virilis admodum animi et masculae virtutis femina." In later life, Lambert commented, her example, together with that of her daughter, aroused many men and women to embrace the ascetic discipline.

[97] Hans Walther, *Proverbia Sensentiaeque Latinitatis Medii Aevi*, II/2 (Göttingen: Vandenhoeck and Ruprecht, 1964), pp. 959–63, and II/9 (Göttingen: Vandenhoeck and Ruprecht, 1986), pp. 796, 799, 800–802.

[98] Cf. *Chronicon*, 4.14; *MGH, SSrrG*, p. 201, an allusion given Otto by his quoted source.

physical beauty and the inward deformity of a person pertains to a man.[99] The association of women with dark powers is illustrated by one atrocity committed during the insurrections in Cologne in 1074. Rioters killed a woman by throwing her from the walls because she was rumored to have used magical arts to drive people (*homines*) mad. But among many atrocities the chronicler mentioned only this one as a crime that would be avenged.[100] As I noted, it was well known that Pope Eugenius III esteemed Hildegard of Bingen "more than lovingly, with a special feeling of charity," and contrasted the wonders divinely revealed to her with his own faltering use of the key of knowledge.[101] The standard repertoire of Christian misogyny is quite absent from the texts under review.

Even so, the evidence of our texts is clear that this segregation was esthetic—that it was grounded in the feelings—and that its Archimedean point was not the mnemonic or the mimetic functions of history but a third: the hedonic.

History was written to give pleasure. Its hedonic function explained its mimetic one in so far as it produced the self-forgetting and desire needed to pass from recollection to emulation. Certainly, the pleasure of history could be considered a recondite pastime, like the singing of a song or the gleeful derision of critics,[102] or a courtly recreation to be mentioned in the same breath as reading sayings of the philosophers, banqueting, and casting dice.[103] For others, philosophy enhanced with its deep colors the pleasures of history. Even though Cosmas of Prague contrasted the clear, thin drink of history with philosophy's deep, strong draft, the intersection of the two enterprises in the minds of readers was assumed, whether in a prosaic, allusive fashion as by Cosmas and Adam of Bremen, or in the actual structure of the work, as when Otto of Freising mingled philosophical excursus with historical for the sake of pleasure (*voluptas*) and to draw his readers to the delight of the high and hidden reasons of things.[104] The authors' conventional, and frequent, disclaimers to eloquence, and praise

[99] See below, nn. 114, 115.

[100] Lambert of Hersfeld, *Annales* (*a*. 1074); *MGH*, *SSrrG*, p. 190.

[101] See above, n. 4.

[102] Cf. Cosmas of Prague, *Chronicon Boemorum, prol. ad Severum*, 2.51; *MGH*, *SSrrG*, pp. 1, 159. See also Adam of Bremen's despair of being able to please his envious rivals. Plainly, he underestimated their delight in finding fault. *Gesta Hammaburgensis Ecclesiae Pontificum, ep. ad Liemarum*; *MGH*, *SSrrG*, p. 3.

[103] Adam of Bremen, *Gesta Hammaburgensis Ecclesiae Pontificum* 3.39(38); *MGH*, *SSrrG*, pp. 181–83. See also chap. 1, n. 3.

[104] Cosmas of Prague, *Chronica Boemorum, ep. ad Clementem*; *MGH*, *SSrrG*, p. 81. Adam of Bremen, *Gesta Hammaburgensis Ecclesiae Pontificum, ep. ad Liemarum*; *MGH*, *SSrrG*, p. 2. Otto of Freising, *Gesta Friderici*, prol., *MGH*, *SSrrG*, p. 12. Cf. Otto's *Chronicon*, 8. prol.; *MGH*, *SSrrG*, pp. 392–93, where Otto defended his mingling of historical accounts with the difficult and hidden testimonies of Scripture.

for the rhetorical skills of others points to another source of pleasure in the words.[105]

Above all, history had a *delectatio morosa* for those aware that the days of man passed more swiftly than a weaver's shuttle, that his life fell away more swiftly than shadow or wind.[106] Like music, life was lost as soon as it seemed to be seen.[107]

Contemplating the random sport of Fortune by no means excluded delight in the horrible. To the contrary, just as according to Aristotle the pleasure of tragic catharsis sprang from pity and fear, so too, Christian writers of history created works of art in which, as Augustine wrote of the theater, spectators could not help the sufferer, but only witness and delight in his misery.[108] Thus, readers cherished accounts of martyrs so that they could bear the sufferings of martyrdom, if not in body, then through compassion of mind.[109] Even John of Salisbury, convinced that in its vanity the life of man on earth was more comic than tragic, and certainly more like comedy than actual fact (*res gesta*), found moral gratification in considering the random play of Fortune that eventually reduced all joy to bitterness.[110]

Compassion and *Schadenfreude* were only two of history's morose pleasures. There was also the erotic pleasure in renouncing pleasure; anhedonia was essential to the ascetic life, crystallized in the treble discipline of poverty, chastity, and obedience. Cosmas of Prague's account of how a certain priest conquered the fires of lust demonstrates one way in which ascetic anhedonia could combine history's mnemonic, mimetic, and hedonic functions. Though the priest had vowed never to know a woman, Cosmas wrote, he was so powerfully assaulted by temptations of the flesh that he almost fell into the devil's snare. But, Cosmas continued, the priest had read in Gregory the Great's *Dialogues* that St. Benedict had extinguished his illicit carnal ardor by afflicting his body with nettles. Imitating that venerable model, he gathered a bundle of nettles and, in solitude, cruelly beat his naked genitals and backside, hanging the flail in his cell so as constantly to have before his fearful eyes a reminder of the torment by which he had cast out the wicked thoughts with which his own heart had tormented him. Cosmas delighted in the "imitable savagery" of the priest.

---

[105] Cf. Rahewin's artful tribute to the eloquence of Otto of Freising. *Gesta Friderici*, 3. prol.; *MGH*, *SSrrG*, p. 163: "Fateor equidem, quod tenuis mihi spiritus est ad excitandam vel minutam tybiam, nedum ad implendam superioris auctoris [et] venerabilis presulis tam magnificam et copiosam scribendi et dicendi tubam."

[106] Rahewin, *Gesta Friderici*, 3. prol.; *MGH*, *SSrrG*, p. 162.

[107] *Musica Enchiriadis*, in Hans Schmid, ed., *Musica et scolica enchiriadis una cum aliquibus tractatulis adiunctis*, Veröffentlichungen der Musikhistorischen Kommission, no. 3 (Munich: Bayerische Akademie der Wissenschaften, 1981), p. 57.

[108] Cf. *Confessions*, 3.2.3; *Corp. Christ.*, *ser. lat.*, 27, p. 28.

[109] Cf. Cosmas of Prague, *Chronica Boemorum*, 2.4; *MGH*, *SSrrG*, p. 89.

[110] *Policraticus*, 3.8; Webb, ed., 1:190–96.

"Ah," he wrote, "if anyone had seen this priest, though sane, raging madly, even if he had buried a dear parent that day, how, willy-nilly, he would have laughed."[111]

Part of the hedonic function of history lay precisely in arousing associations that made it possible to see such scenes of self-denial vicariously, in the mind's eye, that is, in reexperiencing the erotic pleasure of avoidance. The means to avoidance was obstruction of the empathy that might have come through esthetic participation and play.

Given the esthetic function of historical writing as a spur to visualization, it is easy to understand why writers, on the whole, omitted references to the physical appearance of women, notably to their beauty, just as in the discipline of their daily lives they avoided the sight of women. In this regard, their texts provide a remarkable contrast with the literature of courtly love. Occasionally, authors referred to the acquisition of precious ornaments by men for women as an index to collective prosperity and women's loss of their jewelry as one of catastrophe.[112]

But references to the personal beauty of women, as contrasted with their adornments, are extremely rare. When an author did record that a woman as beautiful (as Cosmas of Prague occasionally did), it was by no means clear what his norms of beauty were.[113]

By contrast, references to masculine beauty are so frequent that they appear to have been expected in the portrayal of a great man or of one touched with holiness. Certainly, writers were aware that even among educated prelates handsome exteriors could conceal deformed minds,[114] and that a prince's elegance of body could not save him from succumbing to vice.[115]

---

[111] *Chronica Boemorum*, 3.62; *MGH, SSrrG*, p. 241.

[112] Helmold recounted that the men of a Slavonic tribe, the Rugiani, spent the silver and gold that they gained from raids and ransoms on ornaments for their wives or donations to the treasury of their god. *Cronica Slavorum*, 1.38; *MGH, SSrrG*, p. 77. By contrast, Cosmas recorded that in Prague churches were despoiled and women's ornaments confiscated to pay the tribute that Henry V had demanded. *Cronica Boemorum*, 3.21; *MGH, SSrrG*, p. 187. Likewise, Adam of Bremen considered it a sign of official malfeasance that, while administrators of the church at Hamburg extorted gold and fine raiment from respectable women, harlots and thieves lived in derision of the Archbishop and clergy on the goods of the church. *Gesta Hammaburgensis Ecclesiae Pontificum*, 3.49(48), 58(57); *MGH, SSrrG*, pp. 192, 204. Cf. John of Salisbury's recollection that Pythagoras had inveighed against women's jewelry as "instruments of luxury." *Policraticus*, 7.4; Webb, ed., 2:103.

[113] Fecundity, or the promise of fecundity, certainly appears to have been part of the beauty seen in the Duchess Judith of Bohemia, who produced five sons, and the Empress Mathilda, who, in the event, produced no children. Cosmas of Prague, *Chronica Boemorum* 1.40, 2.1; *MGH, SSrrG*, pp. 73, 82. Ekkehard of Aura, *Chronicon* (a. 1114); *MGH, SS* 6, p. 247.

[114] Helmold, *Chronica Slavorum*, 2.97(1); *MGH, SSrrG*, p. 190.

[115] See the descriptions of Henry IV in Ekkehard of Aura, *Chronicon* (a. 1106); *MGH, SS* 6, p. 239 (extolling the elegance of Henry's whole bearing), and *Vita Heinrici IV. Imperatoris*,

Admittedly, their attributions of physical beauty to men are frequently as general as those to women. It is by no means clear what Ebo meant when he wrote that Bishop Otto of Bamberg was "the most beautiful among his peers," and that, like a most beautiful dawn, he scattered the shadows that had gathered around spiritual discipline.[116] But imprecision does not blunt the contrast with the paucity of comparable references to women, when one realizes that authors felt able to characterize as beautiful, or most beautiful, young brothers whom Otto converted; a member of a monastic community; "a boy of graceful beauty, very full of joy and astonishing in what he could do and say, making everyone glad with his drolleries"; a love-struck and violent duke; a bishop who excelled in hunting; or an archbishop whose thirst for grandeur brought him to a tragic end.[117]

In other portrayals descriptions are very exact, and it is possible to recover the admiration that was felt for bristly hair, dark as pitch, a dense beard, white skin with ruddy accents, dazzling regular and firm teeth, robust limbs, elegance of stature and physical proportion, wholeness of bodies, and the terrible, blinding radiance of a lordly gaze.[118] Many of these

---

chap. 1; *MGH, SSrrG*, p. 12. Correspondence, rather than contrast, worked in Giraldus Cambrensis's reference to Bishop William Longchamps's physical deformities as expressing his wickedness and his "many and horrible sins." *De Vita Galfridi Archiepiscopi Eboracensis*, 2.19; J. S. Brewer, ed., pp., 420, 426. According to Giraldus, William was a beast (*bellua*), rather than a human being (*homo*). Ibid., 2.19; pp. 427, 430.

[116] Ebo, *Vita S. Ottonis Episcopi Babenbergensis*, 1.20; Wikarjak, ed., pp. 36–37.

[117] Herbord, *Dialogus de Vita S. Ottonis Episcopi Babenbergensis*, l. proem., 2.27; Wikarjak, ed., pp. 4, 114. Cosmas of Prague, *Chronica Boemorum*, 1.40, 41; *MGH, SSrrG*, pp. 73–74, 76. Adam of Bremen, *Gesta Hammaburgensis Ecclesiae Pontificum*, 3.1, 2; *MGH, SSrrG*, pp. 143–44. See William of Poitiers, *Gesta Guillelmi Ducis Normannorum et Regis Anglorum*, pt. 2, chap. 44; Raymonde Foreville, ed., Les classiques de l'histoire de France au Moyen Âge, vol. 23 (Paris: "Les belles Lettres," 1952), p. 260, on the enviously handsome youths from the south of France who attended William the Conqueror's Easter court in 1067, and whose beauty yielded in no regard to that of maidens. Despite her vows of celibacy, Christina of Markyate did not fail to notice the beauty of males, with or without beards. Talbot, ed. and trans., *The Life of Christina of Markyate A Twelfth Century Recluse*, chaps. 52, 80; pp. 128, 184. See above, n. 83.

The anonymous biographer of Archbishop Arnold of Mainz employed physical beauty for the sake of dramatic effect. After speaking of the Archbishop's great elegance of person, the elegance of his movements (*gestus*), and his calm and sweet smile (*risus blandus et suavis*), the biographer went on to describe the terrible mutilations inflicted upon his face during his assassination, and the indignities visited on his corpse. *Martyrium Arnoldi Archiepiscopi Magontini*; Böhmer, ed., *Fontes Rerum Germanicarum*, 3:282, 296, 319, 322–23.

[118] Cosmas of Prague, *Chronica Boemorum*, 2.14; *MGH, SSrrG*, p. 103. Rahewin, *Gesta Friderici*, 4.86; *MGH, SSrrG*, pp. 342–43. Ebo, *Vita S. Ottonis Babenbergensis Episcopi*, 2.17; Wikarjak, ed., p. 83. *Vita Heinrici IV. Imperatoris*, chap. 1; *MGH, SSrrG*, p. 12. Lambert of Hersfeld, *Annales* (*a.* 1075); *MGH, SSrrG*, p. 99. See also Lambert, *Annales* (*a.* 1075); *MGH, SSrrG*, p. 243. In a way common among ascetic writers, Lambert described Archbishop Anno of Cologne so as to emphasize the comeliness of Anno's body and, at the same time, the

qualities could be found in the saintly, even when extreme age had changed the color of the hair to angelic whiteness, even when the rigors of asceticism had purified the flesh of its dross. In paragons of masculinity, such physical qualities were found together with moral glory, learning in divine and human writings, eloquence of tongue, and readiness of council.

The opposite of beauty, the ugliness of women, is also passed over, whereas the ugliness of men could have important consequences.[119] Indeed, one author was able to trace to this source the beginning of the Investiture Conflict, that long and destructive warfare between Empire and Papacy. He believed that Hildebrand had once been in service at the Emperor Henry III's court. The Emperor's son, later Henry IV, was then a callow youth. He heaped jibes and indignities on the Italian cleric for his swarthy complexion and malformed appearance. The young Henry often provoked the Emperor to laughter in this way, the annalist wrote, and after he became Pope, Hildebrand remembered the indignities that he had endured.[120] A man who was trifling in stature and disgustingly humpbacked might succeed as Duke of Lorraine, glorious as he was in riches and powerful in men at arms. But when a man of trifling stature, disgusting countenance, and obscure family, someone distinguished by no virtues of soul or body, was nominated to be archbishop of Cologne, the clergy and people recoiled at the unworthiness of the deed. Although the man was a trusted companion of King Henry IV, who had designated him, indigna-

---

ascetic rigors, including fasts and other austerities, with which Anno wore his body down. Lambert added a minute description of the dreadful ravages that Anno's last illness worked on his body. One recalls the enthusiastic assertions by Thomas à Becket's followers that the mutilations of his body by his assassins left his physical beauty intact, and that even as blood poured from the severed crown of his skull, his face carried its habitual expression of happiness and peace.

[119] John of Salisbury provides the fairly redundant information that a misshapen woman ("male formata") was called "informis." *Ep. 110*; Millor, Butler, and Brooke, eds., *The Letters of John of Salisbury*, 1:177. Cf. *Policraticus*, 8.6, among the things that reduce the soul from freedom to captivity, "mulierum formae," Webb, ed., 2:250. The author of the *Vita Godefridi Comitis Capenbergensis* relates that the heiress Aurelia, being "satis elegantis formae," was besieged by men seeking wives; but she gave her fortune "divinis ministeriis" and submitted herself to ascetic discipline (chap. 6; *MGH, SS* 12, p. 521). See Otto of Freising's list of physical uglinesses, including the immense height of giants, the extreme smallness of dwarfs, and the "deformity" of Ethiopians by virtue of their dark color. *Chronicon*, 8.12; *MGH, SSrrG*, p. 408–9. On feminine beauty as a device for enticing men to spiritual death in Herrad of Hohenburg's *Hortus Deliciarum*, see chap. 2, n. 31. For hagiographical traditions emphasizing the physical beauty of women saints (chiefly in thirteenth- and fourteenth-century biographies), see Thomas J. Heffernan, *Sacred Biography: Saints and Their Biographers in the Middle Ages* (Oxford: Oxford University Press, 1988), pp. 279–81. Heffernan interprets feminine beauty as playing a part in the conflict between martyrs and their slayers, which could be interpreted as an erotic conflict in which women triumphed over men (ibid., pp. 283, 292).

[120] *Annalista Saxo* (*a*. 1074); *MGH, SS* 6, p. 702.

tion grew to such a pitch of hatred that whenever he appeared in the precincts of the royal palace everyone raised crude clamors against him and mocked him with songs as though he were some monstrosity of ancient times, and they pelted him with stones and the dust of the earth and whatever else they could snatch up in their raging fury.[121]

It was possible to record that a statue of the Blessed Virgin had miraculously spoken (at least in a dream), but the authors under review had no wish to evoke speaking images of women in their texts.[122] Their esthetics allowed them to introduce into the dramatic play of texts and readers depictions only of men.

Our texts provide another instance in which pleasure was served by blocking empathy by extreme asceticism, namely, in descriptions of Otto of Bamberg's apostolate to the Pomeranians. Here too the senses of the body were used to discipline the sense of the mind to responses of avoidance and acceptance and to transcend the animal in quest of the spiritual.

Accounts of Otto of Bamberg provide striking examples of esthetic thresholds erected by anhedonic gratifications. An earlier missionary Bishop to the Slavs, Bernard, went forth in zeal to exemplify apostolic poverty to the heathen. They looked with contempt at the Bishop's threadbare clothes and bare feet, and cast him forth to preach to the fish of the sea and the birds of the air. Otto was assured by Bernard's calamitous experience that in their spiritual blindness the Pomeranians were animals, judging only by outward appearances. Therefore, while maintaining his personal ascetic discipline, he set forth on his own missionary journey with an abundance of luxurious vestments and furnishings to display and to bestow, winning the favor of the ignorant with sumptuous gifts in order to educate them with his spiritual teaching.[123]

Yet Otto himself had not crossed the illicit threshold of material beauty. His biographer described with admiration the exceptional workmanship of the chief temple at Stettin—its carvings of men and animals so vivid that they seemed to live and breathe, its marvelous combination of painting and sculpture, its vast treasures of rare and gorgeously wrought furniture and ornaments. Otto destroyed the temple and, after exorcising it with holy water, dispersed the treasure. He kept only one image, with three heads on

---

[121] Lambert of Hersfeld, *Annales* (a. 1076); *MGH, SSrrG*, pp. 251, 255. On Duke Gonzilo of Lorraine, see also *Annales* (aa. 1069, 1075); *MGH, SSrrG* pp. 112, 235. Lambert implied a contrast between Anno, the recently deceased Archbishop of Cologne, comely in every respect (a. 1075, p. 243), and Hildolf, the Archbishop-designate. Henry IV insisted that Cologne would have Hildolf or no one, and, eventually he was consecrated. Most of the Colognese, Lambert added, avoided the consecration because of their sense of *indignitas* (a. 1076, p. 257). See above, n. 83.

[122] Helmold, *Cronica Slavorum*, 1.45; *MGH, SSrrG*, p. 89.

[123] Ebo, *Vita Ottonis Episcopi Babenbergensis*, 2.1; Wikarjak, ed., pp. 51–52. Herbord, *Dialogus de Vita Ottonis Episcopi Babenbergensis*, 2.28–29; Wikarjak, ed., pp. 114–17.

one body, which he sent to the Pope so that the entire Church might see what he had achieved by pulling up and planting, by building and destroying. When he destroyed temples, Otto disrupted the ceremonial play of cult and politics, but he also displaced the practice of gathering at the temples for less formal kinds of play.[124]

His esthetic program and his attack on the culture of the Pomeranians that was play also appeared when he forbade baptized children to jeopardize their faith by playing with unbaptized. The affective results were immediately evident. The baptized showed contempt for the unbaptized and excluded them from their games. Expelled and continually exhorted by Otto, the unbaptized eventually begged to be made Christians. "It was a beautiful thing," Otto's biographer recalled, "to see how these [the baptized] glorying in the profession of the Christian name acted as friends together and quite devotedly heeded and heard the Teacher even in the midst of their games, and how the others stood apart as though confounded and terror-stricken in unbelief."[125]

. . .

The passage from criticism through silence to epiphany in the portrayal of women was quite different from that in the portrayal (or nonportrayal) of the Kingdom of God. The criticism behind the silences concerning the Kingdom of God was Scriptural exegesis; that behind those concerning women was moral theology, or at least the moral discipline under which monks and clerics lived. That criticism expressed itself in esthetic judgment, which underscored violence both in the function of historical writing in giving pleasure, and in the pleasures of anhedonia (especially through fear of the power and malice of women) and depictions of the suffering of women as victims. Resentment of political rule by women over men also figured in that esthetic judgment.

Further, although the epiphany sought regarding the Kingdom of God was that of empathetic participation, that sought regarding women required a powerful suppression of empathy. This tactic is represented most directly by the suppression of information concerning all play by women, individually, among themselves, or with men. The barriers that we have encountered to the speculative, mimetic play of imagination regarding women were formidable, but they were also cognitive means to the epiph-

---

[124] Herbord, *Dialogus de Vita S. Ottonis Episcopi Babenbergensis*, 2.32; Wikarjak, ed., p. 124. A similar example of esthetic appreciation and moral revulsion occurs in Thietmar of Merseburg's account of the pagan city, Riedegost as it was ca. 1005. *Chronicon*, 6.23; *MGH*, *SSrrG*, n.s., p. 303.

[125] Herbord, *Dialogus de Vita Ottonis Episcopi Babenbergensis*, 3.19; Wikarjak, ed., pp. 181–82.

any of beauty through the medium of violence that our writers desired, and conditions for the kinds of imaginative play that, they judged, could advance toward that epiphany.

"What motives," Beryl Smalley asked, "led men to write histories and chronicles in the Middle Ages?"[126] From the silences between the lines of our texts, we have now retrieved some of the unspoken principles of inclusion and exclusion by which the texts were shaped. The dominance of history's hedonic function over its mnemonic and mimetic ones is clear, and we have been able to detect some traces of the erotic element of ascetic denial behind the hedonic function. Throughout—in the range of idiosyncratic choices made by authors regarding the portrayal of women, and in the categories of activities commonly ascribed to women (and the reverse)—the writing of history was evidently an esthetic undertaking and, moreover, one that demanded of author and of reader considerable powers in translating verbal into visual associations and visual into affective.

Otto of Freising found it desirable to quote Augustine's argument against those who contended that, at the resurrection, all the saved would be raised men, since according to Scripture all would be raised as a perfect man, conforming with the image of the Son of God. Otto delivered up for his age the Father's judgment that both woman and man were creatures of God and that as he had established so also would he restore both sexes.[127] If the bodies discovered in Braunschweig beneath the sepulchral monument of Henry the Lion and Mathilda were theirs, together with the body of Henry's son by his first marriage, was it in deference to customs in Mathilda's homeland or for other reasons that the woman was wrapped in leather and entombed in a wooden coffin while the two males were buried in stone sarcophagi? The evidence excludes simplistic interpretations.

For it is all fragmentary and segmented. Indeed, the texts with which we have been preoccupied were written as fragmentary, dramatic montages in a total composition of a sacrificial cult. They shared the predicamental ways of thinking demanded by the mysteries of that cult. And, as in all gnostic writings, their coherence rests in their unspoken evocations, rather than in the uttered words. Readers were expected to read the text as a mirror, continually oscillating between the words and the world of cult that they daily saw around them. Where the words spoke of human events as the sport of Fortune, they were expected to supply a contrast with the sphere governed by God's unvarying wisdom. Where texts spoke of man's pomp and power, they were expected to supply a contrast with the Kingdom of God, which, took shape invisibly amidst the visible, passing shadows of this world, be-

[126] Beryl Smalley, *Historians in the Middle Ages* (New York: Scribner's, 1974), p. 9.

[127] *Chronicon*, 8.12; *MGH*, *SSrrG*, p. 408. Augustine, *City of God,*, 22.17; *Corp. Christ.*, *ser. lat.*, 48, pp. 835–38.

ing present in the Eucharist, in visions and miracles, and in the sufferings of martyrs. Like translators seeking the sense, rather than the literal equivalent of words, readers read wholeness, proportion, and clarity into the silences and spaces of texts; they found present before their minds' eyes what was absent from the written words. The technique of reading sense into words consisted of empathetic play and participation, that is, synesthetic kinds of play that enabled readers through paradox, dilemma, and enigma of cult to digest what they had read and to participate affectively in the text.

As to esthetic participation and play in portrayals of women, we have found deliberate strategies blocking the translation of verbal into visual and visual into affective association. In that sense, the portrayals are iconoclastic. They display, in historical writing as an art of visualization, the same idea that Otto of Freising expressed when he wrote, "For, by the words, 'Babylon is fallen, is fallen, and all the graven images of her gods are shattered' (Isa. 21:9), it is inferred that the graven images (so to speak) that we make for ourselves are all the transitory things that we set ahead of God, by loving them inordinately. When Babylon is hurled down, together with its graven images, he who is snatched away to punishment, as the world passes away, must be chastised bitterly in proportion to the tenderness with which, in contempt of God, he has followed his own lust."[128]

This erotic iconoclasm, with its complex longing and aversion, guided the process of translation behind the modelling of our texts. But it does not address the far wider question of why historical writing was one of the genres—including sermons, scriptural commentaries, philosophical discourses, and treatises of political controversy—from whose traditions women partook without requital. Beryl Smalley rightly limited her question about motives for writing histories used chronicles to men. It is likely that, as in all known societies, women acted as conveyers and interpreters of oral histories, such as legends, family stories, and dynastic traditions, and that there were varieties of traditional knowledge, including not least matters having to do with childbirth and reproduction, to which men had no access. Certainly, there were women's songs, *winileodas* from which some ecclesiastical chants may have derived.[129] Women executed historical works; they embroidered the Bayeux "Tapestry"; they copied manuscripts; they heard historical writings concerning Scripture, the deeds of saints,

---

[128] *Chronicon*, 8.20; *MGH*, *SSrrG*, pp. 421–22.

[129] John E. Stevens, *Words and Music in the Middle Ages* (Cambridge: Cambridge University Press, 1986), pp. 110–11. The allusion is not to songs written by male authors who assumed the "voices" or *personae* of women, such as are considered in *"Vox Feminae": Studies in Medieval Woman's Songs*, ed. John F. Plummer (Kalamazoo, Mich.: Medieval Institute, 1981), in which collection William E. Jackson's essay, "The Woman's Song in Medieval German Poetry," pp. 47–94, is especially relevant to the subject of this essay.

and the play of Fortune in their own days. Great princesses such as Adèle of Blois and Eleanor of Aquitaine lived in environments saturated with visual and verbal representations of the past. And yet, while they occasionally composed historical works as Hildegard of Bingen did, the love of learning and the desire for God, which prompted a flood of histories from monasteries, did not produce among female religious a harvest in any of the varieties of historiographic activity, or indeed any single work that found a place among generally recognized authorities. There is no evidence that writings were suppressed as, for example, far later and in another field of endeavor, Fanny Mendelssohn's father and brother suppressed her compositions, thinking them work in a genre unsuitable to a woman.

Perhaps it is true that "men only control women so long as they are able to renegotiate the material basis of their domination and to recreate the symbolic value of its representations."[130] But the materials bearing on the relative womanlessness of the entire western historiographical tradition lie not so much in visible symbols as in the silences between the lines where empathetic translation from word to feeling took place. This is nowhere more true than of the silences that permitted themselves to encompass and enliven the words of women in visionary treatises but not in accounts of Fortune's crazily turning Wheel. It is true of the silences in which, for the authors of our texts, the violent pain of ascetic aversion became the pleasure of redemption. It is also true of silences in modern theories that, on the one hand, recognize that civilization "arises in and as play, and never leaves [play]," and, on the other, leave unexplored the affective grounds on which the artificial world of culture assigns, according to gender, its own integrating forms of play and the wordless conformity by which one sometimes enacts those forms even in defying them.[131]

[130] Henrietta L. Moore, *Space, Text and Gender: An Anthropological Study of the Maraket of Kenya* (Cambridge: Cambridge University Press, 1986), p. 71.

[131] Huizinga, *Homo Ludens*, p. 173. Huizinga refers to the sexual act (p. 43), and to sexual play in animals (p. 9) without attempting to establish the fundamental importance of gender distinctions in the entire network of play by which, according to his theory, civilization was constituted. See also his discussion of the Yin/Yang principles (pp. 54, 117). He refers to five women—Cleopatra (p. 62), Faustina (p. 163), Hildegard of Bingen (p. 140), Marguerite de Navarre (p. 181), and Jane Harrison (p. 81)—but there is nothing to distinguish these references, in kind, from references to men. Hildegard of Bingen is the only woman cited in Umberto Eco's *Art and Beauty in the Middle Ages* (New Haven, Conn.: Yale University Press, 1986. First published in 1959), pp. 36, 47.

## Chapter 7

# TEXT AND TIME AT THE COURT OF EUGENIUS III:
## A SILENCE OF MULTIPLICATION

NOT ALL silences in the text were due to the author's intent. Some were imposed by the deficiencies of the medium of language. The Kingdom of God and women were subjects to be included or excluded by choice. Time represents quite another category of omissions that existed by necessity. Yet, that necessity did not exist because, by thinking of events under the aspect of turning wheels—the Wheel of Fortune or Ezekiel's concentric wheels of prophecy and fulfillment, advancing as they spun—authors negated time. Instead, the necessity existed because those metaphors, and similar ones, expressed assumptions about time and the arts that went far beyond simple affirmation or denial, assumptions that made the circle (or wheel) a figure of narrative discoordination. Discussing the Kingdom of God, we encountered the proposition that writers' intents were directed by esthetic considerations. Discussing the hermeneutic role of women, we were able to go a bit deeper and to explore some rationales that informed the esthetics of historical writing. But, when we turn to the role of time in the hermeneutic projects of our texts, we move a step away from the works of art, with their esthetic of beauty and violence, and toward the conditions that made art, and its rationales, possible.[1]

This is true, in part, because, in leaving the issue of the artist's (or writer's) intentionality, we turn toward the experiences in a particular culture and class that presented a distinct repertoire of choices to artists. Common familiarity with these choices, the artists assumed, would make their work intelligible to others. Thus, when we considered subjects, we had chiefly writers' understandings to deal with. Intelligibility hinged on changing undifferentiated duration into measured *tempi*. Now, thinking directly about time (as one of the silences imposed by the medium), we have to bear in mind two instants at which duration was rendered into *tempi*, two herme-

---

[1] See Donald J. Wilcox, *The Measure of Times Past: Pre-Newtonian Chronologies and the Rhetoric of Relative Time* (Chicago: University of Chicago Press, 1987), p. 137: "Modern scholars have often failed to understand the complexity of medieval chronology, and that failure has affected their use of sources from the period," especially in their complaints about medieval writers' "chronological inadequacies." See also Wilcox's article, "The Sense of Time in Western Historical Narratives from Eusebius to Machiavelli," in *Classical Rhetoric and Medieval Historiography*, ed. Ernst Breisach Studies in Medieval Culture, no. 19 (Kalamazoo, Mich.: Medieval Institute, 1985), pp. 167–237.

neutic moments: those of the artist and those of the audience. And this, as we shall see, was a chief reason for the silences in our texts regarding time. For while the silences regarding the Kingdom of God arose from its character as a "holy secret" apprehended through intuition, and those concerning women arose from a fascinated moral aversion, those having to do with time derived from the dazzling and intricate multiplication of "times" in the minds and experiences of our authors, a multiplication represented not by a single straight line, but by the beginninglessness and endlessness of a wreath. Beauty delighted through ever-amazing diversity.

Of course, neither hermeneutic moment occurs in the text; the author's is before it, the reader's after. However, as in regard to the Kingdom of God and women, these instants are also present by their absence. The hermeneutic moment of the artist is present by residues that it leaves in the text, its memorial. That of the listener or reader is present through the strategy by which the author prepared for it, a web of associations designed to arrest the attention in the rhythm, the *tempi*, of spectacles in the text.

A preliminary word of definition may be helpful. Among all the things absent from historical texts, time is the most conspicuous. Time is of the essence in the performance of a musical text; but in the performance, or reading, of a historical one, only witness to the changing times is possible. There are general and specific reasons.

One general reason is obvious: the flow of time can not be arrested; instants pass away even as they come to be. Meditating on time (*Confessions*, Book 10), Augustine of Hippo observed that the past was present by memory, and the future by anticipation, which is a projection of memory, but the present, he wrote, being always present, could never be retained. The inability to study the present in the act of being present led Wilhelm Dilthey to speak of time's "impenetrability" to thought.[2]

The specific reasons for time's absence from historical texts have to do with the distinction between nature and art. The subject of historical study is the temporal world, and the task of historical writing is to represent the flow of time. But a vast difference stands between the nature of "temporal time" as experienced in the world and the art of "historical time" conveyed by means of written texts. For, while one "reads" time directly through rhythms or *tempi* in poetry and music, one reads about time in historical texts.

At the more exalted level of events and recording angels, this distinction between nature and art was at the core of the theology of sin; for referring to the Last Judgment, Bernard of Clairvaux observed that what was done

[2] "Entwürfe zur Kritik der historischen Vernunft, Teil 1," in *Wilhelm Diltheys gesammelte Schriften* (Leipzig: Teubner, 1927), 7:194.

in time did not pass away with time but remained forever.[3] Lacking the clear view of eternity, historians worked within a more complex temporal field than recording angels.

Natural (or temporal) time is experience of events as they occur. It can be measured in hours, days, and years. Historical time is experience of narrative understanding. It may be acquired cumulatively through the reading of a text or by calculating with stereotypes, such as periods, ages, and eras. This artificial time occurs, not in the words, but in the spaces between the lines of the text, and even in those between the letters.

What makes the difference between temporal and historical time is hermeneutic time. "Hermeneutic" time is the experience out of which the artificial categories of historical time are made: experience, for example, of intellectual and moral formation imposed by a society on its members, and of methods and objectives by which it defines what historians are for. From artifacts, including texts, one may recover the educational norms and analytical strategies of past cultures, but it is far more difficult to regain the experience that they were invented and deployed to serve. They are like a flagon from which perfume has evaporated, leaving only its fragrance.

We have already mentioned the two instants at which the shapeless flow of duration is rendered into the intelligible measures of hermeneutic time: the one, the author's experience prior to the creation of a text; the other, the reader's while digesting the text. Historical time brought about, for author or for reader, through the instrumentality of the text is the point at which these two experiences coincide. And yet traces of the author's pretextual hermeneutic time are most imperfectly left as residues, or traces, in the text; expectations concerning the reader's posttextual time appear there, to be elucidated by reference to other works of criticism and commentary. As I said, evidence of the kind of hermeneutic time that the author intended readers to experience exists in formal aspects of the text's *genre*, style, and organization. (I must stress the difference between the *tempi* of the author and the intended audience and the *tempi* that unintended readers of medieval texts, such as modern critics, may bring to the texts.)

Despite their evanescence, neither the author's nor the intended reader's hermeneutic time has quite the "cognitive impenetrability" that Dilthey (and, much earlier, Augustine) found in temporal time. Some traces left by their evaporation can be recovered, together with other components that are present by their absence. Yet, this is a perspective quite different from the single-image, artist's viewpoint familiar in Western painting since the

[3] *De Consideratione*, 5.12.26; Jean Leclercq and H. M. Rochais eds., *S. Bernardi Opera* (Rome: Editiones Cistercienses, 1963), 3:488. See also Otto of Freising's discussion of how temporal sins merited eternal punishment. *Chronicon*, 8.22; *MGH, SSrrG*, pp. 425–27.

Renaissance (see chap. 4). Its purpose was not to convey the viewer's imagination in one linear course so much as to arrest and provoke it into networks of association, including counterlinear or nonlinear ones. It is a nuclear perspective from within a turning wheel, and, in its most complex form, from within the concentric wheels of prophecy and fulfillment, static, yet ever spinning forward. From this perspective, compartmentalized scenes blended into one another and interpenetrated, as the spokes of a wheel seem to do, as they whirl.

Now, we have to explore a temporal aspect of the nuclear point of view, for historical time mediates between natural (or "temporal") time and the hermeneutic times of author and reader. I wish to explore the hermeneutic times of author and reader, and the mediating third (historical time), chiefly but not exclusively with regard to a cluster of writings composed by authors associated with Pope Eugenius III (1145–53).[4]

Modern scholars have considered all of these works, without exception, characterized by discontinuities and inconsistencies in argument which, in most cases, were judged to have resulted from hasty or ill-considered composition. Yet there are reasons to think that these appraisals mistake the guiding principles of composition itself. Like boredom, the effect that medieval writers labored above all to avert, the perception of narrative disunity actually witnesses to the strategy of artificial, or historical, time in the text. Modern critics of the historical writings in question experience the strategy with expectations that authors intend to make comprehension easy for readers, and that, as means to that end, they employ logical consistency, a narrative progression that moves from beginning to middle to end, and a style that in its clarity conveys the author's message, leaving nothing unsaid in the words.[5]

However, these expectations derive from the Enlightenment, and a series of studies on the texts in question has disclosed another point of view,

---

[4] Anselm of Havelberg, *Antikeimenon*; Migne *PL* 188:1139–1248. Book I only is edited by Gaston Saltet, *Anselme de Havelberg, Dialogues, Livre I*, Sources chrétiennes, vol. 118 (Paris: Cerf, 1966). Bernard of Clairvaux, *De Consideratione*, Leclercq et al., eds., pp. 393–493. Gerhoch of Reichersberg, *Tractatus in Ps. 64*; Migne *PL* 194:13–116, and (partial) *MGH, Ldl* 3, pp. 439–92. Otto of Freising, *Chronicon*; Adolf Hofmeister, ed., 2d ed. (Hannover: Hahn, 1912 [*MGH, SSrrG*]). Otto of Freising and Rahewin, *Gesta Friderici I. Imperatoris*; Georg Waitz and Bernhard von Simson, eds., 3d ed. (Hannover: Leipzig, 1912 [*MGH, SSrrG*]). John of Salisbury, *Historia Pontificalis*; Marjorie Chibnall, ed., *John of Salisbury's Memoirs of the Papal Court* (London: Nelson, 1956).

[5] See Gert Melville, "System und Diachronie: Untersuchungen zur theoretischen Grundlegung geschichtsschreiberischer Praxis im Mittelalter," *Historisches Jahrbuch* 95 (1975): 33, on the distinction between medieval objectives in historical study and modern regard for texts as sources of information; and 325, on the arbitrary character of the medieval author's (and public's) range of interest. Melville did not include time as part of the "implizierte Formungsverständnis von Geschichte."

one whose chief postulate was that the sense of a text was latent in, if not actually concealed by, words.[6] That point of view was canonized in traditions of Scriptural exegesis, traditions that cherished logical contradictions, discontinuous reading of pericopes and anecdotes, and expository methods of deliberate obscurity, all contrived to heighten the pleasure of discovery, the joy of the chase.

The texts were written to provoke thought by dazzling the mind. What, according to norms of modern criticism, appears random and incomplete may actually be evidence of deliberate construction. That construction took as its basis, not the tidy closure of problem and solution, but the inconclusiveness of paradox, enigma, and dilemma. Inevitably, the fact that twelfth-century scholars delighted in the obscure predicament of what was latent in texts while their remote descendants shun it exposes a monumental divergence in ways in which the artificial strategies of time in the texts may be experienced between the lines. It also casts some light on this divergence between the hermeneutic times of twelfth-century and recent scholars. For, in so far as time and space present themselves as a whole "because we can determine space only by reference to time, and vice versa,"[7] we are evidently dealing with a subject known to the visual arts, and not metaphorically, as perspective.

To indicate that the works associated with writers in the circle of Eugenius III were not atypical, I shall occasionally refer to other texts of the same era.

## THE ARTIST'S HERMENEUTIC MOMENT

Of course, the pretextual hermeneutic time of authors and the post-textual ones of intended audiences existed in the same cultural context; at points, they were cognate. My first task must be to sketch out the common ground

---

[6] See, for example, Rupert of Deutz's insistence that the interpreter "hear" or "understand" beneath the text of Scripture (*subaudire, subintellegere*). *Commentum in Apocalypsim*, 1.1, 5.9, 6.10; Migne *PL* 169:851, 1004, 1011. In several articles on related subjects, I have explored the need to recover the unsaid in the said: "Otto of Freising's Quest for the Hermeneutic Circle," *Speculum* 55 (1980): 207–36. "Anselm of Havelberg: Play and the Dilemma of Historical Progress," in *Religion, Culture, and Society in the Early Middle Ages: Studies in Honor of Richard E. Sullivan*, ed. Thomas F. X. Noble and John J. Contreni (Kalamazoo, Mich.: Medieval Institute, 1987), pp. 229–56. "The Church as Play: Gerhoch of Reichersberg's Call for Reform," in *Popes, Teachers, and Canon Law in the Middle Ages: Essays in Honor of Brian Tierney*, ed. Stanley Chodorow and James Ross Sweeney (Ithaca, N.Y.: Cornell University Press, 1989), pp. 114–44. "Hermeneutics and Enigma: Bernard of Clairvaux's *De Consideratione*," *Viator* 19 (1988): 129–51.

[7] Friedrich Schleiermacher, *Manuscript 3: The Compensium of 1819*, "Part I: Grammatical Interpretation," 12.7, in *Hermeneutics: The Handwritten Manuscripts*, trans. James Duke and Jack Forstman, American Academy of Religion, Texts and Translations, no. 1 (Missoula, Mont.: Scholars Press, 1977), p. 120.

from which they sprang. Afterwards, I shall indicate what can be recovered from these texts about the hermeneutic time that the authors expected their readers to experience—in other words, how the authors attempted to pre-shape options for the readers' experience of time in the texts.

Our texts are characterized by a relative indifference toward, if not a categorical rejection of, space, time, and causal connections.[8] The points of view represented by geography and historical positivism were entirely alien to their authors. For them, in general, the topography of a place or the unique convergences of a given instant had no interpretive value. Otto of Freising paused to sketch the topography of his cathedral city and the site where a flash flood with heavy winds engulfed an encampment during the Second Crusade.[9] But these and other exceptions that could be mentioned were brief digressions serving the need for a change in rhetorical pace. They were descriptive, not explanatory. On the whole, the authors left places, though named, without spatial identities, much as, in maps or manuscript illuminations, the same drawing of towers, without fore-ground or background, could be used for every city.

Likewise, the defining contingencies of events were most often ignored, and, when recorded, they were employed to advance narrative, rather than to elucidate the nexus of events. Here, too, there is a counterpart in artistic convention. For illuminators commonly represented a sequence of events with horizontal rows of individual scenes, like friezes or comic strips, with-out any organic unity except that given by the physical dimensions of the pages, and, again, without depth of focus.

To inquire into the hermeneutic role of time, therefore, is indeed to seek

---

[8] This observation was applied to Carolingian texts by Alfred Ebenbauer, *Carmen Histori-cum: Untersuchungen zur historischen Dichtung im karolingischen Europa*, Philologica German-ica, no. 4 (Vienna: Braumüller, 1978), 1:318–19. On causality, see Otto of Freising's state-ment that he would not delve into the causes of things. *Chronicon*, 6.23; *MGH, SSrrG*, p. 286: "Res enim gestas scribere, non rerum gestarum rationem reddere proposuimus." In the *Gesta Friderici*, he did affirm that he was going to insert philosophical excursuses to delight readers of a speculative bent and to keep them going through the text. *Gesta Friderici*, prol.; *MGH, SSrrG*, p. 12. But Otto did not integrate the surviving excursuses into his historical narrative well enough to produce causal explanations. Cf. also his comment that the hidden-ness of causes become clear as historical changes unfold. *Chronicon*, 5. prol.; *MGH, SSrrG*, p. 226. See Wilcox's judgment that Otto had "a complex theoretical perspective." "The Sense of Time in Western Historical Narratives from Eusebius to Machiavelli," p. 210.

The capricious attitude toward space, time, and causality is one reason why Spörl could observe: "Der Begriff der 'historia' im Mittelalter ist schwankend und nicht eindeutig defi-nierbar." Johannes Spörl, *Grundformen hochmittelalterlicher Geschichtsanschauung: Studien zum Weltbild der Geschichtsschreiber des 12. Jahrhunderts* (Munich: Hueber, 1935), p. 18.

[9] *Chronicon*, 5.24; *MGH, SSrrG*, pp. 251–52. *Gesta Friderici*, 1.47(45); *MGH, SSrrG*, pp. 66–67. See Otto's comment on the pious simplicity of those who took literally the prophecy that the Last Judgment would take place in the valley of Jehosephat. *Chronicon*, 8.18; *MGH, SSrrG*, pp. 416–17.

a presence in an absence, perhaps the third dimension implied in two-dimensional perspective. But it is not to be found in the words of the text. Plainly, our writers did not direct themselves by geographical and phenomenal coordinates. How could it be otherwise, when time was regarded as multiple—"the times"—dissonant and disconnected among themselves, comprising in fact "a certain chaos." The Creator's will joined them together as it also did the mutually repellent elements. Thus constrained, they formed a single composition, but its harmony unfolded through the mutual antipathies of times and elements.[10]

As they studied the shuffled materials before them, writers were acutely aware of forming the *"disiecta membra"* of history into the "little body" of a text. But "why," one scholar has asked, "did historians in the Middle Ages so consistently and conscientiously promise truth and then offer something else?"[11]

Among the three functions of history—mnemonic, mimetic, and hedonic—the function of recording events was generally stated to take precedence. However, the mimetic function was by no means understood to mean that a writer of history, even of world history, should give a panorama of the times. Rather, the times were tailored to suit both general and particular conceptions. It was right for a historian to select "a few things out of many" as he "digested truth of deeds, according to the law of the chronicle." It was right, for example, to "cover with silence" the works and teachings of heretics in order to protect "weak listeners" from being smitten with horror.[12] If critics pointed out that an author had omitted more than he wrote, he could magisterially answer that he had rather have less than excess.[13] Deeper considerations, including envy, wrath, greed, and fear made it safer to be silent than to write,[14] and they could also prompt a

[10] Folcuin, *Gesta Abbatum Lobiensium*, prol.; *MGH, SS* 4, pp. 54–55. Ms. Phyllis Jestice kindly drew my attention to this tenth-century passage.

[11] E.g., Lambert of Hersfeld, *Vita Lulli*, chap. 27; *MGH, SSrrG*, p. 340. See also Sigebert of Gembloux, *Gesta Abbatum Gemblacensium*, chap. 1; *MGH, SS* 8, p. 523: "Unde nos quasi particulas discissae vestis recolligentes, et quicquid de eo scriptum ubiubi invenimus simul assuentes, fecimus ut saltem hereat sibi quasi unius corpusculi compages." John O. Ward, "Some Principles of Rhetorical Historiography in the Twelfth Century," in *Classical Rhetoric and Medieval Historiography*, ed. Ernst Breisach p. 105.

[12] Continuator of Sigebert of Gembloux, *Chronicon (a.* 1146); *MGH, SS* 6, p. 389. Otto of Freising argued that no one should consider him untruthful because he told incredible things. Concerning all but events preserved in recent memory, he had chosen "a few out of many things" recorded in writings of trustworthy men. Otto went on to ask God's help in saying things pleasing to him, i.e., in editing out the rest. *Chronicon*, prol.; *MGH, SSrrG*, p. 10. See chap. 1, n. 5; chap. 2, n. 5; chap. 5, n. 32; chap. 6, n. 2; chap. 7, nn. 11–21. On selective omissions, see also chap. 2, nn. 23–49.

[13] Guibert of Nogent, *Gesta Dei per Francos*, 7.50; in *Recueil des historiens des croisades* (Paris: Imprimerie nationale, 1879), 4:260.

[14] Helmold, *Cronica Slavorum*, 2.96; *MGH, SSrrG*, pp. 188–89. William of Tyre, *Chronicon*, prol.; *Corp. Christ., continuatio medievalis*, 63, pp. 98–99.

writer to select materials to suit his own advantage, and "not only [to] disregard chronological order, but actually [to] dissolve it."[15]

The magnitude of omission by authors associated with the court of Eugenius III is astonishing. Though admittedly truncated, John of Salisbury's account of Eugenius's pontificate remarkably omits most the areas of concern reflected in the hundreds of extant letters and decretals issued by the Pope. Given John's conspicuous hostility to Frederick Barbarossa in particular and things German in general,[16] the fact that he ignored Eugenius's preoccupation with central Europe, voluminously attested in the Pope's correspondence, gives a measure of the possible.[17] Although he proposed to give a schematic periodization of Church history in the first book of his *Dialogues*, Anselm of Havelberg excluded all secular history, virtually the entire history of Greek Christianity (a major element in the putative debates occupying Books 2 and 3), and vast and normative sections of Latin ecclesiastical history.

Two authors in our sample provided rationales for their omissions. Lovers of monastic discipline, Gerhoch of Reichersberg wrote, should not feed on "inane tales (*fabulae*) of secular affairs," but on the words of Scripture. He himself rebuked Pope and Curia for usurping the power to inflict blood penalties, which properly belonged to secular courts. But he suppressed what he must have known concerning the popes' own military campaigns and imposition of capital punishment. Fearing retribution, the righteous man, he wrote, might keep silent about such things, as Joseph of Aramathea secretly withheld assent to the condemnation of Christ.[18]

Otto of Freising excluded from subjects worthy of recording for poster-

[15] Alison Goddard Elliott, "The Historian as Artist: Manipulation of History in the Chronicle of Desclot," *Viator* 14 (1983): 209. This comment about a thirteenth-century chronicle is entirely applicable to the twelfth-century historical works under review.

[16] Timothy Reuter, "John of Salisbury and the Germans," in *The World of John of Salisbury*, ed. Michael Wilks (Oxford: Blackwell, 1984), esp. pp. 424–25.

[17] Eugenius's effort to encourage the development of a strong monarchy in Germany distinguished his policies from those of his predecessors and followers. One can mention, for example, Eugenius's canonization (1146) of the Emperor Henry II in an effort to win support from Conrad III against the Romans, and his persistence in seeking rapport with Conrad even after the Emperor turned cool toward the Pope as a result of the disaster of the Second Crusade. See Helmut Gleber, *Papst Eugen III. (1145–1153) unter besonderer Berücksichtigung seiner politischen Tätigkeit*, Beiträge zur mittelalterlichen und neueren Geschichte, Bd. 6 (Jena: Fischer, 1936), pp. 25, 125–28, 133–34, 137. Other examples of Eugenius's continuing interest in Central Europe (never suggested by John of Salisbury) are his correspondence with kings and prelates, his legations to Bohemia and Moravia, and his commission of Anselm of Havelberg's crusade against the Slavs. Cf. John's criticism of Sigebert of Gembloux, whose *Chronicle* he intended to continue, for warping his account through excessive attention to "his Germans." *Historia Pontificalis*, prol.; Chibnall, ed., p. 3.

[18] *De Edificio Dei*, chap. 71; *MGH, Ldl* 3, p. 177. *Tractatus in Ps. 64*, pref. *B*, chaps. 16, 51; *MGH, Ldl* 3, pp. 441, 447, 460. "The Church as Play: Gerhoch of Reichersberg's Call for Reform," pp. 6, 33.

ity the histories of unbelievers (particularly Jews and Muslims). Further-more, since the object of writing history was to provoke the minds of the wise to act virtuously, he wrote, the dark deeds of the craven should be buried in silence, or presented in such a way as to provide wholesome ex-amples of terror.[19] For other omissions, Otto invoked the ratifying exam-ple of John the Evangelist. But the apparently innocent excuse of selecting a few things out of many[20] actually covered massive revisions of the course of events, including Otto's portrayal of the catastrophic reign of his half-brother, Conrad III, as a triumph, and his omission of key events so as to tailor his history of Barbarossa's reign according to the pattern that the Emperor had provided.[21] Even so, he realized that, despite all that prudent revision could do, histories might still give dangerous offence in high places.[22]

Thus, the historical time written into the narrative was a creature of mea-sured artifice; and this attitude toward how the mnemonic function of his-tory was to be served had implications for its mimetic function. With strik-ing redundancy, an analogue was drawn between historical writing and the calculated effects of visual and performing arts on the viewer, including, above all, the impact of the "spectacle" of theater or amphitheater. Histor-ical writing displayed the world itself as a theater in which the human drama was enacted, whether comedy or tragedy, or the random "play of Fortune."[23]

[19] *Gesta Friderici*, proem; *MGH, SSrrG*, p. 9.

[20] *Chronicon*, 8. prol.; *MGH, SSrrG*, p. 392. *Gesta Friderici*, 2.41(26), 4.86; *MGH, SSrrG*, pp. 150, 346.

[21] On Otto's creative omission of the Treaty of Constance (1153) from the *Gesta Friderici*, see Peter Munz, "Why Did Rahewin Stop Writing the *Gesta Frederici*? A Further Consider-ation," *English Historical Review* 84 (1969): 771–79.

[22] *Chronicon, ep. ad Reginaldum*; *MGH, SSrrG*, p. 5.

[23] John of Salisbury, *Policraticus*, 3.8, 9; 7.17; Clement C. J. Webb, ed., *Ioannis Saresberien-sis Episcopi Carnotensis . . . Policratici . . . Libri VIII*, 2 vols. (Oxford: Clarendon, 1909), 1:199, 2:160. Above, chap. 3, nn. 84, 118. Cf. Rupert of Deutz, *Commentum in Apocalypsim*, 10.17; Migne *PL* 169:1133: ". . . imo satiata jam sunt theatra orbis terrarum regum tragoediis. . . ." On the analogies that Gerhoch of Reicherberg drew between his work and *spectacula*, see my essays, *"I Am You": The Hermeneutics of Empathy in Western Literature, Theology, and Art* (Princeton, N.J.: Princeton University Press, 1988), pp. 192, 217–23 and "The Church as Play: Gerhoch of Reichersberg's Call for Reform," pp. 136, 138, 139–40. On Anselm of Havelberg, see "Anselm of Havelberg: Play and the Dilemma of Historical Progress," pp. 232, 244–46. Rupert of Deutz called the dramatic form of a public debate a "spectacle." *Anulus*; Migne *PL* 170:561, 570. Cf. Anselm of Havelberg's effort to produce a vivid descrip-tion in his debate with Nicetas of Nicomedia "similitudine tamquam in scaena contemplari oportet." *Antikeimenon*, 2.19; Migne *PL* 188:1193. Cf. ibid., 2.16; Migne *PL* 188:1187. For the use of *ludus* as in some sense equivalent to *spectaculum theatricale* or *mimicum theatricale*, see Gerhoch of Reichersberg, *Tractatus in Ps. 133*: 3; Migne *PL* 194:890–91; *De Investiga-tione Antichristi*, chap. 5; *MGH, Ldl* 3, pp. 315–16. See also Roger S. Loomis and Gustave

Cohen, "Were There Theatres in the Twelfth and Thirteenth Centuries?," *Speculum* 20 (1945): 93–94.

The question would appear to be answered in part by the experience of Abbot Geoffrey of St. Albans, "a former schoolmaster of Dunstable, who had offered himself as a monk to St. Albans in compensation for the loss of some valuable copes, which he had borrowed from the abbey for a play and which had been accidentally burnt whilst they were in his keeping." C. H. Talbot, ed. and trans., *The Life of Christina of Markyate A Twelfth Century Recluse* (Oxford: Clarendon Press, 1959), p. 28. Geoffrey's experience as a schoolmaster in theater parallels that of Gerhoch of Reichersberg. The theatricality of cult was part and parcel of Bishop Otto of Bamberg's opulent liturgical displays, both in his diocesan monasteries and in his missions to the Pomeranians. See chap. 3, n. 92. See also *Vita Adalberonis Episcopi Wirziburgensis*, chap. 14; *MGH, SS* 12, p. 135, concerning the dedication of the monastery of Lambach: "Omnis ergo ecclesia circumfluae regionis convenerat ad dedicationis diem festum, ad sacri exercitii spectaculum, eratque quadrifidum hac die largitate divina tripudium." The anonymous biographer of Arnold of Mainz drew an implied contrast between the "*pulchrum spectaculum*" of the Archbishop's early pontificate and the "*miserabile spectaculum*" of his gruesome death. *Martyrium Arnoldi Archiepiscopi Magontini*; Johann Friedrich Böhmer, ed., *Fontes Rerum Germanicarum* (Stuttgart: Cotta, 1855), 3:295, 319. Of course, history, cult, and theater coincided in such dramatic performances as that of the "*ludus prophetarum*," staged in Riga to promote the conversion of the Estonians. Henry of Livonia, *Chronicon Lyvoniae*, 9.14; *MGH, SS* 23, p. 242.

On the crosscurrents between historical and theatrical writing, see the proposal that *The Play of Antichrist* (ca. 1160), with its references to contemporary events and frequent appeals to (or aspersions on) the trustworthiness of histories (lines 49, 69, 101, 114d) was written by the chronicler Ekkehard of Aura. Romuald Bauerriss, "Ekkehard von Aura als Verfasser des 'Spiel vom Antichrist,'" *Studien und Mitteilungen zur Geschichte des Benediktiner-Ordens und seiner Zweige* 73 (1962): 41–53. Horst Dieter Rauh, *Das Bild des Antichrist im Mittelalter: Von Tyconius zum deutschen Symbolismus*, Beiträge zur Geschichte der Philosophie und Theologie des Mittelalters, n.f., Bd. 9 (Munich: Aschendorff, 1973), pp. 365, 371–72 (on the *theatrum mundi*).

See also Henry of Bosham's account of Thomas à Becket, who, fighting as Christ's athlete "against the world on the stage of the world was made a spectacle for men and angels." *Ep. 271*. James Craigie Robertson, ed., *Materials for the History of Thomas Becket Archbishop of Canterbury*, Rolls Series, no. 67 (London: Longmans, 1882), 6:122, quoting Augustine's quotation of Paul on Paul cited below.

For earlier citations of this sort, see Augustine on St Paul's struggles in "the theater of this world," making him a "spectacle for [Christ] before angels and men," *City of God*, 14.9; *Corp. Christ., ser. lat.*, 48, p. 427. See also the charge of the Synod of Brixen (1080) that Pope Gregory VII was more devoted than laymen to "obscene theatrical farces." Carl Erdmann, ed., *Die Briefe Heinrichs IV.* (Leipzig: Hiersemann, 1937 [*MGH, Deutsches Mittelalter*, 1]), p. 70. Lambert of Hersfeld, *Annales* (*a.* 1075); *MGH, SSrrG*, p. 240: The clergy of Bamberg stated that they had rather accept anyone else than Rupert, against whom they had appealed to Rome ". . . et cuius vitae institutionisque lugubrem tragediam toto mundi huius theatro decantandum vulgaverant. . . ." See also Lambert of Hersfeld, *Annales* (*a.* 1076); *MGH, SSrrG*, p. 253: Cardinal Hugh the White defended himself against charges before the Pope, "deferens secum de vita et institutione papae scenicis figmentis consimilem tragediam. . . ." A similar phrase ("scenicis figmentis similem esse fabulam") occurs, *Annales* (*a.* 1074); *MGH, SSrrG*, p. 195. See also chap. 3, n. 104; chap. 5, nn. 37, 46; chap. 6, after n. 73; below, n. 46.

Otto of Freising described his *Chronicle* as having been written in the manner of a "tragedy," and both he and Rahewin, his collaborator and continuator, considered part of the historian's task to provide the reader with the illusion of being an eyewitness.[24] In the *De Consideratione*, Bernard of Clairvaux employed the metaphor of spectacle in the amphitheater to portray the reprobate brought out before the eyes of God, angels, men, and themselves, a figure of speech that coincided with his description of his treatise as a mirror in which Eugenius could see his own deformities.[25] Readers were "spectators," and perhaps "benevolent" ones.[26] To achieve this dramatic effect the figures in the written portrayal had, like figures painted in murals, to be seen to stand out from the walls and walk.[27]

The effects of the mimetic function varied according to the reader. As he studied the war in heaven portrayed in the Apocalypse, Rupert of Deutz realized the power of imagination to transform words into spectacle. A great and amazing spectacle of images appeared before the gaze of John's soul, he wrote, such that, by seeing them, he was able correspondingly to conceive an amazing attitude (*sensus*) or habit (*habitus*) of soul. Reading the words of the Apocalypse, he continued, we can only just recover, by dreaming or by imaginings drawn from inward meditation, the summit of wonder mingled with horror that John attained.[28]

Giraldus Cambrensis (ca. 1188) observed the weight that this emphasis on imagination placed on the spectator, rather than on the spectacle, when he contemplated illuminations in an Evangelary from Kildare, which was said to have been dictated by an angel. To the superficial gaze, he said, they seemed to be crude. But the keen-eyed viewer could "transpenetrate" through them to the very secrets of art (*ad artis arcana*) and always find more and more to admire in those inner recesses beneath the surface.[29] William of Tyre used a similar figure alluding to the spectator's work of

---

[24] *Chronicon, ep. ad Fridericum*, 8.20, 33; *MGH, SSrrG*, pp. 2–3, 423, 452. Rahewin, *Gesta Friderici*, 2.41(26); *MGH, SSrrG*, p. 150. On Rahewin's theatrical mode of exposition, sacrificing truth to esthetic effect, see Dietrich Becker, *Die Belagerung von Crema bei Rahewin, im Ligurinus, und im Carmen de gestis Frederici I. imperatoris in Lombardia. Untersuchungen zur literarischen Form staufischer Geschichtsschreibung* (Mannheim: N.p., 1975), pp. 177, 204, 208, 211–12, 217, 221. On Rahewin's employment of "poetic" or "fictive" elements as historical facts, ibid., p. 201. In general, see Hans-Peter Apelt, *Rahewins Gesta Friderici I. Imperatoris: Ein Beitrag zur Geschichtsschreibung des 12. Jahrhunderts* (Munich: N.p., 1971).

[25] See "Hermeneutics and Enigma: Bernard of Clairvaux's *De Consideratione*," pp. 132, 134, 142, 146.

[26] Gerhoch of Reichersberg, *Tractatus in Ps. 64*, chap. 73; *MGH, Ldl* 3, p. 471.

[27] Rupert of Deutz, *Anulus*, bk. 4; Migne *PL* 170:607–8. See chap. 2, n. 54; chap. 6, n. 79.

[28] *Commentum in Apocalypsim*, 7.12; Migne *PL* 169:1050.

[29] *Topographia Hibernia*, dist. 2, chap. 38; James F. Dimock, ed., *Giraldi Cambrensis Opera*, Rolls Series, no. 21 (London: Longman, 1867), 5:123–24.

discovery, or even recomposition. As he introduced his immense *Chronicle* of the Latin Kingdom of Jerusalem, he alleged that his powers had been unequal to the task. He was, he wrote, like the unskilled painters, not yet admitted to the secrets of art (*ad artis arcana*). The unskilled were allowed to prime surfaces and outline figures in earth tones, but wiser hands achieved the beauty of the work by adding nobler colors. So readers, and perhaps more excellent writers among them, could perfect his beginnings.[30]

Thus, both the hermeneutic time of the author and the historical time that the author created for the reader in the text were thought to be related to visual imagination. Because they aroused and drew upon memory, they pertained to the mnemonic and mimetic functions of history. But because the experiences that they constituted were intended to be emotional (or affective), they also served the hedonic function of history, which, as we have seen, could shape historical narrative more powerfully than the other two.

By underscoring the importance of affective response, previous studies have emphasized the difference between the words of a text, the feelings of the author presumed to be in the text, and the feelings of the reader. The comments by Rupert of Deutz and William of Tyre just cited remind us that one result was to distinguish the hermeneutic time of the author from that of the reader, and, moreover, to establish that the hedonic effects of any text might be not only multiple but even mutually exclusive.

Doctrinal conflicts over the meaning of Scripture gave abundant examples. But, of course, we must distinguish between the pretextual hermeneutic time of the author and the posttextual one of the reader. And yet, even when articles of doctrine and order were not at issue, wide variations in readers' hermeneutic times were acknowledged. Gerhoch of Reichersberg, for example, observed that the same Psalm recited on two occasions could have quite different effects, since occasion colored its meaning. And Otto of Freising gave a specific historical witness to the weight of circumstances when he recalled the mass, "Let us rejoice," being sung "with much bitterness of heart," in the wake of disaster, while the cries of the afflicted could still be heard.[31] The same event could be experienced differently by different persons: a creditor and a debtor waited with contrasting attitudes for the same loan to come due.[32] Further, the experience of an individual

[30] *Chronicon*, prol.; *Corp. Christ.*, *continuatio medievalis*, 63, pp. 98–101.

[31] Gerhoch of Reichersberg, *Tractatus in Ps. 37*: 2–5; Damian van den Eynde and Odulph van den Eynde, eds., *Gerhohi Praepositi Reichersbergensis Opera Inedita*, Spicilegium Pontificii Athenaei Antoniani, no. 10 (Rome: Pontificium Athenaeum Antonianum, 1956), vol. 2, pt. 2, p. 588. Otto of Freising, *Gesta Friderici*, 1.47(45); *MGH*, *SSrrG*, p. 67.

[32] John of Salisbury, *ep. 287*; W. J. Millor and C.N.L. Brooke, eds., *The Letters of John of Salisbury* (Oxford: Clarendon, 1979), 2:634.

person at a particular instant could be multiple, as it was when a person chanting a Psalm found his attention lapse through fatigue, reel under sexual fantasies, or succumb to the beauty of music, forgetting the sacred words.[33] The invention of new forms of psalmody, the coordination of voices with every kind of musical instrument necessarily multiplying and entangling *tempi*, alarmed religious conservatives as part of a wide disruption of authentic order in the Church.[34]

Like musical compositions, therefore, hermeneutic experiences of authors—and readers—were understood as being performed in mixed times, certainly another link with theater. In fact, historical texts were occasionally referred to as "songs" (*carmina*), and Scripture itself was known to have mixed many songs with history.[35] The ancient bardic relation between history and music was still vital.[36] The analogy between tales from

[33] Gerhoch of Reichersberg, *Tractatus in Ps. 1*: Gloria, and *Tractatus in Ps. 41*: 6; Migne *PL* 193:655–56, 1505–06. *Tractatus in Ps. 136*: 8; Migne *PL* 194:908–9. *Tractatus in Ps. 37*: 8; *Opera Inedita*, vol. 2, pt. 2, pp. 628–29 on distraction at prayer by "imagines corporum," illusions, not only of sight, but also of touch, smell, and taste. See Augustine's discussion of how music in psalmody could distract him from the words and meanings of the Psalms. *Confessions*, 10.33.49–50; *Corp. Christ., ser. lat.* 27, pp. 181–82. Gerhoch cited this passage in *Tractatus in Ps. 41*: 5; Migne *PL* 193:1505. Gerhoch added that the intellectual sense, heard by the ears of the mind, pleased more than the sound of the chanting heard by ears of the body.

[34] Anselm of Havelberg, *Antikeimenon*, 1.1, 4; Migne *PL* 188: 1142, 1146. On Gerhoch's opposition to mixed choirs because they encouraged polyphony, since men and women could not sing the same tone, see chap. 6, n. 83.

[35] Cosmas of Prague, *Chronica Boemorum*, 2.51; *MGH, SSrrG*, p. 159. See chap. 6, n. 20. As he inserted one of his own poems, the Venerable Bede claimed the precedent of Scripture: ". . . et imitari morem sacrae scripturae cujus historiae carmina plurima indita. . . ." *Historia Ecclesiastica*, 4.20; Bertram Colgrave and R.A.B. Mynors, eds., *Bede's Ecclesiastical History of the English People* (Oxford: Clarendon, 1969), p. 396.

[36] Herbert Grundmann, *Geschichtsschreibung im Mittelalter: Gattungen—Epochen—Eigenart*, 2d ed. (Göttingen: Van den Hoeck und Ruprecht, 1969), pp. 5, 8. Sabine Žak, *Musik als "Ehr und Zier" im mittelalterlichen Reich: Studien zur Musik im höfischen Leben, Recht, und Zeremoniell* (Neuss: Pfäffgen, 1979), pp. 213–15, 223. Manfred Schluck, *Die Vita Heinrici IV. Imperatoris: Ihre zeitgenössischen Quellen und ihr besonderes Verhältnis zum Carmen de bello Saxonico*, Vorträge und Forschungen, Sonderband 26 (Sigmaringen: Thorbecke, 1979). Bernard of Clairvaux referred to the *De Consideratione* as "canticum meum," 2.7.14; Leclercq and Rochais, eds., *S. Bernardi Opera*, 3:422. See also his quotation of Eccl. 22:6 ("Musica in luctu importuna narratio est") in *Vita Malachiae*, 31.72, in the same volume as the *De Consideratione*, p. 376. Common street songs, hunting songs, and songs of ridicule were also in a way historical texts. See Žak, *Musik als "Ehr und Zier,"* pp. 233, 324–25. See Ekkehard of Aura, *Chronicon* (*a*. 1104); *MGH, SS* 6, pp. 225–26, and the songs of ridicule sung against Henry IV's nominee to succeed Anno as Archbishop of Cologne. Lambert of Hersfeld, *Annales* (*a*. 1076); *MGH, SSrrG*, pp. 251, 255. See also *Miracula Adalberonis Episcopi Wirzibergensis*, chap. 7; *MGH, SS* 12, p. 142: ". . . ut quidam de eo satyrizando sic carmine ludit. . . ." See chap. 6, nn. 20, 83.

Giraldus Cambrensis relished the irony by which the kinds of entertainment imported by Bishop William Longchamps for his vainglory and delight were turned to mock him at his fall from power. *De Vita Galfridi Archiepiscopi Eboracensis*, 2.19; J. S. Brewer, ed., *Giraldi Cam-*

history and theatrical spectacles, which were normally enlivened by music, emphasized the mixture of voices in varying *tempi* that could be experienced in reading and reflecting upon historical texts. This was a point of affinity not only with "scurrilous songs and spectacles of plays," but also with fables, or "fictive histories," mimes, fortune-tellers, hunting, gambling and the whole repertoire of play with which writers and readers of histories kept boredom—the experience of dead time—at bay.[37]

Authors were attentive to chronology, but even there a fascination derived from the variety of times with which a given event could be defined.[38]

---

*brensis Opera*, Rolls Series, no. 21 (London: Longman, 1873), 4:427: "Et sicut joculatores de regno Francorum et cantores rythmici ab ipso conducti, in laudem sui nominis epigrammata plurima et cantica praeconiosa fingere consueverunt, sic hodie, vice versa, viri magni et literati super casus huius articulo, notabilique exemplo ad posterorum doctrinam et cautelam, in ignominiam ipsius et confusionem redundantia scripta non pauca et carmina composuere."

On lascivious songs sung by sailors, Rupert of Deutz, *Commentum in Apocalypsim*, 10.18; Migne *PL* 169:1155. For a traveller, stripped naked by thieves of this world and forced to sing for their amusement, *Vita Wicberti*, chap. 3; *MGH, SS* 8, p. 509. For the same topos, Matthew Paris, *Chronica Magna* (*a.* 1253), quoting Juvenal, 10:22; in Henry Richards Luard, ed., *Matthaei Parisiensis Monachi Sancti Albani Chronica Majora*, 7 vols., Rolls Series, no. 57 (London: Longman, 1872–83), 5:401.

[37] See the catalogue of forms of play forbidden to the Knights Templar in Bernard of Clairvaux, *Ad Milites Templi*, 4.7; Migne *PL* 182:926. Bernard included "fabulatores." For the association of history with fable, see John of Salisbury, *Metalogicon*, 1.20; Clement C. J. Webb, ed., *Ioannis Saresberiensis Episcopi Carnotensis Metalogicon Libri IIII* (Oxford: Clarendon, 1929), p. 49: "in historiis aut narrationibus fabulosis"; and *Policraticus*, 1.9; Webb, ed., 1:46: "fictas historias." Adam of Bremen described how, while feasting, Archbishop Adalbert diverted himself with witticisms, histories of kings, and the choice opinions of philosophers, but he drove from his court the pantomimes who entertained the common people with obscene movements of their bodies. *Gesta Hammaburgensis Ecclesiae Pontificum*, 3.39(38); *MGH, SSrrG*, pp. 182–83. See Otto of Freising's interpolations in descriptions of the marriage of Henry III and Agnes, including "omne balatronum et histrionum collegium, quod, ut assolet eo confluxerat, vacuum abire permisit. . . ." *Chronicon*, 6.32; *MGH, SSrrG*, p. 298. See also chap. 6, nn. 70–77.

[38] For example, Ekkehard of Aura recorded that Henry V began to rule in 1106, the eighty-second emperor after Augustus, in the fiftieth year of his father's reign, 1,106 years from the incarnation of Christ, 1,858 years from the founding of Rome, and 5,058 years from the beginning of the world. *Chronicon* (*a.* 1106); *MGH, SS* 6, p. 233. Otto of Freising wrote similarly that the birth of Christ occurred in the forty-second year of Augustus's reign, 752 years after the founding of Rome, in the one hundred ninety-third Olympiad, 5,500 years from Adam, while Herod, the son of Antipater was ruling in Judea, and in the sixty-sixth week according to Daniel's prophecy; and, again when he dated the time of his writing to 1,146 years from the incarnation of the Lord, 1,918 years from the foundation of Rome, the ninth year of the reign of Conrad III (the ninety-third emperor after Augustus), and the second year of the pontificate of Eugenius III. *Chronicon*, 3.6, 7.24; *MGH, SSrrG*, pp. 141, 369. Cf. also Giraldus Cambrensis's dating of the consecration of Geoffrey of York, *De Vita Galfridi Archiepiscopi Eboracensis*, 1.13; J. S. Brewer, ed., p. 384. Giraldus gave these co-ordinates: the age of the consecrand (about forty), the time since the death of his father, King Henry II (two years), the time since Saladin's conquest of Jerusalem (four years), the time since King Philip of France and King Richard of England set out on crusade toward Jerusa-

In rhetoric and in law, time was among the contingencies that defined events (the others being, the cause, place, and mode of occurrence, and the person[s] involved). The variety of relations between one event and others so defined is only one instance of the ornate multiplicity that could be brought to bear by authors in their texts or by readers as they expanded texts with their own associations.[39]

And yet the special delight of events that occurred in time was precisely their "untimeliness" (*inactualité*)[40] that made it possible for all readers, at any time and in any place, to project themselves into the spectacle in the text. Each event could be defined by multiple coordinates that the chronology of no other event could duplicate. But it was also true that, through the categories of figural understanding, events repeated themselves. Henry IV was abandoned; and those who betrayed him installed his son and namesake in his place. Through this sacrilege, one commentator wrote, "Christ, rising in the hearts of all, was crucified again in his Church."[41] In the great dramatic spectacles of history, as in the yearly round of liturgical drama, roles of Scriptural figures were continually reenacted, for spiritual affinity and distance were neither spatial nor temporal. They existed under the aspect of eternity, an "everlasting today." The year of the Lord was a crown, or circle, in which through faith and sacraments Christ's incarnation, passion, and resurrection recurred again and again in converted sin-

---

lem (one year), and the time since the incarnation of the Lord (1,192 years). See the chapter on chronology in Benoît Lacroix, *L'historien au moyen-âge*, Conférence Albert-le-Grand, 1966 (Montréal: Institut d'études médiévales, 1971), pp. 64–98, a study valuable out of proportion to its brevity.

[39] See Gratian, *Concordia discordantium canonum*, dist. 29, chap. 1 (cause, person, place, and time). Ivo of Chartres, prol.; Migne *PL* 161:52 (necessity of times, utility of persons). I am obliged to Mr. Bruce Brasington for these legal references. Bernard of Clairvaux, *De Consideratione*, 3.2.7, referred to place, mode, time, cause and person in appellate jurisdiction. See also ibid., 5.7.16 (times, places, persons, and *res* [*–causae*]); Leclercq and Rochais, eds., *S. Bernardi Opera*, 3:436, 480.

An example of different awarenesses of time occurs in Herbord's biography of Bishop Otto of Bamberg. One participant in the dialogue fears that the history has become overburdened. Another answers that, for those who love Otto, nothing good about him can be superfluous or tedious. *Dialogus de Vita S. Ottonis Episcopi Babenbergensis*, 2.19; Jan Wikarjak, ed., Monumenta Poloniae Historica, n.s., vol. 7, fasc. 3 (Warsaw: Państwowe Wydawnictwo Naukowe, 1974), p. 96.

[40] Roland Barthes, "The Romantic Song," in *The Responsibility of Forms*, trans. Richard Howard (New York: Hill and Wang, 1985), p. 286.

[41] Ekkehard of Aura, *Chronicon* (a. 1106); *MGH*, *SS* 6, p. 238. The combination of chronological distance and atemporality is also exemplified by Rupert of Deutz, particularly in his insistence that, under the aspect of prophecy, all three tenses (past, present, and future) were one and in his typological interpretation of persons. See Rupert's *Commentum in Apocalypsim*, 1.1, 10.17, 11.19; Migne *PL* 169:831, 1130, 1174. For his statement that all the redeemed, past and future, were washed by Christ's blood at the crucifixion, see ibid., 1.1; Migne *PL* 169:840.

ners. Christ died, rose, and ascended but once. Yet one could speak of a "continual resurrection," as sinners were converted, made dead with Christ, and clothed in his Paschal robe.[42] All the numbers by which temporal years were reckoned were gathered up into this "time of times," replicated in the circuit of sun, moon, and stars.[43]

"Time is there for us," Dilthey wrote, "through the synthesizing unity of consciousness."[44] In the twelfth century, in the enactments of cult and in historical writing as an expression of cult, the variety of times was subsumed into the circular year of the Lord, the fullness of time that was already and not yet, and that, like all circles, moved from a beginning without beginning and toward an end without end.[45]

Fortune's spin was plain to see. Writers of history invited their readers to enter with them into the other, more hidden cycles. Thus far, we have been considering the hermeneutic time of authors as they "digested truth." The overarching result of the discussion is summed up in the word "untimeliness" (*inactualité*). To be sure, writers could exhibit great precision in chronology and establish multiple chronological coordinates for a given event (e.g., its length of time from the Creation, Incarnation, and the founding of Rome). But this precision was counterbalanced by a marked and habitual nonchalance toward chronology in dating historical materials. For example, apart from official acts, letters were seldom dated, nor were coins.

We have said something about *tempi* expected by authorial audience and something about the cultural environment that gave the community in which these texts arose and had their original sense common expectations of hermeneutic time. We have encountered an idea of events in which time and space were not necessary coordinates. Therefore, the authors lacked the idea of an event as phenomenon. The hermeneutic event—understanding—was a moment of visualization keyed to the viewer's present, without foreground or background. Without the spectator, the spectacle was empty, empty as an unseen painting, or one that for some reason viewers could not fill with their own associations.[46]

---

[42] Gerhoch of Reichersberg, *Tractatus in Ps. 37*: 2–5; *Opera Inedita*, vol. 2, pt. 2, p. 597. Cf. *Tractatus in Ps. 35*: 9; ibid., p. 438. *Expositio super canonem, "collatio missae"*; *Opera Inedita*, 1:11. *Tractatus in Ps. 7*: 9; Migne *PL* 193:730. *Tractatus in Ps. 64*, chap. 122; Migne *PL* 194:80.

[43] Hildegard of Bingen, *Scivias*, 1.3.21, 3.11.17; *Corp. Christ., continuatio medievalis*, 43, p. 51 and 43A, p. 585.

[44] "Entwürfe zur Kritik der historischen Vernunft, Teil 1," p. 192.

[45] On Christ as the end without end, Otto of Freising, *Chronicle*, 8.34; *MGH, SSrrG*, p. 456. On Christ the Logos, as the point of departure for a history and the end of all things to be done, John of Salisbury, *Historia Pontificalis*, prol.; Chibnall, ed., p. 4. See n. 126.

[46] Pseudo-Cyprian, *De Spectaculis*, chap. 8; *CSEL* 3, pt. 3, p. 11. See *"I Am You,"* pt. 4:

Lacking the requisite properties of phenomena and located in the viewer's perspective, time was indefinitely multiple. Time was multiple in any given event. Measured by the spectator's attention, it was divided as attention was among objects of attention. The spectator experienced mixed times, a variety of times, not merely as shifting, mutating events, and as performance of two or more acts simultaneously (e.g., singing and travelling, or commanding troops in battle and reflecting on Scripture), but also as mixed emotional responses. Of course, time was multiple for participants in the same event (e.g., for the lender and the borrower in the repayment of a loan). Time was multiple in the repetition of events, notably in the reenactment of Scriptural events, such as episodes in the life of Christ, both in the liturgical and sacramental dramas of the Church and in lines of identity that were drawn between past and present (e.g., Christ recrucified in his martyrs).

At a higher level, of course, all times were united in the time of times. Authors could conceive of time's course as circular in the "everlasting today" of God, imitated in the movement of heavenly bodies. In the crown of that everlasting today, even widely separate events could be considered simultaneous.

Our authors were aware that this perception of times was limited to few, even as were the correct understanding of "time" and "the times" in the testimonies of Scripture. They discoursed in Latin, with others whose hands were beautiful, and their limited company displayed an extensive repertoire of ways in which to diversify perceptions of time: among them, ethnic hostilities (represented in the disdainful linguistic epithet, "barbarian"); permeation of thought about time with metaphors and experience of the *tempi* of play (including those in the performing arts and gambling); and, finally, the attitudes toward transience nourished by an ascetic culture of conspicuous waste. This repertoire presupposed the unpredictable, disconnectedness of times, the fitful play that Fortune performed in the theater of the world.

Such were some preconceptions that formed the *cire perdue* of pretextual assumptions that made up the author's perspective. It should be emphasized that all of our texts were written from the viewpoint of the author's present. With the exception of Otto of Freising's *Chronicle*, all deal primarily with contemporary events, referring to the past only for the sake of precedent, or elucidating analogue. Yet, as he presented the *Chronicle* to Frederick Barbarossa, Otto composed the baldest of all statements of authorial presentism. He had woven the work together, he wrote, in the form of a tragedy, because that portrayal corresponded, not with the actual or-

---

"The Emptiness of Painting." See also chap. 3, n. 103; chap. 5, nn. 37, 47; chap. 6, after n. 75; above, n. 23.

der of events, but with his own bitterness of mind.[47] All the works were composed, or commissioned, for specific occasions, with the possible exception of Bernard of Clairvaux's *De Consideratione*. Thus, presentist and occasional, they were also intentionally ephemeral, authentic monuments of the very concept of *inactualité* that they expressed.

. . .

We return, then, to the metaphor of the wheel, that is, to nuclear perspective. This time, the inner wheel of prophecy, which interpreters found in Ezekiel's vision, is omitted, but not the outer one of fulfillment. And, with the metaphor of the turning wheel, we encounter in writings as we did in visual evidence a perspective that both compartmentalized events (as by the spokes) and visually blended them in the turning of the wheel.

In previous inquiries, I have, implicitly and explicitly, identified some traits of the authors and of the readers for whom these texts were intended to serve mnemonic, mimetic, and hedonic functions. Just as place, time, and person were categories of legal and rhetorical analysis, so too were they practical guides for speakers or writers as they calibrated style and message to suit their audience, aiming to draw tears from the stony hearts of the listening multitude and stirring emotions until the whole church resonated with the wails and lamentations.[48] Authors saw themselves in the mirror of their audiences. What profile of an intended reader—and therefore what concept of themselves held by the authors—guided those calculations?

Clearly, our first observation must be that the authorial audience was small. Allowing for the difficulty of copying and the perils of manuscript survival, it is still remarkable that John of Salisbury's *Historia Pontificalis* survives in only one manuscript (written a century after the text was composed), and that Anselm of Havelberg's *Dialogues* are not known to exist in any medieval copies.[49] Two rescensions of Gerhoch of Reichersberg's

[47] *Chronicon, ep. ad Fridericum*; *MGH, SSrrG*, pp. 2–3. Significantly, Otto employed a similar turn of phrase when he referred to a verse account of the Emperor Conrad II by Wipo: "rerum humanarum casum deplorans rhitmum in modum tragediae simplici stilo composuit. . . ." *Chronicon*, 6.31; *MGH, SSrrG*, p. 297.

[48] E.g., Herbord, *Dialogus de Vita S. Ottonis Episcopi Babenbergensis*, 1.10; Wikarjak, ed., p. 12. Lambert of Hersfeld, *Annales (a. 1075)*; *MGH, SSrrG*, p. 244, on Archbishop of Anno's power as a preacher.

[49] Chibnall, *John of Salisbury's Memoirs of the Papal Court*, p. xlvii. The collection of John of Salisbury's letters, some of which constitute important historiographical essays, exists in one "nearly complete" manuscript of the late twelfth or early thirteenth century, in one manuscript of the late twelfth century which contains over half the letters, and in one later fragmentary copy. A fourth, very partial, copy once known has vanished. Millor and Brooke, eds., *The Letters of John of Salisbury*, 2:xlvii–lxiii.

Johann Wilhelm Braun, "Studien zur Überlieferung der Werke Anselms von Havelberg, I:

*Tractate on Psalm 64* are known, each in one twelfth-century manuscript.[50] A modern edition (1912) of Otto of Freising's *Chronicle* inventoried forty-seven manuscripts containing either the entire work or large excerpts. Eleven of these were dated to the twelfth century; seven to the thirteenth; and by far the majority (twenty-five) to the fifteenth and sixteenth.[51] Yet even the distribution of this work, which received imperial sanction, was chiefly limited to Austria and Bavaria. On the whole, it was ignored by other writers in Otto's own day and later, until the fifteenth century; one scholar has concluded that his historiographical methods proved to be a "dead-end."[52]

Otto of Freising concluded his account of the death of Lothar III with a remarkably strange comment. So that they could never be forgotten, he wrote, the Emperor's deeds were inscribed on sheets of lead and buried with him.[53] In fact, a single lead plaque, recovered in 1620, was entombed with Lothar's body (figure 13). One perplexity is how Otto could have thought that entombing a record with the corpse could have been thought to safeguard Lothar's deeds from oblivion. Even taking the very long term into account, it is difficult to imagine circumstances under which those in charge of the Emperor's funeral would have anticipated the exhumation of body and plaque together. A second perplexity arises from the inscription itself, which is far from a comprehensive memoir. In eleven lines, the inscription records Lothar's name and titles, the length of his reign, the date of his death, and a brief eulogy.[54] Perhaps Otto did not know the content of the inscription any more than he knew that there was only one lead plaque. But was there some connection in his mind between the memorial function of the record in the silence of the tomb and that of his own words in the silences of the codex?

Equally, there is no evidence that the other writings in question were read, cited, and absorbed by other writers into their thinking. The scant

Die Überlieferung des Anticimenon," *Deutsches Archiv* 28 (1972): 135–36, lists nineteen manuscripts of Anselm's works, of which thirteen contain the *Dialogues*. Of the thirteen, eleven date from the fifteenth century, and one each from the seventeenth and eighteenth.

[50] Peter Classen, *Gerhoch von Reichersberg: Eine Biographie* (Wiesbaden: Steiner, 1960), p. 419.

[51] Adolf Hofmeister in *MGH, SSrrG*, pp. x–lxxxviii. The edition by Leclercq and Rochais does not systematically provide dates of manuscripts preserving Bernard of Clairvaux's *De Consideratione*.

[52] Martin Haeusler, *Das Ende der Geschichte in der mittelalterlichen Weltchronistik* (Vienna: Böhlau, 1980), p. 41.

[53] *Chronicon*, 7.21; *MGH, SSrrG*, p. 340. This comment is omitted from the account of Lothar's death in Otto's *Gesta Friderici*, 1.23; *MGH, SSrrG*, p. 36.

[54] The inscription eulogizes him as a "man faithful in Christ, simple, truthful, constant, peaceable, gentle, fearless," who died returning from Apulia, where he had visited death and exile on the Saracens. The full inscription is transcribed in Percy Ernst Schramm and Florentine Mütherich, *Denkmale der deutschen Könige und Kaiser* (Munich: Prestel, 1962), p. 179.

*Figure 13.* The degree to which audience response affected historical imagination is called into question by Otto of Freising's statement that the Emperor Lothar III's great deeds were inscribed on lead tablets and buried in his tomb so that they would never be forgotten. The plate shows the one lead tablet and the orb and cross, also in lead, that were recovered from Lothar's tomb in the seventeenth century. *Inv. MA 64165. Herzog Anton Ulrich-Museum, Braunschweig.*

distribution of the histories underscores what we have already determined about their intended audience. The intended readers did not include women, on the whole, nor certainly members of cultural or social categories whose histories were suppressed. Because they were written in Latin, for example, they did not include a Jew of Cologne, the offspring of a prominent family, who conducted business in the Rhineland, becoming the creditor of at least one bishop. This merchant-banker moved easily in Christian society, engaging not only in daily conversations, once with a chaplain to Queen Richenza, but also in frequent theological disputations and public debates. Yet he yet did not master Latin until after his conversion to Christianity and entrance into a monastic community.[55]

Great prejudices were rooted in vernacular languages and other ethnic divisions; and these impeded exchanges even among readers whose ecclesiastical credentials and mastery of Latin was impeccable. Germans, for ex-

---

[55] Gerlinde Niemeyer, *Hermannus quondam Judaeus: Opusculum de Conversione Sua*; *MGH*, Quellen zur Geistesgeschichte, Bd. 4 (Weimar: Böhlau, 1963).

ample, were derided as barbaric by their brethren in Romance countries.[56] Furthermore, geographically, culturally, and linguistically circumscribed, the audience addressed by the texts belonged to social levels that esteemed the contraries of asceticism and conspicuous waste. The authorial audience plainly did not include knights, illiterate men who ought to know more about weapons than about the profession of letters.[57] It did not include "young men of low estate or laborers in the contemptible and mechanic arts whom all peoples repel, like the plague, from the more estimable and liberal pursuits."[58] Nor did it include the "simple and uneducated," the "rude commons" for whom pictures were said to have been invented to serve as books served the literate. Nor in distinguishing, oral, written, and visual perceptions did it include "the illiterate actors and mimes of our age, who deceive the eyes of on-lookers by sleight of hand."[59]

Like courtly love, and its poetry, history was for the few. The authorial audience did include men like Albero of Trier, who, fleeing in disguise, fell into the hands of his enemies, the Pisans. They recognized "from his most beautiful hands, that he was not a man of the plebeian class."[60] Albero

[56] John of Salisbury, *Historia Pontificalis*, chap. 24. Chibnall, ed., p. 55 (on disesteem for the German *barbarus*, Cardinal Theodwin of Porto). Reuter, "John of Salisbury and the Germans," p. 425: The epithets used by John to characterize Germans "were not rhetorical devices which stood in the way of objective understanding, but a necessary means of describing a strange and rather incomprehensible world." To say that, of course, is not to deny the ardent contempt that John did express and that certainly obstructed understanding by obstructing the wish to understand. It is, however, to register an exception to the skeptic's suspension of judgment that was in other regards a feature of John's thought. See Roger Ray, "Rhetorical Scepticism and Verisimilar Narrative in John of Salisbury's *Historia Pontificalis*," in *Classical Rhetoric and Medieval Historiography*, ed. Ernst Breisach, pp. 77–78. For similar animus, see Peter of Eboli, *De Rebus Siculis Carmen*; Ettore Rota, ed., Rerum Italicarum Scriptores, vol. 31, pt. 1 (Città di Castello: S. Lapi, 1904), bk. I, particula 5, ll. 121–23, p. 23: "Teutonicam rabiem quis tolerare potest? / Parce tuis canis: pueri tibi more licebit / Discere barbaricos barbarizare sonos?"

[57] John of Salisbury, *Policraticus*, 6.10; Webb, ed., 2:25.

[58] Rahewin, *Gesta Friderici*, 2.13; *MGH, SSrrG*, p. 116.

[59] Hermannus quondam Judaeus, *Opusculum de Conversione Sua*, chap. 4; *MGH*, Quellen zur Geistesgeschichte, 4:80. Peter the Venerable, *Adversus Iudeorum Inveteratam Duritiem*, chap. 4; *Corp. Christ., continuatio medievalis*, 58, p. 115.

[60] On the elitism of courtly love, see Douglas Kelly, *Medieval Imagination: Rhetoric and the Poetry of Courtly Love* (Madison: University of Wisconsin Press, 1978), p. xv. Balderic, *Gesta Alberonis*, chap. 5; *MGH, SS* 8, p. 247. Two men in John of Salisbury's circle were known for their "fair" or "white" hands, John "Belmeis," Bishop of Poitiers and later Archbishop of Lyons, mentioned at the beginning of the *Policraticus*, and William "of the White Hands," brother-in-law of Louis VII, who died as Archbishop of Rheims. Walter Daniel commented that, in his field labor, the ascetic Ailred did not spare the tender skin and fine fingers of his hands. Walter Daniel, *Vita Ailredi*, chap. 12. F. M. Powicke, ed., *The Life of Ailred of Rievaulx by Walter Daniel* (London: Nelson, 1950), p. 22. Much earlier, Bede recorded that those who observed a certain captive knew from his general bearing, his costume, and his speech that he was not the peasant he pretended to be, but rather a man of noble birth. *Historia Ecclesiastica*,

happened to be carrying with him an ivory box, wrapped in fine cloth of Tyrian purple,[61] and it was characteristic of the intended audience that it, too, was familiar with the conspicuous waste devoted to all the arts—to the theater, which was an appurtenance not only of princes's courts, but also of monasteries and churches; to hunting and the enclosure of great hunting parks often at the cost of peasant villages; to gambling; and to other forms of secular play. Association between historical writing and the conspicuous waste of cult prompted the biographer of a saint to write synesthetically: ". . . his memory will abide forever with us in blessing. For his memory, as is written, rendered as it were the work of a painter in a composition of sweet fragrance, endures to the age of ages, like honey, and as though it were music at a banquet of wine."[62]

It was also characteristic that the authorial audience subscribed to conspicuous waste as practiced in ascetic communities, employing the physical as a necessary instrument of spiritual enlightenment. Our texts presupposed knowledge of the mixed times accessible through liturgy and music, painting and sculpture, monastic architecture and literature, all forms of conspicuous waste in the synesthetic play of cult. The symbiosis of contrasts was striking in the lives of great prelates, renown for the austerity of their own lives, who built majestic edifices and adorned them with the most exquisite splendors. Some sense of this is evident in a question addressed to Bishop Otto of Bamberg. Why, it was asked, did the Bishop devote so much money to founding, elegantly adorning, and richly endowing new monastic establishments, when the world was already full of such institutions? What was the need for more?[63]

The value that the culture placed on conspicuous waste is shown, not only in the lavish devotion of resources to buildings and institutions of cult, but also to the continuing destruction and reconstruction of cult buildings and furniture. With ambition beyond his means, Archbishop

---

4.22; Colgrave and Mynors, eds., p. 403. Even if, as Mégier holds, the range of social classes included by Otto of Freising indicates a far greater elitism than that included by Ordericus Vitalis, the general principle remains intact that the subjects of history and its intended audience were elitist. E. Mégier, "Deux exemples de 'prépurgatoire' chez les historiens: À propos de *La naissance du Purgatoire* de Jacques Le Goff," *Cahiers de civilisation médiévale (Xe–XIIe siècles)*, 8 (1985): 45–62.

[61] Balderic, *Gesta Alberonis*, chap. 5; *MGH, SS* 8, p. 247.

[62] *Vita Godefridi Comitis Capenbergensis*, pref.; *MGH, SS* 12, p. 515. The reference is to Eccl. 49:2, also cited in Ebo, *Vita S. Ottonis Episcopi Babenbergensis*, 1.8; Jan Wikarjak, ed., Monumenta Poloniae Historica, n.s., vol. 7, fasc. 3 (Warsaw: Państwowe Wydawnictwo Naukowe, 1969), p. 19. Evidence of one great donor's wish for objects of luxury devoted to cult to last forever is given by William of Poitiers in his *Gesta Guillelmi Ducis Normannorum et Regis Anglorum*, pt. 2, chap. 42; Raymonde Foreville, ed., Les classiques de l'histoire de France au Moyen Âge, vol. 23 (Paris: "Les belles lettres," 1952), p. 256.

[63] Lambert of Hersfeld, *Annales* (a. 1075); *MGH, SSrrG*, p. 244. Helmold, *Dialogus de Vita S. Ottonis Episcopi Babenbergensis*, 1.12, 18; Wikarjak, ed., pp. 12–13, 18.

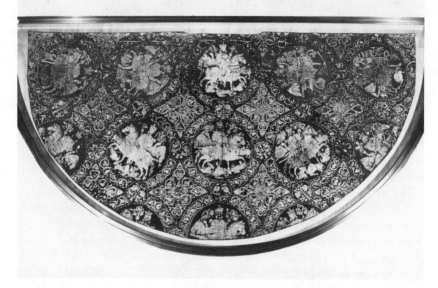

*Figure 14.* Precious fabrics were especially prized in the interplay of ascetic renunciation and conspicuous waste. Depicted here is a large cope, called the *Reiterman-
tel* because the pattern of its medallions is a horseman. The twelfth-century fabric,
possibly from southern Italy, was originally dark blue silk, embroidered in gold.
*Diözesanmuseum Bamberg. Photo: Ingeborg Limmer.*

Adalbert of Bremen expressed the thinking of many when, amidst massive
demolitions, he declared that he would remake in gold those buildings that
had been made in silver. Reality fell short of Adalbert's dreams, but there
were other builders whose churches glittered with figures and plates of
gold.[64]

One symptom of the value placed on the costly and perishable was the
infatuation of the culture with precious fabrics, such as the swathe of Tyrian purple in which Albero wrapped his ivory casket (figure 14). Enumer-
ating the vast array of treasures which he brought St. Denis, Abbot Suger
particularly required the community to exhibit the textiles which the Divine Hand had lavished on it during his abbacy on each anniversary of his
death, in order to propitiate God, increase the devotion of the brethren,
and provide an example to his successors. The production and sale of luxury fabrics was lucrative enough to warrant the itinerancy of workers. For

[64] Adam of Bremen, *Gesta Hammaburgensis Ecclesiae Pontificum*, 3.46(45); *MGH, SSrrG*, p.
189. E.g., Gerhoch of Reichersberg, *Tractatus in Ps. 64*, chaps. 51, 169; *MGH, Ldl* 3, p. 461;
Migne *PL* 194:113.

example, English women were so expert in making embroidered fabrics woven with gold that Germans came to learn from them, and merchants carried the works of their skilled hands to distant regions.[65] It was natural, therefore, that when they described the variations given to the Church by its long history, the equivalence between variety and beauty led authors to employ the metaphor of a queen's robe in cloth of gold, adorned with golden tassels and shimmering in its many-toned iridescent splendor, and yet, like the tunics of Joseph and Christ, woven in seamless unity.[66]

The authorial audience for three of our works specifically included Pope Eugenius III, to whom they were dedicated.[67] Otto of Freising was present in the Curia shortly after his brother Cistercian was elected as Pope; and John of Salisbury's *Historia Pontificalis* was conceived as a memoir of Eugenius. Thus, it is worth observing that the values of asceticism and conspicuous waste just described were cherished by Eugenius and his entourage.

[65] *De Administratione*, chap. 34a. Erwin Panofsky, ed. and trans., *Abbot Suger on the Abbey Church of St.-Denis*, 2d ed. (Princeton, N.J.: Princeton University Press, 1979), p. 80. William of Poitiers, *Gesta Guillelmi Ducis Normannorum et Regis Anglorum*, pt. 2, chap. 42; Foreville, ed., pp. 256–58.

[66] Gerhoch of Reichersberg, *Tractatus in Ps. 64*, chap. 115; Migne *PL* 194:76. Bernard of Clairvaux, *Apologia*, 3.6–4.7; Leclercq and Rochais, eds., *S. Bernardi Opera*, 3:86–88. Cf. the reference to the precious metal that Abbot Godehard of Hersfeld extracted for the poor by melting down two hundred golden stoles. Lambert of Hersfeld, *Institutio Herveldensis Ecclesiae*; *MGH, SSrrG*, p. 349. To depredations of churches charged against two papal legates by Frederick Barbarossa (Rahewin, *Gesta Friderici*, 3.11; *MGH, SSrrG*, p. 179), Gunther added "abrumpere[nt] textibus aurum." *Ligurinus*, 6. line 367; *MGH, SSrrG*, p. 349. To establish a context in which to gauge the magnitude of the love and use of costly fabrics, it may be useful to remember the gifts that Henry IV gave to the desolate church of Hamburg. Clearly re-establishing a treasury at one stroke, Henry gave many objects (including a chasse with a cover allegedly containing nine pounds of gold and three chalices containing ten pounds of gold), books, silver vessels, and one hundred vestments, including dorsals, chasubles, dalmatics, copes, and others. Adam of Bremen, *Gesta Hammaburgensis Ecclesiae Pontificum*, 3.45(44); *MGH, SSrrG*, p. 187. See also the extreme fascination taken by Reginald of Durham (ca. 1175) in the costly and richly patterned fabrics discovered in St. Cuthbert's tomb when it was opened in 1104. Meyer Schapiro, "On the Aesthetic Attitude in Romanesque Art," in *Romanesque Art* (New York: Braziller, 1977), pp. 11–12. The acquisitive instincts aroused by precious fabrics is indicated by the fact that *preciose vestes* are among the temptations besetting climbers of the ladder of Virtue in Herrad of Hohenburg's *Hortus Deliciarum*, in Rosalie Green et al., eds., Studies of the Warburg Institute, vol. 36 (London: Warburg Institute, 1979), vol. 2, illumination no. 296, p. 352. Silk robes and precious ornaments were among the devices of seduction that Bishop Raoul Flambard vainly used against Christina of Markyate. Talbot, ed. and trans., *The Life of Christina of Markyate A Twelfth Century Recluse*, chap. 7, p. 44.

[67] Anselm of Havelberg's *Antikeimenon* (which Eugenius commanded Anselm to write), Gerhoch of Reichersberg's *Tractate on Psalm 64*, and Bernard of Clairvaux's *De Consideratione*, completed after the Pope's death.

Eugenius was celebrated as an incorrupt judge in a venal world. "A man of conspicuous devotion and holiness," he was said to preserve the humility of a Cistercian, wearing the habit of his Order, even as Pope.[68] But above the monastic habit he wore pontifical robes of purple and gold. Sparkling with jewels, he was vested in silks, crowned with plumes, and bedecked with ornaments of precious metals.[69] He constructed (and presumably furnished) two palaces in Italy.[70] His long travels in exile were punctuated with splendid liturgies (including numerous consecrations of altars, churches, and monasteries), exchanges of magnificent gifts, and receptions characterized by sumptuous pomp. "Who," wrote one witness of Eugenius's entry into Trier, "can explain in words what took place so that you, who did not see, can understand or imagine them?"[71]

Eugenius was also familiar with the games of war. One achievement of his armies, generally deployed in the effort to install and maintain the Pope in Rome, was to raze Tivoli to the ground. Eugenius proclaimed a Crusade against the infidel in the Holy Land and a "holy expedition" led by Anselm of Havelberg against the Slavs, and he encouraged war against the Saracens in Spain. With an eye for the distractions of luxurious art, he admonished warriors departing on the Second Crusade not to spend their zeal assembling splendid raiment or weapons of gold and silver, but rather to concentrate all their diligence on weapons, horses, and other equipment with which to fight the unbelievers.[72]

Eugenius's entourage was composed, at least in part, of men whose experience of time combined, as did his, the mixed rhythms of ascetic and luxurious occupations. The authors of our treatises themselves display this combination—Otto of Freising, austere in his Cistercian discipline, lavish in rebuilding his cathedral and city with great splendor; Gerhoch of Reichersberg, inflexible in his devotion to the poverty of the *vita apostolica*, splendid in his devotion to psalmody, in his connoisseur's knowledge of visual and performing arts, and in the skillful drawings with which he illuminated some of his works. Even Bernard of Clairvaux, grim denouncer of lavish visual display as he was, counted the great builder and ornamentor, Abbot Suger of St. Denis, among his spiritual companions, and, in his travels, he moved among the greatest monuments and accumulations of artistic treasures in his day.

To be sure, the balance between asceticism and conspicuous waste varied

[68] Otto of Freising, *Chronicon*, 7.31; *MGH*, *SSrrG*, pp. 359–60. Ernald, *Vita S. Bernardi*, 2.22; *MGH*, *SS* 26, p. 109.

[69] Bernard of Clairvaux, *De Consideratione*, 2.9.18, 4.3.6; Leclercq and Rochais, eds., *S. Bernardi Opera*, 3:425–26, 453.

[70] *Liber Pontificalis*. Louis Duchesne, ed. (Paris: Thorin, 1892), 2:387.

[71] Balderic, *Gesta Alberonis*, chap. 23; *MGH*, *SS* 8, p. 255.

[72] *Ep. 48* to Louis VII; Migne *PL* 180:1065.

in Eugenius's entourage. The princely bishop, Henry of Winchester, was lacking in spiritual rigor, though he devoted great care to his collection of pagan sculpture.[73] Cardinal Octavian, later the Antipope Victor IV, was best known for his nobility of bearing and magnificent liberality.[74] Two others, whom Eugenius ordained and who succeeded him as Pope, were closer to him in his spiritual gifts of learning, eloquence, and elegance of bearing.[75]

Members of such a society were accustomed to experiencing two or more times at the same instant, a time of play, for example, and a time of labor, as a traveller did when singing or telling stories along the journey made the road easier and shorter, or as a bishop did while commanding troops on the battlefield and at the same time giving himself to meditation on the Scriptures.[76] Immersed in the multiplicity of their times, they were also assured by their learning, and by the interplaying symbolic worlds of liturgy and art with which they surrounded themselves, that all that seemed disconnected was one. Characteristically, metaphors of performance were used to explain this unity always in the process of becoming. For, when God combined the diversity of times and fruits into one year, he composed with their contrary parts a single, repeating harmony, and painted, with their diverse colors, the beauty of a single melody.[77]

There is, then, a further lesson to be drawn from the apparently incidental note that Eugenius assembled a store of "most precious fabrics."[78] For as with the round of seasons, the fascination of textiles came not only from their richness, but also from their shifting patterns. Floors were strewn with "pictured" carpets,[79] and the walls with embroidered or woven hang-

[73] John of Salisbury, *Historia Pontificalis*, chap. 40; Chibnall ed., p. 79.

[74] Balderic, *Gesta Alberonis*, chap. 23; *MGH, SS* 8, p. 255. John of Salisbury, who disliked Octavian because he advocated German interests, considered these traits "haughty and pompous." *Historia Pontificalis*, chap. 38; Chibnall, ed., p. 75.

[75] *Liber Pontificalis*; Duchesne, ed., 2:386 (Eugenius III), 388–89 (Hadrian IV), 397 (Alexander III). On Hadrian's palace-building and luxurious court, see John of Salisbury, *Policraticus*, 6.24; Webb, ed., 2:67–68.

[76] John of Salisbury, *Policraticus*, 7. prol.; Webb, ed., 2:90. Rahewin, *Gesta Friderici*, 4.32(29); *MGH, SSrrG*, pp. 274–75.

[77] Cf. Boethius, *De Musica*, 1.2; Migne *PL* 63:1171–72. Hans Schmid, ed., *Musica et scolica enchiriadis una cum aliquibus tractatulis adiunctis*, Veröffentlichungen der Musikhistorischen Kommission, no. 3 (Munich: Bayerische Akademie der Wissenschaften, 1981), p. 189.

[78] John of Salisbury, *Historia Pontificalis*, chap. 29; Chibnall, ed., p. 61: "de suo preciosissimis vestibus." Significantly, when, after long warfare, Eugenius III celebrated his first mass in St. Peter's, he presented for the adornment of the altar *optimum saratasmum* and *pontificale ornamentum*. Thereafter, he did not come with empty hands, but presented offerings of costly fabrics. Petrus Mallius, *Historia basilicae Vaticanae antiquae*, 2.13; *Acta Sanctorum*, 29 June, 6:36* (appendix). On what constituted *pontificale ornamentum*, see chap. 6, n. 59.

[79] *Ligurinus*, 3, lines 206–7; *MGH, SSrrG*, p. 242. See also the description of the draperies

ings that depicted scenes from Scripture, Greek and Roman legends, and recent history.[80]

The powerful robed themselves in cloth figured with repeating geometric, floral, and animal patterns, but also woven, or embroidered, with allegorical symbols and portraits of great men and women. Frederick Barbarossa is described at a moment of glory glittering with jewels and chains of gold, and clad entirely in purple robes, historiated with woven figures.[81] These historiated vestments (which even included footgear, see figure 15) were more even than ostentatious treasure. For such was the power of symbolic, or magical, association of like with like that wearers of such vestments were thought to carry the persons and events depicted with them,

---

on and around Solomon's bed in Herrad of Hohenburg, *Hortus Deliciarum*, in Green et al., eds., vol. 2, text no. 720, p. 345.

[80] Baudry de Bourgueil on the hangings in Adèle of Blois's bedchamber. See F.J.E. Raby, *A History of Secular Latin Poetry in the Middle Ages*, 2d ed. (Oxford: Clarendon, 1957), 1:347. Although there are some references to old vestments, most allusions to precious fabrics appear to indicate cloth that was valued, not for its antiquity or its personal associations, so much as for its costly materials. For two references to vestments left over from previous generations, see *Chronicon S. Huberti Andaginensis*, chaps. 25(35), 32(44); *MGH, SS* 8, pp. 584, 588, accounts of events in 1074 and 1076 that refer to vestments that had belonged to Pope Leo IX (1049–54). Delight in precious fabrics also extended to eastern Europe, where they were counted with cattle as rich booty (Herbord, *Dialogus de Vita S. Ottonis Babenbergensis Episcopi*, 3.2; Wikarjak, ed., p. 150. Henry of Livonia, *Chronicon Lyvoniae*, 4.13.3; *MGH, SS* 23, p. 268). The chief pagan temple at Stettin was adorned with many kinds of precious and intricate art, including much rare cloth, beautiful to see (Herbord, *Dialogus de Vita S. Ottonis Babenbergensis Episcopi*, 2.32; Wikarjak, ed., p. 123).

[81] *Ligurinus*, 4. lines 55–56; *MGH, SSrrG*, p. 267. On Frederick's bestowal of "precious fabrics" ("vestes preciosas") as treasure, together with gold and silver, vessels made of those metals, and fiefs, see Rahewin, *Gesta Friderici*, 4.85; *MGH, SSrrG*, p. 342. For parallel passages from the eleventh century describing diplomatic negotiations between Henry V and eastern Europe, see Lambert of Hersfeld, *Annales* (a. 1075); *MGH, SSrrG*, pp. 202, 225–26. At his state assembly at Fécamp (1067), William the Conqueror saw his entourage in vestments that were woven or encrusted with gold. William of Poitiers, *Gesta Guillelmi Ducis Normannorum et Regis Anglorum*, pt. 2, chap. 44. Foreville, ed., pp. 260–62.

On figured garments, see also Ailred of Rievaulx, *Vita S. Edwardi Regis et Confessoris*; Migne *PL* 195:747: "Ubi non dissoluta otio, nec onerosa fastidio, legere aut operari manibus consuevit [Queen Eadgitha], ornare miro artificio vestes, sericis aurum intexere, quaeque rerum imitari pictura." Otto of Bamberg, who surrounded himself with luxurious fabrics, presented white robes of fine cloth, with edgings of gold, golden belts, and figured shoes (*calciamenta picturata*) to two Pomeranian converts (figure 14). Herbord, *Dialogus de Vita S. Ottonis Episcopi Babenbergensis*, 2.28; Wikarjak, ed., p. 116. Duke Boleslaus of Poland is reported to have sent a gift of a black mantle woven with the figures of two white oxen. Berthold, *Chronicon Zwifaltense*, chap. 13; *MGH, SS* 10, p. 103. See also the burial vestments of St. Cuthbert, which vividly arrested Reginald of Durham's attention (above, n. 66). There are, as well, numerous references to banners with pictorial representations. E.g., the banner of Harald that William the Conqueror sent to Pope Alexander II, "hominis armati imaginem intextam habens ex auro purissimo." William of Poitiers, *Gesta Guillelmi Ducis Normannorum et Regis Anglorum*, pt. 2, chap. 31; Foreville, ed., p. 224.

*Figure 15.* Fragments of buskins, with silver-gilt embroidery on red silk. They were found in a tomb in Worcester Cathedral, possibly that of Bishop Walter Cantelupe (1233–66). The pattern consisted of a series of medallions, showing kings with crowns and scepters, in a foliate trellis. One use of splendid and fragile footgear is indicated by Bishop Otto of Bamberg's gift of "figured sandals" to a Pomeranian convert. *British Museum, M & LA 91.7–13.1.*

just as, long centuries before, according to Philo, the high priest, vested in embroidered robes and precious ornaments representing the cosmos, carried the world with him into the temple "by virtue of the imitations of it which he [bore] about him."[82] Concerning liturgical vestments there was even a Scriptural injunction to this effect: St. Paul's command, "Put on the Lord Jesus Christ. . . ." (Rom. 13:14).

[82] *Life of Moses*, 2.24; in F. H. Colson, ed. and trans., *Philo* (Cambridge, Mass.: Harvard University Press, ca. 1935), 9:504–12. See the description of Archbishop Albero of Trier in Balderic, *Gesta Alberonis*, chap. 26; *MGH, SS* 8, p. 257: "Pontificalibus enim ornamentis indutus angelus Domini videbatur; angelico enim vultu relucebat. . . ." Cf. the description of Bishops Altman of Passau and Adalbero of Würzburg at the dedication of the monastery of Lambach (1089): ". . . procedunt ambo episcopi suo tempore pontificalibus induti iam quasi deificati. . . ." *Vita Adalberonis Episcopi Wirziburgensis*, chap. 13; *MGH, SS* 12, p. 135. This

The blending of conspicuous waste and ascetic devotion in spheres and processes of play—of becoming played out—had one further implication for thought about time. Following where Boethius had led, the circles of which our texts are artifacts postulated a distinction between the stable order that emanated from divine Wisdom and the random world of events governed by Fortune.[83] The motif of Fortune was an old, and continuing, one in medieval historical writing, and it found a ready audience in social classes given to the array of courtiers' pastimes catalogued by John of Salisbury in the *Policraticus*, not least gambling, prognostication, divination, and the interpretation of dreams. In one and the same breath, John himself was able to speak both of God's fixed design in the world and of the all-devouring spin of Fortune's Wheel.[84]

Randomness and suspense between catastrophe and bliss made the play of Fortune a welcome theme in fictional literature written for those classes. There, and in histories, belief in the play of Fortune profoundly affected how people expected to waste and be wasted by time, whether in their own lives, or vicariously, through esthetic imagination. Fortune favored the

---

symbolic identification was particularly likely to occur when, as in the rituals of church and palace, the participants were conscious of mimetic relationships. Cf. Peter of Eboli, *De Rebus Siculis Carmen*, bk. 3, particula 49, lines 1543–48; Rota, ed., p. 201, referring to the palace of Henry VI: "Quave domo genitus fuerit puer, aurea proles, / Quis pater, unde parens, dic, mea Musa, precor. / Est domus, etherei qua ludunt tempora veris, / Ipse domus paries ex adamante riget. / Ante domum patulo preludit sole teatrum, / Quo salit in medio fons, Arethusa, tuus." On the effect of magic on historical writings, see Valerie Flint, "World History in the Early Twelfth Century: The 'Imago Mundi' of Honorius Augustodunensis," in *The Writing of History in the Middle Ages: Essays Presented to Richard William Southern* ed. R.H.C. Davis and J. M. Wallace-Hadrill (Oxford: Clarendon, 1981), pp. 220, 235, 237–38.

[83] See Peter of Eboli, *De Rebus Siculis Carmen*, bk. 3, particula 52 (*Sapientia Convicians Fortune*); Rota, ed., facing p. 213, with an illumination showing Henry VI enthroned in the seat of Wisdom and the victims of Fortune broken into pieces on Fortune's wheel. See chap. 3, n. 151; chap. 4, n. 34; chap. 5, nn. 28–31.

[84] *Ep. 31*; W. J. Millor, H. E. Butler, and C.N.L. Brooke, eds., *The Letters of John of Salisbury* (London: Nelson, 1955), 1:49. See also John's uneasy conclusion that what we ascribe to blind Fortune (if Fortune exists) does not prejudice the powers ascribed to God. *Policraticus*, 3.8; Webb, ed., 1:192–93. John overcame his doubts whether fortune (and fate) existed when he described his friendship with Pope Hadrian IV. *Ep. 235*; Millor and Brooke, eds., 2:434. On Fortuna in Regino of Prüm's writings, see Ebenbauer, *Carmen Historicum*, 1:333–36. See also Hans F. Haefele, *Fortuna Heinrici IV. Imperatoris. Untersuchungen zur Lebensbeschreibung des dritten Saliers*, Veröffentlichungen des Instituts für österreichische Geschichtsforschung, 15 (Vienna: Böhlau, 1954). See also Ekkehard of Aura, *Chronicon* (*a.* 1106); *MGH, SS* 6, p. 235: On Henry IV celebrating Palm Sunday at Cologne: ". . . rursum fortune sinistrorum sibi rotam volvere sentit, dum nimirum [res] inconsultius agitur." Ibid., p. 238: "temptare fortunam." See also Heinz Richter, *Englische Geschichtschreiber des 12. Jahrhunderts* (Berlin: Junker und Dünnhaupt., 1938), pp. 63–64, 73, 152. Douglas Kelly, "Fortune and Narrative Proliferation in the *Berinus*," *Speculum* 51 (1976): 22, stressing recurrence, ramifications, and segmentation in poetry, characteristics that closely resemble materials considered in this essay.

bold. But she was changeable and jealous. She raged. She quietly laid ambushes and savagely hurled her darts, making all her playthings and the butts of her jokes.[85]

On their lofty height of virtue, saints could look down with contempt on the theater of the world and smile with disdain at the play of Fortune, suffering, perhaps, but unconquered by her rage or pranks.[86] But the historical world around them was the theater in which she played her random, crazy sport. To think of time dominated by Fortune was to anticipate disconnected, contingent, and mutually incoherent experiences. And those expectations could widen to include even works of hand or mind. Suppose, some said, that Hescelin the smith takes a mass of hot metal to the anvil. What form is he going to give it with his hammer blows? He is not sure himself—maybe chance will bring the material into the shape of a blade, a scythe, or a ploughshare, or something else—and Hescelin will produce not what he intended but what he could. The skilled worker, they argued, should follow chance, not the judgment of reason. And the same was true, they continued, of intellectual work. Like Hescelin at the forge, Master William at the lectern should seek nothing certain in his disputations; Fortune, and not rational intent, ruled dialectic as well as manual crafts.[87]

Such was also the play that, at God's wink, changed kingdoms,[88] and that provided the delight of history by setting forth the most pitiable examples of those raised and crushed on Fortune's Wheel. One delight of historical mediation was to realize that, whatever their bliss or pain in this world, the saints were secure in the other cycle of the Lord's year, accom-

[85] There is certainly ample justification for Ray's conclusion that "John leaves no doubt that God is indeed the cause of all things"; however, it is also true that John of Salisbury's writings are particularly rich in allusions to Fortune. Ray, "Rational Scepticism and Verisimilar Narrative in John of Salisbury's *Historia Pontificalis*," pp. 70, 72. See, for example: (Fortune aids the bold) *Policraticus*, 6.14, 7.19; Webb, ed., 2:38, 179. (Rage) *Epp. 27, 193*; Millor and Brooke, eds., *The Letters of John of Salisbury*, 1:44, 266. (Jealous) *Ep. 28*; Millor and Brooke, eds., ibid., 1:45–46. (Throws darts) *Ep. 124*; Millor and Brooke, eds., ibid., 1:205. (Lays ambushes) *Policraticus* 2.22; Webb, ed., 1:129. (Jokes) *Ep. 194*; Millor and Brooke, eds., ibid., 1:270 and *Policraticus*, 3.8, 10; 8.12; Webb, ed., 1:191, 194; 2:308. (Whirlwind) *Ep. 194*; Millor and Brooke, eds., ibid., 1:270.

[86] *Policraticus*, 3.9; Webb, ed., 1:199. *Ep. 305*; Millor and Brooke, eds., *The Letters of John of Salisbury*, 2:728 (on Thomas à Becket). Cf. William of Malmesbury's comment on St. Aldhelm's partronage of the church at Malmesbury: "Quanta libertatis naufragia ecclesia nostra pertulerit; quam semper prospere, cum videretur oppressa maxime, per patrocinium sancti caput contra fortunam extulerit." *De Gestis Pontificum Anglorum*, 5. prol.; N.E.S.A. Hamilton, ed., Rolls Series, no. 52 (London: Longman, 1870), p. 331.

[87] John of Salisbury, *Metalogicon*, 3.10; Webb, ed., p. 161.

[88] Otto of Freising, *Chronicon*, 6.9; *MGH, SSrrG*, p. 271. See also Otto's prologue to the *Gesta Friderici*; *MGH, SSrrG,* p. 11. Otto was unwilling, while recounting the deeds of earlier kings and emperors, to suppress Frederick's in silence: "Inter omnes enim Romanorum principes tibi pene soli hoc reservatum est privilegium, ut, quamvis a prima adolescentia bellicis desudasse cognoscaris officiis, obscenum tibi nondum vultum fortuna verterit."

plishing their vocations in the concentric motions of prophecy and fulfillment.

## THE MIXED *TEMPI* OF THE AUDIENCE

Emphasizing again the distinction between the *tempi* of the intended audience and those of unintended readers (including modern critics), I now
turn in greater detail to the posttextual hermeneutic times of the intended
readers.

We cannot pretend to recover those times with any precision, but in the
texts we can find traces of the optional *tempi* that the authors expected
them to experience, contemplating events in the texts "as though on a
stage."[89] Those traces exist in numerous formal devices that authors used
to change mere duration into time; for the historical time that authors
created in texts was the mold into which they intended readers to cast their
hermeneutic time. A modern reader might well imagine that one of those
devices, perhaps the major one, was the narrative line. Yet the inconvenient
absence of a narrative line in our texts is precisely why recent scholars have
commented on their fragmented and occasionally incoherent nature.

However, a confusion of narrative with plot may put a curtain of mis-
comprehension between medieval authors and modern critics. Of the five
(or six) prescribed parts of a rhetorical *oratio*, the narration (*narratio*)
might well be the briefest; it need be no longer than a simple declarative
sentence. Digression was recognized as a device of refreshment for listeners
or readers.[90] Some such guidelines may have been at work in the *oratio* that
Otto of Freising delivered up as history.[91] The project of Otto's *Chronicle*
was an account of the conflict between the City of God and the city of the
world through the ages, but the elaboration of that theme is so meandering
and intermittent that it could hardly be called a line. Repeatedly, Otto

---

[89] Anselm of Havelberg, *Antikeimenon*, 2.19; Migne *PL* 188:1193. See above, n. 23.

[90] On the brevity of the *narratio*, see my essay, "The Church as Play: Gerhoch of Reichersberg's Call for Reform," pp. 124, 143. Melville, "System und Diachronie," p. 44. See Italo
Calvino, *Six Memos for the Next Millennium* (Cambridge, Mass.: Harvard University Press,
1988), p. 46: "Literature has worked out various techniques for slowing down the course of
time. I have already mentioned repetition, and now I will say a word about digression. . . .
Laurence Sterne's great invention was the novel that is completely composed of digressions,
an example followed by Diderot. The digression is a strategy for putting off the ending, a
multiplying of the time within the work, a perpetual evasion or flight."

[91] On historical writing as *oratio*, see *Gesta Friderici*, prol.; *MGH, SSrrG*, p. 12. See also
Otto's frequent allusions to his style, *Chronicon*, 1. prol.; 2. prol.; 5. prol.; 8.35; *MGH, SSrrG*,
pp. 9–10, 68, 226, 457. On a similar usage of the word *oratio*, see Gerhoch of Reichersberg,
*Tractatus in Ps. 64*, chap. 75; Migne *PL* 194:55. See also William of Tyre, *Chronicon*, prol.;
*Corp. Christ., continuatio medievalis*, 63, p. 99: "Nam de reliquo iam non licet ambigere quod
ad impar opus inprudenter enitimur et quod ad rerum dignitatem nostra non satis accedit
oratio."

found it necessary to recall himself from digressions "to the order of history," or, after a long lapse in the theme of conflict, to reintroduce it by way of parenthesis masquerading as apostrophe.

I propose that the absence of narrative line hinges on the understanding of *narratio* as a brief, introductory part of an *oratio*, which is by no means identical with plot. Thus, its absence is indeed a clue to the hermeneutic experience of time that authors expected readers to have as they visualized the spectacles in the texts, or, in other words, to the transition that the authors constructed between their task of thinking through their evidence, or digesting truth for themselves, and the quite different task of composition, or "making a memory" for others.[92]

The metaphors for memory familiar to our authors denoted accumulations, but not necessarily order. The digestive metaphor, already cited, coincided with metaphors of memory as a stomach, where materials were deposited, and from which they were brought up for rumination. Memory was also considered a womb, a cistern (or vat), or a treasury. There were those who considered memory a "glue" retaining what was past, but none of these metaphors implies a "memorial structure."[93] As "compendious memories" (*memoriae compendiosae*),[94] the texts were accumulations of materials. While they may lack the narrative line, they do have three major formal devices that indicated the tracks into which authors tried to channel their readers' minds, optional molds among which readers could choose where to pour their imaginations as they visualized (or played out) the spectacles in the texts and rendered duration into hermeneutic *tempi*: chapter headings, the decision to write in Latin prose, and the organizations of individual works.

The use of chapter headings is quickly dealt with. All the works under review, except the least complete among them (John of Salisbury's *Historia Pontificalis*), provide chapter headings, evidently for the purpose indicated by William of Tyre. "We have divided the whole volume (*volumen*) into twenty-three books (*libros*), and we have marked each of them out with separate chapters so that, among the divisions of the history, the reader can the more easily find whatever seems necessary to him."[95] Like William of

---

[92] Cf. Otto of Freising, *Chronicon*, 1. prol.; *MGH, SSrrG*, p. 9: ". . . quantum ex scripturis colligere potuero, non tacere, sed et civium eius in hac peregrinantium memoriam facere."

[93] Helmut Lippelt applied the term "memorial structure" to the account of Thietmar of Merseburg. *Thietmar von Merseburg: Reichsbischof und Chronist,* Mitteldeutsche Forschungen, Bd. 72 (Vienna: Böhlau, 1973), p. 193.

[94] Godfrey of Viterbo employed the term *"memoria compendiosa"* to describe his own work, the *Memoria Seculorum*. Prol.; *MGH, SS* 22, p. 95.

[95] *Chronicon*, prol.; *Corp. Christ., continuatio medievalis*, 63, p. 101. See Giraldus Cambrensis's comments on quite deliberately shaping the hermeneutic time of the reader with chapter headings and marginal notations. *Topographia Hibernica*, letter to William of Hereford. James F. Dimock, ed., *Giraldi Cambrensis Opera*, Rolls Series, no. 21 (London: Longman, 1867),

Tyre's chapter headings, those in Bernard of Clairvaux's *De Consideratione* and Anselm of Havelberg's *Dialogues* were introduced into the text itself. The verbal keys for Gerhoch of Reichersberg's *Tractate on Psalm 64* were added as marginal notes. The chapter titles for all books of Otto of Freising's *Chronicle* appear together between the prologue and the beginning of the text, and those for Otto's joint effort with Rahewin, the *Gesta Friderici*, were placed at the beginning of each book.

Each arrangement indicates a different mode of consultation. Placement chapter by chapter in the body of the manuscript indicates a gliding perusal of the text; location in margins throughout, a more cursory reconnaissance of the periphery, with occasional incursions into the interior; and a conspectus at the beginning of a text (keyed to chapter numbers in the text), an oscillation between the diagram, as a whole, and the composition, as segments.

In any case, an author plainly judged that, while his work could be read as a continuous exposition, it would most likely be consumed in parts, at the reader's option. His division of his books into chapters might be as arbitrary as his division of the work into books.[96] But there was no need to assume that the text would be considered as a completely self-sufficient work of art, understandable only in its own terms. Therefore, authors placed before their readers the means of dismembering and, perhaps, reassembling the composition in an equally arbitrary fashion. The spectator was expected to select from among the images in the "*memoria compendiosa*" and to form his own *tempi* of understanding.

This proposition can be elaborated as we turn to the second aspect of the mold provided for readers' imaginations: the authors' decision to write in Latin prose rather than in verse. Throughout the post-Classical era, verse had never ceased to be an accepted mode of historical writing. History was close to epic in matter, but written in prose; and, indeed, even for authors who chose to write in prose, the classical models of historical composition included Virgil and Lucan.[97] Few texts indicate what considera-

---

5:203 and *Speculum Ecclesiae*, pref.; J. S. Brewer, ed., *Giraldi Cambrensis Opera*, Rolls Series, no. 21 (London: Longman, 1863), 4:13.

[96] Cf. Rahewin's flat assertion that he and Otto of Freising had decided that the number of books in the *Gesta Friderici* would not exceed the number of the Gospels, a decision that, however lofty in symbolic associations, had nothing, all to do with the nature of the materials. *Gesta Friderici*, 4.85; *MGH, SSrrG,* p. 342.

[97] On Quintilian's statement about history as a kind of epic in prose, see Nancy F. Partner, "The New Cornificius: Medieval History and the Artifice of Words," in *Classical Rhetoric and Medieval Historiography*, ed. Ernst Breisach, p. 13. Grundmann, *Geschichtsschreibung*, p. 49. Otto of Freising appealed to Virgil, Lucan, "and other Roman authors" as precedents for mingling fables and philosophical reflections with histories for the delectation of readers. *Gesta Friderici*, prol.; *MGH, SSrrG*, p. 12. Balderic, *Gesta Alberonis*, chap. 16; *MGH, SS* 8, p. 252, referring to Virgil, Statius, Livy, and Josephus as models. Cf. Fred C. Robinson,

tions led an author to choose verse response. Guibert of Nogent's (1053–after 1121) account of the First Crusade is an exception. Guibert asserted that, when he selected his subject, he hoped to raise a jewel more precious than gold from the dust of neglect. Others had pressed him to write, and, recalling aptitudes that he had displayed as a young man, many asked him to write in meter. But he had outgrown the use of recondite words that commanded applause for their own sake, and verses that clacked in the regularity of their scansion. Josephus's histories of the Jewish war, Guibert judged, demonstrated greater maturity.

He had seen villages, towns, and cities that were hotbeds of grammatical studies. With them in mind, he had no wish to set his own work apart from older histories. The cleavage between prose and verse was not one of style so much as of form; prose did not exclude the poetic. No one should be surprised, he wrote, that he used in the history quite a different style from the one that he had employed in his commentary on Genesis. It was both appropriate and permissible for a history to be adorned with the toilsome elegance of words, but, by contrast, mysteries of Holy Writ were to be considered not with the vanity that inspired the wordiness of poets but with the simplicity of the Church.[98]

In following Josephus as a writer of prose, therefore, Guibert by no means excluded Virgil and Lucan as models of historical writing. He himself included verse passages, some of which are extensive, in his account, occasionally dividing individual sentences into prose and verse members; he normally employed techniques of versification such as terminal rhyme and meter (*cursus*, or *Reimprosa*) in his composition.[99]

In contrast with vernacular poetry of the same era, twelfth-century Latin verse has been described as "mechanical variations on threadbare themes," characteristically "smooth and artificial, but vapid and sterile."[100] Then as earlier, "the classical art of poetry [was] not an art of free composition."[101] Preoccupied with rules of form, writers of verse histories with few exceptions lost sight of everything else, often including narrative, in their pursuit

---

" 'Bede's' Envoi to the Old English *History*: An Experiment in Editing," *Studies in Philology*, Texts and Studies 78, n.s. 5 (1981): 6: "The assumption that verse texts should always be studied apart from those in prose is an odd one to apply to a literary culture in which alternate prose and verse composition within the same text was a common practice."

[98] Guibert of Nogent, *Gesta Dei per Francos*, letter to Bishop Lisiard of Soissons and pref.; *Recueil des historiens des Croisades*, 4:117, 120.

[99] On the use of *cursus*, see James J. Murphy, *Rhetoric in the Middle Ages: A History of Rhetorical Theory from Saint Augustine to the Renaissance* (Berkeley: University of California Press, 1974), p. 78.

[100] Walter Bradbury Sedgwick, "The Style and Vocabulary of the Latin Arts of Poetry of the Twelfth and Thirteenth Centuries," *Speculum* 3 (1928): 349–50.

[101] George A. Kennedy, *Classical Rhetoric and Its Christian and Secular Tradition from Ancient to Modern Times* (Chapel Hill: University of North Carolina Press, 1980), p. 115.

of elevated vocabulary, obscurities of myth and legend, ornate multiplica-
tions of parts, accumulations of epithets, embellishments by repetition,
and ingenious contortions of rhythm.[102]

Yet these characteristics appealed to the esthetic sensibilities of the age,
and about 1186, an anonymous author undertook to render into a verse
paraphrase *The Deeds of Frederick Barbarossa*, completed by Rahewin a generation earlier (ca. 1160). The author, thought by some to have been Gunther of Pairis, a Cistercian monk who served as tutor to a son of Barbarossa, cheerfully cast his dart in the age-old battle between prose and
poetry.[103]

Gunther shared with Otto of Freising and Rahewin the object of celebrating Barbarossa's deeds, but he stated this common purpose in flagrantly panegyrical, rather than in historical, terms. He wished, he declared
to Frederick, to "proclaim your honor, most powerful Caesar, with songs
of praise, and to celebrate your exalted offices, and with eloquence to enu-
merate to the full the brilliance of [your] achievements."[104] Nearly thirty
years earlier, Otto of Freising had also employed "history's plain diction"
for adulation, mingling narrative with excursus on philosophy's "inmost
secrets" to raise the reader's mind to the sublime, but hidden, causes of
events, and so to increase his delight in reading and learning.[105] However,

---

[102] On Stephen of Rouen's *Draco Normannicus* (ca. 1169), see Beryl Smalley, *The Becket
Conflict and the Schools: A Study of Intellectuals in Politics* (Oxford: Blackwell, 1973), pp. 186–
89, and Margaret Gibson, "History at Bec in the Twelfth Century," in *The Writing of History
in the Middle Ages: Essays Presented to Richard William Southern*, ed. R.H.C. Davis and J. M.
Wallace-Hadrill, pp. 181–86. On verse biographies of the first seven abbots of Bec (to 1179),
see Gibson, "History at Bec," p. 180.

For general information, see Raby, *A History of Secular Latin Poetry in the Middle Ages*,
1:405–8 (on works in eleventh-century Germany); 2:69–83 (on works in twelfth-century
France); 2:132–42 (on works in twelfth-century England); 2:147–51 (on works in twelfth-
century Germany); 2:164–70 (on works of the late twelfth century at the imperial court in
Italy). Further, Paul Gerhard Schmidt, "Die Ermordung Thomas Beckets im Spiegel zeitge-
nössischer Dichtungen," *Mittellateinisches Jahrbuch* 9 (1973): 159–72.

[103] Erwin Assmann, ed., *Gunther der Dichter: Ligurinus* (Hannover: Hahn, 1987), pp. 79–
120, elsewhere cited as *MGH, SSrrG*. See the account of Gunther in *Die deutsche Literatur des
Mittelalters: Verfasserlexikon* (Berlin: de Gruyter, 1980), 3:316–22. Munz, "Why Did Rahewin Stop Writing the Gesta Frederici? A Further Consideration," p. 778. Karl Leyser,
"Frederick Barbarossa, Henry II and the Hand of St. James," *English Historical Review* 90
(1975): 502–3. Franz-Josef Schmale, "Die *Gesta Friderici I. imperatoris* Ottos von Freising
und Rahewins: Ursprüngliche Form und Überlieferung," *Deutsches Archiv* 19 (1963): 176,
210. Gunther's reliance on the text by Otto and Rahewin recalls the much earlier statement
by Hrotsvitha of Gandersheim that, to continue her verse *Gesta Ottonis*, she needed a prose
narrative from which to work. Peter Dronke, *Women Writers of the Middle Ages: A Critical
Study of Texts from Perpetua (†203) to Marguerite Poreta (†1310)* (Cambridge: Cambridge
University Press, 1984), p. 77.

[104] *Ligurinus*, 4, lines 33–36; 10, lines 576–654; *MGH, SSrrG*, pp. 266, 491–95.

[105] *Gesta Friderici*, prol.; *MGH, SSrrG*, p. 12. See Becker, *Die Belagerung von Crema*, p. 325.

Gunther considered the best efforts of his predecessors deficient in pleasure.

Repeatedly professing that his abilities were inadequate to his great theme,[106] he declared that his tools were beauty and brevity. Could any poet celebrate the subject of Frederick's greatness with praise enough?[107] The historians, he wrote, had spurned the laws of meter, relying on the splendor of the events that they had to recount, their skill in discourse, and profundity of meaning. It shamed them, he thought, to have disported themselves with boyish pranks and to have woven together a fabric of inane trifles. If anyone could be helped by a fairly prolix order and incorrupt historical accuracy (*historiae fides*), he could consult what the learned men had written (assuming, of course, that he had access to a manuscript containing a complete copy of the *Gesta*). In those pages, the reader would find quite a lot of things that neither augmented Barbarossa's honors nor served the interconnectedness of the subject, but that were simply, as it were, stitched together.

Inelegant in discourse though he was, and faint of heart, he would yet call upon his command of words to veil with overpainting their smeary work. From their full garden, he would gather some flowers, his few from their many. He would not treat everything, but only what was beautiful. For, if he pursued it all, what codex could contain the result, or what reader could peruse it all? Gunther said that he would follow the kingly deeds with a light pen and a certain brevity, and even if someone were annoyed by his unpolished style, still that disgruntled reader might find something praiseworthy, lingering over the structure of the metrical feet and the melody of the verses.[108]

Poetry's warfare with philosophy was as old as that with prose. One of Gunther's most obvious deletions was Book I of the *Gesta*, which deals with Barbarossa's antecedents, but which also contains the only examples of the philosophical excursus that Otto intended to inspire the reader to persist with heightened pleasure.

The point of Gunther's criticism is that pleasure in reading was a matter of how the times were experienced, and that the experience of times (or

[106] *Ligurinus*, 1, lines 8–9, 45–47, 359; 3, lines 223–24; 4. lines 601–2; *MGH, SSrrG*, pp. 151, 154, 172, 243, 295.

[107] *Ligurinus*, 1, lines 112–14; *MGH, SSrrG*, p. 159. See above, n. 104.

[108] *Ligurinus*, 1, lines 100–166; *MGH, SSrrG*, pp. 158–61. Becker, *Die Belagerung von Crema*, pp. 325–35. A very diligent writer in prose, William of Malmesbury entered a similar if more prolix defence of brevity in his *De Gestis Regum Anglorum*, when he came to King Henry I. If he even wrote down all the things that he had heard (much less all the things that were to be found out), he would weary the nerves and burden large bookcases. Cicero himself, the complete master of Latinity, would hardly dare to attempt to tell the whole story in prose, "vel si quis versuum favore Mantuanum lacessit poetam." *De Gestis Regum Anglorum*, 5. prol.; William Stubbs, ed., Rolls Series, no. 90 (London: Stationary Office, 1889), 2:465.

*tempi*) through speech itself—in the stylized rhythm and harmonic pro-
gressions in verse—was more immediate and gratifying than the experience
of times in events, indirectly through the prose filter of historical discourse.
The form of verse gave direct access to the substance of *tempi*. The reading
of his verse was in this sense the experience of temporal events, while the
reading of the *Gesta*'s prose was one step removed from temporal events
(i.e., those in the text). Possibly because he considered painting, like historical prose, an indirect means to the experience of *tempi* in events, he
abandoned both Horace's principle that poetry was like painting and the
analogues that historians drew between their writings and painting. Forgetting also the convention that poetry lied, he held up a celebrated painting of the Emperor Lothar III as suppliant before Pope Innocent II as the
work of a lying painter. Gunther protested that Pope Hadrian IV had asserted papal prerogatives over the imperial office that conformed with the
painting and that he had issued proud documents as empty as the picture.
Mute or speaking, the Pope's letter should be voided, and the lying image,
removed.

It is worth noting particularly Gunther's judgment that the *Gesta* contained many things that were at best marginal to the praise of Barbarossa
or the coherence of its parts and that were merely patched together. This
comment echos a rule set forth by Gunther's contemporary, Matthew of
Vendôme. The versifier, Matthew wrote, "should imitate the degrees of the
actions in clear steps so there may be no break in the narrative." Matthew
was arguing from rules, rather than from observation of life. He illustrated
his proposition with a specific example, namely, the six steps of seduction,
prescribed by rules of style. The continuity on which he insisted depended
upon the regularity of poetic convention, rather than on the unpredictable
course of actual experience. Rules secured the "texture of narration" (*con-
textus narrationis*) and the "discourse" (*colloquium*) governed by them postulated "an orderly succession" (*ordinaria successio*) in human actions represented by the six stages. Matthew did not pause to consider what
experience might have led Ovid to violate the rules when he segmented an
account of seduction by omitting two of the formal stages.[109]

Comparison of two passages will indicate more precisely how the formalist experience of times that Gunther prepared for his reader differed
from the one that he found in the *Gesta*.

The first passage concerns the death of Otto of Freising. In the *Gesta*,
Gunther found an extensive necrology, which, in print, covers just over
eight pages. Writing on command of the Emperor, Otto's nephew, god-

---

[109] *Ars Versificatoria (The Art of the Versemaker)*, 4.13; Roger P. Parr, trans. (Milwaukee,
Wis.: Marquette, 1981), p. 96. Edmond Faral, *Les arts poétiques du XIIe et du XIIIe siècle*,
Bibliothèque de l'École des Hautes Études, fasc. 238 (Paris: Champion, 1962), p. 183.

son, lord, and patron, and writing also about his own master and collaborator, Rahewin had every reason to compose a fulsome account. For him,
the magnitude of Otto's death was underscored by the fire that, the year
after the Bishop died, consumed the glories that he had showered on his
see. Rahewin began and ended the necrology with accounts of the disaster.
Between those somber brackets, he recalled how Otto had restored both
religious life and architectural beauty in Freising, and testimonies to his
exalted lineage, intellectual abilities, education in philosophy, and zealous
representation of the Church's needs before kings and princes. Rahewin
recalled how Otto's greatness had drawn the envy of others upon him, and,
finally, he spoke about the Bishop's devotion to the Cistercian order, an
allegiance so strong that, heeding signs and visions that portended his
death, he returned to his former monastery, Morimund, to die.

Moving toward his dramatic focus, the desolation of Freising by fire,
Rahewin portrayed the Bishop's last moments, fraught with concern about
a passage in the *Gesta* concerning Gilbert of Poitiers. He observed with
satisfaction how—although Otto had chosen an humble place of burial
where his brethren would tread upon his grave—the monks of Morimund
buried him in a place of honor, beside the main altar. In pride of authorship, Rahewin inserted a verse epitaph of fifty-four lines (in two meters)
which he had composed and caused to be carved on his master's tomb. He
then proceeded to the prophetic omens of disaster and the actual desolation of Freising.[110]

Gunther paraphrased all this into ten lines.[111] Evidently, in his eyes, Rahewin had missed the essential point. For, adding that Otto had been Barbarossa's godfather, and that his death had caused the Emperor profound
grief, Gunther drew a parallel between Otto's staunch adherence to the
standards of his earthly king and the death by which he gave what was his
to the King of Heaven, not, he added with a poetic flourish, in the clangor
of military camps or amidst the clash of iron, but among his brethren as
they chanted psalms of lamentation. There are no dates, no places, no
causes or threatening portents, no documents (notably the epitaph), and
certainly no indication of the fire that reduced Otto's beloved church to
dust and ashes.

Barbarossa is the real subject of these lines. Given Gunther's decision,
for his own panegyrical motives, to stress Otto's devoted service to kings
as the single message, his paraphrase did indeed eliminate the many-mem-
bered account that Rahewin had stitched together. Gunther provided little, except allusiveness, and the *tempi* of verbal rhythm and sounds.

The second passage concerns the celebrated audience that Barbarossa

---

[110] *Gesta Friderici*, 4.14(11)–16(12); *MGH, SSrrG*, pp. 248–56.
[111] *Ligurinus*, 9, lines 90–100; *MGH, SSrrG*, pp. 439–40.

granted two papal legates at the diet of Besançon in 1157. The details provided in the *Gesta* are too numerous to be recounted here at length. Outraged by an assault upon the Bishop of Lund as he returned north from Rome through imperial lands, Pope Hadrian IV admonished Barbarossa to avenge the crime. The Emperor, he said, had delayed too long in performing his duties. He should remember how gladly the Pope had conferred the imperial crown upon him, and how he would have bestowed upon him yet greater *beneficia* had that been possible. Construing *beneficia* in the specific legal sense of "benefices" (or "fiefs"), rather than in the general one of "benefits," Barbarossa's entourage broke into a storm of anger at the imputation that he had received the imperial crown as a fief from the Pope's hand. They scented a subversive idea represented, not only in words and texts, but also in the offensive mural of Lothar III in the Pope's own residence, the Lateran palace.

The enthusiastic greed of the legates (including Cardinal Rolando Bandinelli, a protégé of Eugenius III who later, as Pope Alexander III, was Barbarossa's implacable enemy) had already made them unwelcome. They had even, the Emperor reported, plundered altars, confiscated sacred vessels, and stripped crosses of the precious metals and gems with which they were encased. When, raging with bitterness, his nobles at Besançon drew swords against the legates, Barbarossa readily took the cardinals into protective custody and sent them by the quickest road back to Rome. Rahewin did not fail to note that the legates were conspicuous by virtue of their office and authority, but first of all by virtue of their wealth.

Recognizing the prolixity of his account, Rahewin yet held that no one who diligently considered the weight and length of the dispute would object to his details. Indeed, so that the interested reader could draw his own conclusions, instead of relying on secondhand assertions, Rahewin incorporated a little dossier, the very texts of Hadrian's initial letter and Barbarossa's response.[112]

Gunther followed the rule of compression in paraphrasing this account, as he did in rendering Otto of Freising's obituary. Together, compression and the demands of verse composition militated against the inclusion of prose documents, such as the letters of Hadrian and Barbarossa. But a measure of the judgments that guided Gunther is the fact that the vital word *"beneficia"* occurs nowhere in his account of the audience at Besançon or, even more remarkably, in his rendering of a letter that the Pope later sent, and that Otto of Freising translated at the Diet of Augsburg in 1158, specifically clarifying what he meant by the word.[113] Perhaps for the same

---

[112] *Gesta Friderici*, 3.8; *MGH, SSrrG,* pp. 173–74. Cf. John of Salisbury's decision against the prolixity of including documentary texts. *Historia Pontificalis*, chap. 3; Chibnall, ed., p. 8.

[113] Rahewin, *Gesta Friderici*, 3.22–24; *MGH, SSrrG*, pp. 195–97. *Ligurinus*, 6, lines 258–395; 7, lines 119–77; *MGH, SSrrG*, pp. 343–50, 372–74.

reason, he omitted even a paraphrase of the verses inscribed about the objectionable picture in the Lateran (which specifically asserted that Lothar III received the crown after he became the Pope's liegeman). Instead, he referred obliquely to the epigrams added by the vain and lying painter.[114]

Suppressing the specific cause of the dispute, Gunther moved to a higher level of abstraction, namely, to the relations between the imperial and the papal offices. Here, he departed from his texts not by compression but by expansion. One method of incorporating letters into poetic narrative was to recast them as soliloquies. This was Gunther's normal practice, and the letter that Barbarossa issued from Besançon provided the germ of an imaginary discourse on the two swords, representing religious and secular governments. In his letter, Barbarossa asserted that God alone bestowed his kingly office and empire, acting through election by the princes. In the Passion of Christ, his Son, God subjected the earth to the rule of the two swords, and the necessity of there being two was also declared by the Apostle Peter when he commanded, "Fear God; honor the king" (1 Pet. 2:17). Obviously, whoever claimed that Barbarossa had received the imperial crown as a benefice from the Pope withstood the institution of God and the doctrine of Peter and, besides, was guilty of falsehood.[115]

Gunther's very extensive recasting of this single complex sentence retained the insistence that there must be two swords. But Frederick's seventeen years of relentless conflict against Alexander III (1160–77) left their mark in Gunther's shift of responsibility for the affront to imperial dignity from the legates, where Barbarossa had diplomatically placed it in 1157, to Pope Hadrian IV himself. Gunther portrayed Barbarossa asserting with great irony that, although God alone, from whom all power under heaven had its name, was the author of both swords, Hadrian wished to be considered Augustus rather than Pope. Not content with the one sword that was his, he impaired both swords, and stirred them up against himself. Trying to merge the kingly and episcopal offices, he disrupted the mutual bond of alliance in which they were to serve each other; he tore the peace of the Church asunder.

There is no need to pursue the balance of the soliloquy that Gunther assigned to Frederick. Our interest is not in his doctrines so much as in the fact that the rules of poetry, as he understood and applied them, required him to recast historical documents, and that in the recasting he both reshaped the facts that he elected to recount and, through the forms of poetry, presented in his text optional experiences of times altogether different from those available in the *Gesta*. The difference in experience of *tempi* was not due only to the elimination, compression, or elaboration of materials

---

[114] *Ligurinus*, 6, lines 287–90; *MGH, SSrrG*, p. 345.

[115] *Gesta Friderici*, 3.11; *MGH, SSrrG*, p. 179.

for which the poetic enterprise called in its demand that the stylized, formalistic narrative be unbroken. Many other devices were in play. The difference was also due to the diverting baubles of a dead mythology, and to Gunther's comparatively moderate preference for recondite words and names (for example, Gunther referred to Besançon as "Chrysopolis," instead of "Bisuncium," as did Rahewin), a preference that, like circumlocution, was encouraged because in many cases metrical scansion excluded more common words. It was due to the charms in the hypnotically regular clatter of meter that Guibert of Nogent denied himself. Like others, Gunther found that the clatter gratified all the more when it passed over a surface uninterrupted by the irregularities and perplexities that the order of history, with its "stitched together" facts could introduce.[116]

These observations can readily be elucidated by comparing Gunther's verse with the treatment that the metaphor of the two swords received in prose works by the authors with whom we are chiefly concerned. Leaving aside their wide disagreements on the relationship between the two powers, the authors in prose treated the metaphor of the swords as an illustration in more or less technical discourses on matters of law, prerogative, historical precedent, and administrative right.[117] Reducing his freight of

[116] *Ligurinus*, 1, lines 716–39; *MGH*, *SSrrG*, pp. 193–94.

[117] Before Besançon, Bernard of Clairvaux employed the metaphor, rather ambiguously, in the *De Consideratione* to teach Eugenius III that, while both swords belonged to the Church, it exercised only the spiritual one directly. The material sword was wielded by warriors at the behest of the bishop (Did Bernard mean the pope?) and at the command of the emperor. *De Consideratione*, 4.3.7; Leclercq and Rochais, eds., *S. Bernardi Opera*, 3:454. On this highly problematic passage, see my essay, "Hermeneutics and Enigma: Bernard of Clairvaux's *De Consideratione*," *Viator* 19 (1988): 129–51. In general, Hartmut Hoffmann, "Die beiden Schwerter im hohen Mittelalter," *Deutsches Archiv* 20 (1964): 78–114. At about the same time, Otto of Freising, spiritually troubled by the conflict of Empire and Papacy, set down both sides of the argument: on the one hand, the position (later repeated by Gunther) that God had ordained the temporal and spiritual swords to be wielded in the Church over separate jurisdictions and by different officers; and, on the other hand, the contrary position that the temporal power had rightly been subordinate to the ecclesiastical since the Church received royal powers (*regalia*) from the Emperor Constantine. Otto was unsure whether the present exalted state of the Church pleased God more than its humility before Constantine in times of persecution. But he was sure that the Roman Church, made firm in faith by Christ, possessed rightly what she possessed. *Chronicon*, 4. prol.; *MGH*, *SSrrG*, pp. 180–83. Later, in discussing the Investiture Conflict, Otto declared that he could not decide whether those were correct who determined that the kingdom had been laid low, not only by its spiritual, but also by its own material sword, but he did find bishops at fault who turned against the royal office the sword that they held by the grace of kings. *Chronicon*, 7. prol.; *MGH*, *SSrrG*, pp. 308–9.

In the aftermath of the Besançon affair, John of Salisbury and Gerhoch of Reichersberg also adverted to the two swords, but with quite different results. Using a phrase reminiscent of Hadrian's (i.e., Frederick received "*beneficia . . . de manu nostra*"), John contended that the prince, as distinct from the tyrant, held the "sword of blood . . . from the hand of the Church," and that he was therefore a minister of the episcopal office, God's little executioner,

doctrine to the minimum, Gunther by contrast took the metaphor as the *Leitmotif* of his message. Striving for dramatic vividness, he cast the message in the voice of the first person as a soliloquy of the Emperor, rather than in the voice of the third person, as a scholarly demonstration. Finally, crafting his work for beauty, he sought to enchant the ear with the stretched meter of an antique song.

Without by any means exhausting the subject, enough has been said to indicate at least in general what option of temporal experience our authors chose when they elected to write in prose instead of in verse. They did not deny themselves the "poetic garrulity" of quotations from verse compositions (including their own), or the use of techniques of versification to add variety to their prose. History was and long remained a branch of poesy. Yet if Guibert's deliberate choice is in any degree representative of thinking in an age which cherished verse as an instrument of historical writing, it is clear that our authors deliberately chose means that induced readers to visualize spectacles in the text—exactly what Gunther censured in the *Gesta*, that is, prolixity, historical accuracy in detail, immersion in "boyish pranks" and "inane trifles," and selection and arrangement of materials that disrupted narrative coherence and produced an improvised, "stitched-together" effect.

To say this is to describe the optional experiences of times that made chapter headings features in most of the works under review, guides for selected, perhaps idle, diversions in a fabric of patches.

The division of our histories into books and chapters and the implications of choosing prose, rather than verse, lead, finally, to the experiences of *tempi* induced by compositional structure. Gunther's chief objection to the *Gesta* was that it arrested narrative, rather than conducting it. It was full of materials that were tangential, digressive, and perhaps irrelevant to what he considered the main theme. (An extreme example of the deliberate arrest of narrative occurs in Bernard of Clairvaux's life of St. Malachy. There, narrative movement was held in suspense by the recounting of a massive block of twenty-five miracles [sections 42-56], and then resumed.) In fact, Otto himself provided a statement of the rationale that prompted this apparent untidiness. He had decided, he wrote, to begin his account

---

doing for bishops actions unworthy of their consecrated hands. *Policraticus*, 4.3; Webb, ed., 1:239–40. (John's references elsewhere to Barbaraossa as a "tyrant" may suggest a relation between this passage and the dispute at Besançon. E.g., *ep. 219*; Millor and Brooke, eds., *The Letters of John of Salisbury*, 2:376.) Gerhoch interpreted the two swords in a way more compatible with Barbarossa's than any of the other three authors. Convinced that the temporal and spiritual powers were separate, though coordinated as were the sun and the moon, he rebuked prelates who had combined them, whether princely German bishops or the papal Curia, in the exercise of physical coercion and capital punishment. *De Investigatione Antichristi*, chaps. 35–40; *MGH, Ldl* 3, pp. 343–48 (written 1161–62). *Tractatus in Ps. 64*, prol.; *B*, chap. 3; *MGH, Ldl* 3, p. 441 (written 1158?).

of Barbarossa's reign four reigns earlier, omitting reference to Lothar III, who did not belong to the Salian-Staufer dynasty. Without noticing the enormous hole that this omission created in the sequence of events, Otto devoted the entire first book to antecedents "so that, passing down as though by a certain thread of narrative," Frederick's deeds could be seen to have climaxed a progression from brilliant to more brilliant achievements. Postponing the start of his narrative with a digression, Otto also saw fit to interrupt it by inserting here and there in his account deeds of ecclesiastical and secular figures in other lands, since, he argued, the narration of affairs in all kingdoms and peoples eventually led back to a common origin, the Roman Empire. They were all branches on the same tree. Finally, his *oratio* (not *narratio* this time) would occasionally take to the heights of philosophy, so as to enhance the pleasure of the reader and to retain his attention by these excursus into sublime and hidden explanations of things.[118]

Otto's remarks constitute a project not for a narrative line, but for an indefinitely extending web of narratives. The project entailed repeatedly arresting the readers' attention, rather than conducting it by formal stages to esthetic closure. In fact, he spoke of "historical narratives," which he had mingled in the *Chronicle* with "difficult and arcane texts of Scripture,"[119] and it is clear that his reference to a "thread of narrative" implied for him not a single line so much as a complex weaving.[120] Rahewin combined this conception with an ancient figure of speech for making anthologies when he wrote that he and Otto had gathered flowers from the wide meadows of

[118] *Gesta Friderici*, prol.; *MGH, SSrrG*, p. 12.

[119] *Chronicon*, 8. prol.; *MGH, SSrrG*, p. 392.

[120] The phrase "*historiam texere*" occurs frequently enough to indicate a way of thinking. See below, n. 142. Cf. *Chronicon*, 1. prol.; 2. prol.; *MGH, SSrrG*, pp. 8, 9, 68. Cf. the citation of Job 7:6 in Rahewin, *Gesta Friderici*, 3. prol.; *MGH, SSrrG*, p. 162: "dies hominis velocius transire quam a texante tela succiditur." Wilcox notes the metaphor of historical weaving in *The Measure of Times Past*, p. 148, without however commenting on weaving as a metaphor for time. See the parallel phrase used by John of Salisbury, below, n. 124. Cf. Ward, "Some Principles of Rhetorical Historiography in the Twelfth Century," p. 118: "The use of digressions [by Otto of Freising] serves to amplify and diversify the narrative by breaking up long sections, creating the impression of warp and weft, an impression not far from the minds of twelfth-century historians who drew continual analogies between writing and weaving." See also ibid., pp. 118 (William of Malmesbury), 136 (Guibert of Nogent). Rupert of Deutz provided an explanation of how the hairs of Christ's head (mentioned as white as wool in Rev. 1:14) symbolized the way in which the words of prophets were woven together into the text of Scripture. *Commentum in Apocalypsim*, 1.1; Migne *PL* 169:856: "Quare autem lanae isti capilli assimilantur? Videlicet, quomodo ex lana in fusum transmissa, texendo fit vestis aliqua, sic capillis istis, id est multiplicibus Dei verbis, in linguam vocemque prophetarum transfusis, scribendo contexta est sancta Scriptura." The unitive work of charity is also described as weaving in Talbot, ed., *The Life of Christina of Markyate A Twelfth Century Recluse*, chap. 71, p. 162: "Dando siquidem interulas complevit mandatum, retinendo dilectum firmavit promissum, leve rata dispendium texta fila dispergere, ut quem vera contexuerat caritas, a tanto posset labore retinere."

Frederick's deeds and had woven them into a crown for the Emperor.[121] The "fascicle method" of composition could hardly be stated more plainly.

Some such association was at work in analogies between histories and a particular kind of fabric, tapestries or "woven panels" that monks counted with images and precious stones among treasures to be gathered in good fortune and disbursed in ill.[122]

Gunther's formalist criticism was precisely that they had woven together an assortment of trifles, or rather that their materials cohered not as a tightly woven fabric but as a thing of patches.[123] Perhaps he was seeking a pattern that conducted the attention, rather than a web that continually arrested it.[124] Gerhoch described his work with another metaphor drawn from weaving: it was, he said, a basket containing the sayings of the Fathers.[125] Whether web or basket, through all the variations and mutations of times held in the mesh, there could be discerned, as in the Church, one Spirit animating one body in all its diverse members and through all diverse times and ages.[126]

In previous studies, I have indicated reasons for thinking that four of our authors employed apparently digressive, or contradictory, structures precisely as webs in which to capture the reader's attention. The common element in these cases was the construction of a text by fascicles to express predicament. Three works appear to have been deliberately composed, employing partitions entirely conventional in rhetoric, not merely to set predicaments before readers' minds, but actually to enmesh them, through the act of reading, in paradox, enigma, and dilemma.[127] In my opinion, Otto of Freising's *Chronicle* and *Gesta*, considered as one oeuvre composed or reworked at the same time, also intentionally ensnare the reader in hermeneutic predicaments of the author as he followed the complex "line of narrative."[128]

The very incomplete state in which we know John of Salisbury's *Historia*

---

[121] *Gesta Friderici*, 4.86; *MGH, SSrrG*, p. 346.

[122] Balderic, *Gesta Alberonis*, chap. 16; *MGH, SS* 8, p. 252.

[123] *Ligurinus*, 1, line 128; *MGH, SSrrG*, p. 159: "nec contexta rei, sed tanquam adsuta coherent."

[124] John of Salisbury, *Historia Pontificalis*, prol.; Chibnall, ed., p. 2: "telam narrationis ordiens." Chibnall properly translated this phrase as "wove the pattern of his narrative," but the ambiguity of "*telam*" also allows the sense "constructing the web of narrative." See above, n. 120.

[125] *Tractatus in Ps. 64*, chap. 75; Migne *PL* 194:55. See also Gerhoch's preface to the entire *Commentary on the Psalms*: "In Psalmis vero, in quibus texitur historia, de tertio tractandi modo nobis ostenditur forma. . . ."; Migne *PL* 193:633.

[126] E.g., Anselm of Havelberg, *Antikeimenon*, 1.2; Migne *PL* 188:1143–44.

[127] See above, n. 6. The three authors mentioned are Anselm of Havelberg, Gerhoch of Reichersberg, and Bernard of Clairvaux.

[128] See "Otto of Freising's Quest for the Hermeneutic Circle," cited above, n. 6.

*Pontificalis* does not permit a corresponding analysis of the times inserted between the lines of his visible organization. What survives is a collection of detached anecdotes. But some of his comments indicate that the creation of hermeneutic time through the device of multiple narratives was not far from his mind. The intention of all chroniclers, he said, was to relate events so that the invisible things of God might be seen through things that were made (cf. Rom. 1:20). Thus instructed by examples of reward and punishment, readers might be made attentive to fear of God and devotion to justice.[129] Among the "invisible things of God" that he may have wished to become manifest through the fascicles of his account was the Word of God, the beginning of his discourse (*sermo*), the leader of those who walk rightly, and the end of all things that are to be done—the end, as Otto of Freising recalled, without end.[130]

But, John knew, imagination, not the text, opened a reader's view to such invisible things. The form of distinction (*diacrisis*) called "illustration" (*illustratio*) or "picturing" (*picturatio*) was a device by which the most refined authors elucidated "the rude material of history." And the use of imagery stimulated a corresponding response in readers. Aroused by some experience (or "passion"), the power of the soul resorted to the images stored in the treasure room of memory, and from its sifting through the images of things that it wanted, imagination was born, which was not recalled as were rules, but in its vivacity went beyond the rules to confirm them.[131] Meaning, or visualization, preceded words. As Matthew of Vendôme commented: "Imagination precedes the senses, speech follows as the interpreter of thought, and then comes arrangement in the quality of expression."[132]

We have returned to the experience that Rupert of Deutz described when he wrote of recreating by imagination the "spectacle of images" beheld by John the Divine,[133] and that William of Tyre also characterized when he spoke of his own work as a sketch that a more skillful artist might complete with nobler colors.[134] Indeed, Gunther enacted such a project when, he wrote, he overpainted with beauty the smeary lines that Otto and Rahewin had drawn.[135]

As we said at the outset, the crucial act in reading, as conceived by John

[129] *Historia Pontificalis*, prol.; Chibnall, ed., p. 3.

[130] *Historia Pontificalis*, prol.; Chibnall, ed., p. 4. Otto of Freising, *Chronicon*, 8.34; *MGH*, *SSrrG*, p. 456.

[131] John of Salisbury, *Metalogicon*, 1.24, 4.9; Webb, ed., pp. 54, 174–75.

[132] Matthew of Vendôme, *Ars Versificatoria*, 3.52; Parr trans., p. 92. See Jane Chance, "The Artist as Epic Hero in Alan of Lille's 'Anticlaudianus,'" *Mittellateinisches Jahrbuch* 18 (1983): 245.

[133] See above, n. 28.

[134] See above, n. 30.

[135] See above, n. 108.

of Salisbury and the other historical writers in our sample, was visualization. The readers were spectators; they understood by means of the likenesses imagined in the heart,[136] which might be idolatrous.

The text, indeed, was a "memory," or a "memorial," intended like all
such spectacles to stir the readers' memory to imagination, and through
imagination to stir the affects, especially fear and love.[137] But it was imagination that recovered events from the cistern of the readers' memory and
found in them their invisible content and affective power.

The text was an artifact of the author conscious of remembering and
imagining himself. But the times postulated between the lines of the text
were those of the reader (or spectator) as "the remembered or witnessing
self."[138] Just as most of our texts dealt with events contemporary with the
authors, so too they were composed for contemporaries of the authors.
Even texts dealing with events of distant times were viewed as though they
were present. "Although we are placed at the end of ages," Otto of Freising
wrote, "we do not [merely] read the misfortunes of mortals in the codices
[of writers in the patristic era] as the trials of mortals. Rather, by the experiences of our own time, we discover, from them, those misfortunes in
ourselves."[139] Because authors and viewers shared the same (or virtually the
same) moment of remembrance and imagination, the appeal of authors to
known or unknown readers for redactive reading was also an appeal to the
corrective function of social memory.[140] That appeal might be to others
who knew more than the histories included, and who could well amend
their defects by erasing and inserting, as authors invited them to do.

While the moment of viewing might be the same, there was no warrant
to assume identity of perspectives or, indeed, a single perspective on the
part of any given viewer. Since the Enlightenment, the absence of phenomenal time and space is thought to make events unidentifiable.[141] But, as we
have seen, inactualité—in "untimeliness," disorientation, and indifference
to causality—was an integral part of twelfth-century historical writing. We
can now add that it was also crucial to a way of imaginative visualizing that

[136] Gerhoch of Reichersberg, Tractatus in Ps. 44: 2; Migne PL 193:1565.

[137] On "making memory," above, n. 92. On texts as memorials, e.g., Rahewin, Gesta Friderici, 3. prol.; MGH, SSrrG, p. 162. On early Christian texts as monimenta, Otto of Freising,
Chronicon, 1. prol.; MGH, SSrrG, p. 7. See also Gerhoch of Reichersberg, Tractatus in Ps. 76:
14; Migne PL 194:428–29.

[138] Norman Malcolm, Memory and Mind (Ithaca, N.Y.: Cornell University Press, 1977), p.
46.

[139] Otto of Freising, Chronicon, 1. prol.; MGH, SSrrG, p. 7.

[140] E.g., Otto of Freising, Chronicon, 8.25; MGH, SSrrG, p. 457. Rahewin, Gesta Friderici,
3. prol.; 4.86; MGH, SSrrG, pp. 163, 346. Cosmas of Prague, Chronica Boemorum, prol. ad
Gervasium and prol. ad Severum; MGH, SSrrG, pp. 3, 81.

[141] See Peter Munz, The Shapes of Time (Middletown, Conn.: Wesleyan University Press,
1977), p. 117.

took multiple, and optional, perspectives for granted, and that chose not
to fetter the imagination to single images and fixed vantage points set by
the artist.

We have exposed some effects of seeing events from within the perspective of a turning wheel, whether Fortune's Wheel, or the annular year of
the Lord, or Ezekiel's concentric wheels of prophecy and fulfillment. What
the spokes compartmentalized, the turning blended. Now, we have added
the garland to our list of metaphors. Gunther's decision for single images
and an artist's fixed vantage point marked a parting of the ways not only
between verse and prose, but also between literary structures that opened
single perspectives and those that provided multiple ones. His formalist
principles called for the smooth passage of the readers' attention from beginning to end; the esthetic governing our texts required the attention to
be frequently arrested. This is evident even in the ways in which the authors used the cherished metaphor for the fascicles of anthology. Rahewin
wove his flowers into a crown.[142] Repeating the figure of his predecessor,
but with more exalted diction, Gunther affirmed that he had gathered
flowers from a full garden to compose them into a garland worthy of Barbarossa, the prince. In a parallel passage, he equated the "garland" with a
song ("*camoena*," again a recondite word recommended chiefly by its scansion).[143] The difference is not merely in vocabulary and meter, but also in
the deceptively slight fact that Gunther considered his "garland" a "song"
composed as an offering to the Prince. By using the verb "weave," employed earlier to describe the work of writing history, and by leaving any
recipient unspecified, Rahewin conveyed at the end of the *Gesta* the web-

---

[142] Rahewin, *Gesta Friderici*, 4.86; *MGH, SSrrG*, p. 346: "Hos de latissimis gestorum tuo-
rum pratis, augustorum optime, tam dilectus patruus Otto episcopus quam nostrae humili-
tatis diligentia flores legit, unde huius opusculi coronam texeremus. . . ." Otto of Freising
himself commonly used the phrase "*historiam texere*" (and variants). See above n. 120. *Chronicon*, letter to Frederick Barbarossa, 1. prol.; 2.4, 30; 3.22; *MGH, SSrrG*, pp. 2, 8–9, 72,
101, 162. Cf. the related metaphor of a basket woven of evils, *Chronicon*, 2.17; ibid, p. 87.
The term, of course, was generally current. See Ebo, *Vita S. Ottonis Episcopi Babenbergensis*,
2.1; Wikarjak, ed., p. 53: "non sine lacrimis retexit historiam." Giraldus Cambrensis, *Descriptio
Kambriae, pref. prima*; James F. Dimock, ed., *Giraldi Cambrensis Opera*, Rolls Series, no. 21
(London: Longman, 1868), 6:158. The artistic license of weaving made it possible for the
metaphor to be used in reproach, as William of Newburgh used it to disapprove Geoffrey
of Monmouth, "ridicula . . . figmanta contexens." *Historia Rerum Anglicarum*, 1. proem;
Richard Howlett, ed., *Chronicles of the Reigns of Stephen, Henry II., and Richard I.*, Rolls Series, no. 82 (London: Longman, 1884), 1:11.

[143] *Ligurinus*, 1, lines 134–37; *MGH, SSrrG*, p. 160: "Claudendumque manu forma bre-
viore libellum, / Ad demulcendas conflare legentibus aures / Ac velut e pleno, decerptis flori-
bus, orto, / Principe digna suo breviter compingere serta." *Ligurinus*, 4, lines 594–98; *MGH,
SSrrG*, p. 295: "Hec de tam multis generosi principis actis / Credidimus nobis tenui tentanda
camena, / Ac veluti plena raros ex arbore flores / Carpimus, et paucas numeramus in aethere
flammas."

like character of narratives that Otto described at the beginning. They had woven the "formless flow of events" racing toward destruction and forgetfulness into a crown whose opulently varied components (with the aid of chapter headings) could be viewed from any point around the circle.[144] History was a montage of optional vantage points leading from a beginning without beginning to an end without end, rather than a single melodic line, clattering metrically and euphoniously into silence.

. . .

We have found, in assumptions about time, analogues to the nuclear perspective that we found in the visual arts (see chap. 4). Crowns, wreaths, and other woven objects were all composed of distinct elements arranged in recurring patterns. These metaphors for historical writings bring us back to other cyclical patterns that writers found in actual events: the turning of Fortune's Wheel; the hovering, spinning advance of sacred revelation (represented by Ezekiel's wheels) through the centuries; and the cycle (or crown) of the Lord's year, which encompassed all existence. These ideas excluded what is often referred to as "the cyclical view of history," that is, cycles of time in which identical persons and events recur. According to them, chronological time moved in a straight line, but signifying time moved in numbers of other ways, including counterlinear and nonlinear. Thus, within the movement of chronological time, patterns of meaning did recur, and in those patterns there were spaces of hiddenness. Understanding meaning could not be considered a linguistic effort, nor could understanding be equated with that other linguistic effort, interpretation. In fact, there were spaces of hiddenness that understanding could penetrate (for example, by intuition, comprehension, or multiplication of relations), but such verbal exercises as explanation, interpretation, and even description could not, or must not, convey them.

We have now completed a survey of three transits from criticism to epiphany by way of silence. They differed in origin and direction. Criticism regarding the Kingdom of God consisted of Scriptural exegesis; that concerning women, of ascetic morality; and, that concerning time, of formal devices employed by authors to shape and pace readers' experiences of time in the text. Although silences concerning the Kingdom of God can be explained by its character as a holy secret apprehended by intuition, and those concerning women, by their ambiguous character as exemplars and

---

[144] On the formless flow of events, Otto of Freising, *Chronicon*, 1. prol.; *MGH, SSrrG*, p. 6. Ibid., p. 10: Otto affirmed that he wrote in charity so that the zealous inquirer might not find a confused order of past things. On the movement into destruction and forgetfulness, Rahewin, *Gesta Friderici*, 3. prol.; *MGH, SSrrG*, p. 162.

subverters of moral purity, those concerning time derived from the intricate varieties presented by author's and reader's *tempi*.

In each case, we have encountered esthetic judgments of a scholarly, ascetic elite, writing for its own members. But the discussion of time, more than those of the other two subjects, has brought us to consider the cultural context in which the works were written, a context notable for its distinctive combination of asceticism and conspicuous waste. That context, with its joyful delight in the costliness of the costly and its morose delight in the perishability of the perishable, accentuated the multitude of *tempi* that converged in any event, and the diversity of esthetic effects that the same work of art could have in different circumstances. A psalm of victory, for example, would be heard differently by conqueror and vanquished, just as the same person would hear it differently in circumstances of joy or of desolation. However constant principles and methods of criticism might be, epiphanies would vary with the character and circumstances of those to whom they were given, and the choice from a repertory of optional modalities of knowing. Their reality existed in the very act of visualization, of which words or paintings could be only stimuli and memorials.

Perhaps it is true that history is "the least artistic" among the concepts of genre.[145] Our inquiry into the ways in which the capacity for time was created between the lines of some texts, however, indicates that this may not always have been assumed to be true. We have been inclined to turn blind eyes on aspects of these texts, including the fact that among the responses their authors sought to elicit through them were conversion and prayer.[146] And yet, after the passage of so many centuries, we are again in a position to detect in the spaces between their lines the powerful convergence of art, history, and religion. We again confront an esthetic intended to arrest attention rather than to convey it. For there are in the hermeneutic borrowed from theater and the visual arts, and from the experience of play, and in the disconnected, multiple perspectives, optional experiences of *tempi* compatible with others of more recent years: "The world of the romantic song," wrote Roland Barthes, "is the lover's world, the world which the amorous subject has in his head: a single beloved, but a whole population of figures. These figures are not persons but little scenes, each of which consists, in turn, of a memory, a landscape, a movement, a mood, of anything which may be the starting point of a wound, of a nostalgia, of a felicity."[147]

[145] Peter Szondi, *Poetik und Geschichtsphilosophie* (Frankfurt am Main: Suhrkamp, 1974), 1:70.

[146] E.g., Otto of Freising, *Chronicon*, 8.35; *MGH, SSrrG*, p. 457.

[147] Barthes, "The Romantic Song," p. 290.

# Chapter 8

## CONCLUSIONS: A WORD ON "MEDIEVAL HUMANISM"

AT THE OUTSET, I invoked the authority of John Scotus Eriugena. In some Scriptural parables, he found, hidden beneath the surface of the text, a structure of transitions that enabled astute interpreters to move from one figure to another, thus establishing multiple meanings. These transitions constituted an invisible framing structure, but one that was by no means evident to all (see Preface, n. 2). I have suggested that twelfth-century historical writers likewise assumed invisible *transitus* in their own works, as well as in Scripture, and that they indicated as much by the analogies that they drew between their works and representational arts which were more than empty turns of phrase. Historical writing was considered an exercise in play—whether tragedy, comedy, or the hectic spin of Fortune— and readers anticipated game time in their texts. The subject of all our inquiries has been the spectator's imaginative play. We have associated a nuclear perspective with that play, a perspective from which the circle paradoxically became a principle of narrative discoordination. And we have found that, in literature, one way of characterizing it was with metaphors of circles which emphasized the motif of play: the spin of Fortune's Wheel, Ezekiel's wheeled and flying cherubim, the victor's crown (or wreath), and the weaver's basket. Each combined the characteristics of hiddenness and revelation, of expectations reversed, of changed times and repeated patterns implied by "drama" in its original meaning: "racecourse."

Insofar as we may speak of "medieval humanism,"[1] one effect of this exploration has been to disclose a perspective that has grown quite foreign to western scholars. It has been possible to establish some points at which there is little, if any, contact between historical investigations of the present day and the perspectives of the representatives of twelfth-century humanism whose writings we have attempted to read. For, "since Ranke, who

---

[1] Hans Liebeschütz, *Medieval Humanism in the Life and Writings of John of Salisbury*, Studies of the Warburg Institute, vol. 17 (London: Warburg Institute, 1950). R. W. Southern, *Medieval Humanism and Other Studies* (Oxford: Blackwell, 1970), pp. 29–60. See also David Knowles, "The Humanism of the Twelfth Century," in *The Historian and Character and Other Essays* (Cambridge: Cambridge University Press, 1963), pp. 16–30; and Walter Ullmann, *Medieval Foundations of Renaissance Humanism* (Ithaca, N.Y.: Cornell University Press, 1977).

still recognized the dramatic nature of history, there has been a tendency that can not be overlooked to de-dramatize history."[2]

To say this much, of course, is to say that ways of thinking about history that could be taken for granted when historiography was a dramatist's art, a branch of poesy, must also have become foreign. Among these must surely be counted the conception that texts provided readers with an array of narrative options instead of—as has been the ideal since the Renaissance—a single, clear narrative line moving toward closure. Even if they learned by rote such scripts as now survive, "illiterate actors" can only have regarded the written text as something quite separate from what happened on the stage, a cue-sheet for the improvisations that made up actual performance. Performance varied from one day to the next according to the give-and-take between actors and audience. Similarly, historical writers evidently expected readers (and hearers) to combine *ad libitum* the segmented fascicles that comprised their words. Their audience too composed by redactive criticism within options cued by the text, imaginatively expanding the text to include elements that were conspicuously present by their absence. Likewise, our texts display options of poetic discourse through a fabric of meanings, both expressed and implied, discourse even higher than the forms of poetry itself, as long as poetry was not more than the formal, metrical arrangement of words, or the deployment of images as ends in themselves.

Some of what we have discovered about the humanist's eye, seeing invisible things and restlessly darting from one image to another, is not surprising. Most obvious is the fact that the seeing eye and the recording hand were male. The humanist perspectives that are accessible through our texts were achieved and recorded by men, and by men, moreover, who belonged to classes devoted to ascetic discipline and conspicuous waste.

Perhaps there is a connection between our comments on the exclusion of women from histories and the fact that historical works by women are so conspicuously few and meagre. The possible key is the absence of women from forms of play entered into by men. For, as we have seen, play gave the analogues in which historical events were described—gambling, athletic and military competition, and theater. More fundamentally, it also ingrained structures of thought according to which, before texts were composed or even dreamed of, the historical meaning of events was assessed. Thus, women were excluded from the collective activities that, for men, ingrained the mental habits that were the precondition of historical description and, more profoundly, of historical intuition; and these included preeminently the game of honor and vengeance.

Women had peripheral parts to play in the male interpersonal relations

---

[2] Interview with Fritz Stern, *Frankfurter Allgemeine Zeitung*, 13 May 1987, p. 36.

that drove the mechanisms of honor. Chief among them were rivalries in which each tested the worthiness of each, seeking allies in the continual cycles of vengeance. Extraordinary women could display "manly" virtues; but they were playing against type. Lacking manhood, women lacked the worthiness that could be demonstrated in the performance of manly arts. While men were strong, rational, and temperate, women were weak, sensual, and lustful; and it was an irony of nature that the weakness of women was capable of reducing the strength of men to ruin. Rightly, women were excluded from male bonding in real and simulated combat and hence from the commensality of brothers at arms.

Other discoveries are almost as obvious. Our point of departure was the assumption that there was more in the text than we could see in the words. Something was latent in the spaces between the words and the lines. We knew from the beginning that the authors of the works under review were predisposed to expect latency in texts. Was not Christ hidden in the letter of Scripture, even in the words of the Old Testament? St. Paul's axiom, "the letter killeth, but the Spirit giveth life" (2 Cor. 3:6) inspired luxuriant methods of exegesis intended to disclose what was unsaid in what was uttered. Transferring this principle to the Liberal Arts, some argued that in those studies too "the letter was nothing and the spirit, latent in the letter, was on all accounts to be sought."[3]

Thus, it was by no means strange for authors who expected to find in the writings of others an unsaid key to the expressed messages to convey unuttered messages in the coded texts of their own, especially given their zeal for manifesting the invisible things of God, in all the arts, through things that were made. Correspondingly, the beauty (*pulchritudo*) that was a norm of understanding had to be discovered in the silences.

To historians of our day it seems self-evident that once a critic begins with the assumption that there is more to a work than can be seen, inquiries have to be bridled; for, at some point in the inquiry, there may be less, or something other, in the text than the critic sees. This caution, too, was familiar to our authors. They insisted that interpreters should be faithful to the intent of the author.[4] Celebrated teachers found themselves cited as authorities for doctrines set forth by disciples who creatively misunder-

---

[3] E.g., John of Salisbury, *Policraticus*, 7.13; Clement C. J. Webb, ed., *Ioannis Saresberiensis Episcopi Carnotensis Policratici . . . libri VIII* (Oxford: Clarendon, 1909), 2:147. John of Salisbury, *Metalogicon*, 1.3; Clement C. J. Webb, ed., *Ioannis Saresberiensis Episcopi Carnotensis Metalogicon libri IIII* (Oxford: Clarendon, 1929), p. 10.

[4] See Matthew of Vendôme, *Ars Versificatoria (The Art of the Versemaker)*, 1.115, citing the *Rhetorica ad Herennium*, 5.129; Roger P. Parr, trans. (Milwaukee, Wis.: Marquette University Press, 1981), p. 58. John of Salisbury alluded to the same source in *Ep. 248*; W. J. Millor and C.N.L. Brooke, eds., *The Letters of John of Salisbury* (Oxford: Clarendon, 1979), 2:500. See also *Ep. 253*; ibid., 2:510.

stood what they had heard.[5] But there were difficulties in fathoming the author's intent, in establishing the sense (in the author) that created the words, rather than the sense (in readers) that they created. For, even when intended meanings were not multiple, as they were thought to be in Scripture, who with vain imaginings could pretend to unfold the secrets of an author's heart? Only God was judge of such things, and, in the end, the authority of a text might well depend, not on who said it (or with what intent), but on what was said.[6]

Indeed, as was often the case with prophets, inspired authors did not always understand their own words. This was perhaps the case with Virgil, who was considered to have prophesied the Incarnation of Christ, and Ovid, through whom, some said, God spoke as he spoke through Augustine.[7]

These two guiding points—the conviction that there is more than one can see in a work and the caution against seeing more than is there—entered into the making of the texts that we have discussed, and they have also guided our inquiries. More secure controls were available to us than were accessible to Scriptural exegetes in the age of Abelard, and we have been able to profit from comparison of texts, and from an insistence on placing texts in the context of common interpretive traditions.

We have explored the difference in perspective set not by the text but by the point of view from which one expects the text to be viewed. According to post-Enlightenment standards, the writings under review, inspected from outside, lack narrative unity. We have found that organizational structure is not simply something positive in the work, but that it also

[5] See Gilbert of Poitiers's complaint to Pope Eugenius III, at the Council of Rheims in 1148, in John of Salisbury, *Historia Pontificalis*, chap. 10; Marjorie Chibnall, ed., *John of Salisbury's Memoirs of the Papal Court* (London: Nelson, 1956), p. 22: "Videte, pater, qualiter me tractetis, cum in infamiam meam in sacro consistorio vestro alieni recitantur errores. Fateor me plures habuisse discipulos, qui me quidem omnes audierunt, sed quidam minus intellexerunt: quod opinati sunt scripserunt de corde suo, non de spiritu meo." See also John of Salisbury on Abelard, *Metalogicon*, 2.17; Webb, ed., pp. 91–92.

[6] John of Salisbury, *Policraticus*, 2.26; Webb, ed., 1:139–40. John of Salisbury, *Ep. 301*; Millor and Brooke, eds., *The Letters of John of Salisbury*, 2:708. Gerhoch of Reichersberg, *Tractatus in Ps. 64*, chap. 17; *MGH*, *Ldl* 3, p. 447.

[7] On Virgil, see the study by Domenico Comparetti, *Vergil in the Middle Ages*, trans. E.F.M. Benecke (New York: Macmillan, 1895). On Ovid, see the heretical assertions cited by Caesarius of Heisterbach, *Dialogus Miraculorum*, 5.22, an exaggerated statement of a common position. Joseph Strange, ed., (Cologne: Heberle, 1851), 1:304. For the misattribution by King James I of Aragon of a verse by Ovid to Scripture, see Edward Kenneth Rand, *Ovid and His Influence* (New York: Longmans, Green and Co., 1928), p. 136 (in a section on Ovid's reputation in the Middle Ages entitled "Ovid Theologus"). On Virgil and Ovid as quasi-saints in the fourteenth century, see George Kane, *The Liberating Truth: The Concept of Integrity in Chaucer's Writings*, The John Coffin Memorial Lecture, 1979 (London: Athlone Press, 1979), p. 8.

testifies to the *cire perdue* of understanding that was prior to the work. The cognitive structure in our texts was never intended to take shape around a single thread of narrative, *narratio* being one of the briefest members of a discourse. Instead, the thread of narrative was considered to be woven into a basket, a web, or a garland, which contained historical materials contemplated, at option, from multiple points of view inside the structure. The texts presupposed, not the single image, fixed vantage point from outside a work of art such as Renaissance painting presupposed, but the eclectic, darting vagrancy of the eye itself from within the web.

We have also found that understanding was not exclusively linguistic, and by no means identical with the linguistic enterprises of explanation and interpretation. Visual understanding was also acknowledged. The Christian tradition of "symbolic synesthesia," as yet, retained its power.

On every hand, the importance of play as a cognitive strategy has been evident: in establishing the hedonic function of historical writing as prior to the mnemonic and mimetic ones; in applying rationales for including some subjects and excluding others; in deploying the function of drama to baffle or confound logic; and, most fundamentally, in forming the mentality that gave birth to these tactics, a mentality that delighted in playing in mixed *tempi*. That delight was rooted in cult, more precisely in a cult that followed two antithetical religious principles: asceticism and conspicuous waste. The authors of our texts revelled in predicament. They made their home in paradox, enigma, and dilemma. For such were their lives of self-denial and ritual opulence. The variety of *tempi* in the cacophonous flood of actual events and the mixed *tempi* in the polyphonic harmony of cult life alike exemplified that only the predicament of diversity in unity, like the iridescent shimmer of seamless cloth of gold, was authentic.

The esthetic of this cult, centered upon a sacrifice in which a man was killed by men for the honor of God, among other reasons, characteristically embraced violence and death itself as a medium of beauty. The play of sacrificial death and transfiguration was mimetically and continually enacted by those ritually privileged to perform it. Our texts were artifacts made to serve the objects of that continually enacted sacrifice.

The contrast between the formalist mode of Latin poetry (represented by Gunther) and the woven lattices of prose writers contained options. In time, humanists departed from the ways of "symbolic synesthesia" to a more strictly literal understanding. They chose the formalist perspective of the single-image, fixed vantage point outside the work of art, rather than the vagrant perspectives of the spectator's eye darting within a nuclear perspective. A displacement of general cognitive values from imagination to knowledge, and from varied manifestations to individual phenomena had occurred. Beginning in the thirteenth century, changes in the norms of esthetic judgment made it increasingly difficult for humanists to read between the lines of our texts, much less to find there "beauty of style or vivacity of wit,"[8] ironically, two qualities that the authors of the texts especially valued. The texts began their transformation from dramas into documents.

Certainly, the variety of times in the formless flow of events posed quandaries. They presented the spectator no single images of fixed perspectives, no unified self-explanatory work of beginning, middle, and end. But, in their *inactualité*, they did offer provocations to the memory, and spaces where, with the delights of love and terror, empathetic imagination could play its speculative games, as in the circle of a garland or in the round theater of the world, from beginningless beginning to endless end.

A luxurious silk, greatly prized in the twelfth century, displayed a pattern "indicated by a thin sunk outline." When woven in the same color as the ground, the pattern was invisible until the cloth was taken up and moved so that light cast the relief into passing shadows.[9] We have similarly explored patterns in spaces that, from some perspectives, appear to be blank. At the outset, we noted analogues between the quests for spiritual silence in the West with others in Oriental religions and philosophies. In the twelfth century, dominant principles in Western culture had long since begun to depart from analogous ways of understanding in Eastern asceticism, eventually to be covered, among the strata of culture, by norms of fourteenth- and fifteenth-century humanism. But, now, those norms too have lost their dominance. In literature, the concatenation of perspectives, nonlinear narrative, and abstraction of place and character are among the methods of expression that have replaced them. In painting, extremes of abstraction have come forth, only beginning with the fragmentation of the image, or the montage of images, that Cézanne achieved. Such innovations are easily portrayed as rejections of an exhausted legacy. It is more difficult to see, but no less certain, that they have reinvented and affirmed certain principles of understanding that informed an earlier world and gave its arts abundant procreative force. These spontaneous parallels between the ascetic quest for wisdom in East and West, these unconscious reversions to a prior existence, witness to common human needs, a call from within the silences in the texts, a voice like the cry of a great multitude.

[8] Southern, *Medieval Humanism*, p. 60.

[9] A. F. Kendrick, *Catalogue of Early Medieval Woven Fabrics* (London: Victoria and Albert Museum, 1925), p. 41.

# INDEX

Abelard, Peter, 32n.31, 82, 248n.5
abortion, 167. *See also* infanticide
Abraham (patriarch), 163
abuses, clerical, 160, 171, 181. *See also* chastity; reform
actors, 5, 85, 152, 181, 216. *See also* theater
Adalbert, Archbishop of Hamburg-Bremen, 5–9, 75, 142, 149, 150n.38, 209n.37, 218
Adalbert, Bishop of Prague, 177, 183
Adam (protoplast), 28, 31, 35, 39, 44, 100, 114n.63, 183n.87, 209n.38
Adam of Bremen, 142, 170, 186, 188n.112
Adam of Perseigne, 10
Adèle of Blois, Countess, 173, 195, 222n.80
Admont: monastery of, 169n.31, 173
Aelfgyva, 164–65
Agobard, Archbishop of Lyons, 47
Ailred of Rievaulx, 216n.60, 222n.81
Albero, Archbishop of Trier, 10, 66n.62, 158n.9, 216, 223n.82
alchemy, 17
Alcuin, 105n.43
Alexander II, Pope, 222n.81
Alexander III, Pope, 234
Alfonso X, King of Castile, 16n.49
Alice of Blois, Countess, 173
allegory, 6, 52, 63, 69, 129, 132, 141, 143
analogy, xxiv, 51, 85
anhedonia, 187–88, 192. *See also* asceticism
animality, 9, 24, 35, 69, 100, 147, 184n.93, 189n.115, 191
Anno, Archbishop of Cologne, 177n.60, 178n.63, 189n.118, 191n.121, 209n.36, 213n.48
Anselm, Archbishop of Canterbury, 22, 79, 80, 86, 128
Anselm, Bishop of Havelberg, 37n.52, 139, 156, 203, 203n.17, 204n.23, 213, 220, 228
Ansgar, Bishop of Hamburg, 183
Antichrist, 89, 90, 94, 141, 205n.23
Antiquity, xix, 6, 20, 24n.13, 26n.16, 32n.31, 37, 38n.54, 39n.56, 80, 81,

81n.118, 104, 111, 124, 127, 130, 134, 159, 165, 172n.45, 174n.52, 178, 181, 184n.93, 191, 221, 222, 237
apatheia, 81
Apocalypse, 15, 17, 26n.16, 28, 29n.21, 37n.52, 70, 94, 115, 140, 143, 162, 181n.79, 206
Apostles, 51–52, 57, 59, 66n.64, 113, 145
Apuleius, 39n.56
Aquinas, Thomas, xx, 134, 184
architecture, xxi, 10, 17, 28, 39, 49, 53, 54, 61, 64, 73, 75, 96, 97, 144, 149, 173, 217, 220, 221n.75, 233
Aristotle, 24n.13, 52, 80, 132, 147, 151n.1, 187. *See also* philosophy
Arnold, Archbishop of Mainz, 76, 78, 90, 189n.117, 205n.23
art: destruction of, 75–77, 148, 191–92, 217–18, 219n.66, 234; obsolescence of, 46; origins of, 84; as parable of nonexistence, xxiv; recombinant, 28, 104, 113, 228; secrets of, 206, 207; self-concealment of, 9, 13; source of, 84; techniques of, 77, 206. *See also* artists; arts; iconoclasm; individual arts; pagans
artisans, xiv, 39, 49n.5, 61–62, 72, 73, 77, 85, 96–97, 113, 133, 149–50, 159, 176, 194, 207, 216, 220, 225; and patrons, 72–77, fig. 3 (p. 74), 96, 132–33, 159. *See also* patrons
artist: hermeneutic moment of, 196–98, 200–220; rewards of, from God, 97. *See also* artisans
artistic license, 97, 148
arts, 26, 72–73, 171–72, 216, 247; Liberal, 73, 104, 105n.41, 115, fig. 9 (p. 122), fig. 10 (p. 123), 171, 173, 228, 246; performing, xvii, 171, 182; unity of, 36, 84, 84n.142, 85, 104; visual, xvii, xxii, 26n.17, 28, 38, 61, 65, 91, 95, 103, 107–8, 149, 181–82, 200, 220, 243. *See also* literacy; music; painting; sculpture; theater
asceticism, xxii, 23, 34, 36, 44, 53, 63, 68, 73, 74, 77, 81, 86, 96, 99, 99n.28, 101,